# CALIFORNIA STATE UNIVERSITY, SACRAMENTO

This book is due on the last date stamped below.
Failure to return books on the date due will result in assessment
of overdue fees.

# THE SCARECROW AUTHOR BIBLIOGRAPHIES

# ROBERT BLY:

## A
## Primary and Secondary
## Bibliography

by
## WILLIAM H. ROBERSON

*Scarecrow Author Bibliographies, No. 75*

The Scarecrow Press, Inc.
Metuchen, N.J., & London
1986

The author gratefully acknowledges permission to re-
print the following:

"In Search of an American Muse," by Robert Bly (The New
York Times, January 22, 1984).  Copyright © 1984 by The
New York Times Company.  Reprinted by permission.

Library of Congress Cataloging-in-Publication Data

Roberson, William H.
    Robert Bly : a primary and secondary bibliography.

    (Scarecrow author bibliographies ; no. 75)
    Includes indexes.
    1. Bly, Robert--Bibliography.  I. Title.
II. Series.
Z8105.793.R62  1986     016.811'54          86-939
[PS3552.L9]
ISBN 0-8108-1879-5

For Jeannie--

"Shall I flail with words, when love has made the space...."

# CONTENTS

# PREFACE

For over thirty years Robert Bly has been a creative, angry, argumentative, and exciting presence in American poetry. He is a seminal figure in contemporary American letters whose importance is enhanced by his translations of Latin American and European poets, such as Pablo Neruda, César Vallejo, Georg Trakl, Tomas Tranströmer, and Harry Martinson, as well as the fifteenth-century Indian poet Kabir. Through his poetry, translations, and literary criticism Bly has championed new and unorthodox evocations of instinct and intuition and a rejection of orthodox techniques and rhetorical devices. His belief that poets operate under a moral imperative to involve themselves in the political and social struggles of their societies, as evidenced by much of his poetry as well as his co-founding of the American Writers Against the Vietnam War and his donation of the National Book Award prize money to the draft resistance, has threatened the stereotypical notion of the poet as cloistered aesthetic.

Bly's production of books, poetry, criticism, and translations is prodigious. Much of his creative and critical work was originally published by small press book publishers and little magazines. The inadequacy of bibliographic controls and the absence of comprehensive indexing and abstracting services covering these types of publications have, in effect, made much of Bly's work "fugitive" material. To date only five serious, but limited, attempts at a bibliography of Bly's work have been made: the working bibliography included in Ingegerd Friberg's Moving Inward: A Study of Robert Bly's Poetry (Göteborg, Sweden: Acta Universitatis Gothoburgensis, 1977); the bibliography compiled by James Doss and Kate Daniels in Of Solitude and Silence, Writings on Robert Bly (Boston: Beacon Press, 1982); the bibliography accompanying Howard Nelson's Robert Bly: An

Introduction to the Poetry (New York:   Columbia University
Press, 1984); the listing included in Robert Bly:   When
Sleepers Awake, edited by Joyce Peseroff (Ann Arbor:
University of Michigan Press, 1984); and my own two-part
primary bibliography that appeared in Bulletin of Bibliogra-
phy (March 1983 & June 1984).

     Each of these works, however, has serious errors of
omission, and mistakes in citation have been perpetuated
from one source to another.   This bibliography attempts to
present as complete and accurate a record as possible of
Bly's English language work to date and the body of criti-
cism that has resulted from it.   I have utilized all other
bibliographic listings as my starting point, but the accuracy
of no entry has been accepted.   I have endeavored to per-
sonally verify all entries, either in the original works or by
photocopies, to correct previous errors and omissions.   For
those entries that I have been unable to personally verify,
I have cited my source for the entry.

     In compiling this book, my intention was to be inclu-
sive rather than exclusive.   However, works that mention
Bly only in passing or within a larger group of representa-
tive writers, have not been included.   Although the original
intent of this work was to provide access to English language
material regarding Bly, any foreign language sources located
in the course of my research have been included.

     The first part of the bibliography, "Writings by Robert
Bly" is divided into individual sections for "Books" (itself
divided into sections on "Poetry and Prose," "Translations,"
and "Editions"), "Essays and Nonfiction," "Reviews," "Let-
ters," "Poems in Periodicals," "Translations in Periodicals,"
"Poems in Books," "Translations in Books," "Sound Record-
ings," "Videorecordings," "Book Blurbs," "Drama," "Note-
paper," and "Miscellany."   The arrangement is chronological
within each section; within years, the arrangement is alpha-
betical by title with the exception of the sections on trans-
lations, which are arranged by the surname of the original
author.   In the section "Books" a physical description of
first editions of Bly's works is given.   In each case I have
noted the location of the volume that I examined.   The ma-
jority of titles were located in one of five collections:   the
poetry collections at the State University of New York at
Buffalo and Stony Brook, the personal collections of William
Heyen and Anthony Piccione, and my own personal collection.

Part II, "Writings About Robert Bly," is a listing of
secondary material divided into separate sections for "Books,"
"Articles and Parts of Books," "Reviews," "Dissertations,"
"Poems," and "Miscellany." The entries are arranged
chronologically by year of publication and entries within
each year are alphabetically arranged except for the "Re-
views" section, which is alphabetically arranged by the titles
of Bly's works. In those cases where Bly is treated in on-
ly part of any article or essay, the pages cited are those
which are particularly relevant to Bly. The pages for the
entire article are given in brackets. Part II is followed by
an appendix of "Special Collections of Bly Materials" lo-
cated in the United States.

The Name/Title Index to Part I is an alphabetical list
of all authors, editors, compilers, and illustrators appearing
in the bibliography; the titles of Bly's works; works in which
Bly's material appears; and books reviewed by Bly. A sep-
arate Name/Title/Subject Index to Part II includes an alpha-
betical listing of authors and editors; titles of Bly's works;
titles of works about Bly and his writings; and subject head-
ings for material included in the bibliography of secondary
sources.

Bibliographies, by their very nature, are never com-
plete. This is especially true of those concerning living au-
thors. It is the intention of this work to provide as accurate
and solid a starting point as possible for subsequent Bly
scholars, researchers, and bibliographers. May they add
to, revise, and correct this work but also derive assistance
from it.


## ACKNOWLEDGMENTS

I am indebted to a number of people without whose kindness
and help this book would have been more difficult to com-
plete than it was. My thanks to Robert Bly for his always
prompt responses to my inquiries as well as for loaning me
some items I had difficulty locating. I am grateful to the
following people who furnished me with information concern-
ing specific items: Steve Bassett, Steven Ford-Brown, Don-
ald Hall, Pat McClanahan, M. P. Smagorinsky, Jacqueline
Ozon, Rochelle Ratner, R. B. Weber, and Bill Zavatsky.

My thanks and apologies to all those I have forgotten.
Thanks also to Louis Simpson for making his collection of
The Fifties, The Sixties, and The Seventies readily available
to me.  My appreciation to Robert J. Bertholf and the staff
of The Poetry/Rare Books Collection at the State University
of New York at Buffalo.  Special thanks to Evert Volkersz
for his interest and help, and to his staff at Special Col-
lections at the State University of New York at Stony
Brook.  I am especially indebted to Martin Booth and also
to Anthony Piccione for graciously digging out his Bly col-
lection at short notice.  Special warm thanks to Bill Heyen
for his interest and advice and for so joyfully and generous-
ly regaling me with his Bly material from his personal col-
lection.  Heyen's substantial collection of contemporary
poetry is now available at the State University of New York
at Brockport.

        My thanks, as always, to my friends and colleagues
at the Southampton Campus of Long Island University:
Valerie Parry, Frank Wojcik, and Joan Schneider for their
persistence in obtaining material through interlibrary loan,
and Barbara McGuire and Robert Gerbereux for their help
in time of need.  Last here, but, in fact, always foremost,
thanks to my wife--"I look back at my pleasures and they
were you whom I held close in loving."

                                                    W. H. R.

# CHRONOLOGY

1926        born December 23 to Jacob Thomas Bly and Alice
            (Aws) Bly

1944-46     U.S. Navy

1946-47     St. Olaf College, Northfield, Minnesota

1947-50     Harvard University, B.A., magna cum laude

1955        married Carolyn McLean

1956        University of Iowa, Iowa City, M.A.

1956-57     Fulbright Fellowship in Norway

1958        first issue of The Fifties; meets James Wright

1961        Twenty Poems of Georg Trakl

1962        The Lion's Tail and Eyes: Poems Written Out of
            Laziness and Silence; Silence in the Snowy Fields;
            Twenty Poems of César Vallejo

1964        Amy Lowell Travelling Fellowship in England,
            France and Spain

1965        Guggenheim Fellowship; National Institute of Arts
            & Letters grantee

1966        founding, with David Ray, of American Writers
            Against the Vietnam War; A Poetry Reading Against
            the Vietnam War

1967        Rockefeller Fellowship; The Light Around the Body;
            I Do Best Alone at Night; Late Arrival on Earth;
            refusal to accept $5,000 grant from the National
            Endowment for the Arts

1968        recipient National Book Award for Poetry; Twenty
            Poems of Pablo Neruda

1969    The Morning Glory (Kayak); Forty Poems of Juan
        Ramón Jiménez

1970    The Teeth-Mother Naked at Last; Twenty Poems
        of Tomas Tranströmer

1971    Neruda and Vallejo: Selected Poems; The Fish in
        the Sea Is Not Thirsty

1972    Guggenheim Fellowship; Ten Sonnets to Orpheus;
        Basho

1973    Jumping Out of Bed; Sleepers Joining Hands; Lorca
        and Jiménez: Selected Poems

1974    Point Reyes Poems

1975    organized first Conference on the Great Mother;
        Old Man Rubbing His Eyes; Friends, You Drank
        Some Darkness; The Morning Glory (Harper);
        Leaping Poetry

1977    This Body Is Made of Camphor and Gopherwood;
        The Kabir Book; Twenty Poems of Vicente Aleix-
        andre; Twenty Poems of Rolf Jacobsen

1979    divorced; This Tree Will Be Here for a Thousand
        Years

1980    married Ruth Ray; News of the Universe; Talking
        All Morning

1981    The Man in the Black Coat Turns; Selected Poems
        of Rainer Maria Rilke

1983    Times Alone: Selected Poems of Antonio Machado

1985    A Love of Minute Particulars; Loving a Woman in
        Two Worlds

# IN SEARCH OF AN AMERICAN MUSE

## By Robert Bly

Being a poet in the United States has meant for me years of confusion, blundering and self-doubt. The confusion lies in not knowing whether I am writing in the American language or the English or, more exactly, how much of the musical power of Chaucer, Marvell and Keats can be kept in free verse. Not knowing how to live, or even how to make a living, results in blunders. And the self-doubt comes from living in small towns. Yet I think it is a lucky thing to be a poet in the United States. I say that aloud to ward off pity. Some people keep away from poetry and compensate by feeling sorry for poets: "You poets must have a really hard time." William Stafford mentioned to me that if someone asks him, "Why do you write poetry?" he may reply, "Why did you stop?"

When anyone seriously pursues an art--painting, poetry, sculpture, composing--over 20 or 30 years, the sustained discipline carries the artist down to the countryside of grief; and that descent, resisted so long, proves invigorating, just as the goddess Demeter's daughter Persephone, when she went down toward grief in Hades, found herself in a psychic depth different from her mother's.

I come from Norwegian apple farmers on one side, fishermen on the other, who moved to Minnesota in the 19th century. My parents are second generation Norwegian immigrants. Neither of them went to college, though family members in Norway, I found when I went there, are fond of poetry. As a Navy recruit in World War II, I met for the first time a person who wrote poetry, a man named Marcus Eisenstein who I think teaches now at a college in Pennsylvania. During a class on radar, he wrote a poem

as I watched. I had somehow never understood that poems
were written by human beings, and I still remember that
moment with delight. After a year at St. Olaf College in
Minnesota I transferred to Harvard and found myself in the
midst of an intense group of beginning writers that included
John Hawkes, Donald Hall, Adrienne Rich, Frank O'Hara,
Peter Davison, George Plimpton, Harold Brodkey, Kenneth
Koch and John Ashbery. Military service had delayed some
students from going to college and several classes entered
together. Most of us had been in the war and each of us
was obsessed in his own way. I learned to trust my ob-
sessions. It is surely a great calamity for a human being
to have no obsessions.

One day while studying a Yeats poem I decided to
write poetry the rest of my life. I recognized that a single
short poem has room for history, music, psychology, reli-
gious thought, mood, occult speculation, character and
events of one's own life. I still feel surprised that such
various substances can find shelter and nourishment in a
poem. A poem in fact may be a sort of nourishing liquid,
such as one uses to keep amoeba alive. If prepared right,
a poem can keep an image or a thought or insights on his-
tory or the psyche alive for years, as well as our desires
and airy impulses.

So I was lucky to have such a group around me in
college. Writers come in groups; I don't know why. In-
tensities feed each other. In another sense, I began where
so many of us in the United States begin--with no tradition
at all. Yeats's father wrote penetrating and profound let-
ters to his son, guiding him in art, and we know from
Yeats's memoirs that both sides of his family in Ireland were
accustomed to books and pictures. In one branch of his
family, eccentric and creative people went back centuries.
When I would compare Yeats's childhood to my own experi-
ence, I would turn pale, turn--as Juan Ramón Jiménez, the
Spanish poet, said of some window panes on Beacon Hill--
violet, "the color of thought."

To be a poet in the United States is more difficult than
to be a poet in Ireland. If poetry is a harnessed horse, we
can say that in Ireland one finds harnesses still hanging in
a barn. In the United States one has to kill a cow, skin it,
dry the hide, cure it, cut the hide into straps, make buckles

by hand, measure all the straps on a horse that won't stand
still and then buy a riveter from some old man, get a box
of rivets, rivet the straps together, make reins. And then
what about the bridle? What about the collar? And what do
you hitch it to?

Almost all American poets I know suffer each day the
anguish of having no family traditions in art, so they don't
know which sacrifices are proper to make for the sake of
art and which aren't. A Russian poet has specific instruc-
tions on that, and on usable form, from Pushkin: "Art, art,
above all else, art!"

The American poet has much to do alone. He or she
does not inherit a usable style; they have to decide the ques-
tion of form, learn the art, and gain respect. At times a
university offers to help. I don't want to name villains, but
I do think the graduate workshop has caused considerable
damage to American poets during the last 20 years. The
university makes a poet who is teaching an appendage, but
also a special person, which is worse. The poet sees mainly
students, constantly breaks his or her solitude and talks
rather than writes. The university on its part muddles the
whole problem of sacrifice and adds buffers. It welcomes
the writer but balances the scales by saving him from the
constant, deep and humiliating failure the old poets had to
live with, Whitman and Frost among them. These two men
made considerable sacrifices to write poetry, and they lived
many years in isolation, exposed to their own raw side.
Emily Dickinson did too.

If one wants to be and remains a poet in this country,
one can't depend on peers but has to find some way back to
the nourishment of the ancestors. I still read Yeats every
day, and after him Blake, and Chaucer, "Beowulf" and Hor-
ace. In North American poetry, I like to tune my poems to
the interval between Whitman and Frost.

Moving to Europe doesn't seem as essential as it once
did. Joseph Conrad advised, "Immerse yourself in the de-
structive element," but now the destructive element is here.
The United States is the center, and if we listen carefully to
what is happening in our own culture, we have what Gertrude
Stein called the country of the imagination.

Being a poet requires enormous reading. One has to know many things, because so much has happened in psychology, biological thought and sub-atomic physics that the old poets did not know. I personally love the place where poetry and psychology now meet. Blake began contemporary psychological speculation around 1800 and was particularly daring in identifying and naming interior persons, such as those he called Urizen and Orc. Freud continued such work and named the "I" (Ego), the "upper-I" (Superego) and the "It" (Id). Jung continued, describing well, although naming less well, "the anima," "the animus" and "the shadow." Naming interior beings is a task poets have accepted since ancient times. I feel very close in thought to the psychologist James Hillman, particularly to his distinction between image and symbol and his praise of Hades and the soul's desire to descend there. I admire the mythologist Joseph Campbell tremendously, and I have learned from him the distinction between kinetic and stationary art--things T. S. Eliot and Ezra Pound did not teach.

In America the audience for poetry has changed in the last 30 years, and that is partly because of the friendship between psychology and poetry. For whatever reason, the audience is noticeably larger. A book that came out in an edition of 1,000 copies in 1950 would have an edition of 10,000 now. But what is much more important, the texture of the audience has changed. People read poetry for delight and because colleges assign it, but also because poetry represents a private resistance and the stubborn persistence in a commodity society of what the essayist Lewis Hyde calls "gift-giving."

After I graduated from college, I spent several years alone in New York City, then a year at the University of Iowa Writers' Workshop, and then I moved to the country. I didn't choose the rural area for romantic reasons, but because I got a free house to live in on a farm of my father's. Yet, as I realized recently, some self-doubt is always a part of living in a town that doesn't want you or respect art. Yeats said that at times he would debate with himself and:

Wonder how many times I could have proved my worth
In something that all others understand or share.

To augment royalties, I leave my house and family

three months a year--January, March and May.  I make
most of my living now from teaching small groups of people
(some groups are entirely men) who sign up in advance.
I teach fairy tales, and at times Blake.  The memorization
of fairy stories helps later writing.

    Any art form, when pursued over a long period,
gradually reveals hidden dignities, secret thought and its
connection with other art forms.  It asks for more and more
labor.  I finally understand the idea that poetry is a form
of dance.  I may not be able to do it, but I understand it.
As I've gotten older, I find I am able to be nourished more
by sorrow and to distinguish it from depression.

        What is sorrow for?  It is a storehouse far
        in the north for wheat, barley, corn and tears.
        One steps to the door on a round stone.
        The storehouse feeds all the birds of sorrow.
        And I say to myself:  will you have
        sorrow at last?  Go on, be cheerful in autumn,
        be stoic, yes ... be tranquil, calm,
        or in the valley of sorrows spread your wings.

    A Russian fairy story, "The Frog Princess," published
in Aleksandr Afanasyev's "Russian Fairy Tales," describes
what it's like to take up the life of an artist, especially
when one doesn't know what one is doing.  A father tells
his sons to shoot arrows away from the house as a way to
choose their brides.  The older brothers get a prince's
daughter and a general's daughter.  The youngest son's
arrow falls short and lights in a swamp, from which a frog
hops, carrying the arrow in her mouth.  So the youngest
son has to marry a frog.  When you begin to write poetry,
the language doesn't behave, the line won't hold steady,
the poem reveals more than you intended or something dif-
ferent.  You feel clammy and unevolved and, moreover, your
friends can tell by looking at you that you're sleeping with
a frog.

    It's embarrassing to bring this frog forward in public
as your bride, even though you have no other.  It turns
out that the frog bride can slip out of her frogskin at night
and do certain things your older brothers' wives can do--
for example, get a shirt made, get good bread baked, and
so on.  But she is still a frog.  Finally the crisis comes.

The bride offers to appear at the king's ball for the first
time as a human being, and she does, leaving her frogskin
at home.  Everyone is entranced with her.  Without telling
his wife, the man slips out of the ball early, goes home and
burns the frogskin.  That was a bad mistake because, as
we can guess, the bride needs the frogskin.  Now she has
to leave, and much grief for both of them follows from the
husband's secretive act.

Some rationalist inside us urges us to burn our frog-
skins.  I don't know all that "burning the frogskin" implies,
but it suggests losing something that is wet, embarrassing,
precious and private.  Writing a commercial novel can re-
semble burning a frogskin.  By nature, confessional poetry,
because of its lack of reserve, drives and scorches the
frogskin.  Publishing a book of poems when one is too
young is like burning a frogskin; something is damaged.
A poetry reading, when it is done to entice love, can be
a public burning of your frogskin; I have done that.  I
have a longing for love from strangers.  But Boris Paster-
nak gave public readings for years and retained integrity,
so public readings need not damage that which should be
private.

If we get rid of the frog, we lose the way back to
some ancient, instinctive source.  We all burn our frogskins
in different ways.  I have burned mine more than once,
from wanting to evolve while leaving the animal behind.
Pursuing the discipline of poetry then includes studying
the art, experiencing grief, and keeping the frog's skin
wet.

PART I:

WRITINGS BY ROBERT BLY

A.  BOOKS

POETRY AND PROSE

A1.   A BROADSHEET AGAINST THE NEW YORK TIMES BOOK RE-
VIEW   1961

[in red:]   25¢.  /  A Broadsheet  /  Against  /  The New York
Times Book Review  /  1961  /  THE SIXTIES PRESS

Collation:   5 1/4 X 8 3/8".   No sign.   6 leaves.   Pp. [1-12].

Pagination:   p. [1] title-page; p. [2] blank; pp. [3-12]
text; p. [12] "Published by The Sixties Press, Odin House,
Madison, Minnesota.   25¢ / per copy.   Printed in the Re-
public of Ireland."

Binding:   White paper covers.   Title-page is the cover.
Back cover completes text and includes copyright notice.

Location:   SUNY Buffalo

Note:   Interview reprinted from B2.


A2.   THE LION'S TAIL AND EYES   1962

[in blue:] The Lion's Tail and Eyes / [in black:] Poems
written out of laziness / and silence / by / JAMES
WRIGHT, WILLIAM DUFFY, / AND ROBERT BLY /
[in blue:] [publisher's device:  horseman with shield and
spear surrounded by two birds and a snake] / [in black:]
1962 / THE SIXTIES PRESS

Collation:   5 1/4 X 8 7/16".   [1-16]$^3$:   24 leaves.   Pp.
[1-4] 5-6 [7-10] 11-20 [21-22] 23-32 [33-34] 35-45 [46-48]

Pagination:   p. [1] half-title; p. [2] blank; p. [3] title-
page; p. [4] [acknowledgments] / "Library of Congress
Catalogue Card Number: / 62-21532. / Copyright © 1962
by the Sixties Press, / Odin House, Madison, Minnesota.
/ Printed in the Republic of Ireland."; pp. 5-6, "Note"
[by R. B.]; p. [7] second half-title; p. [8] blank; pp.
[9]-[45] text; pp. [46-48] blank.

Binding:  Blue cloth covered boards stamped in black.
Spine, reading downwards:  THE LION'S TAIL AND EYES
THE SIXTIES PRESS.  End-papers front and back of white
paper.

Dust jacket:  Front:  [within black frame:]  [to the left,
in black and white:]  [drawing of lion and tree on blue
field].  [to the right:]  [in white box with black frame:]
[in blue:]  THE / LION'S / TAIL / AND / EYES / [in
black:]  The Sixties Press.  Back cover and spine, paper
white, printed in black.  Spine, reading downwards:
THE LION'S TAIL AND EYES  THE SIXTIES PRESS.
Back:  OTHER BOOKS PUBLISHED BY THE SIXTIES
PRESS / [lists nine titles] / The publisher will be glad
to fill orders directly.  Order from:  THE SIXTIES
PRESS, / ODIN HOUSE, MADISON, MINNESOTA.  All
volumes are $2.00 for cloth bound, / $1.00 for soft cover.
Flyleaves, paper in white.  Front flyleaf:  [in black:]
[twenty line statement on the book] / $2.00.

Back flyleaf:  [twenty-four line statement on The Sixties
Press].

Contents:  James Wright:  Lying in a Hammock at William
Duffy's Farm in Pine Island, Minnesota/A Dream of Burial/
In Fear of Harvests/The Undermining of the Defense Econ-
omy/Spring Images/The Jewel/As I Step Over a Puddle at
the End of Winter, I Think of an Ancient Chinese Governor/
Milkweed/From a Bus Window in Central Ohio, Just Before
a Thunderstorm/Twilights
William Duffy:  Poem on Forgetting the Body/How to Begin
a Poem/Elk/Poem/Slowly/Premonitions/The Horse is Loose/
Marsh Nest/Rendering/This Lion of Loneliness
Robert Bly:  Silence/Snowfall in the Afternoon/Late at Night
During a Visit of Friends/Reading the Translations of Wil-
liam Hung/Poem in Three Parts/"Taking the Hands"/The
Grass-Headed Lion/Traveller Leaves Appomatox/Sparks Of
the Body/Evolution From the Fish

Location:  Columbia University

Note:  Jacket illustration is by Carol Bly [note from Bly to
William Heyen].

First paper edition:  1962

Title page, collation, pagination, and contents same as hard-
bound.

Binding:  White paper covers.  Issued in paper wrappers.

Design on wrappers is same as dust jacket of hardbound,
except front flyleaf: [twenty line statement on the book]
/ $1.00.

Location:  SUNY Stony Brook


A3.  SILENCE IN THE SNOWY FIELDS  1962

Silence in the / Snowy Fields / POEMS BY ROBERT BLY /
Wesleyan University Press:  MIDDLETOWN, CONNECTICUT
[the above against a gray abstract design on a white page].

Collation:  5 15/16 X 8".  [1-16]4:  32 leaves.  Pp. [1-10]
11-21 [22-24] 25-47 [48-50] 51-60 [61-64].

Pagination:  p. [1] half-title; p. [2] blank; p. [3] title-
page; p. [4] "Copyright © 1953, 1959, 1960, 1961, 1962 by
Robert Bly" / [acknowledgments] / "Library of Congress
Catalog Card Number:  62-18340 / Manufactured in the
United States of America / First Edition"; p. [5] "'We are
all asleep in the outward man.' / --Jacob Boehme"; pp.
[6-7] "Contents"; p. [8] blank; pp. [9]-60, text; pp. [61-
64] blank.

Binding:  Gray cloth covered boards, stamped in blue.
Spine, reading downwards:  ROBERT BLY  SILENCE IN
THE SNOWY FIELDS [publisher's device:  shield with a
cross].  End-papers front and back of white paper slightly
heavier than the sheets.


Contents:  Eleven Poems of Solitude:  Three Kinds of
Pleasures/Return to Solitude/Waking from Sleep/Hunting
Pheasants in a Cornfield/Surprised by Evening/Thinking of
Wallace Stevens on the First Snowy Day in December/Sunset
in a Lake/Fall/Approaching Winter/Driving Toward the Lac
Qui Parle River/Poem in Three Parts
Awakening:  Unrest/Awakening/Poem Against the Rich/Poem
Against the British/Where We Must Look For Help/Remember-
ing in Oslo the Old Picture of the Magna Carta/Summer,
1960, Minnesota/With Pale Women in Maryland/Driving
Through Ohio/At the Funeral of Great-Aunt Mary/On the
Ferry Across Chesapeake Bay/A Man Writes to a Part of
Himself/Depression/Driving To Town Late to Mail a Letter/
Getting Up Early/A Late Spring Day in My Life/Love Poem/
"Taking the Hands"/Afternoon Sleep/Images Suggested by
Medieval Music/Solitude Late at Night in the Woods/Watering
the Horse/In a Train.  Silence on the Roads:  After Working/
The Clear Air of October/Laziness and Silence/September
Night With an Old Horse/Night/After Drinking All Night With

a Friend, We Go Out in a Boat at Dawn to See Who Can
Write the Best Poem/Old Boards/Late at Night During a
Visit of Friends/Silence/Snowfall in the Afternoon


First paper edition: 1962

Title page, collation, pagination, and contents same as hard-
bound.

Binding: Stiff paper covers. Front, blue paper with an
abstract design in black. Front: [in white:] poems by
ROBERT BLY / [in gray:] Silence in the / Snowy Fields.
Reading upwards from bottom left corner: [in black:]
Boultinghouse. Spine and back, white paper. Spine, read-
ing downwards: [in black:] Robert Bly [in blue:]
SILENCE IN THE SNOWY FIELDS [in brown:] Wesleyan.
Back: [in brown:] ROBERT / BLY [reading downwards:]
[in blue:] SILENCE IN THE SNOWY FIELDS [in black:]
[twenty-nine line statement on R.B.] / WESLEYAN UNIVER-
SITY PRESS / $1.45 Middletown, Connecticut


A4.  DUCKS  1966

[in black:] DUCKS / Robert Bly

Collation:  4 1/2 X 6".  No sign.  2 leaves.  Pp. [1-4]

Pagination:  p. [1] title-page; p. [2] blank; p. [3]
"DUCKS"; p. [4] blank

Binding:  Light brown paper covers printed in black.
Front: DUCKS / Robert Bly.  Back: OX HEAD PRESS /
Menomonie, Wisconsin.  Tan thread.

Contents:  Ducks [poem]

Location:  Bly

Note:  Approximately 50 copies printed.


Second edition:  1967

Contents same as first edition.

[in black:] ROBERT BLY / [in blue:] DUCKS / [in black:]
Ox Head Press / 1967

Collation:  4 5/8 X 7".  No sign.  4 leaves.  Pp. [1-8]

Pagination: p. [1] title-page; p. [2] "Copyright 1966 by
Robert Bly; p. [3] [inverted A]; p. [4] blank; p. [5]
"DUCKS"; p. [6] blank; p. [7] "This second edition of
Ducks has / been hand-set in Goudy Light / and printed
in an edition of 100 / numbered copies. March, 1967. /
This copy is number [　]."; p. [8] blank.

Binding: Light blue paper covers printed in black. Front:
ROBERT BLY / [rule] / DUCKS. Gray-blue thread.

Location: SUNY Buffalo

Note: Second edition was printed in an edition of 100 num-
bered copies, only 77 copies of which were bound; the rest
of the sheets were destroyed.


Third edition: 1968

Contents same as first edition.

[in black:] ROBERT BLY / [in blue:] DUCKS / [in black:]
Ox Head Press / [rule] / 1968

Collation: 4 1/8 X 6 1/4". No sign. 4 leaves. Pp. [1-8]

Pagination: p. [1] title-page; p. [2] "Copyright © 1966 /
by Robert Bly"; pp. [3-4] blank; p. [5] "DUCKS"; p. [6]
blank; p. [7] "The third Ox Head edition / of DUCKS is
limited to 150 / numbered copies. This is / copy number /
[　] / [ornamental leaf device]

Binding: Gray paper covers printed in black. Front:
ROBERT BLY / [rule] / DUCKS. White thread.

Location: Bly

Note: Limited to 150 numbered copies.


Fourth, or "Migration" edition: 1972

Contents same as first edition.

[in black:] ROBERT BLY / [in red:] DUCKS / [in black:]
Ox Head Press / 1972

Collation: 4 1/8 X 6 1/4". No sign. 6 leaves. Pp. [1-12]

Pagination: pp. [1-2] blank; p. [3] title-page; p. [4]
"Copyright © 1966, 1968, 1972 / by Robert Bly"; p. [5]

"Migration Edition"; p. [6] blank; p. [7] "DUCKS"; p. [8]
blank; p. [9] "A Note on the Migration Edition / Our fourth
edition of DUCKS was printed / at Marshall, Minnesota in
an edition of / 450 copies. The paper is Curtis Rag, the
/ cover is Strathmore Imperial Blue and the / typeface is
Goudy Oldstyle. / D. Olsen, Printer / October 14, 1972";
pp. [10-12] blank.

Binding: Dark blue paper covers printed in black. Front:
ROBERT BLY / [rule] / DUCKS. Blue thread.

Location: Bly

Note: Limited to 450 copies.


A5.  CHRYSANTHEMUMS  1967

ROBERT BLY / [ornament:  leaf] / CHRYSANTHEMUMS /
OX HEAD PRESS - 1967

Collation:  4 1/8 X 6 1/4".  [1-12]:  6 leaves.  Pp. [1-12].

Pagination:  pp. [1-2] blank; p. [3] title-page; p. [4]
"COPYRIGHT 1967 / BY ROBERT BLY"; p. [5] "OX HEAD
4"; p. [6] blank; p. [7] "CHRYSANTHEMUMS" [poem]; p.
[8] blank; p. [9] "CHRYSANTHEMUMS / Has been hand-
set and printed / at Menomonie, Wisconsin, dur- / ing
November-December, 1967, / in an edition of 350 numbered
/ copies. This copy is number / [  ]"; pp. [10-12] blank.

Binding:  Green wrappers.  Front:  [in black:] ROBERT
BLY / [ornament:  leaf] / CHRYSANTHEMUMS.

Contents:  Chrysanthemums.

Location:  SUNY Stony Brook


A6.  [LETTER TO ROGER L. STEVENS]  1967

[white sheet printed in black and blue] [in blue:] THE
SIXTIES PRESS / Odin House / MADISON, MINNESOTA
56256 / UNITED STATES / EDITOR:  ROBERT BLY / [to
the right of the above:  publisher's device:  woodcut of a
horseman with spear and shield surrounded by two birds
and a snake] / [in black:] 12 September 1967 / [text in a
single column ] / [in blue:] [facsimile of R. B.'s signature]

Collation:  9 X 12".  Single sheet printed on one side only.

Binding:  None.  All edges trimmed.

Contents:  Facsimile reproduction of a letter R. B. wrote
the chairman of the National Foundation on the Arts & Hu-
manities refusing a grant offer on the basis of his opposi-
tion to the Vietnam War.

Location:  SUNY Buffalo

Note:  Alternate titles:  "Dear Mr. Stevens," "Letter, 1967
Sept. 12, Madison, Minn., to Roger L. Stevens, Washing-
ton, D.C."  Publisher is Unicorn Press, Santa Barbara,
California.  Part of the Unicorn Folio, Series 1, no. 4, [pt.
4].  Limited to 325 copies.

A7.   THE LIGHT AROUND THE BODY   1967

THE LIGHT / AROUND THE BODY / Poems by / ROBERT
BLY / [publisher's device:  stylized torch dividing the date,
1817, all in an oval] / Harper & Row, Publishers / New
York, Evanston, and London

Collation:  5 1/2 X 8 1/8".  [1-16]$^5$:  40 leaves.  Pp. [a-
b] [i-vi] vii-viii [1-2] 3-10 [11-12] 13-25 [26-28] 29-37
[38-40] 41-50 [51-52] 53-62 [63-70].

Pagination:  pp. [a-b] blank; p. [i] half-title; p. [ii] "by
Robert Bly" [lists two books]; p. [iii] title-page; p. [iv]
[acknowledgments] / "THE LIGHT AROUND THE BODY.
Copyright © 1959, 1960, 1961, 1962, 1963, / 1964, 1965,
1966, 1967 by Robert Bly.  Printed in the United States
of America. / All rights reserved.  No part of this book
may be used or reproduced in any / manner whatsoever
without written permission except in the case of brief quo-
/ tations embodied in critical articles and reviews.  For in-
formation address Harper / & Row, Publishers, Incorporated,
49 East 33rd Street, New York, N.Y. 10016. / FIRST EDI-
TION"; p. [v] dedication:  "For My Mother and Father";
p. [vi] blank; pp. vii-viii, "Contents"; pp. [1]-62, text;
p. [63] "About the Author"; pp. [64-70] blank.

Binding:  Blue paper covered boards, printed in white.
Front:  THE / LIGHT / AROUND / THE BODY / Poems by
/ ROBERT BLY.  Spine, reading downwards:  THE LIGHT
AROUND THE BODY Robert Bly.  End-papers front and
back of cream color paper slightly heavier than the sheets.
Fore edge untrimmed.

Dust jacket:  Front cover and spine, dark blue.  Front:
[in white:] The / Light / Around / The Body / Poems by
/ Robert Bly.  Spine, reading downwards:  [in white:]
The Light Around The Body Robert Bly / [reading across:]

Harper / & Row.  Back:  [photograph of R.B. by Douglas
Hall] / [in blue on white:] Robert Bly.  Flyleaves, paper
in tan.  Front flyleaf:  [in blue:] $3.95 / The Light /
Around The Body / Poems by / Robert Bly / [twenty-four
line statement on R. B. continued on back flyleaf].  Back
flyleaf:  [in blue:] (continued from front flap) / [fifteen
line statement].

Contents:  I. The Two Worlds:  The Executive's Death/The
Busy Man Speaks/Johnson's Cabinet Watched by Ants/Watch-
ing Television/Smothered by the World/A Dream of Suffoca-
tion/Romans Angry about the Inner World
II. The Various Arts of Poverty and Cruelty:  Come with
Me/Those Being Eaten by America/Written in Dejection near
Rome/Listening to President Kennedy Lie about the Cuban
Invasion/The Great Society/Suddenly Turning Away/Three
Presidents/Hearing Men Shout at Night on Macdougal Street/
The Current Administration/Andrew Jackson's Speech/Sleet
Storm on the Merritt Parkway
III. The Vietnam War:  After the Industrial Revolution, All
Things Happen at Once/Asian Peace Offers Rejected without
Publication/War and Silence/Counting Small-Boned Bodies/
As the Asian War Begins/At a March Against the Vietnam
War/Hatred of Men with Black Hair/Driving through Minne-
sota during the Hanoi Bombings
IV. In Praise of Grief:  Melancholia/Turning Away from
Lies/A Home in Dark Grass/Looking at New-Fallen Snow
From a Train/In Danger from the Outer World/The Fire of
Despair Has Been Our Saviour/Looking at Some Flowers
V. A Body Not Yet Born:  Looking into a Face/Hurrying
Away from the Earth/The Hermit/A Journey with Women/
Moving Inward at Last/Riderless Horses/Evolution from the
Fish/Wanting to Experience All Things/Opening an Oyster/
When the Dumb Speak

Location:  SUNY Buffalo


First paper edition:  1967

Collation, pagination, and contents same as hardbound.

THE LIGHT / AROUND THE BODY / Poems by / Robert Bly
/ HARPER & ROW, PUBLISHERS / New York, Hagerstown,
San Francisco, London

Binding:  Stiff paper covers.  Front cover and spine, blue
paper printed in white.  Front:  HARPER [Publisher's de-
vice] COLOPHON BOOKS/CN 786 /$3.95 / The / Light /
Around / The Body / Poems by / Robert Bly.  Spine,
reading downards:  The Light Around the Body  Robert Bly
Harper & Row CN786.  Back cover:  [in blue tones:]

[photograph of R. B. by Douglas Hall] / [in blue on white:]
ROBERT BLY [to right:] DOUGLAS HALL / 0-06-090786-X.

Location:   Roberson


A8.   OPENING AN OYSTER   1967

[tan paper printed in black, illustrated with five seashells
in white] [to left of center:] OPENING AN OYSTER / [text
in a single column] / ROBERT BLY [to right of center:]
On the occasion of Robert Bly's poetry reading / at the
Unicorn Book Shop, April 21, 1967, / 200 copies of this
broadside / were designed and handset by Barbara Bianco,
/ printed by Bill Horton, / and published by Unicorn
Press.

Collation:   17 X 12".   Single sheet printed on one side only.

Binding:   None.   All edges trimmed.

Contents:   Opening an Oyster [poem]

Location:   SUNY Buffalo

Note:   Limited to 200 copies, of which 26 are lettered and
signed by R. B.   Printed for R. B.'s poetry reading at the
Unicorn Book Shop, April 21, 1967.


A9.   SILENCE IN THE SNOWY FIELDS AND OTHER POEMS   1967

SILENCE IN THE SNOWY FIELDS / ROBERT BLY | and Other
Poems | [publisher's device:   ornamental bowl of fruit with
a J to the left and a C to the right, all enclosed in a circle]
| Jonathan Cape / Thirty Bedford Square / London

Collation:   5 3/4 X 8 1/2".   [1-16]$^5$:   40 leaves.   Pp. [1-10]
11-20 [21-22] 23-34 [35-36] 37-51 [52-54] 55-72 [73-74] 75-
78 [79-80].

Pagination:   p. [1] half-title; p. [2] blank; p. [3] title-
page; p. [4] "© 1953, 1959, 1960, 1961, 1963, 1964 by
Robert Bly / New enlarged edition © 1967 by Robert Bly"
/ [acknowledgments] / "The original, somewhat smaller edi-
tion of this book was / published in the United States by
Wesleyan University Press / Made and printed in Great
Britain / by Butler & Tanner Ltd, Frome and London / on
paper made by John Dickinson & Co. Ltd"; pp. [5-7] "Con-
tents"; p. [8] "We are all asleep in the outward man /
Jacob Boehme"; pp. [9]-78, text; pp. [79-80] blank.

Binding:  Aqua blue paper covered boards with white pa-
per covered spine.  Spine, stamped in gold, reading up-
wards:  [publisher's device] SILENCE IN THE SNOWY
FIELDS  ROBERT BLY.  End-papers front and back of
white paper.

Contents:  One/We Know the Road:  Waking from Sleep/
Poem in Three Parts/Solitude Late at Night in the Woods/
After Working/Watering the Horse/Old Boards/Three Kinds
of Pleasures/Surprised by Evening/Return to Solitude/The
Loon
Two/Unrest:  Awakening/Where We Must Look for Help/A
Train Trip in Iowa/Unrest/Hearing Men Shout at Night on
MacDougal Street/On the Ferry Across Chesapeake Bay/A
Man Writes to a Part of Himself/The End of the Old Days/
Ford Cars on their Deathbed/Old and Bad Memories
Three/Private Poems:  Love Poem/'Taking the Hands'/With
Pale Women in Maryland/Laziness and Silence/Driving
through Ohio/Waking from an Afternoon Sleep/Images Sug-
gested by Medieval Music/A Late Spring Day in my Life/
In a Train/Walking at Dusk/Beginning their Empire/Early
Spring/Driving to Town Late to Mail a Letter
Four/In Western Minnesota:  Hunting Pheasants in a Corn-
field/October Evening in Minnesota/At the Funeral of
Great-Aunt Mary/Sunset at a Lake/Night/Driving towards
the Lac Qui Parle River/Summer, 1960, Minnesota/Septem-
ber Night with an Old Horse/Late at Night during a Visit
of Friends/Sitting in a Cornfield/Poem against the British/
Getting up Early/Minnesota Fall/After Drinking all Night
with a Friend, We Go out in a Boat at Dawn to See Who
can Write the Best Poem
Five/Snowfall in the Afternoon:  Poem against the Rich/
Depression/Silence/Snowfall in the Afternoon

Location:  SUNY Buffalo


A10.  ACCEPTANCE SPEECH BY ROBERT BLY ON WINNING THE
      NATIONAL BOOK AWARD FOR POETRY  1968

      [two white mimeographed sheets] Acceptance Speech by
      Robert Bly / on Winning the National Book Award for
      Poetry / [text of speech]

      Collation:  8 1/2 X 11".  Two sheets printed on one side
      only.

      Binding:  None.  All edges trimmed.  Stapled in upper
      left corner.

      Contents:  Text of R. B.'s speech on winning the National
      Book Award for poetry.

Location:   Piccione

Note:   Privately published.   Copy examined had last line
running off the page.

A11.   IN A BOAT ON BIG STONE LAKE   1968

[white sheet with large bright yellow oval in upper center
and five green wavy vertical lines] [in black:] IN A BOAT
ON / BIG STONE LAKE / for Jack Maquire / [text in a
single column] / - Robert Bly / Unicorn Broadsheet Two
/ Silk Screen by Varden Berg / Copyright 1968 Robert Bly.

Collation:   13 X 18 1/4".   Single sheet printed on one side
only.

Binding:   None.   All edges trimmed.

Contents:   In a boat on Big Stone Lake [poem]

Location:   SUNY Stony Brook

Note:   Part of Unicorn Broadsheet Series I, no. 2.   Also
published as a postcard.   See below.

Postcard edition:   1968

Binding, contents same as broadsheet.

[white card] Front:   [large bright yellow oval in center]
[in blue:] IN A BOAT ON BIG STONE LAKE / [text in a
single column] / Robert Bly.   Back:   [in black:] [upper
left corner:] Unicorn Postcard Copyright 1968, Robert Bly
/ from Unicorn Broadsheet Series I (1968-69).   [lettered
down the middle:] UNICORN PRESS BOX 1469 SANTA
BARBARA, CAL. [to the right, across:] TO:

Collation:   4 1/2 X 6 1/2".   Single card printed on both
sides.

Location:   SUNY Buffalo

Note:   Also published as a broadside.   See above.

A12.   THE LIGHT AROUND THE BODY [First British edition].
1968

THE LIGHT / AROUND THE BODY / Poems by / Robert
Bly / Rapp & Whiting London

Collation:  5 3/8 X 8 1/2":  32 leaves.  Pp. [i-vi] [1-2]
3-27 [28-30] 31-45 [46-48] 49-57 [58].

Pagination:  p. [i] half-title / "About the Author"; p.
[ii] "BOOKS BY ROBERT BLY" [lists eleven titles]; p.
[iii] title-page; p. [iv] dedication:  "FOR MY mother AND
father" /[acknowledgments]/ "© 1959, 1960, 1961, 1962,
1963, 1964, 1965, 1966, 1967, 1968 / ROBERT BLY /
FIRST PUBLISHED 1968 IN GREAT BRITAIN BY / RAPP
& WHITING LIMITED / 76 NEW OXFORD STREET LONDON
WC 1 / PRINTED IN ENGLAND BY / THE HOLLEN STREET
PRESS LIMITED / ALL RIGHTS RESERVED"; pp. [v-vi]
"Contents"; pp. [1]-57, text; p. [58] blank.

Binding:  Maroon cloth covered boards, stamped in gold.
Spine, reading downwards:  The Light around the Body /
[device] / Robert Bly.

End-papers front and back of white paper same as the
sheets.

Dust jacket:  Front and spine, paper purple.  Front:
[in black outline:] POETRY USA SERIES / [in white:]
[Series of eleven concentric circles gradually increasing
in thickness and running off the cover on the fore edge.]
[In the last circle, in black:] Robert Bly / The / Light /
around the / Body.  Spine, reading downwards:  [out-
lined in black:] POETRY USA SERIES [in black:] BLY
[reading across:] Rapp & / Whiting.  Back cover, paper
white.  [in purple:] [device] [in black:] Rapp & Whiting
Limited / 128/134 BAKER STREET LONDON W1.  Flyleaves,
paper in white.  Front flyleaf:  [in black:] [thirty-three
line statement on R. B.] / Jacket design by Lawrence Ed-
wards / 21s net.  Back flyleaf:  [in purple outline:]
POETRY USA SERIES / [in black:] [five titles listed] /
Each 21s net / Rapp & Whiting Limited / 128/134 Baker
Street London W1 / Printed in Great Britain.

Contents:  The Various Arts of Poverty and Cruelty:
Come with Me/The Executive's Death/Sleet Storm on the
Merritt Parkway/As the Asian War Begins/The Great Soci-
ety/After the Industrial Revolution, All Things Happen at
Once/Johnson's Cabinet Watched by Ants/Melancholia/A
Dream of Suffocation/Counting Small-Boned Bodies/Watching
Television/Hatred of Men with Black Hair/Three Presidents/
Listening to President Kennedy Lie about the Cuban In-
vasion/Those Being Eaten by America/Andrew Jackson's
Speech/The Current Administration/At a March against the
Vietnam War/War and Silence/Asian Peace Offers Rejected
without Publication/Driving through Minnesota during the
Hanoi Bombings

In Praise of Grief:  The Busy Man Speaks/Romans Angry
about the Inner World/Smothered by the World/In Danger
from the Outer World/The Fire of Despair Has Been Our
Saviour/Hurrying Away from the Earth/When the Dumb
Speak/A Home in Dark Grass/Moving Inward at Last/
Turning Away from Lies/The Hermit/Looking at Some
Flowers/Looking into a Face.  The Two Worlds:  Written in
Dejection near Rome/Wanting to Experience All Things/
Riderless Horses/Looking at New-Fallen Snow from a
Train/Suddenly Turning Away/A Journey with Women/
Evolution from the Fish/Opening an Oyster

Location:  SUNY Buffalo


A13.  THREE SHORT POEMS  1968

[light tan paper printed in red, black, purple, green, and
brown] [in red:] [illustration] [in black:] THREE SHORT
POEMS / [in purple:  first poem:] Writing love poems
again. / Her dark face so close to me, / The longing to
talk of Ice Age things / [four devices] / [in green:
second poem:] I draw near her blouse. / Tiny pieces of
mother-of-pearl. / Glittering over her breasts. / [four
devices] / [in purple:  third poem:] Her nipples are the
color / Of the reeds around / Moses' basket. / [in black:]
ROBERT BLY

Collation:  6 1/2 X 9 1/2".  Single sheet printed on one
side only.

Binding:  None.  All edges trimmed.

Contents:  Three poems

Location:  Heyen

Note:  In a letter to Heyen from Bly, he states that the
broadside was printed by Wang Hui-Ming at Leonard Bas-
kin's Gehenna Press.  It was part of a limited edition of
"pornographic" woodcuts.


A14.  THE MORNING GLORY  1969

[in black:] THE MORNING GLORY / [in green:] ANOTHER
THING THAT WILL NEVER BE MY FRIEND / [in black:]
twelve prose poems by ROBERT BLY with twelve drawings
by TOMIE DE PAOLA

Collation:  6 1/2 X 8 1/4".  [1-36]:  18 leaves.  Pp. [1-6]

7 [8] 9 [10] 11 [12] 13 [14] 15 [16] 17 [18] 19 [20] 21
[22] 23 [24] 25 [26] 27 [28] 29 [30] 31 [32-33] 34-35 [36].

Pagination:   p. [1] blank; pp. [2-3] title-page; pp. [4-5]
blank; p. [6] "Copyright © 1969 by Robert Bly"; p. 7,
"There is an old occult saying:  whoever wants to see the
/ invisible must penetrate more deeply into the visible. /
Everything has a right to exist.  If we examine an animal
/ carefully, we see how independent it is of us.  Its world
is / complete without us.  We feel separated at first; later,
joyful. / Basho says in his wonderful poem: / The morning
glory - / Another thing / that will never be my friend.";
pp. [8]-31, text and drawings; pp. [32]-34, blank; p. 35,
[drawing] / "Eight hundred copies of this book designed
and / printed by George Hitchcock at the Kayak / Press.";
p. [36] blank.

Binding:  White paper covers.  Front:  [in green:] THE
MORNING GLORY / [drawing in purple, green and black]
/ [in black:] ROBERT BLY / [in green:] KAYAK - $ 1.50.
End-papers front and back of brown paper.  Pages 1-4,
11-12, 25-26, and 33-36 are white.  All other pages are
tan.  Some pages have untrimmed edges.  Printed on front
end-paper in black:  A publication of Kayak Books, Inc.,
2808 Laguna St., / San Francisco, California.

Contents:  A Small Bird's Nest Made of White Reed Paper/
Looking at a Dead Wren in My Hand/Seeing Creely For the
First Time/The Hunter/Sitting On Some Rocks In Shaw
Cove, California/Two Prose Poems on Locked-In Animals/
Looking at a Dry Canadian Thistle Brought In From the
Snow/A Hollow Tree/A Turtle/Going In a Helicopter From
Riverside to the LA Airport/A Half-Grown Porcupine/Sketch
for A Renaissance Painting.

Location:  SUNY Stony Brook


A15.   Second, revised and enlarged edition.  1970.

[in brown:] THE MORNING GLORY / ANOTHER THING
THAT WILL NEVER BE MY FRIEND / twelve prose poems
by ROBERT BLY with twelve drawings by TOMIE DE PAOLA

Collation:  6 1/8 X 8 1/2".  [1-48]:  24 leaves.  Pp. [i-ii]
[1-6] 7 [8] 9 [10] 11 [12] 13 [14] 15-17 [18] 19 [20] 21-23
[24] 25 [26] 27-29 [30] 31 [32] 33-35 [36] 37 [38] 39
[40-42] 43 [44-46].

Pagination:  pp. [i-ii] blank; p. [1] blank; pp. [2-3]
title-page; p. [4] blank; p. [5] [acknowledgments]/ "A
publication of Kayak Books, 3965 Bonny Doon Road, /

Santa Cruz, Calif. 95060"; p. [6] "Copyright © 1969, 1970 by Robert Bly."; p. 7, [same as first edition]; pp. [8]-39, text and drawings; pp. [40-42] blank; p. 43, [drawing] / "Fifteen hundred copies of this book designed by / George Hitchcock at the Kayak Press and / printed by Sentinel Printers. / Second, revised and enlarged edition."; pp. [44-46] blank.

Binding: Covers same as first edition. End-papers front and back of light blue paper. All pages are tan. All pages have trimmed edges.

Contents: A Small Bird's Nest Made of White Reed Fiber/ Looking at a Dead Wren in My Hand/Seeing Creeley for the First Time/The Hunter/Looking Into a Tide Pool/Walking on the Sussex Coast/Sitting on Some Rocks in Shaw Cove, California/Two Prose Poems on Locked-In Animals/ At a Fish Hatchery in Story, Wyoming/A Caterpillar on the Desk/Looking at a Dry Canadian Thistle Brought in From the Snow/A Hollow Tree/Grassblades/Frost/A Turtle/ Going in a Helicopter From Riverside to the L.A. Airport/ On the Rocks at Maui/Waterfall Coming Over a Cliff/A Half-Grown Porcupine/Leonardo's Secret.
Location: SUNY Stony Brook


Third edition.  1970.

Title page, collation, pagination, binding, and contents same as A15.
Location: SUNY Stony Brook


A16.   TWO POEMS  1969

Woodcuts by Wang Hui-Ming. [Amherst:] Massachusetts Review. [8] p.

Contents: Two Together/Turtle Climbing from a Rock

Not verified, listed in OCLC by Ball State University, Muncie, IN.


A17.   COUNTING SMALL-BONED BODIES  1970

[gray-green sheet printed in black] Counting Small-Boned Bodies / [text in single column] / Robert Bly [in orange:] free poetry institute for / study of nonviolence palo alto, california

Collation: 7 X 11".  Single sheet printed on one side only.

Binding:  None.  All edges trimmed.

Contents:  Counting Small-Boned Bodies [poem]

Location:  SUNY Buffalo


A18.  [LOOKING INTO A FACE]   1970

THE DEPARTMENT OF ENGLISH / INVITES YOU TO / A
LECTURE/READING / "TWO WORLDS:  A READING" / BY
/ ROBERT BLY / ON WEDNESDAY / MARCH 11, 1970/ AT
/ 8:30 P.M. / IN THE / LOUNGE OF THE / OLD MEMORIAL
UNION / presented by the Brockport Writers Forum / a
series of free lectures and readings / around the creative
process in literature.

Collation:  5 1/2 X 8 1/2".  No sign.  2 leaves.  Pp. [1-
4].

Pagination:  p. [1] title-page; p. [2] [photograph of
R. B.] / [thirteen-line statement on R. B.]; p. [3]
"Looking into a Face" [poem]; p. [4] "PLACE:  MEMORIAL
LOUNGE OF OLD UNION / TIME:  8:30 P.M. / SCHEDULE
/ (SPRING, 1970) / [lists seven dates and the authors who
will be appearing] / No admission charge."

Binding:  Yellow color paper wrappers.  Front, reading
upwards:  [in gray:] [design of sixteen and a half lines
of authors' names separated by formee crosses].  Printed
over this design:  [in black:] DEPARTMENT OF / ENG-
LISH / STATE UNIVERSITY COLLEGE / BROCKPORT.

Contents:  Looking into a Face.

Location:  Roberson


A19.  OUTHOUSE POEM   1970

Santa Barbara, CA:  Unicorn Press.

Card, 22 X 15 cm.

Not verified, listed in OCLC by Ball State University,
Muncie, IN.


A20.  THE TEETH MOTHER NAKED AT LAST   1970

THE / TEETH-MOTHER / NAKED AT LAST / by / ROBERT

BLY / [publisher's device:  a Y with a circle in the groin]
/ City Lights Books.

Collation:  4 13/16 X 6 13/16".  No sign.  12 leaves.  Pp.
[1-4] 5-22 [23-24].

Pagination:  p. [1] title-page; p. [2] "Library of Con-
gress Catalog Card No. 73-11121 / © 1970 by Robert Bly
/ Parts of this poem have been printed earlier in the /
NATION and NEW AMERICAN REVIEW. / Printed in the
United States of America / City Lights Books are edited
by Lawrence Ferlinghetti / and published at the CITY
LIGHTS BOOKSTORE, / 261 Columbus Avenue, San Fran-
cisco, USA."; p. [3] half-title; p. [4] blank; pp. 5-22,
text; pp. [23-24] blank.

Binding:  Stiff white paper.  Front:  [in blue, at top:]
THE POCKET POET SERIES / [in white, on blue-tone
photograph of a Balinese Teeth Mother Mask:] THE
TEETH MOTHER / NAKED AT LAST / ROBERT BLY /
[in blue at bottom:] NUMBER TWENTY-SIX.  Back:
[in blue:] $1.00 / [fifteen line statement by Kenneth
Rexroth] / [eight line statement by publisher].  Spine,
reading downwards:  [in blue:] THE TEETH-MOTHER
NAKED AT LAST  Robert Bly.  Inside back cover:  [in
blue:] [publisher's ad of fifty lines].

Contents:  The Teeth-Mother Naked at Last.

Location:  SUNY Stony Brook

Note:  Also issued in conjunction with The Sixties Press
and made available from American Writers Against the
Vietnam War.  1 folded sheet, [12] p.  "Not to be sold.
Printed as a gift to the Resistance by Robert Bly and
Lawrence Ferlinghetti."


A reprint of the City Lights Books edition by the Kraus
Reprint Company, Millwood, New York, appeared in 1973.


A21.   [A CRICKET IN THE WAINSCOTING] [1971]

[white sheet printed in black] A CRICKET IN THE WAIN-
SCOTING ROBERT BLY / [text of five lines] / [rule] /
NOVEMBER [device] ROBERT BLY / [text of four lines] /
[rule] / [device] POEM [device] ROBERT BLY [device] /
[text of three lines] / [rule] / [device] THE LOON •
ROBERT BLY [device] / [text of three lines] / [rule] /
INSECT HEADS • ROBERT BLY / [text of four lines]

Collation:  9 X 12".  Single sheet printed on one side only.

Binding:  None.  All edges trimmed.

Contents:  A Cricket in the Wainscoting/November/Poem/
The Loon/Insect Heads

Location:  Roberson

Note:  The broadside is a woodcut by Wang Hui-Ming;
place of publication is Amherst, Massachusetts.  Signed by
Bly in lower left corner; signed by Wang in lower right
corner and dated 1971.


A22.  FOUR IMAGES FOR DEATH  1971

[light tan sheet printed in brown] Front:  FOUR IMAGES
FOR DEATH / [four lines, each separated by an asterisk]
/ Robert Bly.  Back:  [centered at bottom:] Copyright
1971 by Robert Bly / Published Free by / The "Slow
Loris" Press / 30 Charter Oaks #3 - Amherst, N.Y. 14221
/ [rule] / Printed in a limited edition of 200 copies / of
which 25 are numbered and / signed by the author

Collation:  8 1/2 X 11".  Single sheet printed on both
sides.

Binding:  None.  Right edge untrimmed.

Contents:  Four Images for Death

Location:  SUNY Buffalo

Note:  Limited to 200 copies of which 25 are numbered and
signed by R. B.


A23.  HEARING GARY SNYDER READ  1971

[white sheet with a red edge along the right side printed
in black and red] [in black:] Hearing Gary Snyder Read /
[text in a single column with stanzas separated by an orna-
mental device in red [a lion] to the left-hand side] / Uni-
corn Broadsheet Series Two Number Three April 20, 1971 /
Written in Albuquerque, N.M. in 1966 by Robert Bly / May
Be Reproduced Without Permission

Collation:  12 1/2 X 19".  Single sheet printed on one side
only.

Binding:  None.  Right edge untrimmed.

Contents:  Hearing Gary Snyder Read [poem]

Location:  SUNY Buffalo

Note:  Unicorn Broadsheet Series 2, number 3.  1010
copies were reprinted and distributed free in late 1971.


A24.  POEMS FOR TENNESSEE  1971

POEMS FOR / TENNESSEE / BY / ROBERT BLY / WILLIAM
STAFFORD / WILLIAM MATTHEWS / MARTIN / TENNESSEE
POETRY PRESS / 1971

Collation:  6 X 9 1/8".  No sign.  20 leaves.  Pp. [1-7]
8-17 [18-19] 20-29 [30-31] 32-40.

Pagination:  p. [1] title-page; p. [2] [acknowledgments]
/ "Copyright 1971 Stephen Mooney / Tennessee Poetry
Press, Box 196, Martin, Tennessee 38237 / Produced by
Laycook Printing Company, Jackson, Tennessee"; p. [3]
dedication:  "To Archie Dykes / for opening doors / to
poetry in Tennessee"; p. [4] blank; p. [5] "Bly, Stafford,
and Matthews" [introduction]; p. [6] blank; pp. [7]-17,
text of Bly poems; p. [18] blank; pp. [19]-29, text of
Stafford poems; p. [30] blank; pp. [31]-40, text of Mat-
thew poems.

Binding:  Stiff cream color paper covers printed in green
with cream color border on all sides.  Front:  [in cream:]
POEMS FOR / TENNESSEE / BY / ROBERT BLY / WILLIAM
STAFFORD / WILLIAM MATTHEWS / MARTIN / TENNESSEE
POETRY PRESS / 1971.  Spine, reading downwards:  [in
green:] POEMS FOR TENNESSEE.  Back:  [in green:]
[device] / POEMS FOR TENNESSEE / BLY, STAFFORD,
MATTHEWS / Tennessee Poetry Press / Stephen Mooney,
Editor / Box 196, Martin, 38237.

Contents:  Robert Bly:  Dawn in Threshing Time/Chrysan-
themums/Walking on the Shore in Late August/An Empty
Place/In a Boat on Big Stone Lake/Thinking of the Destruc-
tion of Hue During an Organ Concert/Driving in Snow/To
Tao Te Ching Running/On the Rocks at Maui/Standing Up
[Tranströmer translation].
William Stafford:  Ferns/The Little Lost Orphans/All My
Life/Questions to Ask in Salzburg/Landowners in the Indian
Country/The R. L. Stevenson Tree on Oahu/Winter Stories/
Final Exam:  American Renaissance/For Certain Little Maga-
zines We Won't Bother to Name/From the Trees in the Forest

William Matthews: The Moon/Rhododendron Leaf/A Field
Made Visible by Lightning/Stone/The Paper Route/Mar-
riage/A Shy Woman in the Snow/Care/Your Face/Your
Eyes, Your Name.

Location: SUNY Buffalo


A25.  RACHEL REBEKAH BLY  1971

[white sheet printed in black] [left side is photograph of
Bly's baby daughter] / Rachel Rebekah Bly / Holy Bap-
tism / Sunday, December 5, 1971 / Old Chatham, New York
[right side] Rachel Rebekah Bly / [text in a single column]
/ Robert Bly / Photo by Wang Hui-Ming

Collation:  11 X 7 1/2".  Single sheet printed on one side
only.

Binding:  None.  All edges trimmed.

Contents:  Rachel Rebekah Bly [poem]

Location:  Heyen


A26.  [SNOWFALL IN THE AFTERNOON]  1971

THE DEPARTMENT OF ENGLISH / INVITES YOU TO / A
READING OF HIS POETRY / by / ROBERT BLY / On
Wednesday / December 1, 1971 / At / 8:30 P.M. / In the
/ Red Room / Edwards Hall (Communications Building)

Collation:  5 1/2 X 8 1/2".  No sign.  2 leaves.  Pp. [1-4].

Pagination:  p. [1] title-page; p. [2] [photograph of
R. B.] / [nineteen line statement on R. B.]; p. [3]
"SNOWFALL IN THE AFTERNOON" [poem]; p. [4] [bottom
of the page: publisher's device].

Binding:  Mustard color paper wrappers.  Front, reading
upwards: [in gray:] [design of sixteen and a half lines
of authors' names separated by formee crosses].  Printed
over this design: [in black:] DEPARTMENT OF / ENG-
LISH / STATE UNIVERSITY COLLEGE / BROCKPORT.

Contents:  Snowfall in the Afternoon.

Location:  Roberson

A27.   [WILD HAY]   [1971]

> [white sheet printed in black] Wild HAY [device:  leaf]
> ROBERT BLY / [text of three lines] / [row of forty-three
> dots] / YES [three devices] ROBERT BLY / [text of three
> lines] / [rule] / SMALL TOWNS • ROBERT BLY / [text of
> four lines] / [rule] / MORNINGS OF WINTER • ROBERT
> BLY / [text of three lines] / [rule] / POEM IN ONE LINE
> • ROBERT BLY / [text]
>
> Collation:  9 X 12".  Single sheet printed on one side only.
>
> Binding:  None.  All edges trimmed.
>
> Contents:  Wild Hay/Yes/Small Towns/Mornings of Winter/
> Poem in One Line
>
> Location:  Heyen
>
> Note:  The broadside is a woodcut by Wang Hui-Ming;
> place of publication is Amherst, Massachusetts.

A28.   ANOTHER DOING NOTHING POEM [&] JUMPING OUT OF BED
[&] NOVEMBER DAY AT MCCLURE'S  1972

> [gray-blue sheet printed in black]  Front:  [upper left
> quadrant:] ROBERT BLY / [centered:] ANOTHER DOING
> NOTHING POEM / [text in a single column] / JUMPING
> OUT OF BED / [text in a single column].  Back:  NOVEM-
> BER DAY AT MCCLURE'S / [text].
>
> Collation:  8 3/4" X 11 1/4".  Single sheet printed on both
> sides.
>
> Binding:  None.  All edges trimmed.
>
> Contents:  Another Doing Nothing Poem/Jumping Out of
> Bed/November Day at McClure's
>
> Location:  Roberson
>
> Note:  This is part of Panjandrum, no. 1, edited by Den-
> nis Koran and published by the Panjandrum Press, San
> Francisco, issued as a folio of twenty-eight sheets.
>
> See A32 and I14.

A29.   CHRISTMAS EVE SERVICE AT MIDNIGHT AT ST. MICHAEL'S
1972

Christmas Eve Service / at Midnight at St. Michael's / for
Father Richter / ROBERT BLY

Collation:   7 3/8 X 7 3/8".   No sign.   2 leaves.   Pp. [1-4].

Pagination:   p. [1] title-page; p. [2] "This edition is lim-
ited to 100 copies, numbered / and printed on laid paper,
with nos 1 to 30 / being signed by the poet. / COPY /
1972 / SCEPTRE PRESS / Rushden, Northamptonshire";
p. [3] poem; p. [4] "Printed by Skelton's Press, Wellings-
borough, Northamptonshire".

Binding:   Gold paper covers.   Front:   [in black:] Christ-
mas Eve Service / at Midnight at St. Michael's / ROBERT
BLY.

Contents:   Christmas Eve Service at St. Michael's [poem].

Location:   SUNY Buffalo.

Note:   "An extra 100 copies were printed in a variant form
without a publisher's normal colophon and were distributed
to the congregation at the church in Madison, Minnesota
on the night of Christmas Eve, 1972."   Note supplied by
Martin Booth.

A30.   A CRICKET IN THE WAINSCOTING   [ca. 1972]

[tan sheet printed in raw umber] [drawing by Franz Albert
Richter] / [text in a single column] / [publisher's device]
THE ALTERNATIVE PRESS / Detroit

Collation:   8 X 12".   Single sheet printed on one side only.

Binding:   None.   All edges trimmed.

Contents:   A Cricket in the Wainscoting [poem]

Location:   SUNY Buffalo

A31.   SIX WINTER PRIVACY POEMS   1972

[gray-blue sheet printed in black] SIX WINTER PRIVACY
POEMS / [text of poems in single column] / Robert Bly /
[to the right:   illustration] / This is No. [   ] of an edition
limited to two hundred fifty copies hand-printed at The
Scarab Press on Nideggen paper. / The illustration is by
Karyl Klopp.   Issued June. 1972 by The Pomegranate
Press, 1713 Massachusetts Avenue, / Cambridge,

Massachusetts. The poem first appeared in Field, Copyright 1970 by Oberlin College. / Copyright 1972 by The Pomegranate Press.

Collation:  12 1/2 X 19".  Single sheet printed on one side only.

Binding:  None.  Right and bottom edges untrimmed.

Contents:  Six Winter Privacy Poems [poems]

Location:  SUNY Buffalo

Note:  Limited to 250 copies of which 150 copies are numbered and signed by R. B. and K. K.


A32.  SUNDAY MORNING IN TOMALES BAY  1972

[white sheet printed in black] Front:  SUNDAY MORNING IN TOMALES BAY / For Michael and Barbara / [text in a single column].  Back:  [pen and ink drawing by Steve Campbell].

Collation:  8 3/4" X 11 1/4".  Single sheet printed on both sides.

Binding:  None.  All edges trimmed.

Contents:  Sunday Morning In Tomales Bay

Location:  Roberson

Note:  This is part of Panjandrum, no. 1, edited by Dennis Koran and published by the Panjandrum Press, San Francisco, issued as a folio of twenty-eight sheets.

See A28 and I14.


A33.  WATER UNDER THE EARTH  1972

Water / Under the Earth / Robert Bly / THE SCEPTRE PRESS / 15 Keats Way, Rushden / Northamptonshire

Collation:  5 1/2 X 8 3/8".  No sign.  4 leaves.  Pp. [1-8].

Pagination:  p. [1] title-page; p. [2] blank; p. [3] "This edition is limited to 150 numbered copies / printed on Abbey Mills laid paper / Nos. 1-50 are signed by the poet / COPY / 1972"; p. [4] blank; pp. [5-6] [poem]; p. [7]

blank; p. [8] "Printed by Skelton's Press, Wellingborough, Northamptonshire."

Binding: Burnt sienna paper wrappers. Front: [in black:] Water / Under the earth / [rule] / ROBERT BLY.

Contents: Water Under the Earth.

Location: SUNY Buffalo

A34.  THE DEAD SEAL NEAR McCLURE'S BEACH  1973

The Dead Seal / near / McClure's Beach / Robert Bly / THE SCEPTRE PRESS / 15 Keats Way, Rushden / Northamptonshire

Collation: 5 X 8 1/8". No sign. 4 leaves. Pp. [1-8].

Pagination: p. [1] title-page; p. [2] blank; p. [3] "An earlier draft of this poem first appeared / in STAND magazine, 1972. / This edition is limited to 150 numbered copies / printed on Abbey Mills laid paper / Nos. 1-50 are signed by the poet / COPY / © 1973"; p. [4] blank; p. [5] poem; p. [6] blank; p. [7] poem (continued); p. [8] "Printed by Skelton's Press / Wellingborough, Northamptonshire / England".

Binding: Burnt sienna paper wrappers. Front: [in black:] The Dead Seal / near / McClure's Beach / [single rule] / ROBERT BLY.

Contents: The Dead Seal Near McClure's Beach [poem].

Location: SUNY Buffalo.

A35.  JUMPING OUT OF BED  1973

JUMPING OUT OF BED / POEMS BY ROBERT BLY / WOODCUTS BY WANG HUI-MING / Barre Publishers, Barre, Massachusetts / 1973

Collation: 8 11/16 X 8 3/4". [1-2] [1-4]$^{11}$ [1-2]: 24 leaves. Pp. [1-48].

Pagination: p. [1] half-title; p. [2] [acknowledgments] / "Copyright © 1972 by Robert Bly and Wang Hui-Ming / All rights reserved / Library of Congress Catalog Number 72-80853 / International Standard Book Number 0-8271-7245-1"; p. [3] title-page; p. [4] [woodcut]; p. [5] [two quotes: from the Tao Te Ching and the Old Testament]; pp. [6-46] text and woodcuts; pp. [47-48] blank.

Binding:  White paper covers.  Front:  [three-color wood-
cut in yellow, green, & brown] [in green, at top right
corner:] $3.95 / [in white, outlined in green on yellow:]
JUMPING / OUT / OF BED [in green on yellow:] POEMS
BY / [outlined in green:] ROBERT / BLY / [in green on
white:] WOODCUTS / BY [in yellow:] WANG / HUI-MING.
Back:  [in green:] JUMPING OUT OF BED / Poems by
Robert Bly / Woodcuts and Calligraphy by Wang Hui-Ming
/ [statement about the collection, and author and artist
statements] / Barre Publishers, Barre, Massachusetts.

Contents:  Turtle Climbing From a Rock/Thinking of "The
Autumn Fields"/Like the New Moon I Will Live My Life/Some
November Privacy Poems/On a Moonlit Road in the North
Woods/The Walnut Tree Orchard/The Hill of Hua-Tzu/
Chrysanthemums/After Long Busyness/Some Images for
Death/A Windy December Night/Sleeping Faces/The Creek
by the Luan House/The Magnolia Grove/Another Doing
Nothing Poem/Walking in the Ditch Grass/Tongues Whirling/
A Doing Nothing Poem/Jumping Out of Bed/Six Winter Pri-
vacy Poems.

Location:  SUNY Stony Brook


A36.  SLEEPERS JOINING HANDS  1973

Sleepers Joining Hands / Robert Bly/ Harper & Row, Pub-
lishers / NEW YORK / EVANSTON / SAN FRANCISCO /
LONDON / [publisher's device:  stylized torch in a rec-
tangle, below which the date, 1817].

Collation:  6 3/16 X 9 5/16".  [1-16]$^5$:  80 leaves.  Pp.
[i-x] [1-2] 3-26 [27-28] 29-50 [51-52] 53-67 [68-70].

Pagination:  p. [1] half-title; p. [ii] "Other Books by
Robert Bly" [lists seventeen titles]; p. [iii] title-page;
p. [iv] [acknowledgments] / "SLEEPERS JOINING HANDS.
Copyright © 1973 by Robert Bly.  All rights reserved.
Printed in / the United States of America.  No part of this
book may be used or reproduced in any / manner whatso-
ever without permission except in the case of brief quota-
tions em- / bodied in critical articles and reviews.  For
information address Harper & Row, Publishers, / Inc.,
10 East 53rd Street, New York, N.Y. 10022.  Published
simultaneously in Canada by / Fitzhenry & Whiteside
Limited, Toronto. / FIRST EDITION"; p. [v] dedication:
"For Carolyn / 'Still, the mist in the garden is simple ...
/ old ideas go up / like the pure mist of the meadow...'
/ - C. Bly"; p. [vi] blank; p. [vii] "Contents"; p. [viii]

blank; p. [ix] "Illustrations"; p. [x] blank; pp. [1]-67,
text; pp. [68-70] blank.

Binding: Red and magenta cloth covered boards. Front,
stamped in gold: [lower left corner:] [R. B.'s signature].
Spine, stamped in gold, reading downwards: ROBERT
BLY SLEEPERS JOINING HANDS Harper & Row. End-
papers front and back of cream color paper slightly heavier
than the sheets. Fore edge of pages untrimmed.

Dust jacket: Front cover and spine, paper white with
gray diagonal stripes from upper right corner to lower left
corner. Front: [in dark orange:] [rule] / [in magenta:]
[rule] / SLEEPERS / JOINING / HANDS / [rule] / [in
orange:] BY / [rule] / ROBERT BLY. Spine, reading
downwards: [in magenta:] [rule] / [in orange:] [rule]
[in magenta:] SLEEPERS JOINING HANDS ROBERT BLY
[rule] HARPER & ROW [rule]. Back cover: [in purple
tones:] [photograph of R. B.] / by Layle Silbert. Fly-
leaves, paper in white. Front flyleaf: [in deep purple:]
$5.95 / SLEEPERS / JOINING / HANDS / [rule] / Robert
Bly / [fifteen line statement on R. B. and the collection]
/ (continued on back flap). Back flyleaf: [printed in
deep purple:] (continued from front flap) / [twenty-four
line statement] / Jacket design by Luba Litwak / Photo-
graph on back of jacket / by Layle Silbert / SBN 06-
010381-7.

Illustrations: p. 35, photograph: "A Good Mother (Egypt-
ian)"; p. 36, photograph: "A Death Mother (Huastec) -
worked into the back of a Quetzalcoatl statue"; p. 45,
photograph: "An Ecstatic Mother (Mycenean)"; p. 46,
photograph: "A Teeth Mother (Balinese) - Mask".

Contents: Six Winter Privacy Poems/The Turtle/Water Un-
der the Earth/Shack Poem/In a Mountain Cabin in Norway/
Hair/Tao Te Ching Running/Condition of the Working
Classes: 1970/Calling to the Badger/Pilgrim Fish Heads/
The Teeth Mother Naked at Last/I Came Out of the Mother
Naked [prose]/Sleepers Joining Hands

Location: Patchogue (N.Y.) Public Library


First paper edition: 1973

Title page, collation, pagination, and contents same as
hardbound.

Binding: Stiff white paper covers. Front: [in brown:]
HARPER [publisher's device] COLOPHON BOOKS/CN 785/

$4.50 / [rule] / [in green-gray:] [rule] / [in brown:]
SLEEPERS / JOINING / HANDS / [in green-gray:] [to the
left:] [rule] / [in brown:] [rule] [in green-gray:] [in
middle:] BY [to the right:] [rule] / [in brown:] [rule] /
[in green-gray:] ROBERT BLY.  Spine, reading downwards:
[in green-gray:] [rule] / [in brown:] [rule] SLEEPERS
JOINING HANDS [in green-gray:] ROBERT BLY [rule] /
[in brown:] [rule] HARPER & ROW [in green-gray:] [rule]
[over which is printed, in brown:] CN 785 / [in brown:]
[rule].  Back cover:  [in brown tones:] [photograph of
R. B.] / [in brown on white bar:] [to right:] Layle Sil-
bert / [four-line quotation from Library Journal] / [to
left:] SBN 06-010382-5 [to right:] 0-06-090785-1.

Location:  Roberson

## A37.  BUFFALO  1974

[bluish-brown sheet printed in brown] [to the left of cen-
ter:] BUFFALO / [text in a single column] / ~ Robert Bly
[to the right of center:] [illustration by Ellen Kennedy]

Collation:  13 3/4 X 7 13/16".  Single sheet printed on one
side only.

Binding:  None.  All edges trimmed.

Contents:  Buffalo [poem]

Location:  Heyen

Note:  Publisher is Smith Park Poetry Series, St. Paul,
Minnesota.

## A38.  THE HOCKEY POEM  1974

THE HOCKEY POEM / [row of sixteen devices] / Robert Bly
/ Knife River Press / 1974

Collation:  4 13/16 X 8 1/2".  No sign.  8 leaves.  Pp.
[1-16].

Pagination:  pp. [1-2] blank; p. [3] title-page; p. [4]
"Copyright 1974 Robert Bly"; p. [5] [in blue:] [illustra-
tion:  wood-cut of a hockey goalie] / "For William Duffy";
p. [6] blank; pp. [7-10] [poem]; pp. [11-12] blank; p.
[13] "THE HOCKEY POEM was hand / printed in an edition
of 500 copies by / Knife River Press, P.O. Box 3082, Dul-
/ uth, Minnesota, 55803, in the spring of / 1974.  Wood-
cut by Ann Jenkins."; pp. [14-16] blank.

Binding:   Blue paper covers printed in black.   Front:
THE HOCKEY POEM / Robert Bly.   Cream-color paper.

Contents:   The Hockey Poem

Location:   Piccione

A39.   A MAN WRITES TO A PART OF HIMSELF.   1974

[New York:] Y[WCA] Poetry Center.

Broadside.

Not verified, cited by Lepper (P122), p. 67.

Note:   SUNY Buffalo lists as holding this item but was un-
able to locate it August 1984 or April 1985.

A40.   POINT REYES POEMS   1974

Point Reyes Poems / [single rule] / Robert Bly / MUDRA:
HALF MOON BAY / [heavy rule] / [thin rule] / 1974.

Collation:   5 1/2 X 8 11/16".   No sign.   10 leaves.   Pp.
[1-20].

Pagination:   pp. [1-2] blank; p. [3] title-page; p. [4]
"Copyright © 1974 by Robert Bly / Distributed by Book
People / 2940 Seventh Street / Berkeley, CA. 94710 /
Cover illustration Beach Rocks from an / oil painting by
Arthur Okamura / Photograph by Steve E. D'Accardo";
pp. [5-17] text; pp. [18-20] blank.

Binding:   Stiff light blue paper.   Front:   [photograph of
a painting of rocks on a beach] / [in black:] POINT
REYES / POEMS / ROBERT BLY.   Back:   [in black:]
[device:   yin-yang] / $1.50.

Contents:   Walking among Limantour Dunes/Sea water pour-
ing back over stones/November day at McClure's/Calm
morning at Drake's Bay/Trespassing on the Pierce Ranch/
Climbing up Mount Vision with my little boy/Finding a sala-
mander on Inverness Ridge/Sunday morning in Tomales
Bay/The dead seal near McClure's Beach/The large starfish.

Location:   SUNY Buffalo

Note:   Limited to 250 copies.   An edition of 50 copies was
printed letterpress and sewn, numbered, and signed by
R. B.   Heyen has copy of limited edition.

A41.  THE FIR   1975

[in black:] Robert Bly / [in green:] THE FIR / [in black:]
Prairie Gate Press / University of Minnesota, Morris

Collation:   4 1/4 X 5 7/8".   No sign.   6 leaves.   Pp.
[1-12].

Pagination:   pp. [1-2] blank; p. [3] title-page; p. [4]
"Copyright 1975"; pp. [5-6] blank; p. [7] [poem]; p. [8]
blank; p. [9] "Our first edition of THE FIR was printed /
with twelve point Garamond type in an / edition of 200
copies.  The paper is 75 / pound Mardi Gras Linweave. /
B. Stamp, Printer / Spring 1975; pp. [10-12] blank.

Binding:   Green paper covers.   Front:  [in black:]
Robert Bly / THE FIR / Prairie Gate Press / University
of Minnesota, Morris.

Contents:   The Fir [poem]

Location:   Piccione

A42.   GRASS FROM TWO YEARS [&] LET'S LEAVE   1975

Grass From Two Years / Let's Leave / (Kabir translation)
/ [ornament] / Robert Bly

Collation:   5 1/2 X 8 9/16".   No sign.   6 leaves.   Pp.
[1-12].

Pagination:   pp. [1-2] blank; p. [3] title-page; p. [4] "©
Robert Bly, 1975 / [publisher's device:  old woman at a
caldron] / The Ally Press / 1764 Gilpin Street / Denver,
Colorado 80218 / Standard Book Number 0-915408-05-8";
p. [5] "This edition limited to 200 numbered copies. /
Nos. 1-50 signed by the author. / Number [   ]"; p. [6]
blank; p. [7] "GRASS FROM TWO YEARS"; p. [8] blank;
p. [9] "LET'S LEAVE"; pp. [10-12] blank.

Binding:   Brown leatherette covered boards.   Orange-
brown paper printed in brown inlaid on front cover:
Grass From Two Years / Let's Leave / (Kabir Translation)
/ [ornament] / Robert Bly.   End-papers front and back
of light brown.

Contents:   Grass from two years/Let's leave.

Location:   SUNY Buffalo

First paper edition:   1976

Title page, collation, pagination, and contents same as hard-bound.

Binding:  Orange-brown wrappers.  Front:  [in black:]
Grass From Two Years / Let's Leave / (Kabir translation)
/ [ornament] / Robert Bly.  Back:  [eleven–line statement
on R. B.] / [fourteen-line statement on Kabir].

Location:  SUNY Stony Brook

A43.   THE MORNING GLORY   1975

[drawing of a morning glory] / THE / MORNING / GLORY
/ Prose Poems by / ROBERT BLY / Harper & Row, Pub-
lishers / New York, Evanston / San Francisco, London

Collation:  5 3/16 X 8".  [1–16]$^{16}$:  96 leaves.  Pp. [A-B]
[i-viii] ix-xi [xii-xiv] [1-2] 3-35 [36-38] 39-56 [57-58]
59-76 [77-80].

Pagination:  pp. [A-B] blank; p. [i] half-title; p. [ii]
blank; p. [iii] "Other books by Robert Bly" [lists eighteen
titles]; p. [iv] blank; p. [v] title-page; p. [vi] [acknowl-
edgments] / "THE MORNING GLORY.  Copyright © 1975
by Robert Bly.  All / rights reserved.  Printed in the
United States of America.  No part / of this book may be
used or reproduced in any manner whatsoever / without
written permission except in the case of brief quotations /
embodied in critical articles and reviews.  For information
address / Harper & Row, Publishers, Inc., 10 East 53rd
Street, New York, / N.Y. 10022.  Published simultaneously
in Canada by Fitzhenry & / Whiteside Limited, Toronto.
/ FIRST EDITION / Designed by Janice Willcocks Stern";
p. [vii] dedication:  "For Mary / who brought me a gift";
p. [viii] blank; pp. ix-xi, "Contents"; p. [xii] blank;
p. [xiii] [forword]; p. [xiv] blank; pp. [1]-76, text;
pp. [77-80] blank.

Binding:  Blue cloth covered boards.  Front:  [blindstamp-
ing of a morning glory in center].  Spine, stamped in yel-
low, reading downwards:  THE MORNING GLORY [vertical
rule] ROBERT BLY [reading across:] Harper / & Row.
End-papers front and back of white paper slightly heavier
than the sheets.

Dust jacket:  Front and spine, paper blue.  Front:  [in
yellow:] THE / MORNING / GLORY / [in white:] Prose
Poems / [drawing of a morning glory in yellow and green

within a green line circle] / [in white:] ROBERT BLY.
Spine, reading downwards: [in yellow:] THE MORNING
GLORY [in white:] Robert Bly [in yellow:] Harper & Row.
Back: [blue-tone photograph of R. B. with white border
at bottom]. Right upper corner, reading upwards: Ed-
ward Lense. Centered, at bottom: [in blue:] ROBERT
BLY. Right lower corner: 0-06-010368-X. Flyleaves,
paper in white. Front flyleaf: [in blue:] [twenty-six-
line statement on the prose poem] / 1075. Back flyleaf:
[in blue:] [seven-line statement on R. B.] / Jacket de-
sign by Muriel Nasser.

Contents: I.: A Bird's Nest Made of White Reed Fiber/
Leonardo's Secret/Looking at a Dead Wren in My Hand/
Sitting on Some Rocks in Shaw Cove, California/At a Fish
Hatchery in Story, Wyoming/The Hunter/A Hollow Tree/
Looking into a Tide Pool/Seeing Creeley for the First Time/
The Hockey Poem/Walking on the Sussex Coast/A Turtle/
Frost on Window Panes/My Three-Year-Old Daughter Brings
Me a Gift/Looking at a Dry Tumbleweed Brought in from
the Snow/Watching Andrei Voznesensky Read in Vancouver/
Standing under a Cherry Tree at Night/Two Prose Poems
on Locked-In Animals/Waterfall Coming Over a Cliff/In the
Courtyard of the Isleta Mission/A Poem about Tennessee/
On the Rocks at Maui/A Rock Inlet on the Pacific
II. The Point Reyes Poems: November Day at McClure's/
Walking among Limantour Dunes/Trespassing on the Pierce
Ranch/Climbing up Mount Vision with My Little Boy/Sunday
Morning in Tomales Bay/Calm Morning at Drake's Bay/Find-
ing a Salamander on Inverness Ridge/Sea Water Pouring
Back over Stones/The Dead Seal near McClure's Beach/The
Large Starfish
III. Going in a Helicopter from Riverside to the L.A. Air-
port/A Half-Grown Porcupine/Visiting Thomas Hart Benton
and His Wife in Kansas City/Walking in the Hardanger
Vidda/Written Forty Miles South of a Sleeping City/A Cat-
erpillar on the Desk/A Windy Day at the Shack/August
Rain/Grass from Two Years/Christmas Eve Service at Mid-
night at St. Michael's/Opening the Door of a Barn I Thought
Was Empty on New Year's Eve.

Location: Patchogue [NY] Public Library

First paper edition: 1979

Title page, collation, pagination, and contents same as hard-
bound.

Binding: Dark blue paper covers. Front: [in white:]
HARPER [publisher's device] COLOPHON BOOKS [vertical

rule] CN 784 [vertical rule] $3.95 / [in yellow:] THE /
MORNING / GLORY / [in white:] PROSE POEMS / [design
of a morning glory in yellow and green within a green line
circle] / [in white:] ROBERT BLY. Spine, reading down-
wards: [in yellow:] THE MORNING GLORY [in white:]
ROBERT BLY [in yellow:] Harper & Row [in white:]
CN 784. Back: [in white:] [twenty-line statement on the
prose poem and R. B.] / 0-06-090784-3.


Location:  Roberson


A44.  OLD MAN RUBBING HIS EYES   1975

[in black:] poems by / ROBERT BLY / drawings by
FRANZ ALLBERT RICHTER / [in brown:] OLD MAN RUB-
BING HIS EYES / Greensboro:  UNICORN PRESS 1975.

Collation:  5 6/16 X 8 7/16".  [1-16]$^4$:  32 leaves.  Pp.
[i-iv] [1-12] 13 [14] 15 [16] 17 [18] 19 [20] 21 [22] 23
[24] 25 [26] 27 [28] 29 [30] 31 [32] 33 [34] 35 [36] 37
[38] 39 [40] 41 [42] 43 [44] 45 [46] 47 [48] 49 [50] 51
[52-60].

Pagination:  pp. [i-iv] blank; pp. [1-2] blank; p. [3]
half-title; pp. [4-5] title-page; p. [6] "Author's Copy-
right © 1975 Robert Bly / Artist's Copyright © 1975
Franz Allbert Richter" / [acknowledgments] / "Library
of Congress Number 72-77913 / Standard Book Number
0-87775-034-3 / Unicorn Press; P.O. Box 3307; Greens-
boro, N.C. 27402"; p. [7] dedication:  "For Arthur Paul-
son"; p. [8] blank; p. [9] "OLD MAN RUBBING HIS EYES"
[table of contents]; p. [10] blank; p. [11] second half-
title; pp. [12]-51, text and drawings; p. [52] blank; p.
[53] "Robert Bly's Old Man Rubbing His Eyes was printed
on / a Mergenthaler 23 Letterpress by Fred Thompson and
/ Alan Brilliant from hand-set 12 pt Joanna type.  The /
stock is 60 lb Warren's Old Style.  The binding was / done
by hand by Olivia Allegrone.  The book was / made at
Unicorn Press, Greensboro, North Carolina. / The first
printing of this new book consists of 235 / cloth-bound,
numbered copies, of which the first 35 / have been signed
by both the poet and the artist."; pp. [54-60] blank.

Binding:  Gray paper covered boards with black cloth
spine.  Front:  [in black:] ROBERT BLY / OLD MAN /
RUBBING HIS EYES / [drawing of man rubbing his eyes].
End-papers front and back of gray paper slightly heavier
than the sheets.

Contents:  October Frost/Writing Again/Fall Poem/Sitting
In Fall Grass/Night Farmyard/Dawn in Threshing Time/

Reading In Fall Rain/Insect Heads/To Live/Cornpicker
Poem/Prophets/A Cricket in The Wainscoting/Thinking of
'Seclusion'/Digging Worms/Walking and Sitting/A Long Walk
Before The Snows Began/A Dream On The Night Of First
Snow/A Walk/Roads/Passing An Orchard By Train.
Location:  SUNY Stony Brook


Second printing.  First paper edition.  1975

Title page and contents same as hardbound.

Collation:  5 X 8 7/16".  [1-16]$^4$:  32 leaves.  Pp.  [1-12]
13 [14]  15 [16]  17 [18]  19 [20]  21 [22]  23 [24]  25 [26]
27 [28]  29 [30]  31 [32]  33 [34]  35 [36]  37 [38]  39 [40]  41
[42]  43 [44]  45 [46]  47 [48]  49 [50]  51 [52-64].

Pagination:  pp. [1-2] blank;  p. [3] half-title;  pp. [4-5]
title-page;  p. [6] "Author's Copyright © 1975 Robert Bly
/ Artist's Copyright © 1975 Franz Allbert Richter" / [ac-
knowledgments] / "Library of Congress Number 72-77913 /
Standard Book Number 0-87775-034-3 / Unicorn Press; P.O.
Box 3307; Greensboro, N.C. 27402";  p. [7] dedication:
"For Arthur Paulson";  p. [8] blank;  p. [9] "OLD MAN
RUBBING HIS EYES" [table of contents];  p. [10] blank;
p. [11] second half-title;  pp. [12]-51, text and drawings;
pp. [52-64] blank.

Binding:  Gray paper covers.  Front:  [in black:]
ROBERT BLY / Old Man / Rubbing His Eyes / [drawing
of a man rubbing his eyes].  Printed in black on spine,
reading downwards:  Robert Bly  Old Man Rubbing His
Eyes.  Back:  [at bottom:] [in black:] $4.00 [ornament]
Unicorn Press.
Location:  SUNY Stony Brook


A45.   CLIMBING UP MOUNT VISION WITH MY LITTLE BOY   1976

[slate-blue sheet printed in brown and black] [on left
side:] [in brown:] [hand printed:] Noah / [child's draw-
ing] / The Slow Loris Broadside, "Climbing Up Mount
Vision With My Little Boy," of Series IV, is an edition of
/ sixty-five numbered and signed broadsides with drawings
printed by the Hoechstetter Printing Company, Pittsburgh,
/ Pennsylvania 15217.  The type composition, Old Century,
is the work of Stanley J. Malinowski, Buffalo, New York.
/ The paper is Strathmore Americana.  The poem first ap-
peared in Point Reyes Poems, copyright 1974 by Robert
Bly. / The drawing is by Noah Bly.  Copyright 1976 by
The Slow Loris Press, a non-profit corporation, 6359 Mor-
rowfield / Number [   ] [to the right:] CLIMBING UP

MOUNT VISION / WITH MY LITTLE BOY / [text in a sin-
gle column] / Robert Bly

Collation:  17 X 11".  Single sheet printed on one side
only.

Binding:  None.  All edges trimmed.

Contents:  Climbing Up Mount Vision With My Little Boy
[poem]

Location:  SUNY Buffalo

Note:  Slow Loris Broadsides, Series IV.  Limited to sixty-
five numbered and signed copies.


A46.  4 POEMS  [ca. 1976/1977]

Birmingham, AL:  Thunder City Press.

Broadside, 11" X 17".

Contents:  [photograph of R. B.] / Looking Into a Face/
Sleeping Faces/Come With Me/Watching Television

Note:  Issued as Thunder City Press Broadside Series No.
10 published in conjunction with a reading at the Univer-
sity of Alabama in Birmingham.  Not verified; the informa-
tion is provided by Steven Ford-Brown, publisher of the
Thunder City Press.


A47.  TAKING THE HANDS  [c. 1976]

Photograph by Walt Seng.  [Pittsburgh:]  Three Rivers
Press, Carnegie-Mellon University.

Broadside, 28 X 71 cm.

Not verified, listed in OCLC by Cornell University, Ithaca,
NY.  See A53 for a verified 1978 edition.


A48.  THE LOON   1977

THE / LOON / [rule] / by Robert Bly / Ox Head Press /
1977

Collation:  4 1/4 X 6 1/4".  [1-28]:  14 leaves.  Pp. [i-iv]
[1-2] 3 [4] 5-18 [19-24].

Pagination: pp. [i-ii] blank; p. [iii] title-page; p. [iv]
"Copyright © 1977 / by Robert Bly"; p. [1] "Ox Head 14";
p. [2] blank; p. 3, "The Poems" [table of contents]; p.
[4] blank; pp. 5-18, text; pp. [19-20] blank; p. [21]
"COLOPHON / This pamphlet was printed at / Marshall,
Minnesota in a first / edition of 500 copies. The leaf /
ornaments were hand painted / with watercolors and brush.
/ D. Olsen, Printer / February, 1977"; pp. [22-24] blank.

Bindings: Blue paper wrappers. Front: [in black:] THE
/ LOON / [rule] / by Robert Bly.

Contents: The Loon/Wind/Alone/The Car/Marietta, Minne-
sota/August Sun/Near Dark/Near Morris/Kabekona Lake/
Love Poem/Winter Grass/Fall/Grass Storm Windows

Location: SUNY Stony Brook
Note: Pp. 3, 5-18 have leaf ornaments to the left of page
headings.


A49.   THIS BODY IS MADE OF CAMPHOR AND GOPHERWOOD   1977

This Body Is Made of Camphor / and Gopherwood / Prose
Poems by ROBERT BLY / [drawing:  shell] / Drawings by
/ GENDRON JENSEN / HARPER & ROW, PUBLISHERS /
NEW YORK, HAGERSTOWN, SAN FRANCISCO, LONDON

Collation:  5 7/8 X 9 1/8".  [1-8]$^8$:  32 leaves.  Pp. [1-8]
9 [10-12] 13 [14] 15 [16] 17 [18] 19 [20] 21 [22] 23 [24]
25 [26] 27 [28] 29 [30] 31-32 [33-34] 35-36 [37-38] 39-41
[42] 43 [44] 45 [46] 47 [48] 49 [50] 51 [52] 53 [54] 55-56
[57-58] 59 [60] 61 [62-64].

Pagination:  p. [1] half-title; p. [2] blank; p. [3] "OTHER
BOOKS BY ROBERT BLY" [lists sixteen titles]; p. [4]
blank;  p. [5] title-page;  p. [6] [acknowledgments] /
"THIS BODY IS MADE OF CAMPHOR AND GOPHERWOOD.
Copyright © 1977 by Robert / Bly.  Drawings copyright ©
1977 by Gendron Jensen.  All rights reserved.  Printed
in the / United States of America.  No part of this book
may be used or reproduced in any manner / whatsoever
without written permission except in the case of brief
quotations embodied / in critical articles and reviews:
For information address Harper & Row, Publishers, Inc., /
10 East 53rd Street, New York, N.Y. 10022.  Published
simultaneously in Canada by / Fitzhenry & Whiteside Lim-
ited, Toronto. / FIRST EDITION / Designed by Gloria
Adelson"; p. [7] dedication:  "Gendron would like to dedi-
cate this book to: / 'All the waters of this world'"; p. [8]
blank; p. 9, "Contents"; p. [10] blank; p. [11] second
half-title; pp. [12]-59, text and drawings; p. [60] blank;

p. 61, "About the Artist" / "About the Author"; pp. [62-
64] blank.

Binding:  Dark gray paper covered boards.  Spine, stamped
in silver, reading downwards:  ROBERT BLY / THIS BODY
IS MADE of CAMPHOR and GOPHERWOOD / Harper & Row.
End-papers front and back of peach color paper slightly
heavier than the sheets.

Contents:  Walking Swiftly/The Left Hand/The Sleeper/
Finding the Father/Looking from Inside My Body/Going Out
to Check the Ewes/Galloping Horses/A Dream of What Is
Missing/Falling into Holes in Our Sentences/Walking to the
Next Farm/The Origin of the Praise of God/Coming In for
Supper/How the Ant Takes Part/When the Wheel Does Not
Move/The Pail/Snow Falling on Snow/We Love This Body/
Wings Folding Up/Snowed In/The Cry Going Out over
Pastures.
Location:  SUNY Buffalo

First paper edition:  1977

Title page, collation, pagination, and contents same as
hardbound.

Binding:  Paper covers.  Front:  [in grays and cream:
enlarged segment of shell drawing].  Printed in purple:
TD277 / $3.95 / This Body Is Made / of Camphor and /
Gopherwood / PROSE POEMS BY / ROBERT BLY / Draw-
ings by / GENDRON JENSEN.  Spine, cream paper printed
in purple, reading downwards:  ROBERT BLY / This
Body Is Made of Camphor and Gopherwood / HARPER &
ROW / TD 277.  Back cover, cream paper:  [in black:]
Robert Bly [photograph by Jim Kalett] / [in purple:
note on R.B.] / [photograph by Greg Booth] [in black:]
Gendron Jensen / Cover design by Gloria Adelson / ISBN
0-06-010-414-7.
Location:  Roberson

A50.  WALKING AT NIGHT  1977

[white placard printed in black with a single rule frame]
[upper left quadrant:] Walking at Night / Robert Bly /
[in center:] [text in a single column] / [to the left:]
Poetry in Public Places* / is made possible with support
from / National Endowment for the Arts, / New York State
Council on the Arts, / Mobil Foundation Inc. / *Poetry in
Public Places, 799 Greenwich St., New York, N. Y. 10014
/ All contributions are tax deductible / [below frame:]
Typography:  Selectype, Inc., New York City [bottom
right corner:] [within frame] Copyright © 1977 by Robert
Bly / [below frame] Design:  Sherwin B. Harris, III.

Collation:   11 X 28".   Single placard printed on one side only.

Binding:   None.   All edges trimmed.

Contents:   Walking at Night [poem]

Location:   Roberson

A51.   THE WHOLE MOISTY NIGHT   [ca. 1977]

[Detroit:] Alternative Press.

Card, 10 X 16 cm.

Not verified, listed in OCLC by Indiana University, Bloomington, IN.

A52.   LOVE POEM   1978

[brown placard printed in black] [printed on a slight diagonal upwards from the left] LOVE POEM / [text in a single column] / poem:   Robert Bly, Minnesota/drawing: James Harrison, New York / [illustration:   within an oval running off bottom of placard, a simple rendering of a road with lightpoles and buildings] / [at bottom, to left of center:] Copyright © 1978 by The Spirit That Moves Us, for the poet & visual artist. / Copies of this, or the entire set of 10 11" X 16" placards & 5" X 7" postcards, available from Morty Sklar, The Spirit That Moves / Us Press, P. O. Box 1585, Iowa City, Iowa 52240.   Discounts available for quantities of 5 or more. / This project was funded in part by a grant from the Iowa Arts Council, the City of Iowa City, CAC and the good people & / merchants of Iowa City, and Mom - Selma Sklar.

Collation:   16 X 11".   Single placard printed on one side.

Binding:   None.   All edges trimmed.

Contents:   Love Poem [poem]

Location:   SUNY Buffalo

Note:   One of eight placards printed in an edition of 500 sets.   The series is a supplement to The Spirit That Moves Us magazine.   Also printed as a postcard.   See below.

Postcard edition:   1978

Design, binding, contents same as placard.

A53.  TAKING THE HANDS  1978

[black placard with white frame printed in white, with a
color photograph of an arm reaching from the left toward
two hands holding a bird] [lower left quadrant:] Taking
the Hands ... / [text in a single column] [upper right
quadrant:] POETRY ON THE BUSES is / supported in part
by the / Department of Transportation, / the National En-
dowment for the / Arts, and the Pennsylvania / Council
on the Arts.  Copyright / © 1978 POETRY ON THE /
BUSES/Carnegie-Mellon / University Press. / Poet:  Robert
Bly / Photo:  Walt Seng © 1976.

Collation:  17 X 11".  Single placard printed on one side
only.

Binding:  None.  All edges trimmed.

Contents:  Taking the Hands [poem]

Location:  SUNY Buffalo

Note:  Poetry on the Buses.


A54.  THIS TREE WILL BE HERE FOR A THOUSAND YEARS  1979

THIS TREE / WILL BE HERE / FOR A / THOUSAND YEARS
/ [picture of a tree] / ROBERT BLY / Harper & Row,
Publishers / New York, Hagerstown, San Francisco, London

Collation:  5 1/4 X 7 15/16".  [1-5] [1-6]$^2$ [1-5]$^3$:  32
leaves.  Pp. [1-5] 6-11 [12-16] 17-38 [39-40] 41-64.

Pagination:  p. [1] half-title; p. [2] "Other Books by
Robert Bly" [lists seventeen titles]; p. [3] title-page;
p. [4] [acknowledgments] / "THIS TREE WILL BE HERE
FOR A THOUSAND YEARS.  Copyright © 1979 by Robert
Bly. / All rights reserved.  Printed in the United States
of America.  No part of this book may / be used or repro-
duced in any manner whatsoever without written permission
except / in the case of brief quotations embodied in critical
articles and reviews.  For informa- / tion address Harper
& Row, Publishers, Inc., 10 East 53rd Street, New York,
N.Y. / 10022.  Published simultaneously in Canada by
Fitzhenry & Whiteside Limited, / Toronto. / FIRST EDITION
/ Designed by Janice Stern"; p. [5] dedication:  "For
Biddy / who came to meet me"; pp. 6-8, "Contents"; pp.
9-64, text.

Binding:  Off-white cloth covered boards.  Blind stamping
of publisher's device on front cover in lower right corner
[torch in a rectangle with 1817 below it].  Spine, stamped
in bronze, reading downwards:  THIS TREE WILL BE
HERE FOR A THOUSAND YEARS  BLY  Harper & Row.
End-papers front and back of brown paper slightly heavier
than the sheets.

Dust jacket:  Front and back covers, spine, paper white.
Front:  [in olive green:]  [rule] / [in black:] THIS TREE
/ WILL BE HERE / FOR A / THOUSAND YEARS / [in
green and brown:] [picture of a tree] / [in olive green:]
POEMS BY / [in black:] ROBERT BLY / [in olive green:]
[rule].  Spine, reading downwards:  [in black:] THIS
TREE WILL BE HERE FOR A THOUSAND YEARS [in olive
green:] BLY [in black, reading across:] HARPER / &
ROW.  Back:  [photograph of R. B. by Jim Kalett] / [in
lower right corner:] 0-06-010358-2.  Flyleaves, paper in
white.  Front flyleaf:  [in black:] $8.95 / [rule] / THIS
TREE / WILL BE HERE / FOR A / THOUSAND YEARS /
[rule] / ROBERT BLY / [twenty-one-line statement on the
collection] / (continued on back flap) / 0879.  Back fly-
leaf:  [in black:] (continued from front flap) / [five-line
statement about the collection] / [thirteen-line statement
on R. B.] / Jacket design by Janice Stern / Author's
photo:  © Jim Kalett / Harper & Row, Publishers / 10 East
53rd Street / New York, NY  10022.

Contents:  The Two Presences/I:  October Frost/Writing
Again/Fall Poem/Sitting in Fall Grass/Night Farmyard/Dawn
in Threshing Time/Reading in Fall Rain/Insect Heads/To
Live/Cornpicker Poem/Prophets/Listening to a Cricket in
the Wainscoting/Thinking of "Seclusion"/Digging Worms/
Walking and Sitting/A Long Walk Before the Snows Began/
A Dream on the Night of First Snow/A Walk/Roads/Passing
an Orchard by Train   II:  Women We Never See Again/
November Fog/Ant Heaps by the Path/Amazed by an Accu-
mulation of Snow/Pulling a Rowboat Up Among Lake Reeds/
Moving Books to a New Study/Driving My Parents Home at
Christmas/After a Day of Work/Walking Where the Plows
Have Been Turning/July Morning/An Empty Place/Prayer
Service in an English Church/Fishing on a Lake at Night/
Night of First Snow/Solitude of the Two Day Snowstorm/
Frost Still in the Ground/Late Moon/A Dream of Retarded
Children/Black Pony Eating Grass/The Fallen Tree/A
Dream of an Afternoon with a Woman I Did Not Know/Nail-
ing a Dock Together/An Evening When the Full Moon Rose
as the Sun Set/Out Picking Up Corn.

Location:  Patchogue (NY) Public Library

First paper edition:   1979

Title page, collation, pagination, and contents same as
hardbound.

Binding:  White paper covers.  Front:  [in olive green:]
[rule] /[in black:] THIS TREE / WILL BE HERE / FOR A
/ THOUSAND YEARS / [in green and brown:] [picture of
a tree] / [in olive green:] POEMS BY / [in black:]
ROBERT BLY / [in olive green:] [rule].  Reading up-
wards from left bottom corner:  [in olive green:] HARPER
[device] COLOPHON BOOKS/CN 713/$4.95.  Spine, reading
downwards:  [in black:] THIS TREE WILL BE HERE FOR
A THOUSAND YEARS [in olive green:] BLY  HARPER
[device] COLOPHON BOOKS CN 713.  Back:  [in olive
green] [rule] / [in black:] THIS TREE / WILL BE HERE /
FOR A / THOUSAND YEARS / [in olive green:] [rule] /
[in black:] ROBERT BLY / [photograph of R. B. by Jim
Kalett] [sixteen–line statement on R. B.] / [in olive green:]
HARPER & ROW, PUBLISHERS / [in black:] Cover design
by Janice Stern  0-06-090713-4.

Location:  Roberson

A55.  VISITING EMILY DICKINSON'S GRAVE AND OTHER POEMS
      1979

VISITING / EMILY / DICKINSON'S / GRAVE / & other
poems / ROBERT BLY / [drawing of vine with flowers,
one of which is printed in blue].

Collation:  5 11/16 X 8 1/4".  No sign.  10 leaves.  Pp.
[1-20].

Pagination:   p. [1] half-title / [drawing]; p. [2] blank;
p. [3] title-page; p. [4] [acknowledgments] / "Copyright
Nineteen hundred and seventy-nine by Robert Bly."; p.
[5] dedication:  "For the one who stays at the bend / of
the river"; pp. [6-17] text; p. [18] blank; p. [19] "Wind
Whipping THROUGH the pressroom.  June tornado /
weather, as this last page is hand-printed at The Red /
Ozier Press by Steve Miller.  Spectrum type was used /
on papers from the Tidepool, Barcham Green, / Fabriano
& Twinrocker Mills.  Marta Anderson did / the illustrations
in this Hotel Washington edition of / two hundred, plus five
patron copies.  Vivaldi is / in the air, winged, & in your
hand is number [  ]. / [drawing in blue]"; p. [20] blank.

Binding:  Brown paper covers with blue paper wrappers.
Blind stamping on front:  VISITING / EMILY / DICKIN-
SON'S / GRAVE / & other poems / ROBERT BLY.  End-

papers of aqua front and back. Bottom and side of pages
are uncut.

Contents:  Words Rising/An Empty Place/Ant Heaps By
The Path/A Woman In A Wheat Field/July Morning/Visiting
Emily Dickinson's Grave with Robert Francis/Snow Falling
On The Water Tank/Women We Never See Again/Aunt
Bertha/For My Son Noah, Ten Years Old/Watching Susan
Matthews Allard Play The Double Bass/An Evening When
the Full Moon Rose As the Sun Set.

Location:  SUNY Stony Brook

Note:  An erratum is inserted:  "ERRATUM:  The last
line of AUNT BERTHA should read / 'long night after
night'."


A56.  WHAT THE FOX AGREED TO DO  1979

[drawing of a girl's head and shoulders] / WHAT THE
FOX / AGREED TO / DO / FOUR POEMS / ROBERT BLY
/ Croissant / & / Company / Athens, Ohio

Collation:  5 1/2 X 8 1/2".  No sign.  6 leaves.  Pp. [1-12].

Pagination:  pp. [1-2] blank; p. [3] title-page; p. [4]
"ACKNOWLEDGEMENTS" / "Copyright  1979 by Robert Bly
/ Published by Croissant & Company / Route 1, Box 51 /
Athens, Ohio 45701 / ISBN 0-912348-02-X / With special
thanks to Franz Richter / for the title page design. /
Croissant Pamphlets No. 12"; pp. [5-9] text; p. [10]
"COLOPHON / This first edition of What the Fox Agreed
To Do by Robert Bly / has been set and printed for
Croissant & Company at the press of / Lettershop Plus,
Athens, Ohio.  The text is 80 lb. Gray Strathmore /
Pastelle, and the covers are 80 lb. Chesnut Simpson Teton
Cover, / sewn by hand. / Of this first edition of What the
Fox Agreed To Do, 85 copies have / been signed and num-
bered by the author, 75 of which are for sale."; pp. [11-
12] blank.

Binding:  Brown paper wrappers.  Front:  [in black:]
[double rule across top and down right hand side] WHAT
THE FOX / AGREED TO / DO / Robert Bly [the y breaks
the rule along the right hand side].  Back:  [in black:]
CROISSANT PAMPHLETS / [lists eleven titles] / Croissant
Pamphlets No. 12.  All pages are of gray paper.

Contents:  A Dream of an Afternoon With a Woman I Did
Not Know/What the Fox Agreed To Do/The Fallen Tree/
Black Pony Eating Grass

Location:   Roberson

A57.   TALKING ALL MORNING   1980

TALKING / ALL / MORNING / Robert Bly / Ann Arbor
The University of Michigan Press

Collation:   5 X 8".   No sign.   160 leaves.   Pp. [A-B] [i-
vii] viii-ix [x] [1-2] 3-70 [71-72] 73-112 [113-114] 115-168
[169-170] 171-237 [238-240] 241-308.

Pagination:   pp. [A-B] blank; p. [i] half-title; p. [ii]
"Poets on Poetry / Donald Hall, General Editor"; p. [iii]
title-page; p. [iv] "Copyright © by The University of
Michigan 1980 / All rights reserved / Published in the
United States of America by / The University of Michigan
Press and simultaneously / in Rexdale, Canada, by John
Wiley & Sons Canada, Limited / Manufactured in the
United States of America / 1984 1983 1982 1981 5 4 3 2";
pp. [v-vi] [acknowledgments]; pp. [vii]-ix, "Contents";
p. [x] blank; pp. [1]-308, text.

Binding:   Aqua blue paper covers.   Front:   [in black:]
[upper right quadrant:] Poets on Poetry / [rule] / [in
white:] [centered:] TALKING / ALL / MORNING / [in
black:] ROBERT BLY / [blue and white design on lower
third of cover].   Spine, reading downwards:   [in black:]
BLY [in white:] Talking All Morning / [publisher's device:
stylized um printed in white on black square] / [design
continued from front cover onto lower third of spine].
Back:   [in black:] [to the left:] ISBN 0-472-15760-4 /
[in white:] ROBERT BLY / Talking All Morning / [in
black:] [eleven-line statement on Poets on Poetry series] /
Other books in the series: / [lists, in white, ten authors,
and, in black, ten titles] / [in black:] [two-line statement
regarding future titles] / Please write for information on
available editions and current prices. / [in white:] The
University of Michigan Press   Ann Arbor.

Contents:   I.   Inwardness and Biology:   Two Long Inter-
views:   The Evolutionary Part of the Mind:   An Interview
with Jay Bail and Geoffrey Cook/Going Out on the Plain
in the Moonlight:   An Interview with Cynthia Lofsness
and Kathy Otto, with Fred Manfred.
II.   On the War and Political Poems:   On Government Sup-
port for the Arts:   An Interview with N. G. Schuessler/
An Argument about "Universal" versus "Political" Art:
An Interview with Gregory FitzGerald and William Heyen/
On Urging Others to refuse the Draft:   An Interview/On
the Lack of Thinking in the Left:   An Interview with

John Maillet and Elliot Rockler/Leaping Up into Political
Poetry:  An Essay/Acceptance of the National Book Award
for Poetry/Three Poems.
III.  Talk About Writing Poetry:  On Writing Prose Poems:
An Interview with Rochelle Ratner/On "Losing the Road":
An Interview with Peter Martin/Two Halves of Life:  An
Interview with Phil Yannella/Poetry Is a Dream That Is
Shared with Others:  An Interview with Paul Feroe, Neil
Klotz, and Don Lee/On Unfinished Poets:  An Interview
with Scott Chisholm/The First Ten Issues of Kayak:  An
Essay/Three Poems.
IV.  An Argument about the Meaning of the Word "Craft":
Craft Interview:  With Mary Jane Fortunato and Cornelia
P. Draves, and Paul Zweig and Saul Galin.
V.  Talk About the "Great Mother":  The Masculine versus
the Feminine in Poetry:  An Interview with William Heyen
and Gregory FitzGerald/About the Conference on the Mother:
An Interview with Bill Siemering/On Split-Brain Experiments
and the Mother:  An Interview with Kevin Powers/Three
Poems.
VI.  Recent Interviews:  The Ascending Energy Arc:
Answers to Students' Questions, Suffolk County Community
College/Infantilism and Adult Swiftness:  An Interview with
Ekbert Faas/Knots of Wild Energy:  An Interview with
Wayne Dodd.

Location:  Southampton Campus Library of Long Island Uni-
versity


A58.  FINDING AN OLD ANT MANSION  1981

[in red-brown:] Finding an / Old Ant Mansion / [in black:]
ROBERT BLY / MARTIN BOOTH / 1981

Collation:  6 1/8 X 7 3/4".  No sign.  6 leaves including
two leaves of tissue paper.  Pp. [1-12].  Printed on cream-
color paper.

Pagination:  p. [1] title-page; p. [2] "The poem is copy-
right: © Robert Bly, 1981"; pp. [3-4] [tissue paper] blank;
pp. [5-8] poem; pp. [9-10] [tissue paper] blank; p. [11]
"FINDING AN OLD ANT MANSION is published by Martin /
Booth at Knotting, Bedford, in the month of April, 1981,
in / an edition of 130 numbered copies, with nos. 1-30
signed by / the poet.  It is printed on Scots Antique laid
paper, set in / 'Monotype' Garamond type, by Christopher
Skelton, at / Skelton's Press, Wellingsborough, England.
/ This copy is numbered"; p. [12] blank.

Binding:  Brown paper wrappers.  Front:  [in white:]
Finding an / Old Ant Mansion / Robert Bly.

Contents:   Finding an Old Ant Mansion [poem].

Location:   SUNY Buffalo.


A59.   THE MAN IN THE BLACK COAT TURNS   1981

[in an ivory rectangle, enclosed by three rules, the last
with ornamental corners, on gray page:] [in black:] THE
/ MAN / in the / BLACK COAT / TURNS / Poems by /
ROBERT BLY / The Dial Press   New York

Collation:   5 7/8 X 8 15/16".   [1-30] [1-20] [1-30].   Pp.
[i-viii] ix-x [xi-xii] [1-2] 3-13 [14-16] 17-30 [31-32] 33-
62 [63-68].

Pagination:   p. [i] "Also by Robert Bly" [list of eighteen
titles]; p. [ii] [list of six titles]; p. [iii] half-title; p.
[iv] blank [gray]; p. [v] title-page; p. [vi] [publisher's
device:   griffen] / "Published by / The Dial Press / 1
Dag Hammarskjold Plaza / New York, New York 10017" /
[acknowledgments] / "Copyright © 1981 by Robert Bly /
All rights reserved. / Manufactured in the United States
of America / First printing / Design by Francesca Belang-
er" / [Library of Congress Cataloging in Publication Data];
p. [vii] dedication:   "For Noah Matthew"; p. [viii] blank;
pp. ix-x, "Contents"; p. [xi] second half-title; p. [xii]
blank; pp. [1]-62, text; pp. [63-64] blank; p. [65]
"About the Author" [twenty-line statement]; pp. [66-68]
blank.

Binding:   Black paper covered boards with white cloth
spine.   Spine, stamped in copper, reading downwards:
Robert Bly   The Man in the Black Coat Turns   The Dial
Press [publisher's device].

Dust jacket:   Black paper.   Front:   [ivory rectangle
bordered with thick green rule, thin green rule, and
brown thin rule with ornamental corners:] [in black within
rectangle:] THE / MAN / in the / BLACK COAT / TURNS
/ [in green:] poems by / [in black:] Robert Bly.   Spine,
reading downwards:   [in black on ivory strip:] Robert
Bly   The Man in the Black Coat Turns   The Dial Press
[publisher's device].   Back:   [photograph of R. B. en-
closed in three brown rules, the last of which is heavy] /
[in ivory:] Robert Bly / [lower right corner:] ISBN:
0-385-27186-7.   Along upper right corner of photograph,
reading upwards:   [in ivory:] BENJAMIN MC CULLOUGH.
Flyleaves, paper in ivory.   Front flyleaf:   [in black:]
$10.95 / [enclosed in a green frame:] [in black:] Robert
Bly / [in brown:] [single rule] / [in black:] The Man /

in the / Black Coat / Turns. [twenty-three-line state-
ment on the collection] / (continued on back flap). Back
flyleaf: [in black:] (continued from front flap) / [thir-
teen-line statement] / [seven-line statement on R. B.] /
Jacket design by Francesca Belanger / [in green:] [pub-
lisher's device] / [in black:] The Dial Press / 1 Dag
Hammarskjold Plaza / New York, New York   10017 / 1081
Printed in U.S.A.

Contents:  I:  Snowbanks North of the House/For My Son
Noah, Ten Years Old/The Prodigal Son/Visiting the Faral-
lones/The Convict and His Radio/Mourning Pablo Neruda
II:  Eleven O'Clock at Night/The Ship's Captain Looking
Over the Rail/The Dried Sturgeon/A Bouquet of Ten Roses
/Visiting Emily Dickinson's Grave with Robert Francis/
Finding an Old Ant Mansion  III:  The Grief of Men/Ken-
nedy's Inauguration/Written at Mule Hollow, Utah/What the
Fox Agreed to Do/Words Rising/A Sacrifice in the Orchard/
A Meditation on Philosophy/My Father's Wedding 1924/Four
Ways of Knowledge/Fifty Males Sitting Together/Crazy Carl-
son's Meadow/Kneeling Down to Look into a Culvert
Location:  Roberson

First paper edition:  1983

Title page and contents same as hardbound except last line
of title page reads "Penguin Books."

Collation:  5 7/8 X 8 15/16".  No sign.  Pp. [i-viii] ix-x
[xi-xii] [1-2] 3-13 [14-16] 17-30 [31-32] 33-62 [63-68].

Pagination:  p. [i] "THE PENGUIN POETS / THE MAN IN
THE BLACK COAT TURNS / [fourteen-line statement on
R. B.] / [publisher's device:  penguin within an oval];
p. [ii] blank; p. [iii] "Also by Robert Bly" [list of eight-
een titles]; p. [iv] [list of six titles]; p. [v] title-page;
p. [vi] "Penguin Books Ltd, Harmondsworth, / Middlesex,
England / Penguin Books, 40 West 23rd Street, / New
York, New York 10010, U.S.A. / Penguin Books Australia
Ltd, Ringwood, / Victoria, Australia / Penguin Books
Canada Limited, 2801 John Street, / Markham, Ontario,
Canada L3R 1B4 / Penguin Books (N.Z.) Ltd, 182-190
Wairau Road, / Auckland 10, New Zealand / First published
in the United States of America by / The Dial Press 1981 /
Published in Penguin Books 1983 / Copyright © Robert Bly,
1981 / All rights reserved" / [Library of Congress Catalog-
ing in Publication Data] / "Printed in the United States of
America by / R. R. Donnelley & Sons Company, Harrison-
burg, Virginia" / [acknowledgments] / "Except in the
United States of America, / this book is sold subject to
the condition / that it shall not, by way of trade or

otherwise, / be lent, re-sold, hired out, or otherwise cir-
culated / without the publisher's prior consent in any form
of / binding or cover other than that in which it is / pub-
lished and without a similar condition / including this con-
dition imposed / on the subsequent purchaser"; p. [vii]
dedication: "For Noah Matthew"; p. [viii] blank; pp. ix-x,
"Contents"; p. [xi] second half-title; p. [xii] blank; pp.
[1]-62, text; p. [63] [within a frame of light and heavy
rules with the publisher's device at the top:] "For a com-
plete list of books available from / Penguin in the United
States, write to Dept. / DG, Penguin Books, 299 Murray
Hill Park- / way, East Rutherford, New Jersey 07073. /
For a complete list of books available from / Penguin in
Canada, write to Penguin Books / Canada Limited, 2801
John Street, Markham, / Ontario L3R 1B4."; pp. [64-68]

Binding:  Front and back paper covers of deep purple |
enclosed by black frames; spine of black paper.  Front:
[upper right quadrant:] [enclosed by six thin black
frames:] [painting of coat above a landscape] / [in
cream:] THE MAN IN THE / BLACK COAT TURNS /
[in black:] [five thin rules] / [in cream:] POEMS BY /
ROBERT BLY / [in lower right corner on black frame:]
[publisher's device].  Spine, reading downwards:  [in
white:] ROBERT BLY   THE MAN IN THE BLACK COAT
TURNS   ISBN 0 14 042.303 6 [reading across:] [publish-
er's device].  Back: [upper left corner:] [in white:]
[publisher's device] / The / Penguin / Poets.  [Upper
right quadrant:] [enclosed by six thin black frames:]
[painting of coat above a landscape] / [in white:]
"Easily Robert Bly's richest, most complex book" / --The
New York Times Book Review / [seven-line statement on
the collection] / "A turning-point collection ... it is fresh,
stark, elegant, and serious." / --Chicago Tribune Book
World / Cover design by Neil Stuart/Cover illustration by
Kevin King / [in lower left corner on black frame:] [in
white:] $6.95 [in lower right corner on black frame:] [in
white:] Poetry/ISBN 0 14 / 042.303 6.


A60.  WALKING AND SITTING  1981

[deep blue placard with white frame printed in white]
[upper left quadrant:] Poet:  Robert Bly / Artist:  George
Segal / Designer: Eddie Byrd / Spanish Translation:
Jose Varela-Ibarra / Poem from This Tree Will Be Here
for a Thousand Years / Copyright © 1974 by Robert Bly /
(Harper & Row) / [in column to right of the above:] Girl
Resting courtesy of / Sidney Janis Gallery Editions, Inc.,
New York, New York / POETRY ON THE BUSESTM is sup-
ported in part / by the National Endowment for the Arts /
and the Pennsylvania Council on the Arts. / © 1981 POETRY

ON THE BUSES / Chatham College, Pittsburgh, PA. [lower left quadrant:] Walking and Sitting / [text in a single column] [in middle of placard:] [illustration] [upper right quadrang:] Caminando y Sentado / [text in Spanish in a single column].

Collation: 17 X 11". Single placard printed on one side.

Binding: None. All edges trimmed.

Contents: Walking and Sitting [poem] and Caminando y Sentado [Spanish translation].

Location: SUNY Buffalo


A61.   THE TRAVELLER WHO REPEATS HIS CRY   1982

The traveller who repeats his cry / [in purple:] Robert Bly / [in pink:] [illustration of a shell with flower buds] / [in purple:] Red Ozier Press

Collation: 5 15/16 X 7". No sign. 8 leaves. Pp. [1-16].

Pagination: pp. [1-2] blank; p. [3] title-page; p. [4] "Copyright 1982 by Robert Bly."; pp. [5-13] text; p. [14] "Barry Moser contributed the drawing to this first / of three pamphlets of love poems by Robert Bly. / There are 160 copies printed on various papers from / the Twinrocker Mill and wrapped in Tidepool / handmade. The Goudy Village type was cast by / Out of Sorts Letter Foundery, & everything else to / do with this speck of optimism in an often dark / world was done by Ken Botnick & Steve Miller at / the Red Ozier Press in New York. This is copy [ ]."; pp. [15-16] blank.

Binding: Pale green paper wrappers. Front: [in black:] The traveller who repeats his cry / Robert Bly. Top edges trimmed.

Contents: A Love that I have in Secret/Poem on Sleep/A Man and a Woman and a Blackbird/At the Time of Peony Blossoming/Here is What I have Experienced/The Ram/Rain on Mountain Grass.

Location: SUNY Buffalo


A62.   AT THE TIME OF PEONY BLOSSOMING   1983

[cream paper printed in red-brown and black] [in red-

brown:] [illustration of a peony] / [in black:] AT THE
TIME OF PEONY BLOSSOMING / [text in a single column]
/ Robert Bly / 225 copies illustrated and printed by Gary
Young at the Greenhouse Review Press for / Poet's Place,
Carmel, California. The type is Garamount; the paper is
hand-made Tovil. / Poem Copyright © 1983 by Robert Bly.

Collation:  15 1/2 X 20 1/2".  Single sheet printed on one
side only.

Binding:  None.  All edges trimmed.

Contents:  At the Time of Peony Blossoming [poem]

Location:  SUNY Buffalo

Note:  Limited to 225 copies.


A63.   THE EIGHT STAGES OF TRANSLATION   1983

THE EIGHT / STAGES / of / TRANSLATION / with a se-
lection / of poems and translations / ROBERT BLY / Rowan
Tree Press / Boston   1983

Collation:  5 1/2 X 7 1/4".  [1-16] [1-13] [1-16] [1-11]:
56 leaves.  Pp. [1-12] 13-49 [50-51] 52-107 [108-112].

Pagination:  pp. [1-2] blank; p. [3] half-title; p. [4]
blank; p. [5] title-page; p. [6] "© Robert Bly, 1983 /
All rights reserved / Library of Congress Catalogue Card
No. 82-060670 / ISBN 0-937672-10-6 / Printed in the
United States of America / ACKNOWLEDGEMENTS / Essay
and poems by Robert Bly / Cover design by Lazarillo /
Photography by Fonville, Baton Rouge" / [acknowledgments]
/ "I'd like here to thank my masters in the labor of trans-
lation, Rich- / ard Wilbur, Kenneth Rexroth, Hardie St.
Martin, Ezra Pound, / Gary Snyder, W. B. Yeats and
H. R. Hays, and to remember many / conversations over
the years of its problems with James Wright, / James
Scherer, Carol Bly, Tomas Tranströmer, Saul Galin, Lisel
/ Mueller, and Donald Hall. / Rowan Tree Press / 124
Chestnut Street / Boston, Massachusetts 02108"; p. [7]
dedication:  "This essay is dedicated to / Hardie St. Mar-
tin / master translator and patient friend"; p. [8] blank;
p. [9] "Contents"; p. [10] blank; pp. [11]-107, text; p.
[108] "ROWAN TREE PRESS [publisher's device] / Poetics
series No. 2 / This book was set in Garamond and printed
/ on acid-free paper by Maple-Vail Press / at Binghamton,
New York. / Rowan Tree Press / 124 Chestnut Street /
Boston, Massachusetts 02108"; pp. [109-111]; p. [112]
[six-line statement about R.B.].

Binding: Gray paper covers. Front: [in black:] [printed over a bouquet:] THE EIGHT STAGES / of / TRANSLATION / ROBERT BLY. Spine, reading downwards: [in black:] BLY   The Eight Stages of Translation   Rowan Tree Press. Back: [in black:] POETICS   $7.95 / ISBN 0-937672-10-6 / [photograph of R.B. by Fonette, Baton Rouge] / [four-line statement by Helen Vendler] / ROWAN TREE PRESS [publisher's device: two chestnut leaves] 124 Chestnut Street, Boston, Massachusetts 02108.

Contents: I. The Eight Stages of Translation / II. Poems and Translations: Old Age-Jacobsen/The Island of Koster, 1973-Sonnevi/Zero-Sonnevi/Holy Longing-Goethe/Old Winter -Quasimodo/Rain-Ponge/Letter to Miguel Otero Silva in Caracas (1948)-Neruda/Ode to My Socks-Neruda/Preciosa and the Wind-García Lorca/In the Great Sweetness of the Spring-Guillaume IX of Poitiers.

Note: This is a bilingual edition with the original texts of the translated poems on facing pages. The essay "The Eight Stages of Translation" is reprinted from B113.

A64.  FOUR RAMAGES  1983

[to the left:] [drawing of a lute] [in black:] FOUR RAM-AGES OF / ROBERT BLY / ILLUSTRATIONS & GRAPHICS / BARBARA LARUE KING

Collation: 7 1/2 X 7 1/2". No sign. 10 leaves. Pp. [1-20].

Pagination: pp. [1-2] [in scarlet:] blank; p. [3] title-page; p. [4] "First Printing. / ISBN 0-935306-11-0 / Publication of this book was assisted by a gift from a patron of The Barn- / wood Press Cooperative, Mrs. Agnes H. Shoaff. / Copyright © 1983 Robert Bly / All rights reserved. No part of this book shall be reproduced in any form / (except by reviewers for the public press) without written permission from / the publisher: / [to the left:] [publisher's device: drawing of a barn] [to the right:] the / Barnwood Press / RIVER HOUSE / R. R. 2 BOX 11C Daleville, Indiana 47334 / Printed in The United States of America."; p. [5] blank; pp. [6-13] text and graphics; pp. [14-17] blank; p. [18] "The poems in this book are printed in 18 point Paladium / Semibold type on Starwhite 65 pound white vellum cover stock. / The cover is 80 pound Legendary Pearl cover, and the fly sheet / is 80 pound Legendry Scarlet text. Of 1000 copies, the first 25 / have been signed by the author and artist and the next 75 have / been signed by the author only. 15 have been hand colored by / the artist."; pp. [19-20] [in scarlet:] blank.

Binding:  Stiff light gray paper covers.  Front:  [in
black:]  [graphic design with lute]  [in lower right quad-
rant:]  [in scarlet:]  FOUR RAMAGES OF / ROBERT BLY
/ ILLUSTRATIONS & GRAPHICS / BARBARA LARUE
KING.

Contents:  "As soon as the master is untied ..."/"Grief
lies close to the roots of laughter."/"Grackles stroll about
on the black floor of sorrow."/"So in the bear's cabin I
come to earth."

Location:  Roberson

Note:  Limited to 1,000 copies of which the first 25 are
signed by R. B. and the artist, and the next 75 are
signed by R. B.  Fifteen copies have been hand colored
by the artist.

A65.    IN THE MONTH OF MAY   1983

[off-white sheet printed in brown, red, and black]  Front:
[in brown:]  [collage of bird & a woman filling a water jug]
/ [in red:]  In the Month of May / [in black:]  [text in a
single column] / - Robert Bly / In the Month of May by
Robert Bly.  With an original collage by John Digby. /
Stone House Press.  Portfolio One / 1983.  Number 2.
Copy [  ].  Back:  [publisher's device:  house]  The
Stone House Press, Box 196, Roslyn, New York 11576 /
The text was set in Poliphilus, the title, in Blado, by the
Out of Sorts Letter Foundery. / Printed by hand in Bas-
ingwerk paper by M. A. Gelfand, in an addition of 150
signed / & numbered copies, with 115 for sale.  Text copy-
right © 1983, by the Atlantic / Monthly, where the poem
was originally published in May 1983.  Illustra- / tion
copyright © 1983, by John Digby.

Collation:  12 X 16".  Single sheet printed on both sides.

Binding:  None.  All edges trimmed.

Contents:  In the Month of May [poem]

Location:  SUNY Buffalo

Note:  Portfolio One consists of ten individually designed
and illustrated poetry broadsides.

A66.    THE WHOLE MOISTY NIGHT   1983

The Whole / Moisty Night / Robert Bly [with a brown-tone

drawing of an opening pod to the left]

Collation:  6 X 7".  No sign.  8 leaves.  Pp. [1-16].

Pagination:  pp. [1-2] blank; p. [3] title-page; p. [4]
blank; p. [5-11] text; p. [12] blank; p. [13] "This is
the second of three pamphlets of love / poems by Robert
Bly with drawings by Barry / Moser.  The papers:
Frankfurt Creme with Carson wrappers.  The types cast
at Out of / Sorts Letter Foundery are Italian Old Style,
/ titling, & Deepdene for text.  Copyright / 1983 by
Robert Bly.  Made in New York / by Ken Botnick &
Steve Miller in this, / the Year of the Boar - 300 copies
- "; pp. [14-16] blank.

Binding:  Dark green wrappers, stamped in black.  Front:
The Whole / Moisty Night / Robert Bly.  Back:  Red Ozier.

Contents:  The White Ground/Covers/Herons/Snowstorm/
The Whole Moisty Night/Affections/Thirst.


A67.   OUT OF THE ROLLING OCEAN   1984

[in black:] OUT OF THE / ROLLING OCEAN / [in maroon:]
[Indian design] / [in black:] & other love poems.

Collation:  5 15/16 X 7 3/4".  No sign.  12 leaves.  Pp.
[1-24].

Pagination:  p. [1] title-page; p. [2] "© Copyright Robert
Bly, 1984" / [Library of Congress Cataloging in Publication
Data] / [acknowledgments] / "The cover and inside illus-
trations are taken from "Indian Designs / from Ancient
Ecuador," edited by Frederick Shaffer, Dover Publica- /
tions. / Ally Press / 524 Orleans St. / St. Paul, MN 55107
/ [publisher's device to the right of the above three lines];
p. [3] "POEMS BY / ROBERT BLY"; pp. [4-23] text [Note:
poems are on odd-numbered pages.  Even-numbered pages
have numbers in black indicating number of the poem, fol-
lowed by an Indian design in maroon in the lower right
corner.]; p. [24] "Robert Bly lives in Moose Lake, Minne-
sota where he is writing a / book about fairy tales.  He
has numerous books, essays and awards / to his credit. /
This first edition of 1000 copies is printed on 80# warm
white Teton / Text and 65# silver Gainsborough Cover.
Book design by Paul / Feroe. / 26 copies have been let-
tered and signed by the author and then / handcased in
boards."

Binding:  Silver-gray paper wrappers.  Front:  [in maroon:]

ROBERT BLY / OUT OF THE / ROLLING / OCEAN / [to
the right of the above two lines, in black:] [four rules,
diagonally cut to the left, running off the cover on the
right / four ornamental devices on a dark gray field /
four rules diagonally cut to the left at both ends / four
ornamental devices on a dark gray field / thin rule /
thick rule [the above two rules are diagonally out to the
left on both ends] / [to the right of last three lines, in
maroon:] & other / love poems.  Back:  [in maroon:]
[lower left corner:] 3.50 / [single rule].

Contents:  In Rainy September/No Mountain Peak Without
Its Rolling Foothills/A Moist Night/Ferns/Secrets/The Black
Hen/At Midocean/Returning Poem/"Out of the Rolling
Ocean, the Crowd ..."/Conversation with A Holy Woman
Not Seen for Many Years.

Location:  Roberson.


A68.   IN THE MONTH OF MAY   1985

[in black:] IN THE MONTH OF MAY / ROBERT BLY / [to
the right:] [in green:] [three ornamental columns] / [in
black:] Red Ozier Press

Collation:   5 X 7 1/2".   No sign.   8 leaves.   Pp. [1-16].

Pagination:  pp. [1-2] blank; p. [3] title-page; p. [4]
blank; pp. [5-13] text; p. [14] "One hundred-forty copies
/ handmade in New York City / Frankfurt papers with
Roma wrappers / Deepdene types / Copyright 1985 by
Robert Bly / Some of these poems first appeared in / The
New Republic, The Atlantic Monthly / The New Yorker, &
The Kenyon Review / [row of seventeen ornamental de-
vices] / This edition was made possible in part / with
public funds from / the New York State Council on the
Arts"; pp. [15-16] blank.

Binding:  Gray-green paper wrappers.  Front:  [top right
quadrant:] [in deep blue:] IN THE MONTH OF MAY /
ROBERT BLY.  Top edges trimmed.

Contents:  The Minnow Turning/The Indigo Bunting/Leaves
On the Highway/Love Poem in Twos and Threes/Lines From
An Old Poem/Two People At Dawn/In the Month of May.

Location:  Roberson

Note:  Pages [1-2], [5-6], [11-12], and [15-16] are off-
white.  Edition limited to 140 copies.

A68a.  A LOVE OF MINUTE PARTICULARS  1985

A Love of / Minute / Particulars / POEMS BY / ROBERT
BLY / With an introduction / by Martin Booth / SCEPTRE
PRESS LIMITED / 1985

Collation:  5 1/2 X 8 1/2".  [1-16]4:  32 leaves.  Pp. [1-
4] 5-7 [8-10] 11-62 [63-64].

Pagination:  p. [1] half-title; p. [2] blank; p. [3] title-
page; p. [4] "SCEPTRE PRESS LIMITED / 7 College Park
Drive, / Westbury-on-Trym, / Bristol BS10 7AN, England
/ Copyright © Robert Bly 1985 / Copyright © Introduction
Martin Booth 1985 / ISBN 0 7068 05194 / ISBN 0 7068 0520
8 (signed, limited edition) / Photoset by Nene Phototype-
setters Ltd, Northampton / Printed in Great Britain by /
The September Press, Wellingborough, Northants"; pp. 5-
7, "Introduction"; p. [8] blank; pp. [9-10] "Contents";
pp. 11-62, text; pp. [63-64] blank.

Binding:  Brown paper covers printed in black.  Front:
ROBERT BLY / A Love / of Minute / Particulars /
SCEPTRE PRESS.  Spine, reading downwards:  A LOVE
OF MINUTE PARTICULARS  SCEPTRE PRESS.  Back:
[seventeen-line statement on R. B.] / Ł4.95  ISBN 0 7068
0519 4.

Contents:  Come with Me/Sleet Storm on the Merritt Park-
way/Watching Television/Those Being Eaten by America/
Condition of the Working Class:  1970/Calling to the Bad-
ger/Pilgrim Fish Heads/Water Under the Earth/The Night
Journey in the Cooking Pot/Visiting Thomas Hart Benton
and His Wife in Kansas City/The Hunter/A Turtle/Walking
on the Sussex Coast/The Dead Seal near McClure's Beach/
Christmas Eve Service at Midnight at St. Michael's/Falling
into Holes in Our Sentences/Going Out to Check the Ewes/
Snowed In/Looking from Inside My Body/Out Picking Up
Corn/Black Pony Eating Grass/A Dream on the Night of
First Snow/Cornpicker Poem/The Dried Sturgeon/Finding
an Old Ant Mansion/Visiting the Farallones/Kennedy's In-
auguration/My Father's Wedding 1924/Crazy Carlson's
Meadow/Here Is What I Have Experienced/In Rainy Septem-
ber/The Whole Moisty Night/A Man and A Woman and A
Blackbird/Returning Poem/At Midocean/The Good Silence/
A Ramage for Sleep/A Ramage for Moonlight/A Ramage for
Limits

Location:  Roberson

Note:  A limited edition of 35 copies, specially bound in
hard covers, numbered and signed by R. B. was published

simultaneously with the trade edition of 750 copies in Au-
gust 1985.


A68b.  LOVING A WOMAN IN TWO WORLDS  1985

[in a single rule frame with ornamental corners:] [in
black:] Loving a Woman / in Two Worlds / ROBERT BLY /
[publisher's device:  griffin] / The Dial Press / Doubleday
& Company, Inc., / Garden City, New York / 1985

Collation:  5 3/8 X 8 1/4".  [1-4]$^5$ [1-14]$^2$ [1-16] [1-20]
[1-4]$^3$:  48 leaves.  Pp. [i-x] xi-xiii [xiv-xvi] [1-2] 3-21
[22-24] 25-57 [58-60] 61-78 [79-80].

Pagination:  pp. [i-ii] blank; p. [iii] half-title; p. [iv]
blank; p. [v] "Books by Robert Bly" [lists 15 titles]; p.
[vi] blank; p. [vii] title-page; p. [viii] [Library of Con-
gress Cataloging in Publication Data] / "Published by The
Dial Press / Copyright © 1985 by Robert Bly / All Rights
Reserved / Manufactured in the United States of America
/ First Printing"; p. [ix] "Acknowledgements"; p. [x]
blank; pp. xi-xiii, "Contents"; p. [xiv] blank; p. [xv]
second half-title; p. [xvi] blank; pp. [1]-78, text; pp.
[79-80] blank.

Binding:  Cream color paper covered boards with maroon
cloth spine.  Spine, stamped in silver, reading downwards:
ROBERT BLY  Loving a Woman in Two Worlds  [publisher's
device] The Dial Press.

Dust jacket:  Black paper.  Front:  [in tan:] [rectangle
formed by intersecting vertical rules, left and right, and
horizontal rules, top and bottom, with an ornament in each
corner:] [in off-white at top of rectangle:] R$^O$BERT BLY
[in tan:] [single rule] / [in red:] L$^O$VING A W$^O$MAN / IN
TW$^O$ W$^O$RLDS / [in tan:] [horizontal line connecting the two
vertical rules of the rectangle] / [full color detail of Goya's
"Gaspar Melchor De Jovellanos"].  Spine:  [in tan:]
[horizontal rule continued from front] / [reading down-
wards:] [in off-white:] R$^O$BERT BLY [in red:] L$^O$VING A
W$^O$MAN IN TW$^O$ W$^O$RLDS [in off-white:] [publisher's device]
THE DIAL PRESS / [in tan:] [horizontal rule continued
from the front].  Back:  [in tan:] [horizontal rule con-
tinued from the spine] / [in white:] [twenty-line statement
on the collection] / [thirteen-line statement on R. B.] /
[in black on a white bar:] ISBN:  0-385-27418-1 / [in tan:]
[horizontal rule continued from spine].  Flyleaves, paper
in white.  Front flyleaf:  [in black:] [at upper right:]
L.A.W.I.T.W / $12.95.  Back flyleaf:  [in black:] [at bot-
tom:] FRONT JACKET PAINTING:  DETAIL FROM /

"GASPAR MELCHOR DE JOVELLANOS" BY GOYA, /
COURTESY MUSEO DEL PRADO, MADRID / JACKET DE-
SIGN BY CATHY SAKSA / Printed in the U. S. A. /
0885.

Contents: ONE: Fifty Males Sitting Together/The Indigo
Bunting/"Out of the Rolling Ocean, the Crowd..."/The
Whole Moisty Night/Secrets/Letter to Her/Two People at
Dawn/Winter Poem/In Rainy September/A Third Body/No
Mountain Peak Without Its Rolling Foothills/Finding Sharks'
Teeth in a Rock / TWO: The Roots/What Frightened Us/
Seeing You Carry Plants In/The Two Rivers/Come with Me/
At Midocean/In the Time of Peony Blossoming/Night Frogs/
The March Buds/The Turtle/Such' Different Wants/Ferns/
The Hummingbird Valley/Love Poem in Twos and Threes/
Returning Poem/The Minty Grass/What We Provide/Poem on
Sleep/The Artist at Fifty/Words Barely Heard/The Condi-
tions/A Man and a Woman and a Blackbird / THREE:
The Minnow Turning/Firmness/Conversation/Shame/The
Horse of Desire/Listening to the Koln Concert/Conversation
with a Holy Woman Not Seen for Many Years/What Moves
and Doesn't Move/Water/The Good Silence/The Hawk/In the
Month of May

Location: Roberson


A69.  STRIPS OF AUGUST SUN  [undated]

[orange card printed in red with a yellow sun] [text in a
single column] / Robert Bly. Back: [reading upwards
from center:] AN ALTERNATIVE PRESS POSTCARD
DETROIT. [Upper right quadrant: device].

Collation: 6 1/2 X 4". Single card printed on both sides.

Binding: None. All edges trimmed.

Contents: "Strips of August sun ..."

Location: Piccione


TRANSLATIONS


A70.  THE ILLUSTRATED BOOK ABOUT REPTILES AND AMPHIBIANS
OF THE WORLD  1960

[in black:] HANS HVASS / The Illustrated Book About /

[in green:] REPTILES / [in black:] and Amphibians of
the World / Text by ROBERT BLY / Illustrations by Wil-
helm Eigener / [color drawing of two frilled lizards] /
GROSSET & DUNLAP • Publishers • NEW YORK

Collation:   7 3/4 X 10 1/2".   No sign.   82 leaves.   Pp.
[1-10]  11-12  [13-15]  16-17  [18-20]  21  [22]  23-24  [25-26]
27-28  [29-30]  31-34  [35-36]  37-39  [40-41]  42-44  [45-46]
47-48  [49-50]  51  [52-54]  55-56  [57]  58-59  [60-61]  62  [63-
65]  66  [67]  68  [69-70]  71  [72]  73-74  [75]  76  [77-78]  79
[80]  81-82  [83-88]  89-90  [91-92]  93-94  [95]  96-97  [98-100]
101  [102-103]  104  [105-106]  107-108  [109]  110  [111]  112-
115  [116-119]  120-122  [123]  124-125  [126-127]  128-129
[130]  131  [132]  133-135  [136]  137-138  [139-140]  141-142
[143]  144-146  [147-148]  149-150  [151-152]  153  [154]  155-
157  [158-164].

Pagination:   pp. [1-4] blank; p. [5] half-title; p. [6]
blank; p. [7] title-page; p. [8] "The author wishes to
thank the herpetologist Kevin Marx of St. Paul / Minne-
sota, for the gift of his time and careful scholarship in
helping estab- / lish names for certain creatures described
in this book, some of which up / till now have not had
any name in English at all." / "© 1960, by Grosset & Dun-
lap, Inc. / The English-language edition is based on the
Danish text by / Hans Hvass, originally entitled Alverdens
Krybdyr. / Art Copyright, 1958, by Politikens Forlag /
All rights reserved under International and Pan-American
Copyright Conventions. / Printed in the United States of
America."; p. [9] "Table of Contents"; pp. [10]-[154]
text and illustrations; pp. 155-157, "INDEX"; pp. [158-
159] [thirteen illustrations]; pp. [160-164] blank.

Binding:   Green cloth covered boards.   Front:   [in dark
green:] The Illustrated Book About / [in red:] REPTILES
/ [in dark green:] AND AMPHIBIANS OF THE WORLD /
[six illustrations in color].   Spine, reading downwards:
[in red on a white bar:] REPTILES AND AMPHIBIANS OF
THE WORLD [in dark green:] BLY.

Contents:   Reptiles and Amphibians/Tuatara/Lizards/Snakes/
Crocodilians/Turtles/Frogs and Toads/Salamanders/Caecilians/
Index

Location:   University of Pennsylvania


A71.   TWENTY POEMS OF GEORG TRAKL   1961

[in red:] Twenty Poems of Georg Trakl / [in black:]
TRANSLATED BY / JAMES WRIGHT AND ROBERT BLY /

[publisher's device:  horseman with shield and spear sur-
rounded by two birds and a snake] / 1961 / THE SIXTIES
PRESS

Collation:  5 1/4 X 8 1/4".  [1-16]$^4$:  32 leaves.  Pp.  [1-
4] 5-10 [11] 12-29 [30-31] 32-47 [48-49] 50-61 [62-64].

Pagination:  p. [1] half-title; p. [2] blank; p. [3] title-
page; p. [4] [acknowledgments] / Library of Congress
Catalogue Card Number: / 61-9805 / Copyright © 1961
by The Sixties Press, / Odin House, Madison, Minnesota.
/ Printed in the Republic of Ireland."; pp. 5-7, "The
Silence of Georg Trakl," by R. B.; pp. 8-10, "A Note
on Trakl," by James Wright; pp. [11]-61, text; pp. [62-
64] blank.

Binding:  Black cloth covered boards, stamped in gold.
Spine, reading downwards:  TWENTY POEMS OF GEORG
TRAKL  THE SIXTIES PRESS.  End-papers front and back
of white paper.

Contents:  The Silence of Georg Trakl-Bly/A Note on Trakl-
Wright/Sumemr/Trumpets/The Sun/Song of the Western
Countries/My Heart at Evening/The Rats/On the Marshy
Pastures/In Hellbrunn/Birth/De Profundis/Descent and De-
feat/The Heart/In Venice/The Mood of Depression/The
Evening/Two Prose Fragments:  A Winter Night & From
Revelation and Defeat/On the Eastern Front/Mourning/
Sleep/Grodek.

Location:  SUNY Buffalo

Note:  This is a bilingual edition with the German texts on
facing pages.

First paper edition:  1961

Title page, collation, pagination, and contents same as
hardbound.

Binding:  Stiff white paper covers with white paper jacket.
Front:  [in red:] TWENTY POEMS OF GEORG TRAKL /
[picture of a child embracing an owl] / [in black:]
CHOSEN AND TRANSLATED / BY / JAMES WRIGHT AND
ROBERT BLY / With introductions by the translators /
THE SIXTIES PRESS.  Spine, reading downwards:  [in
black:] TWENTY POEMS OF GEORG TRAKL  THE SIXTIES
PRESS.  Back:  [in black:] OTHER BOOKS TO BE PUB-
LISHED BY THE SIXTIES PRESS: / [lists eight titles] /
The publishers will be glad to fill orders directly.  Any

book may be ordered in / advance, and if not now avail-
able, will be sent as soon as it is published.  Order /
from:  THE SIXTIES PRESS, ODIN HOUSE, MADISON,
MINNESOTA.  All volumes / are $2.00 for hard cover,
$1.00 for soft cover.  Front flyleaf:  [in black:] [state-
ment on The Sixties Press].  Back flyleaf:  [in black:]
[statement on Trakl].  End-papers front and back of
white paper.

Location:  SUNY Buffalo


A72.   THE STORY OF GOSTA BERLING.  1962

SELMA LAGERLOF / The Story of / GOSTA BERLING /
Translated / and with an Afterword by ROBERT BLY /
[publisher's device:  an "S" within a "C"] / A SIGNET
CLASSIC / Published by THE NEW AMERICAN LIBRARY

Collation:  4 X 6 3/4".  [1–32]$^{10}$:  160 leaves.  Pp. [1–8]
9–318 [319–320].

Pagination:  p. [1] "Selma Lagerlöf" [biographical note];
p. [2] blank; p. [3] title-page; p. [4] [within a frame of
two rules:  three-line statement on Signet Classics ] /
"COPYRIGHT © 1962 BY ROBERT BLY / All rights re-
served / FIRST PRINTING, MAY, 1962 / This translation
is based on an earlier / translation by Pauline Bancroft
Flach. / SIGNET TRADEMARK REG. U.S. PAT. OFF. AND
FOREIGN COUNTRIES / REGISTERED TRADEMARK – MARCA
REGISTRADA / HECHO EN CHICAGO, U.S.A. / SIGNET
CLASSICS are published by / The New American Library
of World Literature, Inc. / 501 Madison Avenue, New York
22, New York / PRINTED IN THE UNITED STATES OF
AMERICA"; pp. [5–6] "Contents"; p. [7] [map of the
Löfven District in Värmland]; p. [8] blank; pp. 9–310,
text; pp. 311–318, "Afterword"; p. [319] "SELECTED BIB-
LIOGRAPHY"; p. [320] "SIGNET CLASSICS from Around
the World" [lists seven titles].

Binding:  Stiff paper covers.  Front cover black with dark
purple frame.  Printed on front:  [drawing of bust of a
man with satan's head emerging from the chest].  At top
in white:  CT125 [publisher's device] 75¢ / The Story of
Gösta Berling / [in blue:] Selma Lagerlöf.  At bottom left,
reading downwards:  [in blue:] A SIGNET CLASSIC.
Spine, white paper, printed in black:  [publisher's device,
printed white on black] / CT / 125 / [reading downwards]
The Story of Gösta Berling  Selma Lagerlöf.  Back cover,
white paper, printed in black:  The Story of Gösta Berling
/ Selma Lagerlöf / [fourteen-line statement on the novel] /

[ten-line statement on the author] / [in red:] Translated
with an Afterword by Robert Bly / [in black:] PUBLISHED
BY THE NEW AMERICAN LIBRARY.

Location:   Southampton Campus Library of Long Island
University

A73.  TWENTY POEMS OF CESAR VALLEJO   1962

[in black:] CESAR VALLEJO / [in red:] TWENTY POEMS
/ [in black:] chosen and translated by / JOHN KNOEPFLE,
JAMES WRIGHT / AND ROBERT BLY / [in red:] [publish-
er's device:  horseman with shield and spear surrounded
by two birds and a snake] / [in black:] 1962 / THE SIX-
TIES PRESS / [in red:] [single rule]

Collation:   5 5/16 X 8 1/4".   [1-16]$^4$:   32 leaves.   Pp.
[1-6]  7-11  [12-13]  14-47  [48-49]  50-61  [62]  63  [64].

Pagination:   p. [1] half-title; p. [2] blank; p. [3] [draw-
ing of Vallejo by Zamorano]; p. [4] blank; p. [5] title-
page; p. [6] [acknowledgments] / "Library of Congress
Catalogue Card Number: / 61-9806 / Copyright © 1962 by
The Sixties Press, / Odin House, Madison, Minnesota /
Printed in the Republic of Ireland"; pp. 7-8, "THOUGHTS
ON CESAR VALLEJO," by J. K.; pp. 9-11, "A NOTE ON
CESAR VALLEJO," by J. W.; p. ]12] blank; pp. [13]-61,
text; p. [62] blank; p. 63, "The translators would like to
thank Hardie St. / Martin for his generous criticism of
these translations / in manuscript. / [six-line statement
about, and endorsement of, H. R. Hays' translations of
Vallejo which Las Americas Press published] / [six-line
statement on the availability of Vallejo's books]; p. [64]
blank.

Binding:   Red cloth covered boards, stamped in black.
Spine, reading downwards:  TWENTY POEMS OF CESAR
VALLEJO   THE SIXTIES PRESS.   End-papers front and
back of white paper.

Dust jacket:   Front and back covers, spine, paper tan.
Front:  [in red:] TWENTY POEMS OF CESAR VALLEJO /
[in black:] [illustration] / CHOSEN AND TRANSLATED /
BY / JOHN KNOEPFLE, JAMES WRIGHT / AND ROBERT
BLY / THE SIXTIES PRESS.   Spine, reading downwards:
[in black:]TWENTY POEMS OF CESAR VALLEJO   THE
SIXTIES PRESS.   Back:  [in black:] OTHER BOOKS
PUBLISHED BY THE SIXTIES PRESS: / [lists nine titles]
/ The publishers will be glad to fill orders directly.   Or-
der from:  THE SIXTIES PRESS, / ODIN HOUSE,

MADISON, MINNESOTA. All volumes are $2.00 for hard
cover, / $1.00 for soft cover. Flyleaves, paper in tan.
Front flyleaf: [in black:] $2.00 / [sixteen-line statement
on C. V.]. Back flyleaf: [in black:] [twenty-four-line
statement on The Sixties and The Sixties Press].

Contents: Thoughts on César Vallejo/A Note on César
Vallejo/The Black Riders/The Distant Footsteps/To My
Brother Miguel/Down to the Dregs/Babble/Agape/The
Spider/White Rose/Twilight/The Black Cup/A Divine Falling
of Leaves/The Weary Circles/Our Daily Bread/The Eternal
Dice/Have You Anything to Say in Your Defense/The Big
People/"I Am Freed"/"The Anger That Breaks a Man"/
Black Stone Lying on a White Stone/Masses

Location:  SUNY Buffalo

Note:  This is a bilingual edition with the Spanish texts
on facing pages.


A74.  FORTY POEMS. JUAN RAMON JIMENEZ.  1967

[in black:] FORTY POEMS / [in red:] JUAN RAMON
JIMENEZ / [in black:] chosen and translated by / ROBERT
BLY / [in red:] [publisher's device: horseman with shield
and spear surrounded by two birds and a snake] / THE
SIXTIES PRESS / [in black:] 1967

Collation:  5 X 8".  [1-16]⁴ [1-18] [1-12] [1-10]:  52
leaves.  Pp. [1-4] 5-10 [11-13] 14-15 [16-17] 18-29 [30-31]
32-41 [42-43] 44-46 [47-49] 50-56 [57] 58-61 [62-63] 64-
100 [101-102] 103-104.

Pagination:  p. [1] half-title; p. [2] blank; p. [3] title-
page; p. [4] "Some of these translations have been pub-
lished / earlier in The Sixties. / The cover shows a detail
from a 12th century / Spanish-Arab water-pitcher. / Li-
brary of Congress Card Catalogue Number: / 67-11594 /
Copyright © 1967 by The Sixties Press, / Odin House,
Madison, Minnesota / PRINTED IN SPAIN / Deposito Legal:
M.9.558-1967 / Graficas BREOGAN - Juan Tornero, 28 -
Madrid - 11 (Espana)"; pp. 5-10, "Juan Ramón Jiménez
Under the Water" [introduction by RB]; p. [11] [quote
from Jiménez]; p. [12] blank; pp. [13]-97, text; pp. 98-
[102] "First Glimpse of Juan Ramón Jiménez" [by Rafael
Alberti]; pp. 103-104, "CONTENTS".

Binding:  Stiff white paper covers with blue paper dust
jacket.  Front:  [in black:] JUAN RAMON / [in red:]
JIMENEZ / [photograph: detail from a 12th-century Spanish-

Arab water pitcher] / [in red:] FORTY POEMS / [in
black:] TRANSLATED BY ROBERT BLY. Spine, reading
downwards: [in black:] JUAN RAMON JIMENEZ  FORTY
POEMS  THE SIXTIES PRESS. Back, printed in black:
OTHER BOOKS PUBLISHED BY THE SIXTIES PRESS /
[lists eight titles] / The publishers will be glad to fill or-
ders directly. Order from: THE SIXTIES / PRESS,
ODIN HOUSE, MADISON, MINNESOTA, 56256. All volumes
are $2.00 / for clothbound, $1.00 for paperbound. Fly-
leaves front and back of blue paper. Front flyleaf: [in
black:] $1.00 / [thirty-line statement on Jiménez]. Back
flyleaf: [in black:] [twenty-four-line statement on The
Sixties Press].

Contents: Juan Ramón Jiménez Under the Water/Early
Poems: Adolescence/"I Was Sitting"/"The Lumber Wagons"
/Winter Scene/"Who Knows What Is Going On"/"A Remem-
brance Is Moving"/"The Lamb Was Bleating Softly"/Return
for an Instant/Diary of a Poet Recently Married: "Some-
thing So Close"/Night Piece/"I Took Off Petal After Petal"/
Cemetery/"In the Subway"/Deep Night/Author's Club/Walt
Whitman/An Imitator of Billy Sunday/Wrong Time/"In New
York"/"Lavender Windowpanes and White Curtains"/Re-
morse/Night Piece
Later Poems: "Intelligence, Give Me"/Oceans/"Music"/
"I Pulled On the Reins"/To Dante/The Memory/Being Awake/
Road/"I Am Not I"/"The Ship, Solid and Black"/"Even
Through My Soul"/Whiteness/Full Moon/"At First She Came
to Me Pure"/Dawns of Moguer/Dawn Outside the City Walls/
The Name Drawn from the Names/Full Consciousness/First
Glimpse of Juan Ramón Jiménez.

Location: University of Wisconsin, Parkside

Note: This is a bilingual edition with the Spanish texts
on facing pages. On four of the five copies examined, the
blue covers had faded to almost white.


A75.  LATE ARRIVAL ON EARTH  1967

Late Arrival on Earth / [rule] / selected poems of /
GUNNAR EKELOF / translated by / Robert Bly and Chris-
tina Paulston / [device: large asterisk] / Rapp & Carroll
London

Collation: 5 1/2 X 8 3/16". [1-16]$^3$: 24 leaves. Pp.
[1-6] 7-8 [9-10] 11-17 [18-20] 21-29 [30-32] 33-47 [48].

Pagination: p. [1] half-title; p. [2] blank; p. [3] title-
page; p. [4] "ACKNOWLEDGEMENTS" / "© 1934, 1936,

1938, 1941, 1945, 1955 BONNIERS FORLAG / STOCKHOLM
/ THIS TRANSLATION © 1967 ROBERT BLY / FIRST PUB-
LISHED IN GREAT BRITAIN 1967 BY / RAPP & CARROLL
LTD 128/134 BAKER STREET LONDON W1 / PRINTED IN
ENGLAND BY W & J MACKAY & CO LTD / CHATHAM
KENT / ALL RIGHTS RESERVED"; p. [5] "CONTENTS";
p. [6] blank; pp. 7-8, "EKELOF'S 'FLAVOR OF THE IN-
FINITE'" by R. B.; pp. [9]-47, text; p. [48] blank.

Binding:  Deep purple-red paper covered boards, stamped
in gold.  On spine, reading downwards:  Late Arrival on
Earth [device]  Gunnar Ekelöf.  End-papers front and
back of white paper.

Dust jacket:  Front and back covers, spine, paper purple-
red.  Front:  [in white:] poetry europe / [in black:]
series / late arrival / on earth / [in white:] gunnar eke-
löf / [in black:] [device].  Spine, reading downwards:
[in black:] late arrival on earth [in white:] gunnar ekelöf
[in black:] [device].  Back:  [photograph of G. E.].
Flyleaves, paper in purple-red.  Front flyleaf:  [in black:]
21s / [twenty-two-line statement from R. B.'s introduction].
Back flyleaf:  [in black:] poetry europe series / RECENT
TITLES / [four titles listed with authors] / FORTHCOMING
TITLES / [two titles listed with authors] / Rapp & Carroll
Limited / 128/134 Baker Street London W1.

Contents:  Introduction/Part I Early Poems:  The Flowers
Doze in the Window/Mirror of October/Sonata Form De-
natured Prose/At Night/Trolldom in Fall/A Dreamt Poem/
The Moon/Part II Poems 1938-45:  In the Forests of Con-
vention/O Sacred Death/There Exists Something That Fits
Nowhere/Night and Stillness/Each Person is a World/Inter-
view/A July Night/Part III Later Poems:  Trionfo della
Morte/Who Is Coming, You Ask/Monologue with its Wife/
For Night Comes/The Silence of the Deep Night is Huge/
The Knight has Rested for a Long Time/So Strange to Me/
I Do Best Alone at Night/Gunnar Ekelöf, A Contemporary
Mystic by Eric Lindegran [excerpts].

Location:  SUNY Buffalo

Introduction reprinted, in part, in B121.


A76.  HUNGER  1967

HUN / GER / Knut Hamsun / Newly translated from the
Norwegian by Robert Bly / With Introductions by ROBERT
BLY and / ISAAC BASHEVIS SINGER / FARRAR, STRAUS
AND GIROUX / NEW YORK / [publisher's device:  three
fish].

Collation:   5 1/2 X 7 15/16".   [1-32]$^8$:   128 leaves.   Pp.
[i-iv] v-xi [xii] xiii-xxii [xxiii-xxiv] [1]2] 3-61 [62-64]
65-113 [114-116] 117-184] [185-186] 187-231 [232].

Pagination:   p. [1] half-title; p. [ii] blank; p. [iii] title-
page; p. [iv] "Copyright © 1967 by Farrar, Straus and
Giroux, Inc. / All rights reserved / Library of Congress
catalog card number:   67-21525 / Published simultaneously
in Canada by Ambassador Books, Ltd., / Rexdale, Ontario
/ Printed in the United States of America / First printing,
1967"; pp. v-[xii] "Introduction by / Isaac Bashevis Sing-
er / KNUT HAMSUN, ARTIST OF SKEPTICISM"; pp. xiii-
[xxiii] "Introduction by / Robert Bly / THE ART OF
HUNGER"; p. [xxiv] blank; pp. [1]-[232] text.

Binding:   Black paper covered boards with tan cloth spine.
Stamped on spine:   [tan on a black field:] HUN / GER /
[in black:] Knut / Hamsun / Farrar, / Straus and / Giroux.
End-papers front and back of olive green slightly heavier
than the sheets.   Top edges tinted red-orange.

Dust jacket:   Front and back covers, spine, paper white.
Front, within a black rectangle:   [in light green:] HUN /
GER [bottom edges of "HUN" and top edges of "GER" are
serated and white] / Knut Hamsun / [in green on white:]
A New Translation by / Robert Bly / with An Introduction
by / Isaac Bashevis Singer.   Spine, within a black rec-
tangle:   [in light green:] HUN / GER [bottom edges of
"HUN" and top edges of "GER" are serated and white] /
[in green on white:] Knut / Hamsun / Farrar, Straus and
/ Giroux.   Back:   [in black:] "From Isaac Bashevis Sing-
er's Introduction:" / [thirty-line excerpt].   Flyleaves of
white paper.   Front flyleaf:   [in black:] $4.95 / [in
green:] [four lines--first sentence of the novel] / [twenty-
five-line statement on K. H. and the novel] / (continued
on back flap).   Back flyleaf:   [in black:] (continued from
front flap) / [seven-line statement] / [thirteen-line state-
ment on present translation] / Jacket design by Milton
Glaser / FARRAR, STRAUS AND GIROUX / 19 UNION
SQUARE WEST / NEW YORK 10003.

Location:   SUNY Buffalo

Note:   R. B.'s introduction, reprinted, in part, in B122.


A77.   THE DICTATORS   1967

[bright green sheet printed in black] Front:   [to left of
center:] THE DICTATORS / Translated by / Robert Bly /
Pablo Neruda / [illustration of a tree] [to right of center:]

THE DICTATORS / [text in a single column] / Pablo Neruda.
Back: [centered at bottom:] Copyright 1967 by the Sixties
Press / Published by / The "Slow Loris" Press / 95 Rand
Avenue - Buffalo, N.Y.  14216 / [rule] / Printed in a lim-
ited edition of 200 copies / of which 25 are numbered and /
signed by the author / Series III.

Collation:  11 X 8 1/2".  Single sheet printed on both
sides.

Binding:  None.  All edges trimmed.

Contents:  The Dictators [poem]

Location:  SUNY Buffalo

Note:  Part of Slow Loris Broadsides, series III.  Limited
to 200 copies, 25 of which are numbered and signed by
R. B.


A78.   TWENTY POEMS OF PABLO NERUDA   1967

[in black:] PABLO NERUDA / [in red:] TWENTY POEMS
/ [in black:] translated by / JAMES WRIGHT AND
ROBERT BLY / [in red:] [publisher's device:  horseman
with shield and spear surrounded by two birds and a snake]
/ THE SIXTIES PRESS / [in black:] 1967

Collation:  5 1/4 X 8 3/16".  [1-16]7:  56 leaves.  Pp.
[1-6] 7-17 [18-19] 20-47 [48-49] 50-87 [88-89] 90-111
[112].

Pagination:  p. [1] half-title; p. [2] blank; p. [3] [draw-
ing of Neruda by Zamorano]; p. [4] blank; p. [5] title-
page; p. [6] [acknowledgments] / "The drawing of Pablo
Neruda was done for this book / by the Spanish artist
Zamorano. / Library of Congress Catalogue Card Number:
/ 66-28654 / Copyright © 1967 by The Sixties Press / Odin
House, Madison, Minnesota / Printed in the Netherlands";
pp. 7-17, "REFUSING TO BE THEOCRITUS," [by R.B.];
p. [18] blank; pp. [19]-101, text; pp. 102-110, "THE
LAMB AND THE PINE CONE" [interview with P. N. by
R. B.]; p. 111, "CONTENTS"; p. [112] blank.

Binding:  Light blue paper covered boards, stamped in
red.  Front:  PABLO NERUDA / TWENTY POEMS.  Spine,
reading downwards:  PABLO NERUDA / TWENTY POEMS
THE SIXTIES PRESS.  End-papers front and back of white
paper slightly heavier than the sheets.

Contents:   Refusing to be Theocritus [introduction]/
Residencia En La Tierra:   Nothing But Death/Melancholy
Inside Families/Sonata and Destructions/Gentleman Without
Company/Sexual Water/Funeral in the East/The Art of
Poetry/There is No Forgetfulness (Sonata)
Canto General:   Some Beasts/The Heights of Macchu Picchu,
III/The Head on the Pole/Toussaint L'Ouverture/The
United Fruit Co./The Dictators/Cristobal Miranda/I Wish
the Wood-Cutter Would Wake Up/The Enigmas/Friends on
the Road
Odas Elementales:   Ode to My Socks/Ode to Salt
The Lamb and the Pine Cone [interview]

Note:   This is a bilingual edition with the Spanish texts
on facing pages.


First paper edition:   1967

Title page, collation, pagination, and contents same as
hardbound.

Binding:   Medium blue paper covers.   Front:   [within a
dark blue frame:] [in red:] PABLO NERUDA / [in blue:]
[drawing of the head of an imaginary animal] / [in red:]
TWENTY POEMS.   Spine, reading downwards:   [in black:]
TWENTY POEMS OF NERUDA   THE SIXTIES PRESS.
Back:   [in black:] OTHER BOOKS PUBLISHED BY THE
SIXTIES PRESS / [lists nine titles] / Write THE SIXTIES
PRESS, Odin House, Madison, Minnesota. / $1.00 paper-
bound; $2.00 clothbound.   Flyleaves, paper in medium
blue.   Front flyleaf:   [in black:] $1.00 / [twenty-two-
line statement on P. N.]   Back flyleaf:   [in black:]
[thirty-one-line statement on The Sixties and The Sixties
Press].

Location:   SUNY Buffalo

Introduction, "Refusing to be Theocritus," is reprinted,
in part, in B125.

See A80.


A79.   I DO BEST ALONE AT NIGHT   1968

[row of eleven stars] / I DO BEST ALONE AT NIGHT /
Poems by GUNNAR EKELOF / Chosen and translated by
Robert Bly / with Christina Paulston / Washington, / The
Charioteer Press / [device]

68                                Writings by Robert Bly

Collation:  4 13/16 X 7 1/2".  [1-8]⁴:  32 leaves.  Pp.
[i-v] vi-vii [viii] ix-x [xi-xii] [1-2] 3-10 [11-12] 13-25
[26-28] 29-50 [51-52].

Pagination:  p. [i] half-title; p. [ii] blank; p. [iii] title-
page; p. [iv] "THIS IS A Charioteer Book / Copyright ©
1968 by Robert Bly. / All rights reserved. / No part of
this book may be reproduced without / permission in writ-
ing from the publisher, except / by a reviewer who may
wish to quote a full poem / or passages. / Published by
The Charioteer Press, 601 19th Street, / N. W., Washing-
ton, D. C. 20006. / Manufactured in the United States of
America. / FIRST EDITION LIMITED TO 300 COPIES.";
p. [v] "ACKNOWLEDGEMENTS"; pp. vi-vii, "CONTENTS";
p. [viii] blank; pp. ix-x, "EKELOF'S 'FLAVOR OF THE /
INFINITE'" [introduction by R. B.]; p. [xi] second half-
title; p. [xii] blank; pp. [1]-42, text; p. 43, "BOOKS BY
GUNNAR EKELOF DRAWN / ON FOR THIS SELECTION";
pp. 44-50, "FROM 'GUNNAR EKELOF A / CONTEMPORARY
MYSTIC'" [by Eric Lindegren, translated by R. B.]; p.
[51] blank; p. [52] "This book was composed on the lino-
type / in Electra & printed by / Theo. Gaus' Sons, Inc.,
Brooklyn, N. Y. 11201."

Binding:  Dark blue cloth covered boards, stamped in gold.
Spine, reading downwards:  Ekelof--Bly  I DO BEST ALONE
AT NIGHT   Charioteer.

Dust jacket:  Front and back covers, spine, paper white.
Front:  [in blue:] I DO BEST / ALONE / AT NIGHT / [in
red:] TRANSLATOR:  ROBERT BLY / [in blue:] POEMS
BY / GUNNAR / EKELOF / [to the right is an illustration
by Sengai].  Spine, reading downwards:  [in blue:]
EKELOF--BLY [in red:] I DO BEST ALONE AT NIGHT
[in blue:] CHARIOTEER.  Back:  [photograph of G. E.
in blue-tone] / [in blue:] ABOUT THE AUTHOR / [nine-
teen-line statement].  Flyleaves, paper in white.  Front
flyleaf:  [in blue:] THE CHARIOTEER PRESS WASHINGTON
/ [star] / ABOUT THE TRANSLATORS / [sixteen-line state-
ment on R. B.] / [five-line statement on C. P.].  Back
flyleaf:  [in blue:] [star] / The drawing on the jacket is
by Sengai and is / used with the kind permission of the
Idemitsu / Gallery (Tokyo).  Sengai's poem goes roughly
like / this. / The Road is without sound and without odor,
/ It has no rules. / It's like his feet with only one shoe.
/ Or riding in a reed-leaf boat. / (Bodhidharma, after his
death, was seen returning to India / carrying one shoe.
The other shoe was found in his grave / in China.)"

Contents:  Introduction/The Flowers Doze in the Window/
Mirror of October/Sonata Form Denatured Prose/At Night/

Trolldom in Fall/A Dreamt Poem/The Moon/In the Forests
of Convention/O Sacred Death/There Exists Something
That Fits Nowhere/Night and Stillness/Each Person is a
World/Interview/A July Night/Trionfo della Morte/Who Is
Coming, You Ask/Monologue with its Wife/For Night Comes
/The Silence of the Deep Night is Huge/The Knight has
Rested for a Long Time/So Strange to Me/I Do Best Alone
at Night/Gunnar Ekelöf, A Contemporary Mystic by Eric
Lindegran [excerpts].

Location:  SUNY Buffalo


A80.  TWENTY POEMS OF PABLO NERUDA [First British edition]
      1968

      Collation and contents same as A78.

      [in black:] PABLO NERUDA / [in red:] TWENTY POEMS
      / [in black:] translated by / JAMES WRIGHT AND ROBERT
      BLY / Rapp & Whiting London

      Pagination:  p. [1] half-title; p. [2] blank; p. [3] [draw-
      ing of Neruda by Zamorano]; p. [4] blank; p. [5] title-
      page; p. 6, "COPYRIGHT © 1967 BY THE SIXTIES PRESS
      / ODIN HOUSE, MADISON MINNESOTA / FIRST PUBLISHED
      IN GREAT BRITAIN 1968 / BY RAPP AND WHITING LIM-
      ITED / 76 NEW OXFORD STREET LONDON WC1 / PRINTED
      IN HOLLAND/ BY G. J. THIEME N.V. NIJMEGEN NETHER-
      LANDS / ALL RIGHTS RESERVED"; pp. 7-17, "REFUSING
      TO BE THEOCRITUS," [by R.B.]; p. [18] blank; pp.
      [19]-101, text; pp. 102-110, "THE LAMB AND THE PINE
      CONE" [interview with P. N. by R.B.]; p. 111, "CON-
      TENTS"; p. [112] blank.

      Binding:  Dark green paper covered boards, stamped in
      gold.  Spine, reading downwards:  Twenty Poems [device]
      Pablo Neruda.  End-papers front and back of white paper
      slightly heavier than the sheets.

      Dust jacket:  Green front and spine.  Front:  [in white:]
      NERUDA / [outlined in black:] 1 7 13 19 / 2 8 14 [in
      white:] 20 / [outlined in black:] 3 9 15 [in white:] poems
      / by / Pablo Neruda / [outlined in black:] 4 10 16 / 5 11
      17 / 6 12 18 / Translated by Robert Bly and James Wright.
      Spine, reading downwards:  [in white:] 20 poems  Pablo
      Neruda [reading across:] [in black:] Rapp & / Whiting.
      Back cover, white.  [in black:] Also by Robert Bly /
      [lists two titles] / Other American poets published by Rapp
      & Whiting / [lists six titles] / [in green:] [device] [in
      black:] Rapp & Whiting Limited / 76 NEW OXFORD STREET
      LONDON WC1.  Flyleaves front and back in white.  Front:

[in black:] [eighteen-line statement on P. N.] / Jacket
design by Lawrence Edwards / 25s net.   Back:   [in black:]
[eleven-line statement on R. B.] / [ten-line statement on
J. W.] / Rapp & Whiting Limited / 76 New Oxford Street
London WC1 / Printed in Great Britain.

Location:  SUNY Buffalo
Note:  This is a bilingual edition with the Spanish texts
on facing pages.


A81.  ISSA:  TEN POEMS  1969

       [in red:] ISSA / [in black:] TEN POEMS / ENGLISH VER-
       SIONS / BY / ROBERT BLY

       Collation:  4 1/4 X 5 1/2".  No sign.  4 leaves.  Pp. [1-8].

       Pagination:  p. [1] title-page; p. [2] "This booklet is a
       gift, and is not to be sold.  /  Copyright 1969 by Robert
       Bly"; pp. [6-7] text; p. [8] [twelve-line note on Issa with
       bibliographical information for further reading].

       Binding:  White paper covers.  Title-page is the cover.

       Contents:  Ten haikus.

       Location:  SUNY Buffalo


A82.  HER VISIT DURING SLEEP, IBN HAZM  [ca. 1970]

       [Boston:] Beacon Press

       Broadside, 28 X 22 cm.

       Not verified, listed in OCLC by Indiana University, Bloom-
       ington, IN.

       Bly could not provide date.


A83.  LETTER TO MIGUEL OTERO SILVA, IN CARACAS (1948)
       [1970?]

       Pablo Neruda: / Letter to Miguel Otero Silva, / in Caracas
       (1948)* / [text begins in a single column] / *Written while
       under pursuit by the Chilean Secret Police on a political
       charge.

       Collation:  7 1/2 X 10".  No sign.  1 folded sheet.  2
       leaves.  Pp. 1-4.

Pagination:   p. 1, title-page; pp. 1-4, text; p. 4, "from
Canto General, Section 12, translated from the Spanish by
Robert Bly / To Be Printed Free Forever.

Binding:   Off-white paper printed in black.   Title-page is
the cover.

Contents:   Letter to Miguel Otero Silva

Location:   SUNY Buffalo

Note:   Printed by Cranium Press, San Francisco.


A84.   TWENTY POEMS OF TOMAS TRANSTROMER   1970

[in black:] TOMAS TRANSTROMER / [in red:] TWENTY
POEMS / [in black:] translated by / ROBERT BLY / [in
red:] [publisher's device:   pig's head] / SEVEnTiES PRESS
(sic)] / [in black:] 1970

Collation:   5 1/4 X 8 1/4".   [1-8]$^4$:   32 leaves.   Pp. [i-ii]
[1-4] 5-7 [8-9] 10-31 [32-33] 34-59 [60-62]

Pagination:   pp. [i-ii] blank; p. [1] half-title; p. [2]
blank; p. [3] title-page; p. [4] [acknowledgments] / "The
jacket drawing was done for this book / by Franz Richter.
/ Library of Congress Catalog Card Number: / 76-147966
/ Copyright © 1970 by The Seventies Press / Odin House,
Madison, Minnesota / Printed in the U.S.A."; pp. 5-7,
"TOMAS TRANSTROMER" [introduction by R. B.]; p. [8]
blank; pp. [9]-59, text; p. [60] blank; p. [61] "The
two editions of this book -- one of 1000 hardbound / copies
and one of 1000 paperback copies -- were printed / hors
commerce, by Morgan Press of Milw., Wisconsin. / The
type, hand set and distributed after each side of a / folio
was printed:   Bookman, from Baltimore Type, based / on
a face designed by A. C. Phemister, c.1860.   The accen- /
ted characters:   supplied by the type foundry or hand cut
/ by the printer.   The text paper:   Becket Text laid fin-
ish / from Bouer Paper Co.   The inks:   Van Son's R.B.P.
The / press:   a Golding no. 7 10X15 hand fed platen press,
c.1900. / [device] Morgan Press / 1970"; p. [62] blank.

Binding:   Blue paper covered boards, stamped in gold.
Spine, reading downwards:   TWENTY POEMS   TRANS-
TROMER.

Dust jacket:   Front and back covers, spine, paper brown.
Front:   [in black:] 20 POEMS / [illustration] / TOMAS
TRANSTROMER.   Spine, reading downwards:   [in black:]

20 POEMS OF TRANSTROMER   Seventies Press.   Back:
[in black:] OTHER SEVENTIES PRESS BOOKS / [sixteen-
line statement on Beacon Press reprinting of Sixties Press
Books] / [three-line statement on The Seventies, no. 1
issue] / The Seventies Press, Odin House, Madison, MN
56256 / A SEVENTIES PRESS BOOK.   Flyleaves, paper in
brown.   Front flyleaf:   [in black:]  [twenty-four-line
statement on T. T.].   Back flyleaf:  [in black:]  [twenty-
three-line statement].

Contents:   Tomas Tranströmer [introduction]/Track/The
Man Awakened by a Song Above His Roof/After the Attack/
Kyrie/Balakierev's Dream (1905)/Lamento/The Couple/Al-
legro/The Half-Finished Heaven/Nocturne/A Few Instants/
Open and Closed Space/Under Pressure/Slow Music/Solitude/
Morning Bird Songs/From an African Diary (1963)/After a
Death/Out in the Open/Night Duty

Location:   Mount Holyoke College

Note:   1,000 copies have been issued in hardbound, and
1,000 copies have been issued in paperback.   This is a
bilingual edition with the Norwegian texts on facing pages.

First paper edition:   1970

Title page, collation, pagination, and contents same as
hardbound.

Binding:   Brown paper wrappers of the identical design as
the dust jacket of hardbound edition.

Location:   Piccione

A85.   THE FISH IN THE SEA IS NOT THIRSTY   1971

[in black:] [arced around an ornate circle of arabesque de-
sign] the fish in the sea is not thirsty / Kabir / [in white
on a black frame:] VERSIONS BY ROBERT BLY

Collation:   5 5/8 X 8 15/16".   No sign.   10 leaves.   Pp.
[1-20].

Pagination:   p. [1] title-page; p. [2] [acknowledgments]
/ "Published by LILLABULERO PRESS, INC. / Northwood
Narrows, N. H. / Distributed by Lillabulero / from Frums
Corners Rd., R. D. 3, / Ithaca, N. Y. 14850 / Designed
by David Sykes; / Hand-set by Tom Stone in 12 pt. Pala-
tino. / Copyright Robert Bly 1971"; p. [3] [statement by

R. B. regarding Kabir and these translations]; p. [4]
blank; pp. [5-18] text; pp. [19-20] blank.

Binding: Stiff blue and white paper covers. Front:
[printed in white on blue:] [arced around an ornate circle
of arabesque design] the fish in the sea is not thirsty /
Kabir / [in blue on a white frame:] VERSIONS BY ROBERT
BLY. Back: [in white:] [publisher's device: stylized
bird] / [in blue on bottom of white frame:] Lillabulero
Pamphlet Number 13. End-papers front and back of gray-
white sheets marked in silver.

Contents: "When my friend is away from me"/"I don't know
what sort of a God we have been talking about"/"Oh friend,
I love you, think this over"/"Student, do the simple purifi-
cation"/"Inside this clay jug there are canyons and pine
mountains"/"Why should we two ever want to part?"/"Shall
I flail with words, when love has made the space..."/"I
laugh when I hear that the fish in the water is thirsty"/
"Knowing nothing shuts the inner gates"/"Between the con-
scious and the unconscious, the mind has put up a swing"
/"My inside, listen to me, the greatest spirit"/"There is a
flag no one sees blowing in the sky-temple"/"There's a
moon in my body, but I can't see it!"/"I said to the want-
ing-creature inside me."

Location: SUNY Stony Brook


A86.  Rainbow Bridge edition: 1971

[in black:] [arced around an ornate circle of arabesque
design] the fish in the sea is not thirsty / Kabir / VER-
SIONS BY ROBERT BLY

Collation: 6 X 8 3/4". No sign. 10 leaves. Pp. [1-20].

Pagination: Same as A85, except p. [2] now reads: [ac-
knowledgments] / "Published by The Rainbow Bridge / A
Publishing and Distributing Company Ltd. / 3548 22nd
Street / San Francisco, California 94114 / ISBN 0-914198-
04-1 / Designed by David Sykes; / Hand-set by Tom Stone
in 12 pt. Palatino. / Copyright Robert Bly 1971 / [pub-
lisher's device] / Rainbow Stars 1;" and p. [19] [line
drawing of Kabir].

Binding: Same as A85, except back cover: [in white:]
[publisher's device] / Rainbow Stars 1 / [in blue on bot-
tom of white frame:] $1.50 ISBN 0-914198-04-1. End-
papers front and back of pale gray sheets.

Contents:    Same as A85.

Location:    SUNY Buffalo


A87.  MASSES, CESAR VALLEJO   [ca. 1971]

Palo Alto, CA:   Frog in the Well

Broadside, 28 cm.

Not verified, listed in OCLC by Indiana University, Bloom-
ington, IN.

Bly could not provide date.


A88.  NERUDA AND VALLEJO:  SELECTED POEMS   1971

[in black:] NERUDA / [in gray:] AND / [in black:]
VALLEJO: / [in gray:] SELECTED / POEMS/ Edited by /
ROBERT BLY / [in black:] Translations by / Robert Bly,
John Knoepfle, / and James Wright / BEACON PRESS /
Boston

Collation:  5 1/4 X 7 15/16".   [1-32]$^9$:  144 leaves.  Pp.
[i-iv] v-xiv [1-2] 3-15 [16-17] 18-21 [22-23] 24-59 [60-
61] 62-63 [64-65] 66-137 [138-139] 140-164 [165-168] 169-
176 [177] 178-219 [220-221] 222-233 [234-235] 236-265
[266-267] 268-269 [270-274].

Pagination:  p. [i] half-title; p. [ii] blank; p. [iii] title-
page; p. [iv] "Copyright © 1971 by Robert Bly / Copyright
© 1962, 1967 by the Sixties Press / Spanish texts copyright
1924, 1933, 1935, 1936, 1938, 1943, 1945, / 1947, 1949,
1950, 1954, 1956 by Pablo Neruda" / [acknowledgments] /
"The translators would like to thank Hardie St. Martin for
his / generous criticism of these translations in manuscript
/ The drawings of Pablo Neruda and César Vallejo were
done specially / for the original Sixties Press edition by
Spanish artist Zamorano / Library of Congress catalog card
number: 76-121825 / International Standard Book Number:
0-8070-6420-3 (casebound) / 0-8070-6421-1 (paperback) /
Beacon Press books are published under the auspices of
the Unitarian / Universalist Association / Published simul-
taneously in Canada by Saunders of Toronto, Ltd. / All
rights reserved / Printed in the United States of America";
pp. v-xiv, "CONTENTS"; p. [1] "Selected Poems of /
PABLO NERUDA"; p. [2] [drawing of P. N.]; pp. 3-15,
"REFUSING TO BE THEOCRITUS" [introduction by R. B.];
p. [16] blank; pp. [17]-164, poems; pp. [165-166]; p.

[167] "Selected Poems of / CESAR VALLEJO"; p.[168]
[drawing of C. V.]; pp. 169-174, "WHAT IF AFTER SO
MANY WINGS / OF BIRDS" [introduction by R. B.]; pp.
175-176, "THOUGHTS ON CESAR VALLEJO" [introduction
by J. W.]; pp. [177]-269, poems; pp. [270-274] blank.

Binding:   Yellow paper covered boards with olive green
cloth spine.  Blind stamping of village buildings on front
center.  Spine, reading downwards:  [stamped in black:]
Robert Bly  NERUDA and VALLEJO Selected Poems
BEACON PRESS.  End-papers front and back of white
paper slightly heavier than the sheets.

Dust jacket:  Front and back covers, spine, lime green
paper.  Front:  [in brown:] NERUDA / AND VALLEJO /
Selected Poems / EDITED BY / Robert Bly / [in red:]
A SEVENTIES PRESS BOOK / [device:  horseman with
shield and spear surrounded by two birds and a snake].
Spine, reading downwards:  [in black:] Robert Bly
NERUDA and VALLEJO Selected Poems  BEACON PRESS.
Back:  [in brown:] Also from Beacon / FORTY POEMS
TOUCHING ON RECENT / AMERICAN HISTORY / edited
by Robert Bly / [twenty-eight-line statement on the book]
/ [publisher's device:  village buildings] / BEACON PRESS
BOSTON   02108 / ISBN 0-8070-0542-8.  Flyleaves, paper
in white.  Front:  [in brown:] $9.95 / NERUDA AND
VALLEJO: / SELECTED POEMS / Edited by Robert Bly /
Translations by Robert Bly, John Knoepfle, / and James
Wright / [twenty-nine-line statement on Neruda and Vallejo
and Bly and The Seventies Press] / (Continued on back
flap).  Back:  [thirty-two-line statement continuing front
flyleaf] / Jacket design by Richard C. Barlett.

Contents:  Selected Poems of Pablo Neruda:  Refusing to
be Theocritus/"Body of a woman, white hills, white thighs"
/"I remember you as you were that final autumn"/Nothing
but Death/Walking Around/The Art of Poetry/Funeral in
the East/Gentleman Without Company/Sonata and Destruc-
tions/The Ruined Street/Melancholy Inside Families/Sexual
Water/There Is No Forgetfulness (Sonata)/Brussels/Some
Beasts/The Heights of Macchu Picchu, III/The Head on the
Pole/Anguish of Death/Discoverers of Chile/Toussaint
L'Ouverture/The United Fruit Company/Hunger in the
South/Youth/The Dictators/America, I Do Not Call Your
Name Without Hope/Hymn and Return/Cristobal Miranda/
I Wish the Woodcutter Would Wake Up/"It was the grape's
autumn"/The Strike/Letter to Miguel Otero Silva, in Cara-
cas/They Receive Instructions Against Chile/Enigmas/
Friends on the Road/Ode to My Socks/Ode to the Water-
melon/Ode to Salt/The Lamb and the Pine Cone [interview]/
Selected Poems of César Vallejo:  What If After So Many

Wings of Birds/Thoughts on César Vallejo/The Black Rid-
ers/The Spider/Pilgrimage/Babble/A Divine Falling of
Leaves/The Black Cup/Down to the Dregs/Twilight/Agape/
White Rose/Our Daily Bread/Pagan Woman/The Eternal Dice/
The Weary Circles/God/The Mule Drivers/The Distant Foot-
steps/To My Brother Miguel/Have You Anything to Say in
Your Defense?/"What time are the big people"/"In that
corner, where we slept together"/"At the border of a
flowering grave"/"I am freed from the burdens of the sea"/
"So much hail that I remember"/The Right Meaning/I am
Going to talk About Hope/"I stayed here, warming the ink
in which I drown"/Poem to Be Read and Sung/Black Stone
Lying on a White Stone/The Rollcall of Bones/"The tennis
player, in the instant he majestically"/"One pillar holding
up consolations"/"And don't bother telling me anything"/
"And so? The pale metalloid heals you?"/"I have a terrible
fear of being an animal"/"And what if after so many words"/
"The anger that breaks a man down into boys"/Masses.

Location:  SUNY Stony Brook

Note:  This is a bilingual edition with the Spanish texts on
facing pages.


A89.  NIGHT VISION  1971

[across two pages with an abstract design in black and
white, with a white frame on all sides] [at the top of the
design:] NIGHT VISION - - TOMAS TRANSTROMER / [at
bottom on white frame:] translated from the Swedish by
Robert Bly

Collation:  6 X 9".  No sign.  26 leaves.  Pp. [i-vii] [1-
3] 4 [5-7] 8 [9-11] 12 [13-15] 16 [17-19] 20 [21-23] 24
[25-27] 28 [29-31] 32 [33-35] 36 [37-39] 40 [41-43] 44
[45].

Pagination:  p. [i] blank; pp. [ii-iii] title-page; p. [iv]
"Also by Tomas Tranströmer: / Twenty Poems of Tomas
Tranströmer (Seventies Press) / Published by LILLABULERO
PRESS, INC. / Northwood Narrows, N.H. / Distributed by
LILLABULERO / from Krums Corners Rd., R.D. 3, /
Ithaca, N.Y. 14850 / frontispiece by Tom Anderson / De-
signed by David Sykes / Hand-set by Tom Stone in Palatino
12 point / Copyright Robert Bly 1971"; p. [v] "INTRO-
DUCTION"; p. [vi] blank; p. [vii] [text of introduction];
p. [1] blank; pp. [2]-44, text; p. [45] blank.

Note:  Only numbered pages contain poems.  All other pages
are either blank or contain the title of the following poem.

Pp. [iv-v] [1-2] [5-6] [9-10] [13-14] [17-18] [21-22] [25-26] [29-30] [33-34] [37-38] and [41-42] all have single rules along tops, bottoms, and outer edges of the page.

Binding: Stiff black paper covers. Front: [in white:] TRANSTROMER / [fifty-seven concentric circles] / NIGHT VISION / translated by Robert Bly. Back: [in white:] [fifty-seven concentric circles with a silhouette of a bird in flight superimposed on the center]. [Along the right-hand edge, reading upwards:] [in white:] Lillabulero Pamphlet 14.

Contents: The Name/A Few Moments/Breathing Space July/ Going With the Current/Outskirts/Traffic/Night Duty/The Open Window/Preludes/Standing Up/The Bookcase.

Location: SUNY Buffalo

A90.   BASHO  1972

[in black with a red accent:] Bashō / Translated by Robert Bly / Illustrated by Arthur Okamura / Mudra San Francisco / 1972

Collation: 10 1/2 X 14 1/2". No sign. 18 leaves. Pp. [1-36].

Pagination: pp. [1-2] blank; p. [3] title-page; p. [4] "Copyright © 1972 by Mudra / Printed by Clifford Burke / at Cranium Press, San Francisco"; p. [5] Bashō; p. [6] blank; pp. [7-33] text and illustrations; pp. [34-36] blank.

Binding: Gray-blue paper covers. Front: [in red-brown:] BASHO.

Contents: Fourteen haikus.

Location: SUNY Buffalo.

Note: Poems and illustrations are on odd-numbered pages, facing pages are blank.

A91.   THE FISH IN THE SEA IS NOT THIRSTY  1972

[in green:] Kabir / [in black:] The Fish / In The Sea / Is Not Thirsty / ENGLISHED BY ROBERT BLY / [in green:] [publisher's device: stylized evergreen tree with a w on either side] / [in black:] A WRITERS WORKSHOP PUBLI-CATION

Collation:  5 5/8 X 8 5/8".  No sign.  16 leaves.  Pp.
[1-32].

Pagination:  pp. [1-2] blank; p. [3]"[rule] / THE FISH
IN THE SEA IS NOT THIRSTY / Kabir / Englished by
Robert Bly / [rule] / [in red:] [device:  drawing of a
bird on a perch] [in black:] Saffronbird transcreation /
Greenbird fiction / Bluebird drama / Greybird criticism /
Redbird poetry / A WRITERS WORKSHOP REDBIRD BOOK
/ [rule] / Hardback Rs 20 / Flexiback Rs 8 / [rule]"; p.
[4] blank; p. [5]"[rule] / THE POET & THE TRANSLATOR
/ [rule] / [nine-line statement on Kabir] / [four-line state-
ment on R. B.["; p. [6] "© 1972 Robert Bly / [rule] /
[in calligraphy:] Hand-set in Univers / typeface & printed
on / an Indian-make hand- / operated machine by / P. K.
Aditya at the / Lake Gardens Press, / Calcutta 45, on
map- / litho paper made in / India.  Layout & / lettering
by P. Lal. / Hand-bound by Tula- / miah Mohiuddeen with
/ cotton handloom sari / cloth woven in India. / [rule] /
Writers Workshop books are pub- / lished by P. Lal from
162/92 / Lake Gardens, Calcutta 45, / India.  Telephone:
46-8325."; p. [7] title-page; p. [8] "[rule] / ACKNOWL-
EDGEMENTS / [rule] / [seven-line statement]"; p. [9]
"[rule] / TRANSCREATOR'S NOTE / [rule] / [twenty-
line statement by R. B.] / ROBERT BLY"; p. [10] blank;
pp. [11-24] text; p. [25] "[publisher's device] / writers
workshop / calcutta / publishers / of creative writing";
p. [26] "[rule] / [in calligraphy:] WRITERS WORKSHOP
/ [thirty-five-line statement on the workshop] / [in callig-
raphy:] Creative Writing / [rule]"; pp. [27-30] [Writers
Workshop Books, a full checklist:  1972]; pp. [31-32]
blank.

Binding:  Bright green cloth covered boards.  Front,
stamped in gold:  [device:  an oval with a tree set in re-
lief in the center with a thin ring of gold around the oval].
Along the fore edge is a decorative woven band of red,
yellow, white, and blue:  [first row to the left:  fifty-two
devices woven in red; second row:  thin line woven in yel-
low; third row:  band of alternating red and white woven
bars; fourth row:  band of blue with twenty-seven yellow
devices woven on top; fifth row:  repetition of third row;
sixth row:  repetition of second row; seventh row:  thin
line woven in red].  Spine, stamped in gold, reading down-
wards:  KABIR  THE FISH IN THE SEA IS NOT THIRSTY.
Back, stamped in gold:  [publisher's device].  Inside front
cover, glued to the bottom:  [light green paper with red
printing:] [in calligraphy:] "[flourish of pen strokes] /
Handbound by Tulamiah with / Indian handloom cloth at /
13 Patwarbagan Lane, Calcutta. / [flourish of pen strokes]".

Contents:  "When my friend is away from me, I am de-
pressed"/"I don't know what sort of a God we have been
talking about"/"Oh friend, I love you"/"Student, do the
simple purification"/"Inside this clay jug there are canyons
and pure mountains"/"Why should we two ever want to
part?"/"Shall I flail with words, when love has made the
space inside me full of light?"/"I laugh when I hear that
the fish in the water is thirsty"/"Knowing nothing shuts
the iron gates"/"Between the conscious and the uncon-
scious, the mind has put up a swing"/"My inside, listen to
me, the greatest spirit"/"There is a flag no one sees blow-
ing in the sky-temple"/"There's a moon in my body, but I
can't see it"/"I said to the wanting-creature inside me."

Location:  University of Connecticut at Storrs

Note:  Not all copies have spine stamped.


A92.  THE MUSK INSIDE THE DEER, KABIR  [ca. 1972]

[n.p.]

Broadside

Not verified, cited by Lepper (P122), p. 71.


A93.  TEN SONNETS TO ORPHEUS  1972

TEN SONNETS TO ORPHEUS / Rainer Maria Rilke / Trans-
lated by / Robert Bly / Zephyrus Image Magazine Number
One [all of the above is framed by ornate ribbon with a
floral design at top center, parts of which have been hand
colored differently on various copies]

Collation:  6 X 8 5/8". No sign. 12 leaves. Pp. [1-24].

Pagination:  p. [1] title-page; p. [2] "1922 / Chateau de
Mozot / Translations © 1972 R. Bly / Cover linocut by
Michael Myers / Aldus & Palatino types used on Curtis
Utopian / Zephyrus Image, 243 Collins, San Francisco,
California"; p. [3] half-title:  pp. [4-23] text; p. [24]
blank.

Binding:  White paper covers.  Title-page is the cover.

Contents:  "A tree rising."/"She was a girl ..."/"A god
can do it."/"O you lovers that are so gentle ..."/"Don't
bother about a stone."/"Is he from our world?"/"To
praise is the only thing!"/"Where praise already is the

only place grief"/"Only the man who has raised his
strings"/"You stone coffins of the ancient world ..."

Location:  SUNY Buffalo

Note:  This is a bilingual edition with the German texts
on facing pages.

Second edition:  1972

Title-page, contents, and note same as first edition, ex-
cept title-page is not hand colored.

Collation:  6 X 8 1/2".  No sign.  14 leaves.  Pp. [1-28].

Pagination:  pp. [1-2] blank; p. [3] half-title; p. [4]
blank; p. [5] title-page; p. [6] "1922 / Chateau de Mozot
/ Translations 1972 R. Bly / Cover linocut by Michael
Myers / Set in Aldus & Palatino types; Second edition /
Distributed by Book People, 2940 Seventh, Berkeley, Ca";
p. [7] blank; pp. [8-27] text; p. [28] blank.

Binding:  Off-white paper covers.  Illustration is the same
as on title-page except the top floral design is printed in
red and green.

Location:  SUNY Buffalo


A94.  NIGHT VISION  1972

NIGHT VISION / Tomas Transtrōmer / Selected and trans-
lated from the Swedish by Robert Bly / [publisher's device:
single leaf with L to the left of stem and M to the right]
/ LONDON MAGAZINE EDITIONS 1972

Collation:  6 X 8".  [1-16]$^3$:  24 leaves.  Pp. [1-4] 5 [6]
7-48.

Pagination:  p. [1] half-title; p. [2] blank; p. [3] title-
page; p. [4] "ACKNOWLEDGEMENTS" / "Published by Lon-
don Magazine Editions / 30 Thurloe Place, London, SW7 /
© London Magazine Editions, 1972 / SBN 9000626 74 7 /
Printed in Great Britain by / Billing & Sons Limited, Guild-
ford and London"; p. 5, "CONTENTS"; p. [6] blank; pp.
7-9, "INTRODUCTION," by R.B.; pp. 10-48, text.

Binding:  Green cloth covered boards, stamped in gold.
Spine, reading downwards:  NIGHT VISION  Tomas
Transtrōmer [publisher's device].  End-papers front and

back of white paper slightly heavier than the sheets.

Contents:  Introduction/After a Death/Track/The Man
Awakened by a Song Above his Roof/After the Attack/
Kyrie/Balakirev's Dream/Lamento/The Couple/Allegro/The
Half-Finished Heaven/Nocturne/Open and Closed Space/
Under Pressure/Slow Music/Solitude-I/Solitude-II/Morning
Bird Songs/From an African Diary (1963)/Out in the Open/
The Name/A Few Moments/Breathing Space, July/Going
with the Current/Outskirts/Traffic/Night Duty/ The Open
Window/Preludes/Standing Up/The Bookcase

Location:  SUNY Buffalo


A95.  LORCA AND JIMENEZ:  SELECTED POEMS  1973

LORCA / AND / JIMENEZ / SELECTED POEMS / Chosen
and Translated by / ROBERT BLY / BEACON PRESS /
Boston

Collation:  5 1/4 X 7 15/16".  [1-32]$^3$ [1-16] [1-32]$^3$:  104
leaves.  Pp. [i-iv] v-xi [xii] 1-5 [6-7] 8-25 [26-27] 28-57
[58-59] 60-97 [98-99] 100-121 [122-123] 124-141 [142-143]
144-181 [182-183] 184-193 [194-196].

Pagination:  p. [i] half-title; p. [ii] blank; p. [iii] title-
page; p. [iv] "Copyright © 1973 by Robert Bly / Copyright
© 1967 by The Sixties Press / Spanish texts:  Juan Ramón
Jiménez, © 1973, Herederos de Juan Ramón / Jiménez, Mad-
rid-España" / [acknowledgments] / "Beacon Press books
are published under the auspices / of the Unitarian Univer-
salist Association / Published simultaneously in hardcover
and paperback editions / Simultaneous publication in Canada
by Saunders of Toronto, Ltd. / All rights reserved /
Printed in the United States of America / 9 8 7 6 5 4 3 2 1";
pp. v-viii, "Contents / Selected Poems of / JUAN RAMON
JIMENEZ"; pp. ix-xi, "Selected Poems of / FEDERICO
GARCIA LORCA"; p. [xii] blank; pp. 1-193, text; pp.
[194-196] blank.

Binding:  Tan paper covered boards with brown cloth
spine.  Blindstamping of village buildings on front cover.
Stamped on spine in black, reading downwards:  Robert
Bly  LORCA AND JIMENEZ:  SELECTED POEMS  Beacon
Press.  End-papers front and back of white paper slightly
heavier than the sheets.

Dust jacket:  Front cover and spine, paper burnt orange.
Front: [in brown:] Selected Poems / LORCA / and /
JIMENEZ / Chosen and / Translated by / Robert Bly / [in
red:] A SEVENTIES PRESS BOOK / [publisher's device:

woodcut of a horseman with shield and spear surrounded
by two birds and a snake]. Spine, reading downwards:
[in brown:] Robert Bly  LORCA AND JIMENEZ:  SELECTED
POEMS  BEACON PRESS.  Back cover, paper yellow: [in
brown:] Other Seventies Press books available from Beacon:
/ [lists four titles] / Also from Beacon:  / [lists one title]
/ [publisher's device:  village buildings] / BEACON
PRESS  BOSTON  ISBN 0-8070-6394-0.  Along right-hand
edge, reading downwards:  Jacket designed by Richard C.
Barlett.  Flyleaves, paper in white.  Front flyleaf:  [in
brown:] $7.95 / LORCA AND JIMENEZ / SELECTED POEMS
/ Chosen and translated by Robert Bly / [thirty-nine-line
statement on García Lorca, Jiménez, and R. B.'s translation
projects] / (continued on back flap).  Back flyleaf:  [in
brown:] (continued from front flap) / [nineteen-line state-
ment] / [six-line statement on R. B.]

Contents:  Juan Ramón Jiménez Under The Water/Adoles-
cence/"I Was Sitting"/"The Lumber Wagons"/Winter Scene/
"Who Knows What Is Going On"/"A Remembrance Is Moving"
/"The Lamb Was Bleating Softly"/Return for an Instant/
"Something So Close"/Night Piece/"I Took Off Petal After
Petal"/Cemetery/"In the Subway"/Deep Night/Author's Club/
Walt Whitman/An Imitator of Billy Sunday/Wrong Time/"In
New York"/Lavender Windowpanes and White Curtains/
Remorse/Night Piece/"Intelligence, Give Me"/Oceans/"Mu-
sic"/"I Pulled on the Reins"/To Dante/The Memory/Being
Awake/Road/"I Am Not I"/"The Ship, Solid and Black"/
"Even Though My Soul"/Whiteness/Full Moon/"At First She
Came to Me Pure"/Dawns of Moguer/Dawn Outside the City
Walls/The Name Drawn from the Names/Full Consciousness/
First Glimpse of Juan Ramón Jiménez by Rafael Alberti/
García Lorca and Crete/Questions/The Boy Unable to Speak/
"Juan Ramón Jiménez"/Malaguena/Song of the Rider/The
Guitar/The Unmarried Woman at Mass/"The Moon Sails Out"
/The Quarrel/Thamar and Amnon/Preciosa and the Wind/
Home from a Walk/Rundown Church/Dance of Death/City
That Does Not Sleep/Sunrise/Death/Landscape with Two
Graves and an Assyrian Hound/Little Infinite Poem/New
York/Song of the Cuban Blacks/Casida of the Rose/Casida
of the Shadowy Pigeons/Casida of Sobbing/Ghazal of the
Terrifying Presence/Ghazal of the Dark Death.

Location:  SUNY Buffalo

Note:  This is a bilingual edition with the Spanish texts
on opposite pages.


A96.  ODE TO SOME YELLOW FLOWERS  1973

[tan-gray sheet printed in dark brown] Ode to Some /

Yellow Flowers / [text in a single column] / Pablo Neruda
/ Translated by Robert Bly

Collation: 7 X 14". Single sheet printed on both sides
which folds twice horizontally. When opened completely,
printed on the back: [top section:] [photograph: "Man
on North Main," by Mark Petty] / [middle section:] Pablo
Neruda/1904-1973 / [bottom section:] Other cards, broad-
sheets, and soon pamphlets will follow. / Cold Mountain
Press would like to see poems from those who / are known
for them, and from those who are not. / 4406 Duval /
Austin, Texas 78751 / "Oda a unas flores amarillas" Copy-
right © 1957 Pablo Neruda / English Translation Copyright
© 1973 Robert Bly / "Man on North Main" photograph Copy-
right © 1973 Mark Petty.

Binding: None. All edges trimmed.

Contents: Ode to Some Yellow Flowers [poem]

Location: SUNY Buffalo

Note: Limited to 1,000 copies.


A97.   ELEGY/SOME OCTOBER NOTES   1973

Elegy / [rule] / Some October / Notes / Robert Bly /
Translated from the Swedish of / Tomas Tranströmer /
THE SCEPTRE PRESS / 15 Keats Way, Rushden / North-
amptonshire

Collation: 5 X 8 1/4". No sign. 4 leaves. Pp. [1-8].

Pagination: p. [1] title-page; p. [2] blank; p. [3] "This
edition is limited to 150 numbered copies / printed on Ab-
bey Mills laid paper / Nos. 1-50 are signed by the poet /
COPY / © 1973"; p. [4] blank; p. [5] "Elegy"; p. [6]
blank; p. [7] "Some October Notes"; p. [8] "Printed by
Skelton's Press / Wellingborough, Northamptonshire / Eng-
land."

Binding: Green paper wrappers. Front: [in black:]
Elegy / [rule] / Some October / Notes / Robert Bly /
Translated from the Swedish of / Tomas Tranströmer.

Contents: Elegy/Some October Notes.

Location: SUNY Buffalo

A98.  HUNGER [First British edition]  1974

HUNGER / Knut Hamsun / Translated from the Norwegian
by Robert Bly / with Introductions by Robert Bly / and
Isaac Bashevis Singer / [publisher's device:  duck]

Collation:  5 X 7 13/16".  [1-32]8:  128 leaves.  Pp. [i-
iv] v-xi [xii] xiii-xxii [xxiii-xxiv] [1-2] 3-61 [62-64] 65-
113 [114-116] 117-184 [185-186] 187-231 [232].

Pagination:  p. [i] half-title; p. [ii] blank; p. [iii] title-
page; p. [iv] "This translation and edition first published
in Great / Britain 1974 / © 1967 Farrar Straus & Giroux,
Inc. / Hunger first published in English by Duckworth in
/ George Egerton's translation 1921 / Gerald Duckworth
and Company Limited / The Old Piano Factory / 43 Glou-
cester Crescent, London NW1 / All rights reserved.  No
part of this publication may b [sic] / reproduced, stored
in a retrieval system, or / transmitted, in any form or by
any means, electronic / mechanical, photocopying, record-
ing or otherwise, / without the prior permission of the
copyright owner. / ISBN 0 7156 0761 8 / Printed in Great
Britain by Unwin Brothers Limited / The Gresham Press,
Old Woking, Surrey / A member of the Staples Printing
Group."; pp. v-[xii] "Introduction by / Isaac Bashevis
Singer / KNUT HAMSUN, ARTIST OF SKEPTICISM"; pp.
xiii-[xxiii] "Introduction by / Robert Bly / THE ART OF
HUNGER"; p. [xxiv] blank; pp. [1]-[232] text.

Binding:  Black paper covered boards, stamped in gold.
Spine, reading downwards:  HUNGER [outlined in gold:]
KNUT HAMSUN  DUCKWORTH.  End-papers front and back
of white paper slightly heavier than the sheets.

Location:  SUNY Buffalo


A99.  THE FLUTE  1974

[card] Front: [printed in black on light yellow:] THE
FLUTE / [rule] / [text in a single column] / Kabir / Ver-
sion by Robert Bly.  Back:  [printed in black on tan-
gray:] [upper left quadrant:] COLD MOUNTAIN PRESS
POETRY POST CARD / Series II, Number 5 / Copyright ©
1974 Robert Bly [reading upwards, middle of the back:]
Cold Mountain Press, 4406 Duval, Austin, Texas 78751.

Collation:  6 1/2 X 5".  Single card printed on both sides.

Binding:  None.  All edges trimmed.

Contents:  The Flute [poem]

Location:   SUNY Buffalo

Note:   Cold Mountain Press Poetry Card Series II, num-
ber 5.

A100.   THE RADIANCE, KABIR   1974

East Lansing, MI:   Old Marble Press.

Wrappers.

Limited to 300 copies.

Not verified, cited in Lepper (P122), p. 72.

A101.   KABIR:   28 POEMS   1975

KABIR / 28 POEMS / VERSIONS BY ROBERT BLY / [de-
vice] / published by / SIDDHA YOGA DHAM / 251 West
95th Street / New York, New York / 10025 / copyright
Robert Bly 1971, 1975 / We are grateful to Robert Bly
and Rainbow Books, San Francisco, / publisher of The
Fish In The Sea Is Not Thirsty:   14 Poems of Kabir, /
for permission to reprint Kabir's poems here.

Collation:   5 7/16 X 7 13/16".   No sign.   18 leaves.   Pp.
[1-36].

Pagination:   pp. [1-2] blank; p. [3] title-page; p. [4]
"This edition is published / in honor of / Sri Gurudev /
Swami Muktananda Paramahansa / on Guru Purnima /
July 23, 1975 / Sadgurunath Maharaj Ki Jaya!"; p. [5]
[statement on Kabir by R. B.]; pp. [6-33] text; p. [34]
[illustration]; pp. [35-36] blank.

Binding:   Stiff orange and red paper covers.   Front:
[in red:] KABIR / [framed illustration in red-tone] /
VERSIONS BY ROBERT BLY.   Back:   [in red:] SIDDHA
YOGA DHAM / 251 West 95th Street / New York, New
York / 10025.

Contents:   "When my friend is away from me"/"I don't
know what sort of a God we have been talking about"/
"Oh friend, I love you, think this over"/"Student, do the
simple purification"/"Inside this clay jug there are canyons
and pine mountains"/"Why should we two ever want to
part?"/"Shall I flail with words, when love has made the
space ..."/"I laugh when I hear that the fish in the water
is thirsty"/"Knowing nothing shuts the inner gates"/

"Between the conscious and the unconscious, the mind
has put up a swing"/"My inside, listen to me, the great-
est spirit"/"There is a flag no one sees blowing in the
sky-temple"/"There's a moon in my body, but I can't see
it!"/"I said to the wanting-creature inside me"/"My body
and my mind are in depression"/"The flute of interior
time is played whether we hear it or not"/"What comes out
of the harp?"/"Friend, hope for the Guest while you are
alive"/"I talk to my inner lover, and I say, why such
rush?"/"I know the sound of the ecstatic flute"/"What has
death and a thick body ..."/"I have been thinking of the
difference between water ..."/"The bhakti path winds in
a delicate way"/"Let's leave for the country where the
Guest lives!"/"Are you looking for me?"/"It is time to put
up a love swing!"/"The darkness of night is coming along
fast ..."/"There is nothing but water in the holy pools."

Location:  SUNY Buffalo


A102.  FRIENDS, YOU DRANK SOME DARKNESS  1975

Friends, You / Drank Some Darkness / THREE SWEDISH
POETS / Harry Martinson / Gunnar Ekelöf / AND / Tomas
Tranströmer / CHOSEN AND TRANSLATED BY / Robert Bly
/ [publisher's device] / BEACON PRESS / BOSTON

Collation:  5 1/4 X 7 15/16".  [1-32]⁴ [1-24] [1-32]⁴:
140 leaves.  Pp. [i-v] vi-xi [xii] [1-2] 3-4 [5] 6-31 [32-
33] 34-65 [66-68] 69-71 [72-73] 74-123 [124-125] 126-155
[156-157] 158-163 [164-166] 167-169 [170-171] 172-221
[222-223] 224-267 [268].

Pagination:  p. [i] half-title; p. [ii] "Seventies Press
Books published by Beacon Press" [lists six titles]; p.
[iii] title-page; p. [iv] "Copyright © 1975 by Robert Bly
/ Copyright © 1970 by the Seventies Press / Swedish
texts:  Harry Martinson poems copyright © 1974 / by
Harry Martinson; Gunnar Ekelöf poems copyright © 1965
by Gunnar Ekelöf; and / Tomas Tranströmer poems copy-
right © 1954, 1958, 1962, 1968 by Tomas Tranströmer /
Beacon Press books are published under the auspices of
the Unitarian Universalist Association / Published simul-
taneously in hardcover and paperback editions / Simul-
taneous publication in Canada by Saunders of Toronto,
Ltd. / All rights reserved / Printed in the United States
of America / 9 8 7 6.5 4 3 2 1" / [acknowledgments] /
Library of Congress Cataloging in Publication Data; pp.
[v]-xi, "Contents"; p. [xii] blank; pp. [1]-267, text;
p. [268] blank.

Binding: Black paper covered boards with blue cloth
spine. Blind stamping of village buildings on front cover.
Stamped in black on spine, reading downwards: Robert
Bly / FRIENDS YOU DRANK SOME DARKNESS / BEACON
PRESS. End-papers front and back of white paper slight-
ly heavier than the sheets.

Contents: Harry Martinson: Introduction/The Cable Ship
/After/Lighthouse Keeper/Out at Sea/I See Women/No Name
for It/Gypsy Laugh/On the Congo/Cotton/Landscape/Crea-
tion Night/March Evening/Letter from a Cattleboat/Fall/
The Birch and the Child/Power/The Sea Wind/From the
Winds of Passage/Dusk in the Country/The Goddess of
Skin/Moon Poem/The Earthworm/from Hades and Euclid/
Old Farmhouse/Henhouse/The Hill in the Woods.
Gunnar Ekelöf: Introduction/"The Flowers Doze in the
Window and the Lamp Gazes Light"/Mirror of October/
Sonataform, Methylated Prose/Chorus/"Paralyzed by the
Night"/At Night/A Dreamt Poem/The Moon/Variations/
Questionnaire/Etudes/A July Night/The Swan/"Who is
Coming, You Ask"/"If You Ask Me Where I Live"/"For
Night Comes"/"The Silence of the Deep Night Is Huge"/
"But Somewhere Else I Have Learned"/Trionfo della Morte/
"So Strange to Me"/Monologue with Its Wife/"When They
Slip Out Through the Churchyard Gate"/"The Knight Has
Rested for a Long Time"/"When One Has Come As Far As
I in Pointlessness"/"In Dreams I Have Met"/"I Do Best
Alone at Night"/From Gunnar Ekelöf: A Contemporary
Mystic by Eric Lindegren.
Tomas Tranströmer: Introduction/Evening-Morning/Sailor's
Tale/The Man Awakened by a Song Above His Roof/Track/
Kyrie/Balakirev's Dream (1905)/After the Attack/The
Couple/Lamento/Allegro/The Half-Finished Heaven/Noc-
turne/From an African Diary (1963)/Morning Bird Songs/
Solitude/After a Death/Under Pressure/Open and Closed
Space/Out in the Open/Slow Music/The Name/A Few Mo-
ments/Breathing Space July/Going with the Current/Out-
skirts/Traffic/Night Duty/The Open Window/Preludes/
Standing Up/The Bookcase/Sentry Duty/Snow-Melting Time,
'66/Further In/Elegy/Seeing Through the Ground/The Scat-
tered Congregation.

Location: SUNY Buffalo

Note: The work is a bilingual edition with the Swedish
texts on facing pages.

First paper edition: 1975

Title page, collation, pagination, and contents same as
hardbound.

Binding: Front and spine, blue paper. Front: [in red:]
BEACON BP 515 $3.95 [upper right corner] / [in black:]
Friends, You / Drank Some Darkness / THREE SWEDISH
POETS / Martinson, Ekelöf, / and Tranströmer / Chosen
and / Translated by / Robert Bly / [in red:] A SEVEN-
TIES PRESS BOOK / [in red:] [device: horseman with
shield and spear surrounded by two birds and a snake].
[In lower right corner, in yellow circle:] NOBEL/ PRIZE
FOR / LITERATURE / [rule] / HARRY / MARTINSON /
[rule] / 1974. Spine, reading downwards: [in red:]
BP / 515 / [in black:] Robert Bly / FRIENDS YOU DRANK
SOME DARKNESS / Beacon Press. Back cover, white
paper printed in black: Beacon Paperback 515 - Litera-
ture / FRIENDS, YOU DRANK SOME DARKNESS / Three
Swedish Poets / Martinson, Ekelöf, and Tranströmer /
Chosen and Translated by Robert Bly / A Seventies
Press Book / [note on R.B., and quotes from Bly's in-
troductions to Martinson, Ekelöf, and Tranströmer].
Lower left corner: [in red:] [publisher's device] / [in
black:] BEACON PRESS  BOSTON.

Location: SUNY Stony Brook

A103.  GRASS FROM TWO YEARS [&] LET'S LEAVE (KABIR)   1975

See A42.

A104.  THE DARKNESS OF NIGHT   1976

[white sheet printed in black] THE DARKNESS OF NIGHT
/ [text in a single column] / Kabir / Version by Robert
Bly / Rook Broadside II, The Darkness of Night, has
been published by The Rook Society, A Non-Profit / Or-
ganization, Derry, Pennsylvania, in an edition of one
hundred numbered copies, of which fifty / copies have
been signed. It has been letterpressed with Garamond
types of Beckett Camric text / paper by Artcraft Print-
ers, Inc., Latrobe, Pennsylvania. Copyright © 1976 by
The Rook Society, / Inc. This is number [   ]

Collation: 8 1/2 X 11. Single sheet printed on one side
only.

Binding: None. All edges trimmed.

Contents: The Darkness of Night [poem]

Location: Heyen

Note:  Rook Broadside 2.  Limited to 100 numbered
copies, of which nos. 1-50 are signed by R. B.


A105.  THE LOVE SWING  1976

[dark pink-red sheet] [row of twenty-six floral devices
printed in silver] / [in black:] THE LOVE SWING / [text
in one column] / Kabir / versions by Robert Bly / [row
of twenty-six floral devices in silver] / [in black:] The
Slow Loris Broadside, "The Love Swing," of Series IV,
is an edition of sixty-five numbered & signed broad- /
sides printed by the Hoechstetter Printing Company,
Pittsburgh, Pennsylvania.  The type composition, Old
Century, / is the work of Stanley J. Malinowski, Buffalo,
New York.  The paper is Strathmore Americana.  Copy-
right 1976 / by the Slow Loris Press, a non-profit cor-
poration, 6359 Morrowfield Avenue, Pittsburgh, Pennsyl-
vania 15217. / Number [   ]

Collation:  8 X 10 3/4".  Single sheet printed on one side
only.

Binding:  None.  All edges trimmed.

Contents:  The Love Swing [poem]

Location:  SUNY Buffalo

Note:  Part of Slow Loris Broadsides, Series IV.  Limited
to sixty-five numbered and signed copies.


A106.  KABIR:  TRY TO LIVE TO SEE THIS!  1976

Kabir / Try to live / to see this! / [design] / Versions
by / Robert Bly

Collation:  5 7/8 X 6 7/8".  No sign.  13 leaves.  Pp.
[a-f] [i-iv] 1-10 [11-12] [g-l].

Pagination:  pp. [a-b] [brown paper heavier than the
sheets]; pp. [c-d] [white paper heavier than the sheets];
pp. [e-f] [onion paper]; p. [i] title-page; p. [ii] "Copy-
right Robert Bly 1976 / Co-published in England by the
Sceptre Press / ISBN 0-915408-12-0 / Cover illustration
from 'Religions of the East' / by Anne Bancroft, courtesy
of William Heinnemann / and Walter Parrish International"
/ [acknowledgments] / [publisher's device:  old woman at
a caldron] / "The Ally Press / 1764 Gilpin Street / Den-
ver, Colorado 80218"; pp. [iii-iv] blank; pp. 1-10, text;

p. [11] blank; p. [12] [six-line statement on Kabir] /
[six-line statement on R. B.]; pp. [g-h] [onion paper];
pp. [i-j] [white paper heavier than the sheets]; pp. [k-
l] [brown paper heavier than the sheets].

Binding: Brown leatherette covered boards. Gray paper
printed in black inlaid on front cover with upper right
corner cut diagonally: Kabir / Try to live / to see this!
/ [in red:] [design] / [in black:] Versions by / Robert
Bly. Single end-papers front and back of printed floral
design in gold, red, brown, blue, green, yellow, and
orange.

Contents: "There is nothing but water in the holy pools"
/"I have been thinking of the difference between water"/
"Are you looking for me?"/"What has death and a thick
body ..."/"I talk to my inner lover ..."/"The bhakti
path winds in a delicate way"/"I know the sound of the
ecstatic flute"/"It is time to put up a love-swing!"/"The
darkness of night is coming along fast ..."/"Friend, hope
for the Guest while you are alive"

Location: SUNY Stony Brook


First paper edition: 1976

Title page and contents same as hardbound.

Collation: 5 7/8 X 6 7/8". No sign. 8 leaves. Pp. [i-
iv] 1-10 [11-12]                                    .

Pagination: p. [i] title-page; p. [ii] "Copyright Robert
Bly 1976 / Co-published in England by the Sceptre Press
/ ISBN 0-915408-12-0 / Cover illustration from 'Religions
of the East' / by Anne Bancroft, courtesy of William
Heinnemann / and Walter Parrish International" / [ac-
knowledgments] / [publisher's device: old woman at a
caldron] / "The Ally Press / 1764 Gilpin Street / Denver,
Colorado 80218"; pp. [iii-iv] blank; pp. 1-10, text; p.
[11] blank; p. [12] [six-line statement on Kabir] / [six-
line statement on R. B.].

Binding: Gray paper wrappers. Front: [in black:]
Kabir / Try to live / to see this! / [in red:] [design] /
[in black:] Versions by / Robert Bly. Back: [in black:]
England / 1 pound / U.S. / $1.75. End-papers of onion
paper front and back.

Location: SUNY Stony Brook

A107.   TWENTY POEMS:  ROLF JACOBSEN  1977

> [in black:] ROLF JACOBSEN / [in red:] TWENTY POEMS
> / [in black:] translated by / Robert Bly / [in red:] [de-
> vice:  woodcut of a pig's head beneath which "SEVEn-
> TiES PRESS" [sic]] / [in black:] 1977
>
> Collation:  5 1/4 X 8 1/4".  No sign.  40 leaves.  Pp.
> [1-6] 7-10 [11] 12-45 [46-47] 48-75 [76-80].
>
> Pagination:  pp. [1-2] blank; p. [3] half-title; p. [4]
> blank; p. [5] title-page; p. [6] [acknowledgments] /
> "The jacket design is from a 17th century / Tantric
> painting of star clusters. / Library of Congress Catalog
> Card Number / 76-50338 / Copyright  by THE SEVENTIES
> PRESS / Odin House, Madison, Minnesota / Printed in
> the U. S. A."; pp. 7-10, "WHITE SHADOW" [introduction
> by R. B.]; pp. [11]-75, text; pp. [76-80] blank.
>
> Binding:  Light brown paper wrappers over stiff white
> paper covers.  Front:  [in blue:] [single rule frame]
> ROLF JACOBSEN / TWENTY POEMS / [in red and blue:]
> [drawing from a seventeenth-century Tantric painting
> of star clusters:  five circles within two larger concentric
> circles].  Spine, reading downwards:  [in blue:] ROLF
> JACOBSEN  TWENTY POEMS  Seventies Press.  Back:
> [in blue:] THE SEVENTIES PRESS / All Sixties Press
> books are now out of print and none should / should
> [sic] be ordered from us.  These books are being re-
> printed by / Beacon Press, 25 Beacon Street, Boston,
> MA.  These books have / been reprinted so far: / [lists
> seven titles].  Flyleaves, paper in light brown.  Front
> flyleaf:  [in blue:] $3.00 / [twenty-six-line statement
> on R. J.'s poetry].  Back flyleaf is blank.
>
> Contents:  White Shadow/Country Roads/Heredity and
> Environment/Melancholy Towers/Sunflower/Stave Churches/
> Old Age/Light Pole/The Age of the Great Symphonies/
> The Grass Shop/The Old Women/Guardian Angel/Towers
> in Bologna/May Moon/Memories of Horses/Moon and Apple/
> The Morning Paper/A Path Through Grass/SSSH/Road's
> End/The Silence Afterwards.
>
> Location:  Roberson
>
> Note:  This is a bilingual edition with the Norwegian texts
> on facing page.

A108.   THE KABIR BOOK:  FORTY-FOUR OF THE ECSTATIC POEMS
         OF KABIR  1977

The / Kabir / Book / Forty-Four / of the / Ecstatic /
Poems of / Kabir / Versions / by / Robert Bly / A
Seventies Press Book / Beacon Press-Boston

Collation:   5 3/8 X 7 15/16".   [1-16]6:   51 leaves.   Pp.
[i-xi] xii [xiii-xiv] 1-18 [19] 20-37 [38-39] 40-59 [60]
61-68 [69-70] 71 [72-82].

Pagination:   p. [i] half-title; p. [ii] "Other Books by
Robert Bly" [lists thirteen titles]; p. [iii] title-page; p.
[iv] "Copyright © 1971, 1977 by Robert Bly / Copyright
© 1977 by the Seventies Press / Beacon Press books are
published under the auspices / of the Unitarian Univer-
salist Association / Published simultaneously in hardcover
and paperback editions / Simultaneous publication in
Canada / by Fitzhenry & Whiteside, Ltd., Toronto / All
rights reserved / Printed in the United States of America
/ (hardcover) 9 8 7 6 5 4 3 2 1 / (paperback) 9 8 7 6 5
4 3 2 1 / Library of Congress Cataloging in Publication
Data" [acknowledgments]; p. [v] dedication:   "Dedicated
to Kabir, and all those working / confused in inner labor
/ Rumi says:   Ecstatic love is an ocean, and the Milky
Way / is a flake of foam floating on it."; p. [vi] blank;
p. [vii] "Acknowledgements"; p. [viii] blank; p. [ix]
"This Book Has Three Groups of Poems / The Fish in the
Sea Is Not Thirsty / The Bhakti Path / The Only Woman
Awake / Is the Woman Who / Has Heard the Flute"; p. [x]
blank; p. [xi] [nineteen-line statement by R.B. on his
versions of Kabir]; p. xii [illustration]; pp. [xiii]-59,
text of poems and illustrations; p. [60] blank; pp. 61-
[69] "Some Rumors About Kabir" by R.B.; p. [70] blank;
p. 71, [acknowledgment of permission to reproduce art
work]; pp. [72-82] blank.

Binding:   Red cloth covered boards, stamped in black.
Spine, reading downwards:   Robert Bly  The Kabir Book
Beacon Press.   Blind stamping of village buildings on front
cover.   End-papers front and back of white paper slightly
heavier than the sheets.

Dust jacket:   Front and back covers, spine, paper white.
Front:   [in dark brown:] [two-line quote from Jonathan
Cott, Rolling Stone] / The / Kabir / Book / Forty-Four /
of the / Ecstatic / Poems of / Kabir / Versions / by /
Robert Bly / [to the left of the above:] [design of a
dancing figure in orange, red, yellow, and brown].
Spine:   [in dark brown:] Robert Bly  The Kabir Book
Beacon Press.   Back:   [in dark brown:] Also available
from Beacon Press: / [lists five titles] / [publisher's de-
vice:   village buildings] / BEACON PRESS 25 BEACON
ST. BOSTON, MA   02108 / ISBN 0-8070-6378-9.

Flyleaves: paper in white. Front flyleaf: [in brown:]
7.95 / THE KABIR BOOK / FORTY-FOUR OF THE
ECSTATIC POEMS / OF KABIR  / Versions by Robert
Bly / A SEVENTIES PRESS BOOK /[thirty-five-line state-
ment on the edition] / (continued on back flap).  Back
flyleaf: [in brown:] (continued from front flap) /
[thirty-eight-line statement on the edition and R. B.]
/ BEACON PRESS / 25 Beacon Street, Boston, MA  02108.

Contents:  The Fish in the Sea Is Not Thirsty:  "When
my friend is away from me"/"I don't know what sort of a
God ..."/"Oh friend, I love you, think this over"/"Stu-
dent, do the simple purification"/"Inside this clay jug
there are canyons and pine"/"Why should we two ever
want to part?"/"Why should I flail about with words"/"I
laugh when I hear that the fish in the water is thirsty"/
"Knowing nothing shuts the iron gates"/"Between the
conscious and the unconscious"/"My inside, listen to me"/
"There is a flag no one sees blowing in the sky-temple"/
"There's a moon in my body, but I can't see it!"/"I said
to the wanting-creature inside me"/The Bhakti Path:
"My body and my mind are in depression ..."/"The flute
of interior time is played whether we hear it or not"/
"What comes out of the harp?"/"I talk to my inner lover,
and I say, why such rush?"/"Friend, hope for the Guest
while you are alive"/"I know the sound of the ecstatic
flute"/"What has death and a thick body dances ..."/"I
have been thinking of the difference ..."/"The bhakti
path winds in a delicate way"/"Let's leave for the country
where the Guest lives!"/"Are you looking for me?  I am
in the next seat"/"The darkness of night is coming along
fast ..."/"It is time to put up a love-swing!"/"There is
nothing but water in the holy pools"/The Only Woman
Awake Is the Woman Who Has Heard the Flute:  "Clouds
grow heavy; thunder goes"/"Friend, wake up!  Why do
you go on sleeping?"/"I played for ten years with the
girls my own age"/"I married my Lord, and meant to
live with him"/"The small ruby everyone wants has fallen
out on the road"/"Swan, I'd like you to tell me your whole
story!"/"Listen friend, this body is his dulcimer"/"Don't
go outside your house to see flowers"/"The spiritual ath-
lete often changes the color of his clothes"/"Friend, please
tell me what I can do about this world"/"The Holy One
disguised as an old person in a cheap hotel"/"At last the
notes of his flute come in"/"How hard it is to meet the
Guest!"/"Have you heard the music that no fingers enter
into?"/"The Guest is inside you, and also inside me"/
"The woman who is separated from her lover ..."/Some
Rumors About Kabir by R.B.

Location:  SUNY Buffalo

First paper edition:   1977

Title page, collation, pagination, and contents same as
hardbound. p. [iv] "Copyright 1971, 1977 by Robert
Bly / Copyright 1977 by The Seventies Press / Beacon
Press books are published under the auspices / of the
Unitarian Universalist Association / Simultaneous publica-
tion in Canada / by Fitzhenry & Whiteside, Ltd., Toronto
/ All rights reserved / Printed in the United States of
America / (paperback) 9 8 7 6 5 4 / [Library of Congress
Cataloging in Publication Data] / ISBN 0-8070-6379-7
(pbk.)" / [acknowledgments].

Binding:  Stiff white paper covers. Front:  [to the right
with right margin justification:] [in black:] The / Kabir /
Book / Forty-Four / of the / Ecstatic / Poems of / Kabir
/ Versions / by / Robert Bly  [to the left:] [design of
a dancing figure in orange, red, yellow, and black above
a star shaped design in red, yellow, orange, and black
[in lower left corner, reading upwards:] [in black:] BP
544 > $4.95.  Spine, reading across:  [in black:] BP /
544 [reading downwards:] Robert Bly The Kabir Book
ISBN 6379-7 BEACON PRESS. Back:  [in black:] Poetry,
World Literature / THE KABIR BOOK / Forty-four of the
Ecstatic Poems of Kabir / versions by Robert Bly / A
Seventies Press Book / [twenty-five-line statement on Kab-
ir and RB] / [to the left:] [publisher's device] / BEACON
PRESS  BOSTON  ISBN 0-8070-6379-7 / Beacon Paperback
544 / Cover design by Karyl Klopp / 0147676

Location:   Roberson


A109.   THE VOICES   1977

[in black:] Rainer Maria Rilke / [in red:] The Voices /
[in black:] translated by / Robert Bly

Collation:   6 X 7 1/2".  No sign.  8 leaves.  Pp. [1-16].

Pagination:  p. [1] title-page; p. [2] "Copyright Robert
Bly 1977 / Co-published in England by the Sceptre Press
/ Distributed by Bookpeople and Rainbow Bridge. /
Thanks to The Minnesota Review, / where these versions
first appeared. / ISBN 0-915408-15-5 paper. / ISBN 0-
915408-16-3 signed, handcased. / [rule] / THE ALLY
PRESS / Denver, Colorado" / [publisher's device to the
right of the above two lines]; p. [3] [rule] / "THE
VOICES / nine poems with a title poem" / [rule]; p. [4]
blank; pp. [5-14] text; p. [15] blank; p. [16] [ten-
line statement on R. M. R.] / [facsimile of R. M. R.'s

signature] / eight-line statement on R. B.].

Binding: White paper covers. Front: [in brown:]
Rainer Maria Rilke / [within a brown frame:] [in yellow:]
[illustration of a rose branch] / [in brown:] the voices
/ Translated by Robert Bly. Back: [in brown:] THE
ALLY PRESS / $1.95. End-papers front and back of
dark yellow.

Contents: Title poem/The Song the Beggar Sings/The
Song the Drunkard Sings/The Song the Blind Man Sings/
The Song the Suicide Sings/The Song the Widow Sings/
The Song the Idiot Sings/The Song the Orphan Sings/
The Song the Dwarf Sings/The Song the Leper Sings.

Location: SUNY Buffalo

A110. ALONG THE LINES, TOMAS TRANSTROMER 1979

[n.p.]: Square Zero Editions.

Broadside, 51 X 22 cm.

Limited to 150 copies. Designed and printed at the Black
Stone Press.

Not verified, listed in OCLC by the University of North
Carolina, Chapel Hill, NC.

A111. I NEVER WANTED FAME 1979

[across two pages] [in black:] I NEVER WANTED FAME
/ [on left hand side] 10 poems & proverbs translated by
/ ROBERT BLY / Ally Press :: St. Paul, Minnesota ::
May, 1979 [on right hand side] ANTONIO MACHADO /
[in blue:] [drawing of a figure within an oval]

Collation: 6 5/8 X 4 7/8". No sign. 10 leaves. Pp.
[1-20].

Pagination: p. [1] blank; pp. [2-3] title-page; p. [4]
"© 1979 by Robert Bly / FIRST EDITION / Ally Press
Translation Series #2 / Distributed by Bookpeople and
Bookslinger / [Library of Congress Cataloging in Pub-
lication Data] / [publisher's device] / Ally Press / P.O.
Box 30340 / St. Paul, Minnesota 55175"; p. [5] half-title;
p. [6] blank; pp. [7-16] text; p. [17] blank; p. [18]
"About the Author and Translator" / [five-line statement
on A. M.] / [four-line statement on R. B.]; p. [19]

"Also available from Ally Press" / [lists three titles]:
p. [20] "Colophon / This volume was handset from Bul-
mer and Homewood types, then printed on an / ATF
Little Giant. From a run of 1,626 copies, 26 are let-
tered A-Z, handcased in / boards & signed by the trans-
lator and binding craftsman. 100 copies are printed /
on Ragston paper, numbered and signed by the trans-
lator. The illustration was / created on scratchboard by
Randall W. Scholes. Printed at The Toothpaste Press."

Binding: Light blue paper wrappers. Front: [in black:]
Antonio Machado / I NEVER WANTED FAME / TRANS-
LATED BY ROBERT BLY / [in dark blue:] [drawing of
a figure within an oval]. Back: [in black:] $2.50 /
[publisher's device] / Ally Press / P.O. Box 30340 / St.
Paul, Minnesota 55175. End-papers front and back of
dark blue paper.

Contents: "I have never wanted fame"/"Why should we
call"/"Let us sing together: know?/"I love Jesus, who
said to us:"/"It is good knowing that glasses"/"All things
die and all things live forever;"/"To die ... To fall like
a drop"/"Mankind owns four things".

Location: Roberson


A112.   ARCHAIC TORSO OF APOLLO, RAINER MARIA RILKE   [ca.
        1980]

        [n.p.]: Square Zero Editions

        Broadside, 43 X 35 cm.

        Limited to 126 copies

        Not verified, listed in OCLC by Indiana University,
        Bloomington, IN.


A113.   CANCIONES   1980

        ANTONIO MACHADO / CANCIONES / Translated by
        Robert Bly / The Toothpaste Press / West Branch, Iowa
        / [publisher's device]

        Collation:  4 1/4 X 8".  No sign.  12 leaves.  Pp. [1-24].

        Pagination:  pp. [1-2] blank; p. [3] title-page; p. [4]
        "Five of these translations appeared in The / Sixties, &
        one in The Sea and the Honeycomb (Beacon Press). / The
        original poems form a group which / Antonio Machado

wrote in homage to / the Spanish folk tradition, & pub-
lished / under the title 'Canciones' in his book, / Nuevas
Canciones, [in italics] 1930. / © 1980 by Robert Bly"
/ [Library of Congress Cataloging in Publication data] /
"The National Endowment for the Arts & the Iowa / Arts
Council helped an appreciative publisher."; p. [5] half-
title; p. [6] blank; pp. [7-21] text; p. [22] "Handset
in Blado & Poliphilus types by / Al Buck. Designed &
printed by Allan / Kornblum. Cover calligraphy by
Sandy / Gourlay. 1,450 copies printed on Strath- / more
Pastelle text & sewn into Fabriano / Ingres wrappers.
150 copies printed on / Rives; numbered & signed by the
trans- / lator; and cased in Fabriano Ingres over /
boards by Constance Syare at the Black / Oak Bindery.";
pp. [23-24] blank.

Binding: Dark green wrappers, stamped in gold. Front:
Antonio Machado / CANCIONES / Translated by Robert
Bly / [underscored in a spiral of ten lines]. Back:
[in black:] [fourteen-line statement on Machado by
R.B.] / [publisher's device] THE TOOTHPASTE PRESS /
Box 546 : West Branch, Iowa 52358 / $4.00.

Contents: "The huge sea drives"/"Not far from the black
water."/"The spring has arrived."/"Full moon, full moon,"
/"Night of Castille!"/"Sing, sing in crisp sound"/"The
fountain and the four"/"White inn"/"The Roman aqueduct,"
/"In words of love"/"High mass"/"There is a fiesta in the
green field"/"With you in Valonsadero,"/"While you are
dancing in a ring,".

Location: Roberson


A114. MIRABAI VERSIONS 1980

[across two pages[ [to left:] [in dark blue:] MIRABAI
[in black:] VERSIONS BY ROBERT BLY / [in lavender:]
ILLUSTRATED BY ELLEN LANYON [to right:] [in deep
purple:] [illustration of a snake] / [in black:] THE RED
OZIER PRESS

Collation: 6 3/4 X 10 1/8". No sign. 8 leaves. Pp.
[1-16].

Pagination: p. [1] blank; pp. [2-3] title-page; p. [4]
[in lavender:] "We are grateful to the editors of East /
West Journal where some of these poems first appeared.
/ Copyright Nineteen-hundred & eighty, the Year of the
Monkey, by / Robert Bly. Mirabai, who wrote in Rajast-
hani, became part / of the renewal of ecstatic religious
life in North India / in the sixteenth century. When her

husband was / killed in a war, she was about twenty-
/ seven and decided to leave the compound:   she did,
writ- / ing her poems, composing the music for them, / and
dancing them.   Her husband's family / insisted she made
a bad bargain.  / Mirabai answers them in / 'It's True I
Went To / The Market' / Robert Bly"; p. [5] blank; pp.
[6-13] text and illustrations; p. [14] blank; p. [15] [in
black:] "These Two-hundred & twenty / copies were
handmade by Steve Miller with / the assistance of Ken
Botnick during the spring & summer / of Nineteen-
hundred & eighty.   Ten copies are hand / colored by
the artist & bound in boards by / Gray Parrot.  Basker-
ville is the type / & the papers are Arches Text / &
Tidepool handmade. / [in lavender:] Number [   ]"; p.
[16] blank.

Binding:   Red-purple paper covers.   Front:   [in deep
purple:] [illustration of a snake].   Three sets of end-
papers front and back.   First set of red-purple paper;
the other two sets of lavender paper.   Top-edge trimmed.

Contents:   It's True I Went to the Market/All I Was Do-
ing Was Breathing/Why Mira Can't Go Back to Her Old
House/Where Did You Go?/The Clouds/Don't Go, Don't Go

Location:   SUNY Buffalo

Note:   Limited to 220 copies.   Ten copies are hand colored
by the artist and bound in boards.   A first facsimile edi-
tion of 2,000 copies was printed from proofs of the orig-
inal limited edition the same year.

A115.   THE DELIGHTS OF THE DOOR   1980

[in green:] THE DELIGHTS OF THE DOOR / [in blue-
gray:] a poem by Francis Ponge translated by Robert
Bly / [in green:] [rule] / [in blue-gray:] Bedouin Press
New York City / [in green:] [rule]

Collation:   6 1/8 X 5 1/4".   No sign.   4 leaves.   Pp.
[1-8].

Pagination:   p. [1] title-page; p. [2] "copyright 1980
Robert Bly"; p. [3] blank; p. [4] [illustration]; p. [5]
[poem]; p. [6] blank; p. [7] "One hundred fifty chap-
books were hand / printed using Baskerville in Arches
and / wrapped in Tidepool at 73 Warren St. / This poem
appears in News of the U- / niverse, a Sierra Club Book.
[in green:] [device:  arm and hammer] All / thanks to
Dr. Miller."; p. [8] blank.

Binding: Blue-gray paper covers. Front: [blindstamp-
ing:] THE DELIGHTS OF THE DOOR. End-papers front
and back of gray-pink. Top edge trimmed.

Contents: The Delights of the Door

Location: SUNY Buffalo


A116.  I AM TOO ALONE IN THE WORLD  1980

[in green:] I Am Too Alone In The World / [in gold:]
Ten Poems / By / Rainer Maria Rilke / Translated by
Robert Bly / [publisher's device] / [in green:] The Sil-
ver Hands Press  New York City

Collation:  6 1/2 X 9 7/8". No sign. 10 leaves. Pp.
[1-20].

Pagination:  p. [1] title-page; p. [2] "Copyright © by
Robert Bly Nineteen hundred and eighty"; p. [3] half-
title; p. [4] [illustration]; pp. [5-19] text; p. [20] [in
green:] "Autumn 1980 / With this Robert Bly translation
of / Rainer Maria Rilke, The Silver Hands / Press begins
to publish hand printed / limited editions of fine poetry.
The / type is Bembo, printed on our number / four Van-
dercook Press in the sunlit loft / at 115 West 23rd Street
New York City. / The papers are Arches, Dewint and /
Kizuki. Illustrations by Pat Apatovsky." / [illustration
in gold] / "There are two hundred twenty hand / sewn
copies of this edition. One hundred / twenty are signed
and numbered. The / Press thanks Alex Mead, Diana
Rivers, / and Micha Taubman. / [in gold:] Number [   ]".

Binding:  Beige paper wrappers. Front: [in olive green:]
[illustration]. End-papers front and back of gray-green
paper lighter than the sheets. Page edges are not trimmed.
Poems are printed in green.

Contents:  "I live my life in growing orbits"/"I have many
brothers in the South"/"We don't care to do paintings of
you as we want to"/"I love the dark hours of my being"/
"You darkness, that I come from"/"I have faith in all those
things that are not yet said"/"I am too alone in the world"/
"You see, I want a lot"/"I can hardly believe that this tiny
death"/"I find you in all these things of the world."

Location: SUNY Buffalo

A117.   "I LIVE MY LIFE IN GROWING ORBITS"   [c. 1980]

> [ivory card printed in brown]   Front:   [text in a single
> column]  /  Rainer Maria Rilke  translated by Robert Bly.
> Back:   [in upper left quadrant:] from  I AM TOO ALONE
> IN THE WORLD   10 poems  /  Published by Silver Hands
> Press   115 W 23 Street New York City 10011.
>
> Collation:   6 1/2 X 3 7/8".   Single card printed on both
> sides.
>
> Binding:   None.   All edges trimmed.
>
> Contents:   "I live my life in growing orbits."   [poem]
>
> Location:   Roberson

A118.   TRUTH BARRIERS   1980

> Truth Barriers  /  Poems by  /  Tomas Tranströmer  /  Trans-
> lated and Introduced by  /  Robert Bly  /  Sierra Club Books
> San Francisco
>
> Collation:   6 X 8 15/16".   [1-16]$^2$:   32 leaves.   Pp. [i-
> vi] 1-10 [11] 12-18 [19] 20-23 [24-25] 26-30 [31] 32-39
> [40-41] 42-55 [56-58].
>
> Pagination:   p. [i] half-title; p. [ii] [illustration]; p.
> [iii] title-page; p. [iv] [fourteen-line statement on the
> Sierra Club]  /  "Copyright © 1980 by Robert Bly  /  All
> rights reserved.   No part of this book may be reproduced
> in  /  any form or by any electronic or mechanical means,
> including  /  information storage and retrieval systems,
> without permission  /  in writing from the publisher.  /
> This book was originally published in Sweden under the
> title  /  Sanningsbarriaren by Bonniers Forlag, Stockholm,
> in 1978."  /  [Library of Congress Cataloging in Publication
> Data]  /  "Illustrations by Joseph Stubblefield  /  Printed in
> the United States of America  /  10 9 8 7 6 5 4 3 2 1"; p.
> [v] "CONTENTS"; p. [vi] blank; pp. 1-10, "The Bound-
> ary Between Worlds" [introduction by R. B.]; pp. [11]-
> 39, illustrations and text of translations; p. [40] blank;
> pp. [41]-55, "Sanningsbarriaren:   Original Swedish Texts";
> pp. [56-58] blank.
>
> Binding:   Gray paper covered boards with off-white cloth
> spine, stamped in black.   Spine, reading downwards:
> TRUTH BARRIERS  Tranströmer  •  Bly  Sierra Club
> Books.   End-papers front and back of white paper slight-
> ly heavier than the sheets.

Contents:  Introduction/Citoyens/Street Crossing/The
Clearing/Start of a Late Autumn Novel/For Mats and
Laila/From the Winter of 1947/Schubertiana/The Gallery/
Below Freezing/Boat, Town/Montenegro/Calling Home/
After a Long Dry Spell/A Place in the Woods/At Funchal/
Sanningsbarriaren:  Original Swedish Texts.

Location:  Colgate University Library

Note:  This is a bilingual edition with the Swedish texts
following the translations at the end of the book.

First paper edition:  1980

Title-page, collation, pagination, and contents same as
hardbound, except signatures are [1-15] [1-5] [1-12].

Binding:  Stiff paper covers.  Front:  [light gray with
design in black over lower two thirds] [at top, in black:]
Truth Barriers / POEMS BY TOMAS TRANSTROMER /
Translated and Introduced by ROBERT BLY.  Spine,
white paper printed in black, reading downwards:
TRUTH BARRIERS  Transtromer • Bly  Sierra Club Books.
Back cover, white paper printed in black:  [eighteen-
line statement on T. T. and Truth Barriers] / [nine-
line statement on T. T.] / [seven-line statement on
R. B.] / ISBN:  87156-239-1.  $.595.

Location:  Roberson


A119.   THE EYE THERE IS NOT   1981

[white placard printed in black, illustrated in black, blue,
and purple] [to left side:] El ojo que ves no es / ojo
porque tu lo veas; / es ojo porque te ve. [middle:] [il-
lustration in black, blue, and purple] [to right:] The
eye there is not / an eye because you see it; / it is an
eye because it sees you. / [in two columns:] [first col-
umn:] Poet:  Antonio Machado / Artist:  Paul Veress /
English Translation:  Robert Bly / Graphic Design:  Ed-
die Byrd / Poem from "Proverbios Y Cantares" [second
column, to right:] POETRY ON THE BUSES$^{TM}$ / is sup-
ported in part by the / National Endowment for the Arts
/ and the Pennsylvania Council on the Arts. / Copyright
© 1981 POETRY ON THE BUSES / Carnegie-Mellon Univer-
sity

Collation:  28 X 11".  Single placard printed on one side.

Binding:  None.  All edges trimmed.

Contents:  "El ojo que ves no es" and an English trans-
lation, "The eye there is not."

Location:  SUNY Buffalo


A120.  NIGHT & SLEEP  1981

Night / & / Sleep

Collation:  6 X 9 3/16".  [1-16]$^3$:  24 leaves.  Pp. [1-48].

Pagination:  pp. [1-2] blank; p. [3] title-page; p. [4]
"Copyright © 1981 by Yellow Moon Press / Copyright re-
verts to authors upon publication. / ISBN 0-938756-01-X
(Signed limited edition) / ISBN 0-938756-02-8 (Paperback)
/ Typeset by Ed Hogan/Aspect Composition / 13 Robinson
St., Somerville, Mass. 02145 / Yellow Moon Press / 1725
Commonwealth Ave. / Brighton, MA 02135"; p. [5] "Thank
you for the gifts of love / that make up this book. /
YELLOW MOON PRESS"; p. [6] blank; p. [7] "The Mys-
tery"; p. [8] blank; pp. [9-11] "WHY RUMI DIDN'T SIGN
HIS POEMS" [by Coleman Barks]; p. [12] blank; p. [13]
Night / & / Sleep [within an ornamental floral frame];
pp. [14-39] drawings and text; p. [40] blank; p. [41]
[ornamental floral design]; p. [42] blank; p. [43] "Notes
on the Versions" / [six-line statement on C. B.'s ver-
sions] / [five-line statement on R. B.'s versions]; p. [44]
blank; p. [45] "Notes on the Gift Givers" / [six-line state-
ment on C. B.] / [seven-line statement on R. B.] / [two-
line statement on Laurie Graybeal, graphic designer];
p. [46] [three-line statement on John Moyne] / [nine-
line statement on Rita Schumaker]; pp. [47-48] blank.

Binding:  Stiff light brown paper covers.  Front:  [in
black:] [ornamental floral design frame] [in center:]
Night / & / Sleep / [floral design] / Rumi.  Spine, read-
ing downwards:  [in black:] Rumi  NIGHT & SLEEP
Barks & Bly  Yellow Moon Press.  Back:  [in black:]
[ornamental floral design frame] [in center, in calligra-
phy:] The clear bead at the center / changes everything.
/ There are no edges to / my loving now. / I've heard
it said, there's a window / that opens from one mind to
another. / But if there's no wall, there's no need / for
fitting the window, or the latch. / [floral design] /
Versions by / Coleman Barks & Robert Bly / [floral de-
sign] / Illustrations by Rita Shumaker / [floral design]
/ $6.00 / [floral design].

Contents:  Night and Sleep/Maybe They're Shy/Solomon

and all His Wives/Idle Questions/Praising Manners/The
Hidden/Longing for the Birds of Solomon/The Ears/When
Things Are Heard/Who Says Words with My Mouth/The
Friend/Someone Digging in the Ground/The Ground/No
Wall/The Instruments/The Elusive Ones/Across the Doorsill.

Location:  Roberson

A121.  OCTOBER DAY & OTHER POEMS  1981

OCTOBER / DAY AND / OTHER POEMS / BY RAINER
MARIA RILKE / SELECTED AND TRANSLATED BY /
ROBERT BLY [all of the above is printed over a print
in gray of an iris] / CALLIOPEA PRESS • SEBASTOPOL
CA

Collation:  6 3/8 X 9 9/16".  [1-6] [1-8] [1-6]:  20
leaves.  Pp. [1-40].

Pagination:  pp. [1-2] blank; p. [3] half-title; p. [4]
blank; p. [5] title-page; p. [6] "These poems are part
of Rainer Maria Rilke:  [in italics] / Selected Poems, [in
italics] published by Harper and Row. / COPYRIGHT ©
1981 ROBERT BLY / ISBN 0933888-11-2"; p. [7] "CON-
TENTS"; p. [8] blank; pp. [9-35] text; p. [36] blank;
p. [37] "October Day and Other Poems was designed and
printed / in an edition of 1500 by Carol Denison at Cal-
liopea Press.  The / text, monotype Bembo, was set by
Mackenzie-Harris; the paper is / Ragston.  The cover
and title page were adapted from an / original etching
by Donna Guardino."; pp. [38-40] blank.

Binding:  Ivory paper covers.  Front:  [in black:]
[single rule frame] [blind stamping of an iris with a cen-
ter rectangle of the flower colored a brownish-red] /
[in black:] OCTOBER DAY & OTHER POEMS / RAINER
M. RILKE • ROBERT BLY.  Spine, reading downwards:
[in black:] OCTOBER DAY AND OTHER POEMS • RAINER
M. RILKE • TRANSLATED BY ROBERT BLY.  Back:
[in black:] [single rule frame].

Contents:  Childhood/From Childhood/Sense of Something
Coming/Loneliness/Human Beings at Night/Sunset/The
Solitary Person/The Neighbor/Pont Du Carrousel/The
Ashantis (Jardin D'Acclimation)/Moving Forward/October
Day.

Location:  SUNY Buffalo

Note:  This is a bilingual edition with the German texts
on facing pages.

A122.   SELECTED POEMS OF RAINER MARIA RILKE   1981

> Selected Poems of / RAINER MARIA RILKE / A Transla-
> tion from the German / and Commentary by ROBERT BLY
> / [single rule] / [publisher's device:  stylized torch in
> rectangle below which the date 1817] HARPER & ROW,
> PUBLISHERS, New York / Cambridge, Hagerstown, Phila-
> delphia, San Francisco / London, Mexico City, São Paulo,
> Sydney

Collation:  6 X 9 1/4".  [1-32]$^5$ [1-16]  [1-32]$^2$:   120
leaves.  Pp. [i-iv] v-xi [xii]  [1-2] 3-59 [60-62] 63-107
[108-109] 110-129 [130-132] 133-151 [152-154] 155-181
[182-184] 185-213 [214-216] 217-224 [225-226].

Pagination:  p. [i] half-title; p. [ii] "Other Books by
Robert Bly" [lists twenty-one titles]; p. [iii] title-page;
p. [iv] [acknowledgments] / "SELECTED POEMS OF
RAINER MARIA RILKE.  Copyright © 1981 by Robert
Bly.  All rights / reserved.  Printed in the United
States of America.  No part of this book may be used /
or reproduced in any manner whatsoever without written
permission except in the case / of brief quotations em-
bodied in critical articles and reviews.  For information
address / Harper & Row, Publishers, Inc., 10 East 53rd
Street, New York, N.Y. 10022.  Published / simultane-
ously in Canada by Fitzhenry & Whiteside Limited, Tor-
onto. / FIRST EDITION / Designed by Sidney Feinberg"
/ Library of Congress Cataloging in Publication Data;
pp. v-xi, "Contents"; p. [xii] blank; p. [1]-213, text;
p. [214] blank; p. [215] "Indexes"; p. [216] blank; pp.
217-218, "Index of Titles in German"; pp. 219-220, "In-
dex of Titles in English"; pp. 221-222, "Index of First
Lines in German"; pp. 223-224, "Index of First Lines in
English"; pp. [225-226] blank.

Binding:  Black cloth covered boards.  Stamped in gold
on spine, reading downwards:  Selected Poems of RAINER
MARIA RILKE / Robert Bly EDITOR / HARPER / & ROW.
End-papers front and back of white paper slightly than
the sheets.

Contents:  From A Book for the Hours of Prayer:  I live
my life/I have many brothers/We don't care/I love the dark
hours/You darkness, that I come from/I have faith/I am
too alone/You see, I want a lot/Because One Man/My life
is not/I find you/And then that girl/I can hardly believe/
This is my labor/All of you undisturbed cities/How many
thousands/Just as the watchman/In this town/Sometimes
a man stands up/The kings of the world/Already the
ripening barberries/It's possible/And the great cities/
And where is he

From the Book of Pictures:  The Way In/Childhood/From
Childhood/Sense of Something Coming/Loneliness/Human
Beings at Night/Sunset/The Solitary Person/Autumn/
Storm/The Neighbor/Pont du Carrousel/The Ashantis/
Evening in Skane/Moving Forward/October Day/The Man
Watching/The Voices:  Title Poem/The Song the Beggar
Sings/The Song the Blind Man Sings/The Song the Drunk-
ard Sings/The Song the Suicide Sings/The Song the
Widow Sings/The Song the Idiot Sings/The Song the
Orphan Sings/The Song the Dwarf Sings/The Song the
Leper Sings
From New Poems:  The Panther/The Swan/Roman Coun-
tryside/Leda/Archaic Torso of Apollo/The Solitary Man/
Buddha Inside the Light
From The Uncollected and Occasional Poems:  "We Must
Die Because We Have Known Them"/Mourning/Left Out
to Die/Again, Again/On Music/Imaginary Biography/Fox
Fire/Just as the Winged Energy of Delight/A Walk/Palm/
For Erika
From Sonnets to Orpheus:  A tree rising/It was a girl,
really/A god can do it/O you lovers that are so gentle/
Don't bother about a stone/Is he from our world/To
praise is the whole thing/Where praise already is/Only
the man who has raised his strings/You stone coffins
of the ancient world

Location:  SUNY Stony Brook


First paper edition:  1981

Title page, collation, pagination, and contents same as
hardbound.

Binding:  Purple paper covers.  On front:  [drawing of
Rilke within single rule red frame, below which, printed
in white:] Selected Poems of / RAINER MARIA RILKE /
A Translation from the German / and Commentary by
Robert Bly / HARPER [device] COLOPHON BOOKS/CN
727/ $7.95.  On back, in light purple box framed by sin-
gle red rule:  [in black:] POETRY / [extended statement
concerning Rilke's poetry and Bly's selections] / HARPER
& ROW, PUBLISHERS / $7.95 / Cover design by Honi
Werner  ISBN 0-06-090727-4.  On spine, printed in white,
reading downwards:  Selected Poems of RAINER MARIA
RILKE  Robert Bly, Editor / HARPER / COLOPHON
BOOKS / [device] / [horizontal at bottom:] CN 727.

Location:  Roberson

A123.   TWENTY PROVERBS   1981

        TWENTY / PROVERBS / by Antonio Machado / [ornamen-
        tal device] / Translated by / Robert Bly & Don Olsen /
        Ox Head Press [ornamental device] 1981

        Collation:   4 1/8 X 6 1/4".   No sign.   12 leaves.   Pp.
        [1-24].

        Pagination:   pp. [1-4] blank; p. [5] title-page; p. [6]
        "Two hundred seventy-five copies / printed at the Ox
        Head Press / Marshall, Minnesota / Copyright © 1981";
        p. [7] "Ox Head 17"; p. [8] blank; pp. [9-19] text; p.
        [20] blank; p. [21] "A NOTE ON THE TRANSLATORS /
        Proverbs numbered three, four, six, seven, / ten and
        twelve were translated by Robert / Bly; the remainder
        were translated / by Don Olsen. / [ornamental device];
        pp. [22-24] blank.

        Binding:   Deep yellow-green paper covers.   Front:
        [in black:] [row of twelve ornamental devices] /
        TWENTY / PROVERBS / by / ANTONIO MACHADO /
        [ornamental device] / [row of twelve ornamental devices].
        [Vertical rules connect the two rows of ornamental de-
        vices on either side of the title.]

        Contents:   Twenty proverbs.

        Location:   SUNY Buffalo


A124.   THE ECONOMY SPINNING FASTER AND FAST   1982

        The Economy / Spinning / Faster / and / Faster / poems
        by / Göran Sonnevi / chosen and translated / from the
        Swedish by / Robert Bly / SUN / New York 1982

        Collation:   5 1/2 X 8".   No sign.   28 leaves.   Pp. [A-H]
        i-iii   2-45 [46].

        Pagination:   p. [A] half-title; p. [B] OTHER BOOKS BY
        GORAN SONNEVI / In Swedish / [lists eleven titles] / In
        English Translation / [lists two titles]; p. [C] title-page;
        p. [D] "ACKNOWLEDGEMENTS / Swedish poems copyright
        © 1965, 1967, 1970, 1972, and 1975 by / Göran Sonnevi.
        / English translations copyright © 1979 and 1982 by
        Robert Bly. / This edition copyright © 1982 by SUN. /
        Swedish texts published with the kind permission of their
        original / publisher, Bonniers Förlag, Stockholm, Sweden.
        / SUN wishes to thank the following individuals and or-
        ganizations for / their assistance in the production of this

volume: Richard Jones and / Kate Daniels, editors of
the Scandinavian Review; Marna Feldt of / the Swedish
Information Service; and Linda Snider, Kathleen Hayes, /
and Dolores Schaefer of Tiffany Communications, New
York City. / All rights reserved. No part of this pub-
lication may be reproduced or / transmitted in any form
by any means, electronic or mechanical, in- / cluding
photocopy, recording, or any information storage and /
retrieval system without the written permission of the
publisher, ex- / cept in the case of brief quotations em-
bodied in critical articles and / reviews. For information
address SUN, 347 W. 39 St., New York, / N. Y. 10018.
/ Printed in the United States of America / First Edition"
/ [Library of Congress Cataloging in Publication Data] /
"The publication of this book is supported by a grant
from the / National Endowment for the Arts in Washing-
ton, D. C., a Federal / agency."; p. [E] second half-
title; p. [F] blank; p. [G] "CONTENTS"; p. [H] blank;
pp. i-iii, "INTRODUCTION" [by R. B.]; pp. 2-45, text;
p. [46] blank.

Binding: Stiff paper covers. Front cover and spine,
paper yellow with gray collage of stock market reports.
Front: [in black:] [printed around arcs of seven con-
centric circles:] [on fifth circle:] The Economy / [on
top of outer edge of sixth circle:] Spinning / [on top of
outer edge of seventh circle:] Faster / [on bottom of in-
ner edge of seventh circle:] and / [on bottom of inner
edge of sixth circle:] Faster / poems by / Göran Sonnevi
/ chosen and translated / from the Swedish by / Robert
Bly. Spine, reading downwards: [in black:] THE
ECONOMY SPINNING FASTER AND FASTER • SONNEVI.
Back cover paper white: [in olive green:] [thin rule] /
[thick rule] / [to left of center:] [in black:] The Econ-
omy / Spinning / Faster and Faster / Göran Sonnevi /
chosen and translated / by Robert Bly [to right of cen-
ter] [photograph of G. S. by Monika Englund] / [twenty-
nine-line statement on G. S.] / [five-line statement on
R. B.] / [in olive green:] [thick rule] / [thin rule] /
[in black:] Design: Mary Albanese / Photograph by
Monika Englund / $5.00 SUN ISBN 915342-39-1.

Contents: Introduction/Clarity/On the War in Vietnam/
Zero/Through the Open Door/A Ball/The Double Move-
ment/"You Shouted to me and said"/"Speaking literally"/
"That Small"/The Island of Koster, 1973.

Location: Roberson

Note: This is a bilingual edition with the Swedish texts
on facing pages.

A125.  TIMES ALONE  1982

[in dark pink:] TIMES ALONE / [in black:] [illustration]
/ TRANSLATED BY ROBERT BLY / GRAYWOLF PRESS
/ PORT TOWNSEND

Collation:  5 1/2 X 8 15/16".  No sign.  18 leaves.  Pp.
[1-36].

Pagination:  p. [1] blank; p. [2] [in dark pink:] "12 /
POEMS FROM SOLEDADES / BY ANTONIO MACHADO";
p. [3] title-page; p. [4] "Translation copyright © by
Robert Bly / Funding for this project was provided in
part by a / grant from the National Endowment for the
Arts. / Published by Graywolf Press, Post Office Box
142, / Port Townsend, Washington 98368."; p. [5] half-
title; pp. [6-29] text; p. [30] blank; p. [31] "Using
Bembo type for the text and for poem titles, / and
Lydian Bold for the numerals and book title, / approxi-
mately 1000 copies of TIMES ALONE / were printed on
Warren's Olde Style paper and / saddle-stitched into
Curtis Tweedweave covers. / An additional 30 numbered
copies were printed on / Nideggan paper, signed by the
translator and case / bound by Marsha Hollingsworth.
The illustration / is by Helen Byers.  David Romtvedt
& Kim Staf- / ford assisted with design and printing.";
pp. [32-36] blank.

Binding:  Orange-red paper covers.  Front:  [in dark
red:] TIMES ALONE / [in black:] [illustration] /
TWELVE POEMS FROM SOLEDADES / BY ANTONIO
MACHADO / TRANSLATED BY ROBERT BLY.  Back:
[in black:] $5.00 (ISBN 0-915308-38-X) / THE ILLUSTRA-
TION IS BY HELEN BYERS / [in dark red:] [publisher's
device:  three wolves] / GRAYWOLF PRESS.

Contents:  Memory from Childhood/"Like Anacreonte"/
"Clouds ripped open"/"The house I loved so much"/On
the Burial of a Friend/"The wind, one brilliant day ..."/
"And he was the demon of my dreams ..."/"From the
doorsill of a dream they call my name ..."/"It doesn't
matter now if the golden wine ..."/"It's possible that
asleep the hand ..."/"If I were a poet"/Field.

Location:  SUNY Buffalo

Note:  Thirty numbered copies were printed on Nideggan
paper, signed by R. B. and case bound by Marsha Hol-
lingsworth.  Poems are on odd-numbered pages with
numerals 1-12 in dark pink on facing pages.

A126.  TIMES ALONE  1983

TIMES ALONE / [row of sixteen ornaments] / SELECTED
POEMS OF / ANTONIO MACHADO / [row of sixteen orna-
ments] / Chosen And Translated By / ROBERT BLY /
[publisher's device:   shield with a cross and five orna-
ments] / Wesleyan University Press / Middletown, Con-
necticut

Collation:  5 3/8 X 8 1/2".  [1-36]$^6$:  96 leaves.  Pp.
[i-xiv] [1] 2-8 [9-10] 11-14 [15] 16-73 [74-76] 77-80
[81] 82-115 [116-118] 119-124 [125] 126-167 [168] 169-173
[174-178].

Pagination:  pp. [i-ii] blank; p. [iii] half-title; p. [iv]
"Other Books By Robert Bly" [lists twenty-one titles];
p. [v] title-page; p. [vi] "Copyright © Antonio Machado
/ Translation copyright  1983 by Robert Bly / All rights
reserved." / [acknowledgments] / "All inquiries and per-
missions requests should be addressed to the Publisher, /
Wesleyan University Press, 110 Mt. Vernon Street, Mid-
dletown, Connecticut / 06457 / Distributed by Harper &
Row Publishers, Keystone Industrial Park, Scranton, /
Pennsylvania 18512" / [Library of Congress Cataloging in
Publication Data] / "Manufactured in the United States of
America / First Edition"; p. [vii] dedication:  "to James
Wright / (1927-1980) / Making things well / is more im-
portant than making them / (A. Machado)"; p. [viii]
blank; pp. [ix-xii] "Contents"; p. [xiii] second half-title;
p. [xiv] blank; pp. [1]-172, text; p. 173, "Translations
of Machado / Available in English"; p. [174] blank; p.
[175] "Times Alone has been composed in Linotype Basker-
/ ville and printed on 60 pound Warren's Olde Style by /
Heritage Printers, Inc., and bound by The Delmar /
Company. / Designed by Joyce Kachergis. / Wesleyan
University Press, 1983. / Robert Bly is the author of ten
books of poetry. / Antonio Machado was a strong influence
on his first / book of poetry, Silence in the Snowy Fields.
Bly has / edited and translated works of Swedish, Ger-
man, Nor- / wegian, and Persian poetry, including that
of Neruba [sic] / and Rilke.  He received the National
Book Award for / poetry in 1968.  His home is in Moose
Lake, Minnesota."; pp. [176-178] blank.

Binding:  Gray cloth covered boards.  Stamped in gold
on spine: [reading across:] BLY / [reading downwards:]
TIMES ALONE  Wesleyan [publisher's device].  End-
papers front and back of white paper slightly heavier
than the sheets.

Contents:  A Few Notes on Antonio Machado/I have walked

along many roads/Memory from Childhood/The square and
the brilliant orange trees/The Burial of a Friend/I listen
to the songs/... The clock struck twelve times .../
Dreams have winding/Faint sound of robes brushing/In
the shady parts of the square/Close to the road we sit
down one day/The Water Wheel/Commentary/Last night,
as I was sleeping/Is my soul asleep?/Clouds ripped open/
... And he was the demon of my dreams .../From the
door sill of a dream they called my name/If I were a poet/
It doesn't matter now if the golden wine/The wind, one
brilliant day, called/The house I loved so much/Like
Anacreonte/Oh, evening full of light!/The evening is
greyish and gloomy/Field/Rebirth/It's possible that while
sleeping the hand/You can know yourself, if you bring
up/Oh, Guadarrama Range/Fall Down/Two poems from
"The Countryside of Soria"/Country Roads/Lord, You
Have Ripped Away/Hope says:  Someday you will/There,
in that high plateau/I dreamt you guided me/One summer
night/Fourteen Poems Chosen from "Moral Proverbs and
Folk Songs"/For Don Francisco Giner de los Rios/Passage-
ways/Rainbow at Night/Songs/Forty Poems Chosen from
"Moral Proverbs and Folk Songs"/To the Great Circle of
Nothing/Abel Martin's Last Lamentations/Siesta/The Death
of the Wounded Child/Coplas/Today's Meditation/Afterword:
An Homage To Machado In 1966/Translations of Machado
Available in English

Location:  SUNY Stony Brook

Note:  This is a bilingual edition with the Spanish texts
on facing pages.


First paper edition:  1983

Title page, collation, pagination, and contents same as
hardbound, except collation has no signatures.

Binding:  Stiff paper covers.  Front cover:  [within a
frame of burnt orange:] [top:  on white banner:] [in
black:] TIMES ALONE / Selected Poems of Antonio
Machado / Translated by Robert Bly / [in black and
white:] [photograph of Machado].  Spine, of burnt
orange:  [reading across:] [in black:] BLY / [reading
downwards:] TIMES ALONE  WESLEYAN [publisher's de-
vice].  Back cover, white with burnt orange bar along
right margin:  [in black:] Poetry / [in burnt orange:]
TIMES ALONE / [in black:] Selected Poems of Antonio
Machado / Translated by Robert Bly / [in burnt orange:]
"The poems written while we are awake ... are / more
original and more beautiful, and sometimes / more wild

than those made from dreams," / Antonio Machado. / [in
black:] [eleven-line statement on Machado] / Cover
photograph: Antonio Machado, Madrid. Foto Alphonso
/ Cover design by Joyce Kachergis / [publisher's device]
[in burnt orange:] WESLEYAN UNIVERSITY PRESS /
Middletown, Connecticut / [in black:] Distributed by
Harper & Row, Publishers / Printed in U.S.A. ISBN
0-8195-6081-2.

Location:   Roberson

A127.   WHEN GRAPES TURN TO WINE   1983

[in purple:] [rule] / [in green:] [row of thirteen orna-
mental devices] / [in purple:] WHEN GRAPES TURN TO
WINE / Versions of Rumi by Robert Bly / Firefly Press,
Cambridge, Mass., 1983 / [in green:] [row of thirteen
ornamental devices] / [in purple:] [rule]

Collation:   7 3/4 X 5 1/2". No sign. 12 leaves. Pp.
[1-24].

Pagination:   p. [1] half-title; p. [2] blank; p. [3] title-
page; p. [4] "Copyright © 1983 by Robert Bly / All
rights reserved. / Printed in the United States of America.
/ ISBN 0-937876-06-2 Trade edition / ISBN 0-937876-07-0
Limited signed edition / FIREFLY PRESS / 607 Franklin
Street / Cambridge MA 02139 / (617) 661-9784" / [ac-
knowledgments for illustration]; p. [5] [twenty-two-line
statement on Rumi and R. B.'s interest in the mystic
poets Kabir, Mirabai, and Rumi; also contains a drawing,
"Two Dervishes."]; p. [6] blank; pp. [7-21] text; p.
[22] blank; p. [23] [in purple, printed over two orna-
mental devices in green:] COLOPHON / [to the left:]
"Five hundred copies have been printed, at / last,
around Hallowe'en, 1983. This book / was designed by
Carl Kay and John / Kristensen and printed by John
Kristensen / on the new 1938 printing press. Dan Carr /
set the Janson type at Golgonooza Letter / Foundry.
The paper is Ticonderoga Text / with Grandee Cover.
The drawings were / printed offset by Red Sun Press. /
Fifty copies are signed by Robert Bly and / bound in
covers made by Bernie Toale / and Joe Zina of Rugg
Road Handmade / Papers. [to the right:] Thanks to
Janet Morgan, Carolyn Lieff, / and to Abraham for the
songs. / The kitten jumped over a wall we cannot / see.
The publisher prays that she will / always land on her
feet. / Firefly Press is now five years old."; p. [24]
blank.

Binding:  Green paper covers printed in purple.  Front:
[rule] / [row of thirteen ornamental devices] / WHEN
GRAPES TURN TO WINE / Versions of Rumi by Robert
Bly / [row of thirteen ornamental devices] / [rule].

Contents:  Winning or losing/Names/It was Adam Who
Wept/When Grapes Turn to Wine/The Edge of the Roof/
The Jar With the Dry Rim/That Journeys are Good/Eating
Poetry/The Mill, the Stone, and the Water/Two Kinds of
Miracles/The Hawk/The Drunkards

Location:  Roberson

Note:  Limited to five hundred copies.  Fifty copies are
signed by R. B. and bound in hardcovers.


A128.  THE RUBY  [Undated]

[white sheet printed in a deep brown-red] [illustration]
/ THE RUBY / [text in a single column] / KABIR / Ver-
sion by Robert Bly

Collation:  7 X 5 1/16".  Single sheet printed on one side
only.

Binding:  None.  All edges trimmed.

Contents:  The Ruby [poem]

Location:  Heyen


EDITIONS


A129.  A POETRY READING AGAINST THE VIETNAM WAR   1966

A / POETRY READING / AGAINST THE / VIETNAM WAR
/ collection gathered by / ROBERT BLY and DAVID RAY
/ published by THE AMERICAN WRITERS / AGAINST THE
VIETNAM WAR / 1966 / Distributed by The Sixties Press

Collation:  5 3/8 X 8 3/8".  [1-8]$^4$:  32 leaves.  Pp.
[1-4] 5-20 [21-24 cut] 25-63 [64].

Pagination:  p. [1] half-title; p. [2] dedication:  "This
book is dedicated / to Senator Fulbright, Senator Morse
/ and Mr. Kennan"; p. [3] title-page; p. [4] [acknowl-
edgments] / "Copyright © 1966 by the Sixties Press, /

Odin House, Madison, Minnesota / Printed in the U.S.A.
By H. Gantt, New York 40, N. Y."; pp. 5-63, text; p.
[64] blank. Note: Pp. 21-24 have been removed from
some copies. They are blank pages. One copy that
was examined had two pages numbered 25.

Binding: Dark blue and white paper covers. Front,
blue paper, [in white:] A / POETRY READING /
AGAINST THE / VIETNAM WAR / Poems and Prose Pieces
By General Araki, / Abraham Lincoln, Galway Kinnell,
[e. e. cum- / mings (name is blacked out with crayon)]
Lawrence Ferlinghetti, Adolf Hitler, / John F. Kennedy,
Louis Simpson, David Ray, / William Stafford, Robinson
Jeffers, I. F. Stone, / George Hitchcock, Lyndon B.
Johnson, Thu- / cydides, James Wright, Walt Whitman,
Rob- / ert Peterson, Robert Bly, Robert Creeley, The /
Author of Ecclesiastes and Others. Spine and back cov-
er, paper white. Spine, reading downwards: [in blue:]
A POETRY READING AGAINST THE VIETNAM WAR.
Back: [in blue:] [seven line statement on the collection]
/ [four-line statement on the American Writers Against the
Vietnam War organization] / Members in April, 1966 /
Robert Bly / Robert Creeley / Lawrence Ferlinghetti /
Donald Hall / George Hitchcock / Galway Kinnell / John
Logan / Robert Lowell / Robert Peterson / David Ray /
Louis Simpson / James Schevill / William Stafford / James
Wright / $1.00. Inside front cover: [in blue:] Walt
Whitman's "To the States."

Contents: Giving to Johnson What Is Johnson's-Bly /
From a Speech Attacking the President in War Time-
Lincoln/To the States-Whitman/Rearmament-Jeffers/The
Way With Dissent-Ray/The Inner Part-Simpson/The Words
of a famous Statesman-Hitler/Where Is Vietnam?-Ferling-
hetti/To Kill in War is Not Murder-Jeffers/from Counter-
Attack-Sasson/A Sonnet-Sasson/Autumn Begins in Martins
Ferry, Ohio-Wright/Life at War-Levertov/[quote from Los
Angeles Times re: napalm]/[quote from Mark Twain] /
Up Rising, Passages 25-Duncan/An American Bombing in
South Vietnam-from Liberation/On the War in Vietnam-
Sonnevi/Johnson's Cabinet Watched by Ants-Bly/Asian
Peace Offers Rejected Without Publication-Bly/Selections
from Thucydides on the Peloponnesian War/At the Bomb
Testing Site-Stafford/Watching the Jet Planes Dive-Staf-
ford/[quote from Johnson's 1964 campaign platform] /
Thought-Whitman/Scattering Flowers-Hitchcock/For the
Minority-Peterson/No Complaints-L. L. Case/On Looking
Through A Book of Photographs Entitled LBJ Country-
Ray/Democracy-Rimbaud/Who Said This [quotes from
General Sadao Araki and Lyndon Johnson]
Part II: On Fallout-Campbell/For No Clear Reason-

Creeley/from Instead of Squash: A Catalog Apropos
Swindle-Burke and Hohn/The U. S. Sailor with the
Japanese Skull-Scott/Reconciliation-Whitman/Who Said
This? [quotes from Hermann Goering and Heinz Schaef-
fer]/Some U. S. Pilots Rebel at Genocide-Fernand Gigon/
Two Paragraphs by Sigmund Freud/American Dreams-
Simpson/Washington Refuses to Aid Burned Vietnamese
Children/[quote from John F. Kennedy]/Napalm [two ex-
cerpts from New York Times]/Hatred of Men With Black
Hair-Bly/Containment but Not Isolation-I. F. Stone/Who
Said This? [quote from Matsuzo Nagai]/Vapor Trail Re-
flected in the Frog Pond-Kinnell/Encouraging Debate-
I. F. Stone.

Location: SUNY Buffalo

Note: Pp. 15, 25, and 41 contain blacked-out passages
"in mourning for the poems of E. E. Cummings, for which
permission was refused by Harcourt Brace."


Second edition: 1967

Title-page, collation, pagination, and contents same as
first edition, except pagination is correct with all blank
pages removed; p. [4] now reads: [acknowledgments]
/ "Library of Congress Catalog Number 66-4861 / Copy-
right © 1966 by the Sixties Press, / Odin House, Madison,
Minnesota / SECOND PRINTING, MARCH 1967 / Printed
in the U. S. A. By H. Gantt, New York 40, N. Y.";
and the blacked-out poems of E. E. Cummings have been
removed and "The Discourse on Peace," by Jacques Pre-
vert added.

Binding: Gray-blue paper covers. Front: [in red:]
A POETRY READING / AGAINST THE VIETNAM WAR /
[illustration in black] / [in red:] Poems and Prose Pieces
By General Araki, Abraham / Lincoln, Galway Kinnell,
Robert Duncan, Lawrence / Ferlinghetti, Adolf Hitler,
John F. Kennedy, Louis / Simpson, David Ray, Herman
Goering, William / Stafford, Robinson Jeffers, I. F.
Stone, George / Hitchcock, Lyndon B. Johnson, Walt
Whitman, James / Wright, Robert Peterson, Robert Cree-
ley, Denise / Levertov, Jacques Prevert, Thucydides
and Others. Spine, reading downwards: [in red:] A
POETRY READING AGAINST THE VIETNAM WAR. Back:
[in red:] [seven-line statement on the collection] / [four-
line statement on the American Writers Against the Viet-
nam War organization] / . / Members in April 1967 /
Robert Bly / Robert Creeley / Lawrence Ferlinghetti /
Mitchell Goodman / Donald Hall / George Hitchcock /

Galway Kinnell / Denise Livertov / John Logan / Robert Lowell / Robert Peterson / David Ray / Louis Simpson / James Schevill / William Stafford / James Wright / $1.00.

Location:  SUNY Buffalo

A130.  THE SEA AND THE HONEYCOMB 1966

[in red:] THE SEA / AND / THE HONEYCOMB / [in black:] A book of poems / Edited by / ROBERT BLY / [in red:] [publisher's device:  horseman with shield and spear surrounded by two birds and a snake] / THE SIX-TIES PRESS / [in black:] 1966

Collation:  5 1/4 X 8 3/16".  [1-8]$^3$ [1-4] [1-8]:  36 leaves.  Pp. [1-4] 5-7 [8-10] 11-20 [21-22] 23-32 [33-34] 35-44 [45-46] 47-56 [57] 58-70 [71-72].

Pagination:  p. [1] half-title; p. [2] blank; p. [3] title-page; p. [4] "Library of Congress Card Catalog Number: / 62-21969 / The drawing on the cover is 'Oiseau' by / Odilon Redon / Printed in The Netherlands"; pp. 5-7, "DROPPING THE READER," [introduction by R. B.]; pp. [8-10] blank; pp. 11-66, text; pp. 67-68, "NOTES AND ACKNOWLEDGEMENTS"; pp. 69-70, "CONTENTS"; pp. [71-72] blank.

Binding:  Gray cloth covered boards, stamped in red. Front:  THE SEA / AND / THE HONEYCOMB.  Spine, reading downwards:  THE SEA AND THE HONEYCOMB THE SIXTIES PRESS.  End-papers front and back of white paper.

Dust jacket:  Front and back covers, spine, paper white. Front:  [in red:] THE SEA AND / [in black:] [illustra-tion] / [in red:] THE HONEYCOMB.  Spine, reading down-wards:  [in red:] THE SEA AND THE HONEYCOMB  THE SIXTIES PRESS.  Back:  [in black:] OTHER BOOKS PUB-LISHED BY THE SIXTIES PRESS / [lists nine titles]. Flyleaves, paper in white.  Front flyleaf:  [in black:] [eighteen-line statement on edition].  Back flyleaf:  [in black:] [thirty-line statement on The Sixties and The Six-ties Press].

Contents:  The Mole-Al-Muntafil/"And sometimes we look"-Azeddin Al Mocadecci/Galley with Oars-Ali Ben Hariq/ Walnut-Andrade/The Owl-Apollinaire/The Fly-Apollinaire/ The Lion-Apollinaire/Fall-Aspenström/The Oriole-Char/To the Tree-Brother-Char/Her Visit During Sleep-Hazm/ Seeds-Hazm/Meetings-Hazm/Separation By Death-Hazm/

Whiteness-Rabbihi/The Storm-Suhaid/"Music"-Jiménez/The
White Horse-Lawrence/"Little Mary"-De Vega/"People pos-
sess four things"-Machado/"If it is good to live"-Machado/
"Near the flowering mountain"-Machado/"In the sea called
woman"-Machado/"Lord, you took from me"-Machado/Fans
XVI-Mallarmé/"Only the birds"-Nabokov/And Suddenly It's
Evening-Quasimono/Death-St. Geraud/"On nights like this"-
St. Geraud/"When our hands are alone"-St. Geraud/
Goodbye-St. Geraud/At the desk-Storm/The Monkey-
Tablata/"Sometimes I go about"-Anonymous/"The moon has
set"-Anonymous/"My Mother"-Anonymous/I Stand and Look-
Whitman/Look Down, Fair Moon-Whitman/The Runner-
Whitman/The Torch-Whitman.

Location:  Piccione

Note:  Original texts of translations appear on pp. 58-66.


First paper edition:  1966

Title page, collation, pagination, and contents same as
hardbound.

Binding:  White paper covers with paper wrappers. De-
sign of wrappers is same as dust jacket design of hard-
bound.

Location:  Piccione


A131.   FORTY POEMS TOUCHING ON RECENT AMERICAN HISTORY
        1970

        FORTY POEMS / TOUCHING ON / RECENT AMERICAN /
        HISTORY / edited by / ROBERT BLY / [publisher's de-
        vice:  horseman with shield and spear surrounded by two
        birds and a snake] / BEACON PRESS BOSTON / [rule] / 3

        Collation:  5 3/8 X 8".  [1-32] [1-16] [1-32]$^2$:  56 leaves.
        Pp. 1-105 [106-112].

        Pagination:  p. 1, half-title; p. 2, blank; p. 3, title-
        page; p. 4, "Copyright © 1970 by Robert Bly / Additional
        copyright notices and acknowledgements appear / at the
        back of the book / Library of Congress catalog card num-
        ber:  76-116906 / Simultaneous casebound and paperback
        editions / International Standard Book Number:  0-8070-
        6422-X (casebound) / 0-8070-6423-8 (paperback) / Beacon
        Press books are published under the auspices of the /
        Unitarian Universalist Association / Published simultaneously

in Canada by Saunders of Toronto, Ltd. / All rights reserved / Printed in the United States of America"; pp. 5-6, "Contents"; pp. 7-17, "Leaping Up Into Political Poetry"; pp. 18-104, text; pp. 105-[106] "Acknowledgements"; pp. [107-112] blank.

Binding: Yellow paper covered boards with olive green cloth spine. Blind stamping of village buildings on front cover. Stamped in black on spine, reading downwards: Robert Bly / 40 Poems Touching on RECENT AMERICAN HISTORY / Beacon Press. End-papers front and back of white paper slightly heavier than the sheets.

Dust jacket: Front and back covers, spine, green paper. Front: [in brown:] FORTY POEMS / Touching on Recent / American History / EDITED BY / Robert Bly / [device] / A SEVENTIES PRESS BOOK. Back: [extended statement by Bly] / [device: village buildings] BEACON PRESS BOSTON 02108. Spine, reading downwards: [in brown:] Robert Bly 40 Poems Touching on RECENT AMERICAN HISTORY Beacon Press.

Contents: To the States: To the States-Whitman/"Iowa, Kansas, Nebraska"-Frumkin/Eisenhower's Visit to Franco, 1959-Wright/How Come?-Ignatow/I Know A Man-Creeley/ In the Oregon Country-Stafford/from Canto 89-Pound/A Warming to Abraham Lincoln-Fombona-Pachano The Dictatorship Of The Flies: On American Island Wars-Moody/Imperator Victus-Crane/To Theodore Roosevelt-Daríŏ/The United Fruit Co.-Neruda/The Dictators-Neruda Recent Wars: The Odor of Blood-McGrath/Carentan O Carentan-Simpson/Night-McGrath/from Ode for the American Dead in Korea-McGrath/Rearmament-Jeffers/I Wish the Wood-Cutter Would Wake Up-Neruda/At the Bomb Testing Site-Stafford/On the Eve-Simpson The People: A Christmas Note for Geraldine Udell-Rexroth /The People-Creeley/from "Paterson: Book II"-Williams/ "Night Here"-Snyder/Los Angeles-Alexander/America-Ginsberg/An Imitator of Billy Sunday-Jiménez/from Dance of Death-García Lorca/The United States-Goethe/The Man in the Dead Machine-Hall/from A Poem Beginning with a Line by Pindar-Duncan/Autumn Begins in Martins Ferry, Ohio-Wright/The Ambassadors-Burford/Shaman Song 12-Fowler/The Mouth of the Hudson-Lowell/Night Journey-Roethke/from The River-Crane/The Dream-Ignatow/Sunrise-García Lorca

Note: Originals of the Poems in Spanish and German

Location: SUNY Buffalo

A132.    THE SEA AND THE HONEYCOMB:    A BOOK OF TINY POEMS
         1971

         THE SEA / AND THE HONEYCOMB / A Book of Tiny
         Poems / edited by / ROBERT BLY / Beacon Press  Boston

         Collation:  5 1/4 X 7 15/16".  [1-32]⁴:  64 leaves.  Pp.
         [i-iv] v-xi [xii-xiv] [1-2] 3-12 [13-14] 15-24 [25-26] 27-
         36 [37-38] 39-48 [49-50] 51-60 [61-62] 63-72 [73-74] 75-
         84 [85-86] 87-101 [102] 103-107 [108-114].

         Pagination:  p. [i] half-title; p. [ii] blank; p. [iii] title-
         page; p. [iv] "Copyright © 1971 by Robert Bly / Library
         of Congress catalog card number:  75-156447 / Interna-
         tional Standard Book Number:  0-8070-6410-6 (casebound)
         / 0-8070-6411-4 (paperback) / Beacon Press books are
         published under the auspices / of the Unitarian Univer-
         salist Association / Published simultaneously in Canada
         by Saunders of Toronto, Ltd. / All rights reserved /
         Printed in the United States of America"; pp. v-viii,
         "Contents"; pp. ix-xi, "Dropping the Reader"; p. [xii]
         blank; p. [1]-101, text; p. [102] blank; pp. 103-104,
         "Notes"; pp. 105-107, "Acknowledgements"; pp. [108-114]
         blank.

         Binding:  Light blue paper covered boards with olive
         green cloth spine.  Blind stamping of village buildings
         on front cover.  Stamped in black on spine, reading
         downwards:  Robert Bly / THE SEA AND THE HONEY-
         COMB / BEACON PRESS.  End-papers front and back of
         white paper slightly heavier than the sheets.

         Contents:  Dropping the Reader-Bly/I. Horsehair in the
         Wild Rose Bushes:  And Suddenly It's Evening-Quasimodo/
         Fall-Aspenström/The Storm-Suhaid/"Sometimes I go about
         pitying myself"-Anonymous/The White Horse-Lawrence/
         The Glow of Wine-Hisn/The Mole-Al-Muntafil/"Music!"-
         Jiménez/"It is good knowing that"-Machado/"Why should
         we call"-Machado
         II.  Divinities of the Snow:  The Owl-Apollinaire/The
         Fly-Apollinaire/"If it is good to live"-Machado/To the
         Tree-Brother with a Few Days Left-Char/"This slowly
         drifting cloud is pitiful"-Dogen/"In this world of infinite
         possibilities"-Ghalib/Walnut-Andrade/"The moon has set"-
         Anonymous/"White inn"-Machado/"Near the flowering moun-
         tain"-Machado
         III.  The Dead on Their Backs:  Look Down, Fair Moon-
         Whitman/The Lion-Apollinaire/The Oriole-Char/At the
         Desk-Storm/The Runner-Whitman/Fans-Mallarmé/Galley
         with Oars-Hariq/"People possess four things"-Machado/
         "In the sea called woman"-Machado/"Lord, you took from
         me what I loved most"-Machado

IV.  Issa:  Ten Haikus
V.  If You Are Still Alive ...:  The Torch-Whitman/A
Farm Picture-Whitman/Sleep-Saint Geraud/Death-Saint
Geraud/"On nights like this the heart journeys to other
islands"-Saint Geraud/"When our hands are alone"-Saint
Geraud/Goodbye-Saint Geraud/"Only the birds are able
to throw off their shadow"-Nabukov [sic]/Earth Hard-
Ignatow/I Stand and Look-Whitman
VI.  The Hill In the Mist:  The Monkey-Tablata/"The
ferryboat, with a bull"-Shiki/"Millionaires"-Shiki/"There
are high clouds"-Shiki/Frightening Things-Shonagon/
The sea grows dark"-Bashō/"The temple bell stops"-
Bashō/"Storm on Mount Asama!"-Bashō/"Dried salmon"-
Bashō/"It's spring, all right"-Bashō
VII.  Love Poems;  Whiteness-Rabbihi/Seeds-Hazm/The
Dawn-Malik/"My mother"-Anonymous/Call it Romance-
Anonymous/"Little Mary"-De Vega/Her Visit During Sleep-
Hazm/Meetings of Those in Love-Hazm/Separation by
Death-Hazm/"And sometimes we look to the end"-Mocadecci

Location:  SUNY Stony Brook

Note:  Originals of Poems in Foreign Languages


First paper edition:  1971

Title page, collation, pagination, and contents same as
hardbound.

Binding:  Stiff paper covers.  Front cover and spine,
paper green-blue.  Front:  [in black:]  BEACON BP
399 $2.45 / THE SEA / AND THE / HONEYCOMB / A
BOOK OF / Tiny Poems / EDITED BY / Robert Bly / [in
red:] A SEVENTIES PRESS BOOK / [publisher's device:
woodcut of horseman with shield and spear surrounded
by two birds and a snake].  Spine, reading across:  [in
black:] BP / 399 [reading downwards:] Robert Bly  THE
SEA AND THE HONEYCOMB  ISBN 6411-4 / BEACON
PRESS.  Back cover, paper white:  [in black:] Beacon
Paperback 399 - Poetry / THE SEA AND THE HONEY-
COMB / edited by Robert Bly / [seventeen-line statement
on the edition] /[four-line statement on R. B.] / Also
Available from Beacon / [lists two titles] / [in red:]
[publisher's device:  village buildings] / BEACON PRESS
BOSTON  02108 / ISBN 0-8070-6411-4.  Along spine edge,
reading downwards:  [in red:] Cover designed by R. C.
Barlett.

Location:  Piccione.

A133.   DAVID IGNATOW:   SELECTED POEMS   1975

> DAVID / IGNATOW / Selected Poems / Chosen, with In-
> troductory Notes / and an Afterword, by / ROBERT BLY
> / Wesleyan University Press / MIDDLETOWN, CONNECTI-
> CUT

Collation:   5 1/2 X 8 7/16".   [1-32]$^4$:   64 leaves.   Pp.
[1-12] 13-27 [28-30] 31-42 [43-44] 45-73 [74-76] 77-90
[91-92] 93-106 [107-108] 109-125 [126] 127-128

Pagination:   p. [1] half-title; p. [2] "BY DAVID IGNA-
TOW" [lists eight titles]; p. [3] title-page; p. [4] "Copy-
right © 1948, 1955, 1956, 1960, 1961, 1962, 1963, 1964,
1965, / 1966, 1967, 1968, 1969, 1970 by David Ignatow /
Copyright © 1975 by Wesleyan University" / [Library of
Congress Cataloging in Publication Data] / "Manufactured
in the United States of America / First edition"; p. [5]
dedication:   "For Bill Bueno / with affection, admiration
/ and fondest memories"; p. [6] "I feel along the edges
of life / for a way / that will lead to open land."; pp.
[7-10] "Contents"; pp. [11]-125, text; p. [126] blank;
pp. 127-128, "An Afterword".

Binding:   Blue cloth covered boards, stamped in silver.
Spine, reading downwards:   DAVID IGNATOW:   Selected
Poems / WESLEYAN.   End-papers front and back of light
brown paper slightly heavier than the sheets.

Contents:   I.   Images of the Wild, Third Thing:   My
beard rough as the beginning/Mystique/Poem (A view of
the mountain from the valley floor)/The Gentle Weight
Lifter/Brief Elegy/To an Apple/Two Voices/Doctor/Earth
Hard/Say Pardon/The Song/A Loose Gown/The Bagel/East
Bronx
II.   Working for a Living:   The Paper Cutter/I See a
Truck/For One Moment/Love Poem for the Forty-Second
Street Library/The Errand Boy I/I Want/Lunchtime/Notes
for a Lecture/The Fisherwoman/Paymaster/The Dream/An
Ecology
III.   What Clings like the Odor of a Goat:   Communion/
News Report/And That Night/No Theory/Sunday at the
State Hospital/Blessing Myself/1960/A Political Cartoon/
How Come?/Against the Evidence/Leaping from Ambush/
Ritual One/Ritual Two/Self-Employed/Spring/Dilemma/
Epitaph/And the Same Words/For My Mother Ill/Playfully/
Last Night/Beautiful and Kind/Brief Cases
IV.   The Struggle between the Statistical Mentality and
Eros:   A First on TV/In Place of Love/Emergency Clinic/
The White Ceiling/With the Door Open/Content/The busi-
nessman is a traitor to himself first/The Business Life/

Nice Guy/The faces that judge me/A Guided Tour through
the Zoo/The Debate/Nurse
V. Living in the City: The Zoo lion/Sales Talk/Where
Nothing is Hidden/Promenade/Pricing/Moving Picture/Get
the Gasworks/An Illusion/Off to the Cemetery/Side by
Side/The Appointment Card
VI. A New Theme: For My Daughter/The Room/Secretly/
The Derelict/A Dialogue/The Open Boat/On the Death of
Winston Churchill/While I Live/All Quiet/An American
Parable/The Life Dance/I wish I understood the beauty/
From a Dream/An Allegory/Rescue the Dead
An Afterword

Location: Southampton Campus Library, Long Island U.

"An Afterward" is reprinted, in part, in B101.

A134. LEAPING POETRY: AN IDEA WITH POEMS AND TRANSLA-
TIONS 1975

LEAPING POETRY / AN IDEA / with POEMS / and /
TRANSLATIONS / ROBERT BLY / A Seventies Press Book
/ BEACON PRESS : BOSTON

Collation: 5 5/16 X 7 15/16". [1-28]⁴: 56 leaves. Pp.
[i-x] 1-93 [94-102].

Pagination: p. [i] half-title; p. [ii] "SEVENTIES PRESS
BOOKS PUBLISHED BY BEACON PRESS" [lists seven ti-
tles]; p. [iii] title-page; p. [iv] "Copyright © 1975 by
Robert Bly / Copyright © 1972 by The Seventies Press /
Beacon Press books are published under the auspices /
of the Unitarian Universalist Association / Published simul-
taneously in hardcover and paperback editions / Simul-
taneous publication in Canada by Saunders of Toronto,
Ltd. / All rights reserved / Printed in the United States
of America / 9 8 7 6 5 4 3 2 1 "; p. [v] [quotations from
Ortega y Gasset and García Lorca]; p. [vi] blank; pp.
[vii-viii] "Contents"; p. [ix] second half-title; p. [x]
blank; pp. 1-93, text; p. [94] blank; pp. [95-96] "Ac-
knowledgements"; pp. [97-102] blank.

Binding: Yellow marbled paper covered boards with brown
cloth spine. Blind stamping of village buildings on front
cover. End-papers front and back of white paper slightly
heavier than the sheets.

Contents: Looking for Dragon Smoke-Bly/Landscape with
Two Graves and an Assyrian Hound-García Lorca/Little
Infinite Poem-García Lorca/The Holy One of the River-

ChuYuan/Fish-Takahashi/Spanish Leaping-Bly/Potato-
Takahashi/Poem to Be Read and Sung-Vallejo/I Have a
Terrible Fear-Vallejo/The Ruined Street-Neruda/And What
if After So Many Words ...-Vallejo/Wild Association-Bly/
Loyalty-Otero/Rundown Church-García Lorca/Something
Like A-Otero/And So?  The Pale Metalloid Heals You ...-
Vallejo/Poetry of Steady Light-Bly/Leaping in Narrative
Poetry-Bly/The Quarrel-García Lorca/Hopping-Bly/Mono-
logue with Its Wife-Ekelöf/Out in the Open-Tranströmer/
The Three Brains-Bly/City That Does Not Sleep-García
Lorca/Surrealism, Rilke, and Listening-Bly/Sonnets to
Orpheus-Rilke/Home Grown Poems-[Bly]/This Life Like
No Other-Orr/Prosepoem to Hart Crane-Knott/from The
Car Crash Poem-Ginsberg/Conjugal-Edson/Repose of Rivers-
Crane/Winter Scene-Young/from Sleepers Joining Hands-
Bly/Two Years Later-Wieners/Crazy Dog Events-Rothen-
berg/Threads IX-Zdonek/Silence-Orr/The Way West Under-
ground-Snyder/from The Newcastle Poem-Pickard.

Location:  Southampton Campus Library of Long Island
University

Note:  This is a partial bilingual edition with the Spanish
texts of selected poems on facing pages.

First paper edition:  1975

Title page and contents same as hardbound.

Collation:  5 5/16 X 7 15/16".  [1-28] [1-36] [1-40]:
52 leaves.  Pp. [i-vi] 1-93 [94-98].

Pagination:  p. [i] half-title; p. [ii] "SEVENTIES PRESS
BOOKS PUBLISHED BY BEACON PRESS" [lists seven ti-
tles]; p. [iii] title-page; p. [iv] copyright notice; pp.
[v-vi] "Contents"; pp. 1-6, "Looking for Dragon Smoke";
pp. 7-93, text; p. [94] blank; pp. [95-96] "Acknowl-
edgements"; pp. [97-98] blank.

Binding:  Front and spine, yellow paper.  Front:  [in
red:] BEACON BP 462 $2.95 / [in black:] LEAPING /
POETRY / An Idea with Poems / and Translations /
Chosen by / Robert Bly / [in red:] A SEVENTIES PRESS
BOOK / [device:  horseman with shield and spear sur-
rounded by two birds and a snake].  Spine, reading
downwards:  [in red:] BP 462  [in black:] Robert Bly
  LEAPING POETRY  [in red:] ISBN 6393-2  BEACON
PRESS.  Back cover, white paper printed in black:
Beacon Paperback 462--Poetry / LEAPING POETRY / An
Idea With Poems And Translations / by Robert Bly /

[note on anthology and R.B.] / [in red:] [publisher's device] / [in black:] BEACON PRESS  BOSTON.

Location:  Patchogue [N. Y.] Public Library

A135.  NEWS OF THE UNIVERSE  1980

NEWS OF THE / UNIVERSE poems / of twofold conscious-ness / chosen and introduced by ROBERT BLY / [photo-graph of a feather] / SIERRA CLUB BOOKS  SAN FRANCISCO

Collation:  6 1/16 X 8 1/2".  [1-16]$^{20}$:  160 leaves. Pp. [i-vi] vii-xiv [1-2] 3-5 [6-7] 8-27 [28-29] 30-77 [78-79] 80-122 [123] 124-181 [182] 183-207 [208-209] 210-248 [249] 250-277 [278-279] 280-293 [294] 295-299 [300] 301-305 [306].

Pagination:  p. [i] half-title; p. [ii] blank; p. [iii] title-page; p. [iv] [eleven-line statement by the Sierra Club] / "Copyright © 1980 by Robert Bly. / All rights reserved. No part of this book may be reproduced in any form / or by any electronic or mechanical means, including in-formation storage and / retrieval systems, without per-mission in writing from the publisher." / [Library of Con-gress Cataloging in Publication Data] / "Designed by James Robertson and Diana Fairbanks, / The Yolla Bolly Press, Covelo, California. / Typeset in Kennerley by Mackenzie-Harris Corp. / Cover photograph by John Hendrickson. / Printed in the United States of America. / 10 9 8 7 6 5 4 3 2 1"; erratum slip inserted between p. [iv] and p. [v]:  "ERRATUM / Please note / The correct ISBN for this title, / NEWS OF THE UNIVERSE:  Poems of / Twofold Consciousness / is:  87156-198-0 / 87156-199-9 pbk."; p. [v] dedication:  "for Kenneth Rexroth / 'One Day the master imagined / a new blossoming.'"; p. [vi] blank; pp. [vii-xiv] "Contents"; pp. [1]-293, text; p. [294] blank; pp. 295-299, "Acknowledgements"; p. [300] blank; pp. 301-305, "Index"; p. [306] blank.

Binding:  Blue paper covered boards, stamped in white. Spine:  NEWS / OF THE / UNI- / VERSE / BLY / SIERRA. End-papers front and back of white paper slightly heavier than the sheets.

Contents:  An Introductory Note/Part One:  The Old Position/The Three Kingdoms of Nature-Lessing/Song of the Cape of Good Hope-Schubart/Lines, from An Essay on Man-Pope/"Lo, the Poor Indian," from An Essay on Man-Pope/A Gentle Echo on Women-Swift/Adam Speaks,

from Paradise Lost-Milton/Dover Beach-Arnold/Part Two:
The Attack on the Old Position/Golden Lines-Nerval/The
Sanctimonious Poets-Hölderlin/The Voice of the Devil, from
The Marriage of Heaven and Hell-Blake/A Memorable Fan-
cy, from The Marriage of Heaven and Hell-Blake/"When
Geometric Diagrams ..."-Novalis/Delfica-Nerval/Intimate
Associations-Baudelaire/The Second Poem the Night-Walker
Wrote-Goethe/"All the Fruit ..."-Hölderlin/Bread and Wine,
Part 7-Hölderlin/Aphorisms, from Pollen and Fragments-
Novalis/The Second Hymn to the Night-Novalis/"Hear the
Voice of the Bard!", from Songs of Experience-Blake/
From a Letter-Keats/A Memorable Fancy, from The Mar-
riage of Heaven and Hell-Blake/The Badger-Clare/Autumn-
Clare/Of Jeoffry, His Cat-Smart/Nutting-Wordsworth/From
"Lines Composed a Few Miles Above Tintern Abbey"-
Wordsworth/To Autumn-Keats/Lines, from The Prelude-
Wordsworth/The Invisible King-Goethe/Mignon-Goethe/
The Holy Longing-Goethe/"Her Face Was in a Bed of Hair"-
Dickinson/From "Walden"-Thoreau/From "The Shepherd's
House"-Vigny/From "Song of Myself"-Whitman/"I Live My
Life," from Book for the Hours of Prayer-Rilke/From
"Introductory Lines," published with The Shadowy Waters-
Yeats/Part Three:  Poems of Twofold Consciousness, Early
Twentieth Century/The Most of It-Frost/Sometimes-Hesse/
Two Look at Two-Frost/After Apple-Picking-Frost/Country
Roads-Jacobsen/Sunflower-Jacobsen/Road's End-Jacobsen/
The First Psalm-Brecht/The Sea-Elephant-Williams/Whales
Weep Not!-Lawrence/Science-Jeffers/Animals-Jeffers/
Voyages II-Crane/Oceans-Jiménez/"The Lamb was Bleating
Softly"-Jiménez/Full Consciousness-Jiménez/Rebirth-
Machado/Casida of the Rose-García Lorca/New York-García
Lorca/Enigmas-Neruda/The Snow Man-Stevens/On the Road
Home-Stevens/Winter Scene-Young/Leda-Rilke/"The Kings
of the World ..."-Rilke/Moving Ahead-Rilke/The Man
Watching-Rilke/ Part Four:  Poems of Twofold Conscious-
ness, 1945-1979/The Signature of all Things-Rexroth/The
Heart of Herakles, from The Lights in the Sky Are Stars-
Rexroth/Autumn Rain, from Mary and the Seasons, Rex-
roth/Waxwings-Francis/This Poem is for Bear-Snyder/
Foxtail Pine-Snyder/Journeys-Snyder/An Embroidery-
Levertov/Come into Animal Presence-Levertov/The Depths-
Levertov/The Owl-Bjørnvig/To Drink-Mistral/The Call-
Supervielle/If the Owl Calls Again-Haines/Dream of the
Lynx-Haines/First Winter Storm-Everson/Winter Ploughing-
Everson/Often I am Permitted to Return to a Meadow-
Duncan/The Experiment That Failed-Logan/Milkweed-
Wright/Her Longing-Roethke/The List-McClure/Beasts-
Wilbur/"A Land Not Mine"-Akhmatova/The Night-Blooming
Cereus-Hayden/A Coal Fire in Winter-McGrath/November
Day at McClure's-Bly/The Origin of the Praise of God-
Bly/Middle of the Way-Kinnell/The Peace of Wild Things-

Berry/Kadish-Ignatow/Darkmotherscream-Voznesensky/
Sayings from the Northern Ice-Stafford/Ultimate Problems-
Stafford/Poets Who Have Appeared in the Last Few Years/
Bunch Grass #37-Sund/All Hallows-Glück/The Voice of the
Power of this World-Hall/Just as the Small Waves Came
Where No Waves Were-Millward/The Death of an Elephant-
Pagnucci/V, from The Angelic Poems-Anhelaki-Rooke/
Lamb-Browne/Silica Carbonate Rock-Berry/Couplets 20-
Mezey/Sleeping in the Forest-Oliver/Mussels-Oliver/The
Power of Maples-Stern/Differences-Bear/The Cows Near
the Graveyard-Nelson/Schubertiana-Tranströmer/On the
Morning of the Third Night Above Nisqually-Ransom/
Library-Jenkins/Violence on Television-Jenkins/Part Five:
The Object Poem/The Delights of the Door-Ponge/The
Oyster-Ponge/Trees Lose Parts of Themselves Inside a
Circle of Fog-Ponge/The Horse-Ponge/The End of Fall-
Ponge/Snake-Lawrence/Study of Two Pears-Stevens/
Rigorists-Moore/The Groundhog-Eberhart/The Sea Wind-
Martinson/The Fish-Bishop/Bats-Jarrell/The Dead Seal
Near McClure's Beach-Bly/Ode to Salt-Neruda/Ode to the
Watermelon-Neruda/Archaic Torso of Apollo-Rilke/The
Panther-Rilke/Palm of the Hand-Rilke/Stone-Simic/Part
Six:   Leaving the house/The Great Sea/Magic Words-after
Nalungiaq/Poor Wolf Speaks-Poor Wolf (Gros Ventre)/Of-
fering-Zuni/Foot Race Song-Pima/Grendel, from Beowulf/
The Daemon Lover/The Falcon/The Name-Rumi/The Drunk-
ards-Rumi/Two Drinking Songs-Tao Yuan-ming/The Simple
Purification-Kabir/The Clay Jug-Kabir/Fish-Takahashi/
Snail-Takahashi/Sparrow in Winter-Takahashi/The Clouds-
Mirabai/Why Mira Can't Return to Her Old House-Mirabai/
Two Meditations as an Afterword/A Meditation on a Poem
of Goethe's/A Meditation on a Yeats Poem.

Location:  SUNY Stony Brook


First paper edition:  1980

Title page, collation, pagination, and contents same as
hardbound, except no erratum is inserted.

Binding:  White paper covers.  Front:  [in black:] NEWS
OF THE / UNIVERSE poems / of twofold consciousness /
[photograph of the sky with a feather floating down] /
chosen and introduced by ROBERT BLY.  Spine:  [in
black:] NEWS / OF THE / UNI- / VERSE / BLY / SIERRA
/ CLUB / BOOKS.  Back:  [in black:] [sixteen-line
statement on the anthology] / [photograph of R.B. by
Jim Kalett] [fourteen-line statement on R.B.] / ISBN 0-
87156-199-9  $7.95.

Location:   Southampton Campus Library of Long Island
University

A136.   TEN LOVE POEMS   1981

TEN / LOVE / POEMS / [drawing of a reindeer] / Anthol-
ogized By / Robert Bly

Collation:   6 x 9".   No sign.   32 leaves.   Pp. [1-16].

Pagination:   p. [1] title-page; p. [2] "© Copyright
Robert Bly 1981 / From Robert Creeley, For Love:   Poems
1950-1960. / Copyright © 1962 by Robert Creeley (New
York: / Charles Scribner's Sons, 1962) Reprinted with
the / permission of Charles Scribner's Sons / Passing
Remark from Stories That Could Be True / by William
Stafford Copyright © 1961 by / William E. Stafford.
Reprinted by permission of / Harper & Row, Publishers,
Inc." / [Library of Congress Cataloging in Publication
Data] / "[publisher's device] Ally Press / P.O. Box
30340 / St. Paul, Minnesota 55175"; p. [3] "Ten Love
Poems" [statement by R. B.]; p. [4] blank; pp. [5-14]
text; p. [15] "CONTRIBUTORS"; p. [16] [ornamental
device of two birds and flowers] / "Ten Love Poems is
set in 12 point Schoolbook / and printed on Howard
Permanlife stock, / formulated to last 250 years."

Binding:   Stiff light blue paper covers.   Front:   [within
a single rule frame in dark blue:] [in dark blue:] TEN
/ LOVE / POEMS / [in black:] [drawing of a reindeer]
/ Anthologized By / Robert Bly.   Back:   [in black:]
$3.50 / [publisher's device] / Ally Press.   End-papers
front and back in blue.

Contents:   The Greeting-Haba/Meetings of Those in Love-
Ibn Hazm/Six-Neruda/My Darling-Goethe/Equal to the
Gods-Sappho/Love Comes Quietly-Creeley/Passing Remark-
Stafford/At Funchal-Tranströmer/Western Wind-Bly/A
Land Not Mine-Akhmatova.

Location:   Roberson

Note:   Twenty-six copies were handcased, signed by
R. B., and lettered A-Z.

Binding:   Dark blue cloth over boards.   Front, stamped
in gold:   TEN / LOVE / POEMS / [rule] / Robert Bly.
Two sets of end-papers front and back.   The first is of
white sheets; the second is of blue-gray sheets.

Location:   SUNY Buffalo

## B. ESSAYS AND NONFICTION

### 1958

B1. "Five Decades of Modern American Poetry." The Fifties, no.
  1, pp. 36–39.
      In 1910 a new imagination appeared heralding a generation
of poets stronger than in the previous forty or fifty years. In
subsequent decades, there was a gradual moving away from this
new imagination and a return to conventional and traditional verse
lacking a new, fresh style. Contributions to this new imagination
are now being made by Spanish, South American, and Swedish
poets. They are writing poetry with a "magnificence of suggestion
and association." American poets must invent a new style to deal
with new subject matter. The most important contemporary experi-
ences will be lost if poets continue to write in the old style.

B2. "Interview with the Head of The New York Times Book Review.
      (May 2, 1958, Mr. Francis Brown)." The Fifties, no. 1,
      pp. 47–51.
      A discussion concerning the credentials of Brown for his
position and the policy of choosing and assigning reviewers. Bly
charges that the reviewing policy is pressured by book advertisers
desiring positive reviews.
      Reprinted in A1.

B3. "The Work of Louis Simpson." Crunk. The Fifties, no. 1,
      pp. 22–25.
      There is a conflict between form and content in Simpson's
poems. While the content denotes a sense of an ending of one age
and the beginning of something new, the forms used are not new,
but traditional. The resulting conflict, while sometimes effective,
is most often self-destructive. Simpson needs to experiment and
utilize new forms. His extensive experiences and worldliness are
evident in his poetry.

### 1959

B4. "Gottfried Benn." The Fifties, no. 2, p. 53.
      An extended contributor note giving biographical informa-
tion and discussing Benn's concept of poetry.

B5. "Juan Ramón Jiménez." The Fifties, no. 2, pp. 54–55.

A contributor note which discusses Jiménez's ideas of soli-
tude and naked poetry as well as providing biographical information.

B6.    "Mirko Tuma." The Fifties, no. 2, p. 59.
       A biographical note.

B7.    "On English and American Poetry." The Fifties, no. 2, pp.
       45-47.
       The British introduced abstraction and the subjection of
emotions to the intellect into poetry. English poetry was becoming
more abstract and intellectual in the process of gradual sterility
and petrification, while American poetry was growing. However,
the effect of English poetry on American poetry in the last one
hundred years has been disastrous. The English tradition should
be abandoned. Teachers of new vigorous poetry are to be found
in the Spanish, French, and German traditions. They are closer
to the mood of modern life and the joy of the unconscious.

B8.    "Paul Celan." The Fifties, no. 3, p. 58.
       A contributor note commenting on the surrealistic nature
of Celan's poems which are deeply sunk in the inward world.

B9.    "The Possibility of New Poetry." The Fifties, no. 2, p. 36.
       Brief statements on the iambic style and repetition. The
iambic style is like a man who gestures too much. The new poetry
has no necessity in the form itself for continuous gesture. When a
gesture is made, therefore, it has great meaning.
       The repetition derived from the Old English style of poetry
tries to explain emotion but has none in it.

B10.   "Some Thoughts on Lorca and Rene Char." The Fifties, no.
       3, pp. 7-9.
       Why hasn't America been able to produce a poet like Gar-
cía Lorca or Char, or to develop new poetry? Other poetries have
passed through surrealism but American poets have not. America
needs to balance her puritanism with poems in which the uncon-
scious winds over the mind.

B11.   "The Work of Donald Hall." Crunk. The Fifties, no. 3,
       pp. 32-46.
       In tracing the development of a relationship between the
poet and middle-class society, Bly notes that Hall's first book,
Exiles and Marriages, is a good example of the poet's unwillingness
to offend the dominating middle-class society which represents "cul-
tural 'father' English." Hall's second book, The Dark Houses, ex-
hibits a dissolution of the "poetic marriage" with the middle class.
Although he is still unable to get away from the middle class, poems
within the book show him capable of development and movement,
and certain poems exhibit an absence of the middle class and a
transition toward an independent state.
       Bly believes that the past ten years have shown poetry and
the middle class to be uncompatible.

B12. "The Work of Robert Creeley." Crunk. The Fifties, no. 2,
      pp. 10-21.
      This essay provides an overview of the work of the Black
Mountain poets and the publication of the Black Mountain Review as
well as Creeley's poetry. The Black Mountain poets and the "San
Francisco" people (Ginsberg, Snyder, Rumaker, et al.) are an
amorphous group, sharing a common respect for William Carlos Wil-
liams and Ezra Pound, independent thought, a dislike of hacks and
innocents, and a kind of American isolationism from the newer po-
etry of Europe.
      Creeley's weaknesses, like the others within the Black Moun-
tain/San Francisco group, is that he does not share in any of the
great traditions of modern poetry:  use of imagery, going deeply
into one's self, simple description of modern life, or daring self-
revelation.  What is modern about him is his use of words, his
honest and convincing utilization of language, and the presence of
women in his poems.
      His poetry is isolated from the great richness of daring of
Spanish and French poetry, and is too entirely based on the Amer-
ican tradition which is not rich enough.  He should try to deepen
his own imagination by searching for more richness of language and
image.


                                1960


B13. "A Note on Antonio Machado." The Sixties, no. 4 (Fall),
      14-15.
      A biographical and anecdotal note.

B14. "On Current Poetry in America." The Sixties, no. 4 (Fall),
      28-29.
      There is a disharmony between form and content in Amer-
ican poetry.  The form must begin to reflect the content, as in the
poetry of Jiménez and Trakl.

B15. "The Work of W. S. Merwin." Crunk. The Sixties, no. 4
      (Fall), 32-43.
      Merwin's best poems show a "strange kind of genius,"
yet the predominant characteristic of the poems is a "wastage of
words."  The poems do not dive to the core of emotions.  He is
representative of the contemporary poet caught midway between be-
ing a prose writer and being a poet.  Poets are using written lan-
guage (prose language) rather than spoken language.  The poems
become about things rather than about the poet himself.  There is
a lack of personal speech.
      The essay is something less than an analysis of Merwin's
work, and more a vehicle for Bly to examine the idea of prose
language appearing in poetry.

1961

B16.   "Poetry in an Age of Expansion."  Nation, 192 (22 April),
       350-354.
       A prevailing mood of constriction in the nineteenth cen-
tury resulted in the iconoclastic tradition.  Today the condition is
reversed--the prevailing mood is of infinite expansion.  Iconoclasm,
therefore, is out of place; old forms and ideas are not criticized
and replaced.  The poem, in response to the expansiveness, will
become shorter and more intense, and great work will emerge from
a vision of life different from the present mood of expansion.
There will come a poetry of things that do not yet exist and
"thoughts not yet thought"; a poetry of instinct.

B17.   "Some Notes on French Poetry."  The Sixties, no. 5 (Fall),
       66-70.
       French poetry is distinguished by its "voyage into the
sea of imagination."  There is a true interest in the deep interior
life beneath the reason.  American poets have a fear of the uncon-
scious.  A false impression of French poetry is gained from the
writings of T. S. Eliot and Ezra Pound because of their belief that
only ugly things emerge from the unconscious.  American poets
must begin to trust the unconscious and live more in solitude.

B18.   "The Work of John Logan."  Crunk.  The Sixties, no. 5
       (Fall), 77-87.
       Logan is a poet of authentic vigor and originality.  His
poems express the sense of greatness inside certain human beings.
The content of his poems is against the generally accepted ideas,
whether of personality, sainthood, love, or poetry.


1962

B19.   "A Fable."  The Sixties, no. 6 (Spring), 62.
       A brief satiric piece concerning the "violent criticism"
that greeted the first edition of New Poets of England and America
from the older generation of poets and critics.
       Reprinted in B32.

B20.   "On the Necessary Aestheticism of Modern Poetry."  The
       Sixties, no. 6 (Spring), 22-24.
       In taking exception to John Crowe Ransom's essay "Poets
Without Laurels" (in The World's Body), which states that there is
no interest in moral questions or public life in modern poetry, Bly
argues that modern poetry is not restricted to English language
and that Ransom should read the contemporary French, Spanish,
or German poets.  The aesthetic and moral interests of a poem are
equally important and must be present.  The greatness of modern
poetry lies in the very fact that it is able to describe the sights and
sounds of modern life as well as deal with powerful ideas.

B21.  "Translations from Gunnar Ekelöf."  Hudson Review, 15
      (Winter 1962/1963), 546-547.
      A brief note prefacing poems translated by Christina
Bratt and Bly.  The popularity of Ekelöf, despite his difficulty,
is cited.  "He is an uncomfortable poet, who tries to make the
reader conscious of lies.  His work attacks the moralistic personal-
ity.  He divides all personalities into the innocent, the moralistic,
and the uncommitted."
      Reprinted, in part, in B121.


## 1963


B22.  "Henrik Ibsen:  On the Murder of Abraham Lincoln."  Na-
      tion, 196 (16 February), 142.
      A note prefacing the poem.  Ibsen was struck by the
Europeans' reaction to Lincoln's assassination when they take their
own brutal acts so calmly.  He utilized the poem to remind readers
of European atrocities.  Ibsen believed betrayal had become a cor-
nerstone of European civilization and was now spreading to America.
Bly comments that his translation is faithful in meaning, but does
not reproduce the poem's rhyme or meter.

B23.  "A Wrong Turning in American Poetry."  Choice:  A Magazine
      of Poetry and Photography, no. 3, pp. 33-47.
      One of the most well presented of Bly's major poetic
statements.  Twentieth-century American poetry has evolved through
three clearly marked psychic steps:  objectivist generation--Eliot,
Pound, Moore, and Williams; metaphysical generation--Eberhart and
Tate; and hysterical--Lowell, Berryman, Schwartz, et al.  Develop-
ing out of Eliot's concept of the "objective correlative," American
poetry is without a center.  Its trust is in the outward world and
it drifts aimlessly in this outer world.  It is a poetry devoid of
politics and revolutionary feelings resulting in "fabricated gross-
ness."  It places intellectual statements about passion above passion.
This is poetry without spiritual life.  In sharp contrast to it is the
work of the European poets, especially the Spanish, whose poetry
participates in an inward movement and involves the consciousness
in the poem.
      Reprinted in B118.


## 1964


B24.  "The Surprise of Neruda."  The Sixties, no. 7 (Winter),
      18-19.
      Pablo Neruda's imagination can see the hidden connections
between conscious and unconscious substance with assurance.  He
has confidence in what is hidden.  He proves literary conventions
wrong:  that to a surrealist the outer world has no reality, that
political poetry cannot be good poetry, and that sophisticated poetry
can also be wildly romantic.

B25.  "The Work of James Dickey."  Crunk.  The Sixties, no. 7
      (Winter), 41-57.
          Bly traces the spiritual struggle in Dickey's poems of "an
      animal to become a man" and examines the predominance of animals
      in Dickey's early poems.  There is a constant mingling of the idea
      of divinity and the idea of the animal world in In the Stone and
      Drowning with Others.  Dickey has a staggering gift for the image.
      He discards a mediocre charade and ignores everything that is or-
      dinary and average.  He has the ability to carry tremendous physi-
      cal energy into his poems.  However, his narcissism pushes other
      people out of the poems.  His lines exhibit little texture and have
      a forced dactyllic rhythm.  He uses ordinary language too much
      and is too long-winded, relying on rhetorical structures.


                                  1966

B26.  "Concerning the Little Magazines:  Something Like a Sym-
          posium."  Carleton Miscellany, 7 (Spring), 20-22.
          Following his self-created role, Bly typically feels he
      must insert a "few rude words."  American little magazines are,
      for the most part, utterly pointless.  The editors have become
      permissive.  Daring poems are no longer printed.  They continue
      the mediocrity of the status quo.  The quarterlies should publish
      only when they have something good to say, not to follow a set
      schedule of publication.

B27.  "The Dead World and the Live World."  The Sixties, no. 8
          (Spring), 2-7.
          An essential statement of Bly's belief in a poetry that
      embodies the "news of the universe."  He differentiates between
      two types of poetry:  poetry that is locked inside the ego and
      poetry that reaches out in waves over everything that is alive.
      The former type studies the human mind as if it was locked off
      from the universe, isolated and independent.  There is a need for
      more of the latter type of poetry which possesses an awareness of
      the "Gott-natur," the holy-nature, which is an inner energy that
      senses the interdependence of all things alive, and longs to bring
      them together inside a work of art.  Poetry needs to go deep
      within the human being, beyond the ego, and, at the same time,
      to be aware of other beings.

B28.  "A Statement About 'Hatred of Men with Black Hair'."  In
          Poems for Young Readers:  Selections from Their Own
          Writing by Poets Attending the Houston Festival of Con-
          temporary Poetry.  56th Annual NCTE Convention, Novem-
          ber 24-26, 1966.  [Champaign, IL:]  National Council of
          Teachers of English, [1967?], p. 14.
          It is wrong to study a poem by meter or form; the con-
      tent is the important consideration.  The poem is concerned with
      the Vietnam War.

B29.   "Voznesensky and His Translators."   Kayak, no. 9, pp. 46-
          48.
          Voznesensky's message to both the young and old is to
have compassion, be responsible, be a human being.   In the two
available selections in English, Antiworlds and Selected Poems, the
translators are at a loss emotionally.   They do not know what to
do with the spontaneous and fiery feelings of the originals.
See B33 and P18.

B30.   "The Work of James Wright."   Crunk.   The Sixties, no. 8
          (Spring), 52-78.
          A wide ranging and commendatory essay on Wright's
poetry.   From his first volume, The Green Wall, Wright's poetry
goes against the dominant tendency in American and English poetry
to be tame and divorced from the wild world.   He introduces feroc-
ity and terror in his work.
          The evolution of his work from Saint Judas to The Branch
Will Not Break is examined with particular attention to the influ-
ence of Trakl.
          A discussion of the critical response to Wright's poetry leads
into a discourse on the two different views of poetry which emerge
from two different areas of consciousness.   This involves an exam-
ination of the reaction to the last line in "Lying in a Hammock at
William Duffy's Farm in Pine Island, Minnesota."
          There is a tendency in his poems not to look deeply enough
into hard material, but to gloss over it.   This results in a kind of
softness and romanticization; a tendency to evade practical prob-
lems.   Wright's instinct is to push everything to extremes.   He has
an unusual intellectual enthusiasm and a personality that drives him
forward regardless of the consequences.
          Reprinted in B117.


                                          1967


B31.   "A Conversation About [Miguel] Hernandez."   [Interview with
          Pablo Neruda, June 12, 1966].   The Sixties, no. 9 (Spring),
          4-6.
          Neruda speaks of his first meeting with Hernandez as well
as his perceptions of him as a person.   He also discusses the pub-
lication of Hernandez's poems and his treatment by Franco.   Neruda
briefly gives his opinion on recent Spanish poetry.
          Reprinted in B68.

B32.   "A Fable by Robert Bly."   Tennessee Poetry Journal, 1
          (Fall), 41.
          Reprint of B19.

B33.   "Answers to Correspondents."   Kayak, no. 11, pp. 28-31.
          A reply to George Bowering's letter concerning Anselm
Hollo's translations of Andrei Voznesensky.   Bly admits that he

missed Hollo's translations but states that they are no better than
the others he previously reviewed, and, in effect, continues his
review by focusing on Hollo's work. As a translator, Hollo is "an
Anglo-Finnish version of Robert Lowell." He makes mistakes deli-
berately. Translators like Lowell and Hollo have a "fantastic arro-
gance" deciding to rewrite anyone. Bly concludes with "some fine
things" concerning Hollo's translations. See B29 and P18.

B34.  "The First Ten Issues of Kayak, no. 12, pp. 45-49.
        The different types of criticism are discussed and Bly
calls for a criticism by those interested in the same type of poetry
attacking each other sharply but still maintaining respect and af-
fection for each other. He then proceeds to put into practice his
theory.
        George Hitchcock is too permissive an editor. He encourages
poets' weaknesses. The "foggy" imagery of Kayak poems is dis-
cussed and the typical Kayak poet is defined. The poet mistakes
a way of living for a style. The poet leads an over-socialized life
and must seek solitude to write true poetry. Despite its shortcom-
ings, Kayak offers an alternative to the "trapped, small-boned,
apologetic, feverish, glassy, intellectual fluttering."

B35.  "Leaping Up into Political Poetry." London Magazine, 7
        (Spring), 82-87.
        An examination of why America has had so few real politi-
cal poets. American poets can, generally, be divided into two
groups: those occasionally courageous in public statements but
whose poetry lacks political energy, and those who utilize political
language in their poetry but negate it by acting "like clowns."
Political poems and personal poems are compared and contrasted.
Yeats and Neruda have written the greatest political poetry of the
twentieth century to date, and Whitman was the "first true politi-
cal poet" in the United States.
        This is the introduction to Forty Poems Touching on Recent
American History.
        Reprinted in B124. See B37.

B36.  "Looking for Dragon Smoke." Stand, 9 (no. 1), 10-12.
        An important essay, central to an understanding of Bly's
poetics. Ancient and classical literature contained leaps from the
known to the unknown parts of the mind. As Christianity became
dominant, this leaping occurred less and less often. In forming a
distinction between spiritual and animal energy, Christianity worked
against the leap. There was a loss of associative freedom in Euro-
pean poetry after the thirteenth century. A rationalist intelligence
developed at the expense of psychic flight. William Blake took the
initial step in bringing the psychic life back to poetry. By the
end of the nineteenth century, helped by the influence of Freud,
the poem and dream had been set free, and a fantastic energy and
excitement was given to modern European poetry.
        Association has not taken hold in the United States. There

has been a constant loss and recovery of it in American poetry.
The swift movement of the psyche in American poetry is always
sidetracked by technique which constrains. The emphasis in United
States poetry is erroneously placed on technique. Technique can-
not aid in the writing of the intense poem.
   Reprinted in B50, B58, and B67. This is the shorter original
essay which was later expanded. The annotation given here is for
Bly's final version.

B37. "On Political Poetry." Nation, 204 (24 April), 522-524.
   A shortened version of B35.

B38. "The Work of Denise Levertov." Crunk. The Sixties, no. 9
   (Spring), 48-65.
   The weaknesses of Levertov's earlier works were a lack
of vision (most of her objective poems end as evasions of herself)
and the absence of real ideas. She offered only liberal attitudes
derived mostly from William Carlos Williams. Her later work tends
toward the sentimental and talky connected by a humorless egotism.
She has been freed from English literary language by the influence
of Robert Creeley and Williams, yet she clings so closely to Creeley
and Robert Duncan that she has blocked her recent development.
She has, however, the touch of a "genuine artist." Her "words
come alive by mysterious, almost occult means."

1968

B39. "Harry Martinson." Unicorn Journal, (Spring), 58.
   Brief introduction to eight poems.

B40. "My Counsel: Stop War." American Dialog, 5 (Winter, 1968-
   69), 29.
   Text of acceptance speech for 1968 National Book Award
for Poetry. See B46 and B49.

B41. "Note." Tennessee Poetry Journal, 1 (Winter), 18.
   Reprint of the introduction to The Lion's Tail and Eyes.

B42. "A Note on Olaf Bull." The Sixties, no. 10 (Summer), 38-39.
   Bull is a poet of suffering. He is not embarrassed by his
suffering; he allows it to be seen in a clear light.

B43. "Notes on Five Norwegian Poets." The Sixties, no. 10 (Sum-
   mer), 54-55.
   Brief entries on Ibsen, Gunnar Reiss-Anderson, Emil
Boyson, Claes Gill, and Peter Holm.

B44. "On Pablo Neruda." Nation, 206 (25 March), 414-417.
   An appreciation of Neruda as a poet and a person. The
essay consists of Bly's usual mixture of biographical fact, long

quotations from Neruda poems, and his espousal of critical theory
which places American poets in a comparatively lesser light than
Neruda.  Much of the discussion is centered around the poems in
Residencia en Tierra which contains "the greatest surrealist poems
yet written in a Western language."
This is probably the best single source for Bly's thoughts on
Neruda and his poetry.
Reprinted in B45.

B45.  "On Pablo Neruda."  London Magazine NS, 8 (July), 24-35.
Reprint of B44.

B46.  "A Poet on Vietnam; Murder as a Prudent Policy."  Common-
weal, 88 (22 March), 17.
Text of acceptance speech for 1968 National Book Award
for Poetry.  See B40 and B49.

B47.  "Poetry--What Is It Saying and to Whom?"  American Dialog,
5 (Winter 1968-69), 28.
American poets are the only artists not losing their
dreams.  Writers of fiction and playwrights are showing very little
energy.  They have lost faith in the power of their work.  Poetry
has considerable and increasing political and private energy.  Only
poetry has come into a higher state of consciousness, yet it must
find ways to go into still more intense states of consciousness.

B48.  "Rolf Jacobsen."  The Sixties, no. 10 (Summer), 54-55.
Jacobsen is the most "modern" Norwegian poet and one of
the freshest and most original poets in Europe.  His poetry reflects
a realization of language and self-acceptance.


1969

B49.  "Acceptance of the National Book Award for Poetry, March 6,
1968."  Tennessee Poetry Journal, 2 (Winter), 14-15.
Text of acceptance speech for 1968 National Book Award
for Poetry.  See B40 and B46.

B50.  "Looking for Dragon Smoke."  In Naked Poetry: Recent
American Poetry in Open Forms.  Ed. Stephen Berg and
Robert Mezey.  Indianapolis:  Bobbs-Merrill, pp. 161-164.
Reprint of B36.

B51.  "Private Gardens, Cloisters, Silent Women."  Nation, 209 (7
July), 17.
A variation of the introduction to Forty Poems of Juan
Ramón Jiménez.  Jiménez's poetry "pulls the psyche toward pleasure.
His poems are an elaborate defense of the pleasure principle."
Jiménez emphasizes how the poet lives--one must live to feel ecstasy
--and a poem means ecstasy.
See A74.

B52. "Tomas Tranströmer." Field, no. 1 (Fall), 60-61.
      Tranströmer is the best poet to appear in Sweden in
some years. He has a strange genius for the image. The beauti-
ful quality of his poems is the space that is in them. They have
a surprise and mystery that never fails.

## 1970

B53. "For Alden Nowlan, with Admiration." In Playing the Jesus
      Game: Selected Poems. Alden Nowlan. Trumansburg,
      NY: New/Books, pp. 5-10.
      A tribute to Nowlan and his poetry. Bly emphasizes the
clarity and descriptive quality of his language, and Nowlan's will-
ingness to confront and explore the chaos of life.
      Reprinted in B54.

B54. "For Alden Nowlan, with Admiration." Tennessee Poetry
      Journal, 4 (Fall), 6-10.
      Reprint of B53.

B55. "Some Notes on Donald Hall." Field, no. 2 (Spring), 57-61.
      Hall is not a prolific poet. He does not have a large
number of good poems, but when they are good, they are solid all
the way through and absolutely genuine. Two dominant character-
istics of his poetry are the grief for the permanent loss to civili-
zation--the loss of manliness and moral nobility, and the wonder at
the natural processes--animal processes, vegetable processes, and
instinctual change.

B56. "What About Poetry." Prairie Schooner, 44 (Summer), 146
      [146-150].
      A brief statement entitled "Crossing Roads." What Bly
loves in poetry are the mysterious lines that cross: the roads that
start as political energy and end in spiritual energy, those that
start in solitude and end in human love, or those that begin in
primitive energy and become spiritual energy.

## 1971

B57. "Commentary" [on "A Missouri Traveller Writes Home: 1846"
      and "Hatred of Men with Black Hair"]. In The Literature
      of the American West. Ed. J. Golden Taylor. Boston:
      Houghton Mifflin Co., pp. 395-396.
      Bly links the two poems by the identification of the mur-
der of the American Indian with the murder of Asian peoples. The
Vietnam War is like a ritual of repetition in regard to the white
man's relationship with the Indian.

B58. "En Quete de Fumee de Dragon." Les Lettres Nouvelles,

(December 1971/January 1972), 199–205.
Reprint of B 36.

B 59.   "John Logan's Field of Force."  <u>Voyages</u>, 4 (Spring 1971/
        Spring 1972), 29–36.
            A tribute to Logan and his ability to achieve a prominent
and respectful position as a poet despite the lack of support from
major schools or their magazines because of Logan's concept of
Christianity.
            Powerful phrasing and extraordinary range of language are
characteristic of Logan's poetry.  The language is used to build
rather than reflect something; it is muscular and masculine.  He is
one of the very few masters of sound we now have alive.  His
poetry is able to move the reader because of its openness and body
sound.

B 60.   "Symposium:  What's New in American and Canadian Poetry."
        <u>New</u>, 15 (April/May), 17–20.
            Either because of editing or Bly's style, this essay begins
as if it were the middle of a conversation.  Bly typically uses long
poem passages when he would be better off expanding his own ideas
and then supporting them with the poems.
            There is a new stage of father-consciousness emerging, one
of spiritual inflation.  The poetry of spiritual inflation is marked
by obsessive disorder, great heartiness toward daily life, and an
assumption of unearned tenderness.

B 61.   "Words Emerging from Objects Again."  In <u>Everything Falling</u>.
        William Pillin.  Santa Cruz, CA:  Kayak Books, pp. 5–11.
            The foreword to the book and a tribute to Pillin's poetry.
Pillin's good poems have a curious mingling of mind sediments in
them (different layers of the mind).  He is able to free his mental
powers because of the physical labor he must perform to support
himself.  This labor has contributed to the growth of this art.
Brief biographical material is given, and a few poems are briefly
analyzed.


                              <u>1972</u>

B 62.   "American Poetry:  On the Way to the Hermetic."  <u>Books
        Abroad</u>, 46 (Winter), 17–24.
            A cogent essay in which Bly delineates five stages or
descents.  The first stage is when the soul and invisible world
enter into a poem but the poet has no faith in it.  Stage two is
when language brings forward the eternal world and an unseen
state side by side.  When the poet is still drawn to the external
world but the inner energies are triumphant, he is at the third
stage.  This is where many American poets are now.  Poetry ᵒf
the fourth descent moves forward on inner energies; the battle
with the world is no longer in the poem.  In the final stage the

poet's energy is separated from his dominant personality. The poem is able to avoid the past. The outer world falls away and what is left is the psyche moving in the psyche.

The fault of Westerners is their desire to go immediately to the deepest level without going through the other stages on the way.

B63.  "García Lorca and Desire." New Letters, 38 (Summer), [3]-6.

Desire-energy pervades García Lorca's poems. All he writes about is what he loves, what he takes delight in, what he wants. When García Lorca came to New York City his desire-energy became pent up and burst out in wild images in poems of desperate power and compassion.

Reprinted in B120.

B64.  "Home Grown Poems." The Seventies, no. 1 (Spring), 81.

American poets tend to be specialists in one world. They are exclusively literary. When it comes to writing leaping poetry, American poets are "the dolts."

B65.  "Hopping." The Seventies, no. 1 (Spring), 54-56.

The St. Mark's and Bolinas group of poets after John Ashbery do not approach the poem with emotion, but rather pleasure. This is not to deny the talent, but they are not able to make leaps from one point to another; they are merely staying within one part of the mind, hopping, as it were. They have a leisure-class mood about them, products of a rich country, seeing nothing to fight for, and never fighting.

Reprinted in B102.

B66.  "Living Out Dreams." Stinktree, no. 2 (November), 18-19.

Thoughts on John Haines in reaction to his Stone Harp and Twenty Poems. Haines is a "mysterious poet," i.e., a genuine poet. He is living out a dream of a disintegrating community. He must avoid developing a sense of superiority; a chilling of the heart.

B67.  "Looking for Dragon Smoke." The Seventies, no. 1 (Spring), 3-8.

The revised essay in which the beginning discussion concerning leaping is expanded.

See B36. Reprinted in B102.

B68.  "Pablo Neruda: Conversation About Hernandez." In Miguel Hernandez and Blas De Otero: Selected Poems. Ed. Timothy Baland and Hardie St. Martin. Boston: Beacon Press, pp. 38-40.

Reprint of B31.

B69.  "Poetry of Steady Light." The Seventies, no. 1 (Spring), 48-49.

Leaping poetry is not the only good kind of poetry.
There are two types of poetry that do not leap: the dull poetry
where the poet dislikes all parts of his psyche, and the poetry
where the poet remains by choice in one part of his psyche. In
this latter type, the poem gives off a steady light. Robert Creeley
is this type of poet.

B70. "Spanish Leaping." The Seventies, no. 1 (Spring), 16-21.
The difference between Spanish and French surrealism
is that the Spanish has a great deal of emotion. The poet enters
the poem excited, with emotions alive. Powerful feelings make the
mind associate faster. An important concept is that of "duende,"
a sense of the presence of death which allows the poet to brush
past death and in that presence to associate faster.
Reprinted in B102.

B71. "Stephen Mooney...." Chelsea, no. 30/31 (June), 117-119.
A tribute to and reminiscence of Stephen Mooney, poet,
teacher, and editor of the Tennessee Poetry Journal.

B72. "Surrealism, Rilke, and Listening." The Seventies, no. 1
(Spring), 74-76.
García Lorca, as a leaping poet, is discussed in relation-
ship to surrealism. Surrealism is weak in the United States be-
cause North Americans are obsessed with unity and identity.
Rilke is the greatest spiritual poet of the twentieth century,
and the greatest poet of the new brain. He described the powers
of leaping from one part of the brain to another as listening.

B73. "The Three Brains." The Seventies, no. 1 (Spring), 61-69.
An expansion of Paul MacLean's theory of three brains,
each being independent to some extent: the reptile brain, the
mammal brain, and the new brain. Poets, like anyone, can be
dominated by one of the brains. There is a constant competition
among the three brains for available energy. Through meditation,
transfer of energy can be achieved from the reptile brain to the
mammal brain, and from the mammal brain to the ecstasy of the
new brain. Poets should try to bring all three brains into their
poetry.
Reprinted in B102.

B74. "Wild Association." The Seventies, no. 1 (Spring), 30-32.
There is an absence of the concept of association in
American critical thought regarding poetry. Association is not con-
sidered to be a form of content. Spanish poets of this century,
however, loved the new paths of association. Their ecstatic widen-
ing of association has been denied to American poets because Span-
ish poetry is underrated and underread. The great Spanish leaps
were lost in the academic translations of the 1940's and 1950's, and
there was a grudge by American critics and academics against sur-
realism.
Reprinted in B102.

## 1973

B75.  "Developing the Underneath." <u>American Poetry Review</u>, 2
      (November/December), 44-45.
      Bly applies jung's four-intelligences theory to Louis
Simpson, James Tate, Ai, and Galway Kinnell.  Poets must respect
and develop their inferior functions.  If the underneath or weaker
function is not developed, there is no poetry, or the poetry will
die out.  Literary theory is achieved through the development of
the weaker function.  Critics do not encourage the development of
auxiliary powers.  They prefer to categorize poets by the function
that appears first.
      See P91 and P99.

B76.  "The Problem with Exclusive Rights." <u>American Poetry Re-</u>
      <u>view</u>, 2 (May/June) 48-50.
      A discussion of the situation regarding the translation
of Pablo Neruda because of the granting of exclusive rights, speci-
fically New Directions' exclusive rights to <u>Residencia en la Tierra</u>,
and Donald Walsh's translation of <u>Residencia One</u> as opposed to
that of Lewis Hyde.  Bly opposes lengthy exclusive rights, stating
that "great poetry ought to be translated every ten years or so."
Exclusive rights also favor older, recognized translators, thus
locking out younger ones and thereby stiffling their development.
      In comparing the two translators, Bly finds "Hyde's tone [to
be] closer to Neruda's."  Walsh's translations are hasty.  Bly advo-
cates that all American poets and translators "never sign a contract
that provides for exclusive rights on poems," and that they "never
translate any foreign poet who ... signs exclusive contracts."

B77.  "Translations from Harry Martinson." <u>New Letters</u>, 39
      (Spring), [58].
      A brief introductory note to three poems.

B78.  "The War Between Memory and Imagination." <u>American Poetry</u>
      <u>Review</u>, 2 (September/October), 49-50.
      "There is a mental war going on always between the two
principles of 'memory' and 'imagination'," between recording experi-
ence and actual experience itself.  Harold Bloom is an advocate of
memory and academic influence.  Bly fears that academic critics will
attempt to affect the course of poetry by overpriaisng poets of
"memory."  He further criticizes Bloom's work concerning contempo-
rary poetry, or the new academia he believes American poetry is
entering.
      Reprinted, in part, in B87.

## 1974

B79.  "The Network and the Community." <u>American Poetry Review</u>,
      3 (January/February), 19-21.

Further speculations on the four-intelligences system or the "four ways of grasping the world." The weakest mode is the "channel opening you to the rest of humanity." He discusses Philip Slater's distinction between a community and a network. Networks have no territory and are composed of people with the same dominant function; they are closed circuits. A community consists of whole ranges of people with different functions developed.

Poets are analyzed in terms of networks and communities. There is a network of poets rather than a community. They constitute "flying fragments" with no sense of a community or of the importance of the group itself and its continuity. David Ignatow is cited as the American poet with the greatest sense of community.

B80.   "Reflections on the Origins of Poetic Form." Field, no. 10
       (Spring), 31-35.
       Some thoughts in response to Donald Hall's essay on the origins of poetic form ("Goatfoot, Milktongue, Twinbird:  The Psychic Origins of Poetic Form," Field, no. 9). Hall speculates that three sensualities, all linked with infancy, lie behind what is called "poetic form": mouth-sensibility, dance-sensibility, and appearance-disappearance sensibility. Bly agrees that the three sensibilities are present, but emphasizes that this infantile influence is on form only. The content pole is influenced by adulthood. He briefly applies this concept to free verse.
       There is a very abrupt end to the essay, leaving the reader with a strong sense of incomplete thoughts.
       Reprinted in B103.

B81.   "Starting a Cooperative House." American Poetry Review, 3
       (March/April), 12-13.
       A description of the Minnesota Writers' Publishing House, a publishing venture based on the Swedish Writers' Publishing House. The purpose is to allow poets, especially younger poets, the opportunity to publish at affordable prices.
       Reprinted in B82.

B82.   "Starting a Cooperative House." Urban Review, 7 (no. 4),
       [327]-330.
       Reprint of B81.


                                  1975

B83.   "The Guest Word: Eugenio Montale: Ascending." New
       York Times Book Review, 9 November, p. 63.
       A tribute to Montale on the occasion of his being awarded the Nobel Prize. He has an intense relation to objects, energy flows from the object into him, hypnotizing him. Also discussed is Montale's sound (magnificent and powerful) as well as the relationship of his three main books to the movement in Dante's Divine Comedy and their similar dependency upon women for the ascent.

B84. "Growing Up in Minnesota." American Poetry Review, 4
    (January/February), 4-6.
    An autobiographical essay which offers interesting hints
at Bly's childhood and the relationship with his mother and father.
He was a typical "boy-god," the son towards whom the mother di-
rects a good deal of energy. He developed a sense of somehow be-
ing eternal, out of the stream of life, as if he were floating above
it. He sensed he was something special and acted with correspond-
ing aloofness and a general lack of compassion for others. This
was compounded by his Lutheran upbringing.
    Bly also reminisces about Minnesota farm experience, present-
ing an idealization of farm life and the pleasure of physical labor.
He relates a story about his father that proves that "one moral
example will do for a lifetime," and which showed him that "the in-
dignation of the solitary man is the stone pin that connects this
world to the next."
    Although this article appears a year before the publication of
Growing Up in Minnesota, it is actually drawn from the essay which
appears in that collection.
    See B88.

B85. "Lowell, Robert." In Contemporary Literary Criticism. Vol.
    4. Ed. Carolyn Riley. Detroit: Gale Research Co., p.
    297.
    Reprint, in part, of C5.

B86. "The Writer's Sense of Place." South Dakota Review, 13 (Au-
    tumn), 73-75.
    As one of a number of writers contributing articles on
regional art, Bly instead talks of the division between "head" writ-
ers and "earth" writers and turns the essay into a lament for the
development of academic writing programs. An earth artist can
reach through the words to actually touch some nonverbal experi-
ence. Just because one is a regional writer does not mean that
the he is an "earth" writer. The power of head art is strong and
is supported by the universities and writing workshops. Writers
must take great works of earth art as their models. Among these
are Whitman's Long Island poems, Gogol's Dead Souls, Lewis Thomas'
The Lives of the Cell, and Dürer's rabbit.


1976


B87. "Ammons, A. R." In Contemporary Literary Criticism. Vol.
    5. Ed. Carolyn Riley and Phyllis Carmel Mendelson.
    Detroit: Gale Research Co., p. 28.
    Reprint, in part, of B78.

B88. "Being a Lutheran Boy-god in Minnesota." In Growing Up
    in Minnesota: Ten Writers Remember Their Childhood.
    Ed. Chester G. Anderson. Minneapolis: University of
    Minnesota Press, pp. 205-219.

A slightly expanded version of "Growing Up in Minnesota."
The additional section provides selections from the diary Bly kept
at age eleven.
See B84.

B89.   "I Came Out of the Mother Naked."   East West Journal, 6
       (August), 12–13.
       Reprinted from A36.

B90.   "Wallace Stevens and Dr. Jekyll."  In American Poets in
       1976.  Ed. William Heyen.  Indianapolis:  Bobbs-Merrill,
       pp. 4–19.
       Stevens and his work are representative of the group of
shadow poets born in the last quarter of the nineteenth century.
Their poetry consisted of shadow energies from the dark side, in
opposition to the idealist position.  Stevens' early poetry expressed
an extraordinary richness of sensual intelligence and awareness of
all the senses.  The influence of William James on Stevens' develop-
ment of the shadow energies is discussed.  These qualities are,
however, found only in Harmonium.  His poetry degenerates after-
wards, and Bly looks to Stevens' life for the cause.  He speculates
that Stevens brought the darkness into his poems but made no
changes in his life.  He did not listen to his own poetry and allow
the shadow energies to enter his life.


                                   1977

B91.   "Introduction."  In Flame People.  Gregory Hall.  Santa
       Cruz, CA:  Green House Press, pp. [5–7].
       There is a need to express our grief.  The strength of
Hall's poetry is that he can see others not related to him in their
grief.

B92.   "A Note on James Wright."  Ironwood, no. 10, pp. 64–65.
       A personal tribute to Wright and his powers of transfor-
mation:  his ability to work with an experience with assurance and
energy.

B93.   "Two Poets Translating."  With Tomas Tranströmer.  Trans-
       lation, 4 (Spring/Summer), [47]–58.
       A record of a discussion between Bly and Tranströmer at
a translation seminar at Columbia University.  Bly recounts how he
began translating poetry and describes the five steps involved in
doing so.  Bly and Tranströmer discuss several poems that Bly has
translated from the Swedish and the differences between the English
version and the original to illustrate the difficulties involved in
translating.  This presents a good understanding of both poets'
philosophies concerning translation and offers insights on one poet's
view of Bly as his translator.

B94.  "What the Prose Poem Carries with It."  American Poetry
        Review, 6 (May/June), 44-45.
        Prose poems allow the poet's original perceptions to live.
By not asking for general statements, the form urges a return to
the original perception.  It frees the poet from the demands of past
poets and poetry, the "needy divinities," trying to give poetry
back "to the muse of museums."


## 1978

B95.  "Rilke's Book of Hours."  Field, no. 18 (Spring), 93-94.
        A brief introduction to five translations of Rilke.  The
poems can be understood as Rilke's "inner life."  He realized that
he could have a life that flowed from an inner source.

B96.  "Where Have All the Critics Gone?"  Nation, 226 (22 April),
        456, 458-459.
        A discussion of the general absence of criticism and re-
views of poetry compared to the amount of poetry now being pub-
lished and the fact that "more bad poetry is being published now
than ever before...."  Bly feels young poets are being overencour-
aged and overindulged by poetry workshops and university writing
programs.  Too many critics are elevating selected poets rather than
doing the critics' job of separating the "rotten grain from the
sound."  He states his belief in "a healthy pugnacity in criticism,"
and the need for "people willing to do the hard work around litera-
ture, separate weak from strong..., people with a joy in their own
intellect and judging capacity."


## 1979

B97.  "Holding On to One Rope."  In Modern Swedish Poetry in
        Translation.  Ed. Gunnar Harding and Anselm Hollo.
        Minneapolis:  University of Minnesota Press, pp. vi-viii.
        A presentation of a "one-sided view" of Swedish poetry.
The Swedish citizen must confront two walls:  one is the demand
for political engagement, the second is the pressing dissatisfaction
coming from inside the personality--the absence of love and the
sense of emptiness in the civilized psyche.  Poets must either
wrestle with the walls or escape their crush by entering the space
of imagination.  Swedish poets are divided by how they confront
the wall.

B98.  "The Story in Three Stages."  Foreword to The Spirit of the
        Valley:  The Masculine and Feminine in the Human Psyche.
        Sukie Colegrave.  Los Angeles:  J. P. Tarcher, Inc.,
        pp. [ix]-xiii.
        Society, as well as each person individually, passes
through three stages:  matriarchy, patriarchy, and the two souls--

feminine and masculine--talking to each other. If they talk to each
other and join, the psyche achieves a new life. Bly illustrates this
concept by inventing a narrative centered around a cow, a man,
and a woman.

B99.   "Tranströmer and 'The Memory'." Ironwood, no. 13, pp.
       84-87.
       Bly introduces the concept of a layer in the conscious-
ness or memory that runs alongside the life-experience but is not
it. It is older, the before-birth intensities or the intensities not
ours. The sound of poems resonate somewhere inside us and can
pierce this layer. Transtömer is an elegant and humorous servant
of this "memory," and his work is steadied by this concept.


                                1980

B100.  "Castaneda, Carlos." In Contemporary Literary Criticism.
       Vol. 12. Ed. Dedria Bryfonski. Detroit:  Gale Research
       Co. pp. 94-95.
       Reprint, in part, of C15.


B101.  "Ignatow, David." In Contemporary Literary Criticism.
       Vol. 14. Ed. Dedria Bryfonski and Laurie Lanzen Har-
       ris. Detroit:  Gale Research Co., p. 274.
       Reprint, in part, of "An Afterword" from A133.


B102.  "Leaping Poetry." In Editor's Choice:  Literature and
       Graphics from the U.S. Small Press, 1965-1977.  Ed.
       Morty Sklar and Jim Mulac.  Iowa City:  The Spirit That
       Moves Us Press, pp. 322-341.
       Compilation of "Looking for Dragon Smoke," "Spanish
Leaping," "Wild Association," "Hopping," and "The Three Brains."
See B65, B67, B70, B73, and B74.


B103.  "Reflections on the Origins of Poetic Form." In A "Field"
       Guide to Contemporary Poetry and Poetics.  Ed. Stuart
       Friebert and David Young.  New York and London:
       Longman. pp. 37-40.
       Reprint of B80.


B104.  "Two Stages of an Artist's Life." Georgia Review, 34
       (Spring), 105-109.
       The object or thing poem allows the artist to pass from
an introspective, narcissistic stage to a second stage of spontane-
ous, sober observation of the external world.  The two great
practitioners of this type of poetry are Rainer Maria Rilke in his
"seeing poems" and Francis Ponge in his "object" poems.  They
possess the ability to concentrate on an object and not return to
the "I."
       This is an important essay that delimits Bly's increasing in-
terest in objects.

1981

B105.  "Form That Is Neither In nor Out."  Poetry East, no. 4/5
        (Spring/Summer), 29-34.
        In these "preliminary and inadequate" notes on form,
the concept of in-between form is examined.  This is a living form
derived from the economy of nature rather than human conditions,
and lies between open form and mechanical form.  The more a poem's
form can draw from nature the faster it moves, the greater its
leaps, and the better it can escape from "tigers and professors."
        Reprinted in B114.

B106.  "Ponge, Francis."  In Contemporary Literary Criticism.
        Vol. 18.  Ed. Sharon R. Gunton.  Detroit:  Gale Re-
        search Co., p. 419.
        Reprint, in part, of B104.

B107.  "Recognizing the Image as a Form of Intelligence."  Field,
        no. 24 (Spring), 17-27.
        A discussion of the place of image among the other ele-
ments that constitute a good poem.  There are six energies:  image,
sense of speaking voice, psychic weight, sound (resonating interior
sounds), sounds (as related to the drum beat), and power of the
story.  The image cannot be overpraised but it can be overempha-
sized, allowing the other elements in the poem to suffer.  Attention
is given to considering Owen Barfield's ideas on the discipline of
creating images as an exercise of intelligence essential to the poet's
mind.  The image can join the light and dark words, what we know
and don't know, or what is visible and what is invisible.  Equally
important, it can reach beyond human consciousness to touch some-
thing else--the non-human universe.
        Reprinted as "What the Image Can Do" in B116.

B108.  "Response to Frederick Turner."  Missouri Review, 5 (Win-
        ter 1981/1982), 189-191.
        A reply to Turner's "'Mighty Poets in Their Misery Dead':
A Polemic on the Contemporary Poetic Scene."  Turner's judgments
are not good; his generalizations are too sweeping, but he offers
ideas and we are in need of these.  Bly responds to a number of
points made in the article.  He believes that American poets have
produced great poetry since World War II, but it is of a curiously
modest tone.  Wallace Stevens is cited as one of the few American
poets whose work carries the values of an entire class.  The re-
sponse should, of course, be read in conjunction with Turner's
original essay.
        See P199.

B109.  "Symposium on Chinese Poetry and the American Imagina-
        tion."  Ironwood, no. 17, pp. 20, 39-40 [11-21, 38-51].
        Bly is one of ten participants.  He briefly speaks of the
Chinese ability to root the poem instantly in the body.  Concerning

the translation of Chinese poetry, he believes that, in general,
English translations have been too mental, and he expresses his
thoughts on "grounding" the poem inside the body.

B110.   "What Whitman Did Not Give Us." In Walt Whitman:   The
        Measure of His Song.  Ed. Jim Perlman, Ed Folsom, and
        Dan Campion.  Minneapolis:  Holy Cow! Press, pp. 321-
        334.
        An interesting and well composed essay in which Bly
delineates seven areas of deficiency in Whitman's legacy.  Since he
states that these areas tend to narrow poets who follow Whitman,
the criticisms he offers are not only of Whitman but many contempo-
rary poets as well, including himself.  The seven areas that are
discussed are these:   care for male masters (lack of any sense of
spiritual fathers), the problem of pain, the emphasis on audience
(in contrast to art), care for small sounds (loss of vivid, large
sounds by overuse of little words), care for pauses, the problem
of observation vs. participation, and the question of whether pri-
vate or public speech is appropriate to poetry.  Bly draws on vari-
ous sources--particularly Pushkin and Russian poetry, Rilke, and
Beowulf--to offer background and contrast to Whitman's poetry.

B111.   "The Witch, The Swan, and The Middle Class:  Some Con-
        versations at the Great Mother Conference, Ocoee, Ten-
        nessee, June, 1981."  Plainsong, 3 (Fall), 18-29.
        Some entertaining and unusual comments from Bly on a
number of not necessarily connected topics:   object poems, the
need for more discipline, moods and poetry ("A poem is a mood!"),
introduction to the witch, and the swan.  The last two topics are
commented upon the most.  Bly explores the development of the
witch mythology in western civilizaiton and the concept of the boy-
swan in terms of psychology and the absorption of the mother's
sexual energy by her son.  The spiritual laziness of a mother,
caused, in part, by her presence within a collective, contributed
to turning her son into a swan.  Here a connection between the
last two topics is made in terms of visible and invisible witches.
A witch appearing invisibly is the mother taking the form of spirit-
ual laziness.


                              1982

B112.   "Antonio Machado."  River Styx, no. 13, p. 21.
        A brief biographical note.

B113.   "The Eight Stages of Translation."  Kenyon Review NS, 4
        (Spring), 68-89.
        An answer to the question, "What is it like to translate
a poem?"  The difficulties inherent in the process are emphasized
as the task is delineated through stages involving literal translation,
meaning and problems, English language and American language,

tone, and sound. A Rilke sonnet from the first series of the Son-
nets to Orpheus is used as an example throughout. A cogent and
interesting essay for what it reveals of Bly's translating process
as well as its points on the process in general.
Reprinted in B119.

B114. "Form That Is Neither In nor Out." In Of Solitude and
      Silence: Writings on Robert Bly. Ed. Richard Jones
      and Kate Daniels. Boston: Beacon Press, pp. 22-27.
      Reprint of B105.

B115. "The Visionary Prose Poems of Louis Jenkins." Poetry East,
      no. 8 (Autumn), 6-7.
      In these prose poems the reader is confronted with an
aggressive, ominous and vegetative form of the unknown. There
is a sense of a force that is not obeying; there is no sense of op-
timism about these forces.

B116. "What the Image Can Do." In Claims for Poetry. Ed. Don-
      ald Hall. Ann Arbor: The University of Michigan Press,
      pp. 38-49.
      Reprint of B107.

B117. "The Work of James Wright." In The Pure Clear Word:
      Essays on the Poetry of James Wright. Ed. Dave Smith.
      Urbana: University of Illinois Press, pp. 78-98
      Reprint of B30. A final paragraph is added by Bly.
He dislikes the insistence on polarizing that he now finds in the
essay, and its section on Wright's faults amount to unrealized criti-
cism of his own poems. He stands by his words of praise for the
man and his work.

B118. "A Wrong Turning in American Poetry." In Claims for
      Poetry. Ed. Donald Hall. Ann Arbor: The University
      of Michigan Press, pp. 17-37.
      Reprint of B23.


                              1983

B119. "The Eight Stages of Translation." In The Pushcart Prize,
      VIII: Best of the Small Presses. Ed. Bill Henderson.
      New York: Avon, pp. 451-475.
      Reprint of B113.

B120. "García Lorca and Desire." New Letters, 49 (Spring/Sum-
      mer), 83-88.
      Reprint of B63.

1984

B121.  "Ekelöf, Gunnar."  In Contemporary Literary Criticism.
        Vol. 27.  Ed. Jean C. Stine.  Detroit:  Gale Research
        Co., pp. 111, 115.
        Reprint, in part, of "Ekelöf's 'Flavor of the Infinite',"
the introduction to A75, and B21.

B122.  "Hamsun, Knut."  In Twentieth Century Literary Criticism.
        Vol. 14.  Ed. Dennis Poupard and James E. Person, Jr.
        Detroit:  Gale Research Co., pp. 238-239.
        Reprint, in part, of "The Art of Hunger," the introduc-
tion to A76.

B123.  "In Search of an American Muse."  New York Times Book
        Review, (22 January), pp. 1, 29.
        Personal recollections and thoughts on the pursuit of the
discipline of poetry in America.  It is a nicely written and concise
summarization of many of Bly's dominant ideas.  There is a lack of
family tradition in art; American poets have much to do alone.
They do not inherit a useable style.  To be a poet one must study
the art and experience the grief.

B124.  "Leaping Up into Political Poetry."  In Poetry and Politics:
        An Anthology of Essays.  Ed. Richard Jones.  New York:
        William Morrow & Co., pp. 129-137.
        Reprint of B35.

B125.  "Neruda, Pablo."  In Contemporary Literary Criticism.  Vol.
        28.  Ed. Jean C. Stine.  Detroit:  Gale Research Co.,
        pp. 306-307, 315.
        Reprint, in part, of "Refusing to Be Theocritus," the
introduction to A78, and of "Song of Himself," C18.

B126.  "Where the Wildmen Are."  Utne Reader, no. 7 (December
        1984/January 1985), 49.
        In this brief piece drawn from Bly's 1982 interview with
New Age Journal, he advances his theory of the wildman, "a large,
primitive man covered with hair down to his feet," which exists at
the bottom of each man's psyche.  The wildman symbolizes forceful
action undertaken with resolve.  The male loses touch with the wild-
man when he comes under the influence of the mother's field of
energy.  Men must throw off this energy and discover what the
father and masculinity are.  When he is in touch with the wildman,
man has true strength.
        See P210.

# C. REVIEWS

## 1960

C1. "Louis Simpson's New Book." The Sixties, no. 4 (Fall), 58-
61. "Crunk."
An evenhanded review of A Dream of Governors. Simpson
is complimented for his willingness to examine the "unpleasant pub-
lic realities" in his poetry. However, Bly is critical of Simpson's
continual use of traditional forms, and feels that he, at times, will
"simply choose any form that will do."


## 1962

C2. "Prose vs. Poetry." Choice: A Magazine of Poetry and Pho-
tography, no. 2, pp. 65-80.
A classic Bly review-essay which begins with a note con-
cerning how it was originally rejected by The Hudson Review be-
cause Bly refused to accept the editors' cuts.
James Dickey, Drowning with Others/Denise Levertov, The
Jacob's Ladder/Richard Wilbur, Advice to a Prophet/X. J. Kennedy,
Nude Descending the Staircase/Horace Gregory, Medusa in Gramercy
Park/Harold Witt, Beasts in Clothes/Harold Norse, Dancing Beasts/
Frances Golffing, Selected Poems/Lawrence Ferlinghetti, Starting
from San Francisco/Revel Denney, In Praise of Adam/Philip Booth,
The Island/Alan Ansen, Disorderly Houses/Hayden Carruth, Journey
to a Known Place/Isabella Gardner, The Looking Glass/Richard
Hugo, A Run of Jacks/John Woods, On the Morning of Color/Ernest
Sandeen, Children and Older Strangers/Michael Benedikt, Changes/
Robert Hazel, Poems/Thom Gunn, My Sad Captains/Geoffrey Hill,
For the Unfallen/A. D. Hope, Poems/Hugh MacDiarmid, Collected
Poems.

C3. "Rewriting vs. Translation." Hudson Review, 15 (Autumn),
[469]-475.
Selected Poems of Pablo Neruda, tr. Ben Nelitt/Selected
Works, Vol. II, R. M. Rilke, tr. J. B. Leishman/Dunio Elegies,
R. M. Rilke, tr. C. F. MacIntyre/The Satires of Persius, tr. W. S.
Merwin/Poem of the Cid, tr. W. S. Merwin/An Anthology of Spanish
Poetry, ed. Angel Flores.

1966

C4.   "Recent German Anthologies."  The Sixties, no. 8 (Spring),
       84-88.
            Twentieth Century German Verse, ed. Patrick Bridgwater/
      Contemporary German Poetry, tr. Gertrude Clorvis Schwebell/
      Modern German Poetry:  1910-1960, ed. Michael Hamburger and
      Christopher Middleton.

C5.   "Robert Lowell's For the Union Dead."  The Sixties, no. 8
       (Spring), 93-96.
            People are trying to make Lowell the "great living poet,"
      and he is succumbing to their influence.  Two bankrupt intellectual
      traditions have come together in this book:  the intellectual longings
      represented by the history of the Partisan Review, and the notion
      that an artist must never be calm, but must always be excited.
      The result is a book of poetry that is a melodrama.  It has no life
      of its own; the ideas are banal and journalistic.  Lowell does not
      achieve poetic excitement, only nervous excitement.
            Reprinted in B85 and C9.  See P148.


1967

C6.   "Buckdancer's Choice."  [The Collapse of James Dickey].
       The Sixties, no. 9 (Spring), 70-79.
            A classic piece of contemporary vitriolic literary criticism.
      The content of the book is "repulsive."  Its subject is power and
      the tone of the book is gloating--gloating about power over others.
      The poem "Slave Quarters" is "one of the most repulsive poems
      ever written in American literature."  It is bad, tasteless, slurping
      verse.  The language is without feeling, and the quality of the
      imagination is paralytic.  There is no grief in the poem.  It is a
      perpetuation of the old romantic lying picture.  All Southern preju-
      dices are accepted.  The poem "Firebombing" replaces the Negro
      women with the civilian population of Asia.  There is no real anguish
      in the poem.  Dickey emphasizes the picturesque quality of the bomb-
      ing.  The language of the poems is inflated, and the rhythm is
      manufactured.
            Bly blames the blind acceptance of these poems by reviewers
      on the New Critics.  Their concept of the "personae" excuses
      Dickey.  He, however, is not standing outside of the poem.  There
      is no personae.  The new critical ideas do not apply to it.  Bly
      further notes Dickey's support of the Vietnam War and the unity of
      the man and his work.  Dickey's decision to make poetry a "career"
      is associated with the abrupt decline in the quality of his work.
            This is an important essay which demonstrates Bly's belief in
      the moral, social, and political imperative of poetry.

## 1968

C7.  "Not Very Near the Ocean."  Michigan Quarterly Review, 7
      (Summer), 211-212.
      A review of Robert Lowell's Near the Ocean.  The book
is an almost total loss.  It is full of bloated and rhetorical language;
it is plotless and virtually emotionless.  The translations are dread-
ful.

C8.  "Slipping Toward the Instincts."  The New Leader, 51 (May
      20), 31-33.
      A review of David Ignatow's Rescue the Dead.  In its
implications, Ignatow's work has a harshness like Robert Lowell's,
but it is more interesting because of his ideas.  His ideas make him
an important poet.  Like Rilke, he recognizes that emotions are
more insistent and that they have a greater influence upon events.
Reprinted in a slightly revised version in C10.

## 1970

C9.  "Robert Lowell's For the Union Dead."  In Robert Lowell:  A
      Portrait of the Artist in His Time.  Ed. Michael London
      and Robert Boyers.  New York:  David Lewis, pp. 73-76.
      Reprint of C5.

C10.  "Some Thoughts on Rescue the Dead."  Tennessee Poetry
       Journal, 3 (Winter) 17-21.
       Slightly revised version of C8.

## 1971

C11.  Review of Octavio Paz's Configurations (New Directions edi-
       tion).  New York Times Book Review, 18 April 1971, pp.
       6, 20, 21.
       This book is used as an excuse to praise Neruda, Vallejo,
and Machado.  Bly strangely takes Paz's poems and states what they
may sound like if Machado wrote them.  This is essentially a dis-
course on the Spanish-American literary tradition of which, accord-
ing to Bly, Paz is a victim.

## 1973

C12.  "Three Great Photographers."  New Letters, 39 (Spring),
       80, 85.
       Edward S. Curtis, In a Sacred Manner We Live, Photo-
graphs of the North American Indian/H. W. Gleason, The Western
Wilderness of North America/Nell Dorr, Mother and Child.

## 1974

C13.  "Difficult Questions, Easy Answers."  New York Times Book
      Review, 17 March, p. 6.
         An admiring review of Robert Graves' book, Difficult
Questions, Easy Answers.  Graves' speculations and prose are both
marvelous.  Bly discusses a number of Graves' speculations that
appear in these essays.  He concludes that Graves is "one of the
very finest writers in English."

## 1976

C14.  "Fragrance of the Unknown."  Moons and Lion Tailes, 2
      (no. 2), 49-53.
         A review of Searching for the Ox by Louis Simpson.  Al-
though Simpson has a considerable gift for the image with uncon-
scious ingredients, he is here focusing on the banal, ordinary de-
tails of daily life.  In his "brave attempt" to give the hard objects
of the world attention, he has given them too much; they become
permanent.  The poems can become circular and suffocating, just
as daily life can be.  This difficult unusual discipline does result,
however, in a number of "rich and brilliant" poems that contain
the fragrance of the unknown.

## 1978

C15.  "Carlos Castaneda Meets Madame Solitude."  New York Times
      Book Review, 22 January, pp. 7, 22.
         A review of Castaneda's The Second Ring of Power.  The
conversations with Don Juan are a hoax, but Castaneda's instruction
is charming and good-natured.  He has found ideas in other people's
works and rephrased them.  While he has good taste in the ideas he
borrows, there is an air of regression that surrounds the language.
The predominant attitude is that of the pre-genital stage.
         Bly focuses the review upon the "anti-female" material in
Castaneda's work.
         Reprinted, in part, B100.  See P139, P144, and P150.

C16.  "Mixed Parables."  New York Times Book Review, 5 February,
      pp. 14-15.
         A review of W. S. Merwin's Houses and Travellers.  While
praising the persistent energy and air of intelligence in the work,
Bly is critical of its insistent generality and the connection to "the
collective unconsciousness."  Too often Merwin gives in to the imi-
tation collective unconscious.  Bly believes the book lacks editing.
He charges that books by established poets are accepted without
editing.  He criticizes, generally, the lack of editing in poetry to-
day.
         See P142.

## 1981

C17.  Review of Robert Peters' The Great American Poetry Bake-
      Off.  American Book Review, 3 (January), 11-12.
           Peters shares Bly's view of criticism; critics should not
      be maternal (reluctant to be nasty in print).  Criticism should en-
      courage and confront the poet.  Bly briefly admires four "harsh"
      pieces on W. S. Merwin, Galway Kinnell, Diane Wakoski, and Allen
      Ginsberg.  He summarizes some points made regarding poets who do
      not receive enough attention, and also focuses upon "the essay I
      enjoyed most," an admiring one, of Robert Creeley's For Love.


## 1982

C18.  "Songs of Himself."  New York Times Book Review, 23 May,
      pp. 9, 26.
           A review of Isla Negra:  A Notebook by Pablo Neruda,
      translated by Alastair Reid.  The book is rambling and loosely put
      together.  The poems give evidence of the astounding abundance
      human imagination has when mingled with memory.  A comparison
      is drawn between Neruda and Yeats.  The book has been translated
      elegantly.  The solutions are calm, lively, lucid, and attentive.
           Reprinted, in part, in B125.

# D. LETTERS

## 1969

D1. "Correspondence." American Dialog, 5 (Spring/Summer), 39.
A congratulatory note on the Winter 1968/1969 issue.

D2. "Letters." Kayak, no. 19, p. 51.
A response to Elizabeth Bishop's claim that three of Bly's prose poems are imitations of hers. Bly gives the dates and locations from his journals for the writing of the three poems. They are all before the appearance of Bishop's poems in print.
See P.45.

## 1971

D3. "A Letter from Robert Bly." Poet and Critic, 6 (no. 2), 30.
A response to David Cummings' article clarifying some points made in reference to "Looking for Dragon Smoke."
See P65.

## 1973

D4. "Letters (Robert Bly Replies to Donald D. Walsh)." American Poetry Review, 2 (September/October), 59.
Bly calls for the withdrawal of exclusive rights for Walsh's translations of Neruda's Residencia because of the poor quality of the translations and the fact that changes have been made in the poem without proof of textual evidence of original terms in the text or the permission of Neruda.
See P89 and P90.

## 1974

D5. "Letters." American Poetry Review, 3 (January/February), 53.
A continuation of Bly's correspondence with David Walsh regarding Neruda's Residencia I Poems. Bly has found a first edition of Residencia that supports his claims.
See P89 and P90.

## 1980

D6. "A Letter from Minnesota." Bachy, no. 16 (Winter), 158.
Bly compliments the editors on Bachy no. 15 and the tribute to Bert Meyers. He also defends Robert Peters from attacks stating, "it's a critic's job to be nasty--he's not a mother or an uncle."

## 1981

D7. [Letter from R. B. to Richard Jones and Kate Daniels].
Poetry East, no. 4/5 (Spring/Summer), [back cover].
A reproduction of Bly's original letter in reply to Jones and Daniels' suggestion of a special issue. He offers his thanks and states his willingness to help with the issue.

## 1982

D8. "On Translating Rilke." New Republic, 186 (28 April), 2-3.
A response to Erich Heller's review of Bly's Selected Poems of Rainer Maria Rilke which Bly finds "absurd." He believes that Heller is "not really reviewing, but bragging that he's a cultured European." Bly writes that German academics in the United States have consistently written as if they wanted to keep German literature to themselves. He evokes Ezra Pound's belief that the purpose of translation is to assist the poet in becoming useful to, and nourishing in, another culture, not to convert the poem perfectly into another language.
See Q146 and P206.

E.   POEMS IN PERIODICALS

1953

E1.   Choral Stanza. Paris Review, no. 2 (Summer), [79].

E2.   Two Choral Stanzas. Paris Review, no. 1 (Spring), [27].

1957

E3.   The Man Whom the Sea Kept Awake. Paris Review, no. 16
        (Spring/Summer), [141].

E4.   What Burns and Is Consumed. New World Writing, no. 11,
        pp. 115-116.

1958

E5.   The Fire of Despair Has Been Our Saviour. Paris Review,
        no. 18 (Spring), [123].

E6.   The Sorb Is the Tree of Thor, Who Hung Nine Days Wounded.
        Paris Review, no. 20 (Autumn/Winter 1958/1959), [26].

1959

E7.   The Army of Advertising Men. The Fifties, no. 2, p. 40.

E8.   Poem. The Fifties, no. 3, p. 3.

E9.   Poem in Three Parts. The Fifties, no. 2, p. 41.

E10.  Poems for the Ascension of J. P. Morgan. New World Writing,
        no. 15, pp. 61-77. [Group includes entries E11-E26.]

E11.  The Ascension of J. P. Morgan, p. 61

E12.  The Westerns, p. 62

E13.  [Gloria Dei Lutheran Church, St. Paul, Minnesota], p. 63

E14.  Warning to the Reader, p. 65

E15.  America Is Dancing, p. 65

E16.  Mr. Mcelroy [from The New York Herald Tribune], p. 66

E17.  We Have Overlooked Something, p. 68

E18.  [From a review of a book on Herbert Hoover], p. 69

E19.  MacDougal Street, New York, p. 70

E20.  Each Day I Live, p. 71

E21.  [From Look], p. 72

E22.  For Three American Heroes, p. 73

E23.  The Search Back Through Memory, p. 74

E24.  Proclamation [of Alex Dewar] [From The Madison Press],
       p. 75

E25.  Thinking of Wallace Stevens on the First Snowy Day in De-
       cember, p. 76

E26.  Remembering in Oslo the Old Picture of the Magna Charta,
       p. 77

E27.  Salute to All the Countries Which Helped Franco.  Paris Re-
       view, no. 21 (Spring/Summer), [73].

E28.  What We Have Inherited from the Intellectual Leadership of
       New England.  Paris Review, no. 21 (Spring/Summer),
       [72].


                                1960

E29.  Driving Through Ohio.  Poetry, 96 (April), 32.

E30.  Merchants Have Multiplied.  Chelsea, no. 8 (October), 64.

E31.  The Possibility of New Poetry.  Poetry, 96 (April), 31.

E32.  Restless in the Fall Afternoon.  The Sixties, no. 4 (Fall), 50.

E33.  This World is a Confusion of Three Worlds.  Poetry, 96
       (April), 31.

<u>1961</u>

E34.   Archaic Torso of Apollo (after reading Rainer Maria Rilke).
       <u>Choice: A Magazine of Poetry and Photography</u>, no. 1
       (Spring), 13.

E35.   Awakening. <u>Poetry</u>, 99 (October), 43.

E36.   Clear Air of October. <u>Poetry</u>, 99 (October), 40.

E37.   The Confusion of America. <u>Poetry</u>, 99 (October), 42.

E38.   Fall Rain. <u>Poetry</u>, 99 (October), 44.

E39.   Getting Up Early. <u>Nation</u>, 193 (30 December), 534.

E40.   Images Suggested by Medieval Music. <u>Poetry</u>, 99 (October),
       41.

E41.   On Ancient Death. <u>Poetry</u>, 98 (July), 234. [As Charles
       Reynolds].

E42.   Poem. <u>Poetry</u>, 99 (October), 40-41.

E43.   from "Poems for J. P. Morgan." <u>Choice: A Magazine of
       Poetry and Photography</u>, no. 1 (Spring), 13.


<u>1962</u>

E44.   After Drinking All Night with a Friend, We Go Out in a Boat
       at Dawn to See Who Can Write the Best Poem. <u>Hudson
       Review</u>, 15 (Spring), 78-79.

E45.   After the Industrial Revolution, All Things Happen at Once.
       <u>The Sixties</u>, no. 6 (Spring), 7.

E46.   After Working. <u>Poetry</u>, 100 (August), 281.

E47.   Andrew Jackson's Speech. <u>Paris Review</u>, no. 27 (Winter/
       Spring), [21].

E48.   Boards on the Ground. <u>Poetry</u>, 100 (August), 278.

E49.   A Busy Man Speaks. <u>San Francisco Review</u>, no. 12 (June),
       56-57.

E50.   The Coming of Night. <u>San Francisco Review</u>, no. 12 (June),
       56.

E51.   Condition of the Working Class. <u>The Sixties</u>, no. 6 (Spring),
       9.

E52.  Hunting Pheasants in a Cornfield. Poetry, 100 (August),
      279.

E53.  In a Train. Nation, 195 (22 September), 166.

E54.  Late at Night After an Early November Snow. Hudson Review,
      15 (Spring), 78.

E55.  Late at Night During a Visit of Friends. Poetry, 100 (Au-
      gust), 282.

E56.  Legion Night at the Armory. Midwest, no. 4 (Summer), 11.

E57.  Morning. San Francisco Review, no. 12 (June), 57.

E58.  Nearing the Middle West. Paris Review, no. 27 (Winter/
      Spring), [20].

E59.  On Listening to Stevenson and Kennedy Lie About the First
      Cuban Invasion. Coastlines, no. 19, p. 61.

E60.  Poem. Paris Review, no. 27 (Winter/Spring), [18].

E61.  Poems on the Voyage. Quarterly Review of Literature, 12
      (Fall), 144-148.

E62.  September. Hudson Review, 15 (Spring), 76-77.

E63.  Sleet Storm on the Merritt Parkway. The Sixties, no. 6
      (Spring), 8.

E64.  Snowfall in the November Afternoon. Poetry, 100 (August),
      280.

E65.  Summer in Minnesota. Hudson Review, 15 (Spring), 76.

E66.  Taking the Hands. Poetry, 100 (August), 278.

E67.  Thoughts on Alger Hiss. The Sixties, no. 6 (Spring), 12.
      [As Charles Reynolds].

E68.  Three Kinds of Pleasure. Hudson Review, 15 (Spring), 77.

E69.  The Traveller. Audience, 8 (Winter), 70.

E70.  Walking to a Good Friday Service in New York at Night.
      Audience, 8 (Winter), 71.

E71.  Watering the Horse. Poetry, 100 (August), 280.

E72.  Wind. Paris Review, no. 27 (Winter/Spring), [19]. Poem
      later entitled "Poem Against the British."

E73.  With Pale Women in Maryland.  Paris Review, no. 27 (Winter/
      Spring), [19].


                                   1963

E74.  April.  Choice:  A Magazine of Poetry and Photography, no.
      3, p. 110.

E75.  At the Ranch.  Epoch, 13 (Fall), 42.

E76.  Dusk in the Sixties.  Epoch, 13 (Fall), 42.

E77.  Evolution from the Fish.  Choice:  A Magazine of Poetry and
      Photography, no. 3, p. 109.

E78.  Fear of the Boar with Tusks.  Choice:  A Magazine of Poetry
      and Photography, no. 3, p. 108.

E79.  Hamilton's Dream.  Choice:  A Magazine of Poetry and Photog-
      raphy, no. 3, p. 107.

E80.  Leaving Ithaca (for Ruth and Dave).  Choice:  A Magazine
      of Poetry and Photography, no. 3, p. 109.

E81.  Suffocation.  Choice:  A Magazine of Poetry and Photography,
      no. 3, p. 111.

E82.  Supper.  Epoch, 13 (Fall), 42.

E83.  Watching Fall Dust Inside Sheds.  Beloit Poetry Journal, 14
      (Fall), 42.

E84.  Watching Television.  Choice:  A Magazine of Poetry and
      Photography, no. 3, p. 111.


                                   1964

E85.  The Beauty of Women.  Poetry, 104 (September), 366.

E86.  Come With Me.  Poetry, 104 (September), 365.

E87.  Cricket Calling from a Hiding Place.  Kayak, no. 1 (Autumn),
      31.

E88.  Cricket on a Doorstep in September.  Kayak, no. 1 (Autumn),
      31.

E89.  Driving North From San Francisco.  Poetry, 104 (September),
      366-367.

E90.  Driving to Town Late to Mail a Letter.  Agenda, no. 3
      (September), 19.

E91.  Fall.  Poetry, 104 (September), 366.

E92.  Listening to the Radio.  Midwest, no. 7 (Summer), 30.

E93.  Looking Backward.  Paris Review, no. 31 (Winter/Spring),
      [107].

E94.  Meditation on Olai and Pete Bly.  Paris Review, no. 32
      (Summer/Fall), [96].

E95.  The Moon.  Kayak, no. 1 (Autumn), 30.

E96.  On a Cliff.  Poetry, 104 (September), 367.

E97.  Poem for the Drunkard President.  Paris Review, no. 31
      (Winter/Spring), [106].

E98.  The Son of Black Waves.  Midwest, no. 7 (Summer), 31.

E99.  The Testament.  Poetry, 104 (September), 367-368.

E100. Thinking of Troubles.  Kayak, no. 1 (Autumn), 30.

E101. Unanswered Letters.  Poetry, 104 (September), 365.

E102. Walking Near a Pasture.  Kayak, no. 1 (Autumn), 30.


                              1965

E103. About to Drink Wine.  Kayak, no. 2, p. 31.

E104. With a Naked Girl, Up to See the Spring Dawn.  Kayak,
      no. 2, p. 30.


                              1966

E105. Afternoon Sleep.  Crazy Horse, no. 2, p. 6.

E106. An American Dream.  Poetry, 108 (September), 382.

E107. As the Asian War Begins.  Solstice, 4, p. 19.

E108. Asian Peace Offers Rejected Without Publication.  American
      Dialog, 3 (Summer), 3.

E109. The Current Administration.  Kayak, no. 5, p. 31.

E110.  Death.  Agenda, no. 4 (Summer), 4.

E111.  Difficulties of Living.  East Side Review, 1 (January/February), 73.

E112.  Full Moon, Thinking of High School Girls.  Poetry, 108 (September), 385.

E113.  Going Down.  Agenda, no. 4 (Summer), 4.

E114.  Hatred of Men with Black Hair.  Nation, 203 (5 September), 192.

E115.  In Italy.  Solstice, 4, p. 19.

E116.  In the North Atlantic.  Kayak, no. 5, p. 33.

E117.  Johnson's Cabinet Watched by Ants.  Nation, 202 (30 May), 653.

E118.  A Journey with Women.  Poetry, 108 (September), 386.

E119.  Late at Night During a Visit of Friends.  Plaintiff (Mankato State College), (Spring), p. 14.

E120.  The Life of Weeds.  Poetry, 108 (September), 384.

E121.  Looking at New Fallen Snow from a Train.  Polemic, 11 (Winter), 11.

E122.  March in Washington Against the Vietnam War; November 27th, 1965.  Poetry, 108 (September), 387.

E123.  On a Night of Conversation.  East Side Review, 1 (January/February), 73.

E124.  Revolution.  Kayak, no. 5, p. 32.

E125.  Running Over the River.  Kayak, no. 5, p. 33.

E126.  The Sadness of American Unrest in 1961.  Crazy Horse, no. 2, p. 17.

E127.  Sunset at a Lake.  Plaintiff (Mankato State College), (Spring), p. 14.

E128.  Taking the Hands.  Plaintiff (Mankato State College), (Spring), p. 14.

E129.  Three Presidents (Andrew Jackson, Theodore Roosevelt, John F. Kennedy).  Nation, 202 (24 January), 108.

E130. Vietnam. Some thing, no. 2 (Winter), 61.

E131. Written Near Rome. Poetry, 108 (September), 383.

## 1967

E132. Counting Small-Boned Bodies. Crazy Horse, no. 3, p. 14.

E133. Driving Through Minnesota During the Hanoi Bombings. Nation, 205 (28 August), 152.

E134. Early Winter. Crazy Horse, no. 3, p. 13.

E135. The Executive's Death. Stand, 9, no. 1, p. 14.

E136. Foreign Policy. Nation, 205 (18 September), 251.

E137. The Hermit. Poetry, 110 (June), 183.

E138. Hurrying Away from the Earth. Poetry, 110 (June), 181.

E139. Johnson's Cabinet Watched by Ants. Stand, 9, no. 1, p. 13.

E140. Looking at Some Flowers. Poetry, 110 (June), 182.

E141. Melancholia. Crazy Horse, no. 3, p. 15.

E142. Poem for Max Ernst. Crazy Horse, no. 3, p. 13.

E143. Prepared to Experience All Things. Crazy Horse, no. 3, p. 13.

E144. Riderless Horses. Poetry, 110 (June), 183.

E145. Suddenly Turning Away. Poetry, 110 (June), 182.

E146. Visiting Italy. Nation, 204 (19 June), 793.

E147. When the Dumb Speak. Poetry, 110 (June), 180.

## 1968

E148. Dark Eyebrows Swim Like Turtles. Chelsea, no. 22/23 (June), 17.

E149. How Beautiful the Shiny Turtle. Chelsea, no. 22/23 (June), 16.

E150. Lies. Nation, 206 (25 March), 417.

166                                      Writings by Robert Bly

E151.  From "Poems for Max Ernst."  Chelsea, no. 22/23 (June),
       16-18.

E152.  Romans Angry About the Inner World.  Chelsea, no. 22/23
       (June), 17-18.


                              1969

E153.  Ants.  Nation, 208 (9 June), 739.

E154.  Dawn in the Threshing Time.  Tennessee Poetry Journal, 2
       (Winter), 7.

E155.  The Hunter.  Kayak, no. 18, p. 39.

E156.  Looking at a Dead Wren in My Hand.  Kayak, no. 18, p. 39.

E157.  New Snow.  Hearse, no. 11, p. [15].

E158.  November Fog.  Tennessee Poetry Journal, 2 (Winter), 13.

E159.  A Pilgrim Settlement.  Tennessee Poetry Journal, 2 (Winter),
       6.

E160.  Scene with Respectable Men.  Tennessee Poetry Journal, 2
       (Winter), 11.

E161.  Sea Scene, Night.  Tempest, 1, no. 1, p. 9.

E162.  Seeing Creeley For the First Time.  Tennessee Poetry Jour-
       nal, 2 (Winter), 5.

E163.  Sitting on Some Rocks in Shaw Cove, California.  Kayak,
       no. 18, p. 38.

E164.  The Sleeper in the Mountain.  Tennessee Poetry Journal, 2
       (Winter), 12.

E165.  A Small Bird's Nest of White Reed Fiber.  Tennessee Poetry
       Journal, 2 (Winter), 3.

E166.  The Snail.  Tennessee Poetry Journal, 2 (Winter), 9.

E167.  Thoughts in the North Woods.  Hearse, no. 11, p. [15].

E168.  A Turtle.  Tennessee Poetry Journal, 2 (Winter), 4.

E169.  Turtle Climbing from a Rock.  Massachusetts Review, 10
       (Autumn), [763].

E170.  Two Together.  Massachusetts Review, 10 (Autumn), [761].

E171.  Writing Again.  Tennessee Poetry Journal, 2 (Winter), 10.

E172.  Written Late at Night.  Tempest, 1, no. 1, p. 8.

## 1970

E173.  Anarchists Fainting.  Harper's Magazine, 240 (April), 118.

E174.  At a Fish Hatchery in Story, Wyoming.  Crazy Horse, no.
       5, p. [4].

E175.  A High Waterfall Coming Over a Cliff.  Crazy Horse, no. 5,
       p. [4].

E176.  Love Poem.  Chelsea, no. 28 (August), 81.

E177.  Owning Homes.  Nation, 211 (26 October), 411.

E178.  The President About to Address the Whole Nation in the
       Eighth Year of the Vietnam War.  Tennessee Poetry
       Journal, 4 (Fall), 5.

E179.  A Review of James Wright's Shall We Gather at the River.
       Cafe Solo, 2, p. 69.

E180.  Six Winter Privacy Poems.  Field, no. 2 (Spring), 8-9.

E181.  Some November Privacy Poems.  Antioch Review, 30 (Fall/
       Winter 1970/1971), 322.

E182.  _____.  Phoenix, 3 (Winter), 99.

E183.  Sons and Cornpickers.  Crazy Horse, no. 5, p. [5].

E184.  Still Trying to Describe a Valley Between Two Mountains
       Near Grace, Idaho.  Dragonfly, 2 (Fall/Winter), 2.

E185.  The Teeth-Mother Naked at Last.  Stand, 11, no. 2, pp.
       48-56.

E186.  Trying to Describe a Valley Between Two Mountains Near
       Grace, Idaho.  Dragonfly, 2 (Fall/Winter), 2.

E187.  Thinking of 'The Autumn Fields'.  Phoenix, 3 (Winter), 98.

E188.  Walking in Spring Ditches.  Field, no. 2 (Spring), 9.

## 1971

E189. After Long Business. Poetry, 118 (April), 33.

E190. A Caterpillar on the Desk. Poetry, 118 (April), 34.

E191. Christmas Day. Greenfield Review, 1 (Winter), 26.

E192. Collapsing Bridge. (Some Poems for Max Ernst). New Directions in Prose and Poetry, 23, p. 23.

E193. Deciding to Go to Inverness for a Few Months. Tennessee Poetry Journal, 4 (Spring), 42.

E194. A Dream on the Night of First Snow. Poetry, 118 (April), 33.

E195. Driving in Snow. Midwest Quarterly, 12 (January), 144.

E196. Finding a Salamander on Inverness Ridge. New Letters, 38 (Autumn), 94.

E197. For My Father. (Some Poems for Max Ernst). New Directions in Prose and Poetry, 23, p. 25.

E198. Frost. Iowa Review, 2 (Winter), 22.

E199. Gibbon's Body. (Some Poems for Max Ernst). New Directions in Prose and Poetry, 23, p. 26.

E200. Hair. Field, no. 5 (Autumn), 17.

E201. Looking at the Moon from the Point Reyes Peninsula. Tennessee Poetry Journal, 4 (Spring), 43.

E202. Mother Coming. (Some Poems for Max Ernst). New Directions in Prose and Poetry, 23, p. 24.

E203. On the West Short of Maui. New Letters, 38 (Autumn), 95.

E204. Poem for William Stafford at Martin. Tennessee Poetry Journal, 4 (Spring), 42.

E205. Reading Old Books. (Some Poems for Max Ernst). New Directions in Prose and Poetry, 23, p. 24.

E206. Reelfoot Lake, West Tennessee. Tennessee Poetry Journal, 4 (Spring), 44.

E207. Riding Around Big Stone Lake. Voyages, 4 (Spring 1971/ Spring 1972), 37.

E208.  Shack Poem. Iowa Review, 2 (Winter), 23.

E209.  Small Scene with Winged Man. (Some Poems for Max Ernst).
       New Directions in Prose and Poetry, 23, p. 23.

E210.  To the Reader. (Some Poems for Max Ernst). New Direc-
       tions for Prose and Poetry, 23, p. 26.

E211.  Train Wreck in Midocean. (Some Poems for Max Ernst).
       New Directions in Prose and Poetry, 23, pp. 22-23.

E212.  Turtle Climbing From a Rock. (Some Poems for Max Ernst).
       New Directions in Prose and Poetry, 23, p. 25.

E213.  Waking Up In a Car. Iowa Review, 2 (Winter), 22.

E214.  Watching Andrei Voznesensky Read. New York Times, 19
       November, p. 45.

E215.  Winter Privacy Poems. Kayak, no. 27 (Autumn), 14.


                              1972

E216.  Affection (for John and Muriel Ridland). The Lamp in the
       Spine, 3 (Winter), 68.

E217.  Another Poem for Wallace Stevens. Iowa Review, 3 (Summer),
       91.

E218.  The Dead Seal Near McClure's Beach. Stand, 13, no. 4,
       p. 19.

E219.  _____. Straight Creek Journal, 1 (October 24), 10-11.

E220.  Fall Poem from Minnesota. Vanderbilt Poetry Review, 1
       (Spring), 5.

E221.  Fall Solitude. The Lamp in the Spine, 3 (Winter), 67.

E222.  Insect Heads. Modern Occasions, 1 (Winter), 210.

E223.  Looking Into a Tide Pool. Modern Occasions, 1 (Winter),
       211.

E224.  New Fallen Snow. Modern Occasions, 1 (Winter), 211.

E225.  Night Farmyard. Stone Drum, 1 (Spring), 15.

E226.  On a Farm. New York Times, 28 April, p. 41.

E227.   On a Moonlit Road in the North Woods. Stone Drum, 1
        (Spring), 14.

E228.   Orchard Grass. Stone Drum, 1 (Spring), 15.

E229.   Pilgrim Fish Heads. Stand, 13, no. 4, p. 18.

E230.   Poem Adapted from the Chinese. Unmuzzeled Ox, 1 (Febru-
        ary), 28.

E231.   Pulling the Boat Up Among Lake Reeds. Kayak, no. 28,
        p. 54.

E232.   Reading Wallace Stevens on New Year's Eve. Vanderbilt
        Poetry Review, 1 (Spring), 4.

E233.   From "The Shadow Poem:" Someone is asleep in the back of
        my house. New York Quarterly, no. 11 (Summer), 44.

E234.   From "Sleepers Joining Hands:" There are fears that come
        up from underneath. The Seventies, no. 1 (Spring), 88.

E235.   So Much Is Not Spoken. Iowa Review, 3 (Summer), 89-90.

E236.   Thinking of Tedious Ways Eight. Unmuzzeled Ox, 1 (Febru-
        ary), 29.

E237.   Time to Be.... Ohio Review, 13 (Spring), 17.

E238.   Visiting Thomas Hart Benton in Kansas City. New Letters,
        38 (Summer), [29]-30.

E239.   A Walk. UT Review, 1, no. 2, p. 3.

E240.   Water Reconcilation. Iowa Review, 3 (Summer), 91.

E241.   Windy Day. UT Review, 1, no. 2, p. 3.

E242.   Writing Again. Ohio Review, 14 (Autumn), 41.

E243.   Written at Island Lake. Ohio Review, 13 (Spring), 18.


                            1973

E244.   August Rain. Field, no. 8 (Spring), 30.

E245.   A Hollow Tree. Prospice, 1 (November), 30.

E246.   Nonsense Poem. Twin Cities Express, no. 1, p. 37.

E247. November Fog. Prospice, 1 (November), 30.

E248. Pilgrim Fish Heads. National Observer, 9 June, p. 23.

E249. The Shadow Goes Away. Prospice, 1 (November), 28-29.

E250. Surf and Water Sounds. Chicago Review, 24 (Winter), 138.

E251. Two Poems Written on a Visit to Hawaii: 1. Sitting on the
Shore Near Lahaina at Dusk; 2. Sitting on a Rock Cove
on Kaena Point. Hawaii Review, 1 (Winter), 3.

## 1974

E252. After a Day of Work. New Salt Creek Reader, 6 (Spring),
70.

E253. Afternoon Sleep. Paintbrush, no. 1 (Spring), 10.

E254. At Night. Field, no. 10 (Spring), 36.

E255. Being Born. Field, no. 10 (Spring), 36.

E256. Buffalo. Kayak, no. 34 (March), 52.

E257. Christmas Eve Service at Midnight at St. Michael's. Madrona,
no. 7, p. 36.

E258. December. Poetry Now, 1, no. 3, p. 27.

E259. A Dream. Kayak, no. 34 (March), 52.

E260. Hearing Gary Snyder Read. Fiction International, no. 2/3,
pp. 118-119.

E261. The Hockey Poem. Ohio Review, 15 (Spring), 5.

E262. Late October. Rapport, no. 7, p. 9.

E263. Looking at the Moon in a Cottonwood Tree. New Salt Creek
Reader, 6 (Spring), 70.

E264. _____. Poetry Now, 1, no. 6, p. 26.

E265. The Moth. Kayak, no. 34 (March), 51.

E266. My Three Year Old Daughter Brings a Gift. Poetry Now,
1, no. 4, p. 5.

E267. Poem After Kabir. Kayak, no. 34 (March), 53.

E268.  Poems on the Voyage. Quarterly Review of Literature, 19,
       no. 1/2, p. 245.

E269.  From "Sleepers Joining Hands": The woman chained to the
       shore stands bewildered as night comes. Lillabulero, no.
       13 (Spring), 15.


## 1975

E270.  Ant Heaps on the Road. Partisan Review, 42, no. 1, p.
       60.

E271.  A Bird's Nest Made of White Reed Fiber. New York Times
       Book Review, 26 October, p. 63.

E272.  The Climber. North Stone Review, no. 7 (Fall/Winter 1975/
       1976), 16.

E273.  Coming Home After Weeks Away. Montana Gothic, 3 (Au-
       tumn), 75.

E274.  A December Dream. Small Farm, no. 2 (October), 8.

E275.  Finding the Father. Field, no. 13 (Autumn), 97.

E276.  The Hockey Poem. New York Times Book Review, 26 Octo-
       ber, p. 63.

E277.  A Long Walk Before the Snows Began. North Stone Review,
       no. 7 (Fall/Winter 1975/1976), 15.

E278.  Opening the Door of a Barn I Thought Was Empty on New
       Year's Eve. Boundary 2, 4 (Fall), 158.

E279.  The Pail. Field, no. 13 (Autumn), 96.

E280.  The Sleeper. Field, no. 13 (Autumn), 95.

E281.  Snowbanks North of the House. American Poetry Review,
       4 (January/February), 1.

E282.  Winds. Partisan Review, 42, no. 1, p. 60.


## 1976

E283.  The Aeroplane. Boundary 2, 4 (Spring), 704.

E284.  Alone in a Blizzard. Boundary 2, 4 (Spring), 702.

E285. Black Pony Eating Grass. New Letters, 42 (Summer), 15.

E286. Doing Some Moon-Viewing. Seneca Review, 6 (January), 5.

E287. A Dream About Tiles on the Floor. Paris Review, no. 65 (Spring), [150].

E288. Driving. Some, no. 7/8, First Installment, p. [3].

E289. Falling into Holes in Our Sentences. Iowa Review, 7 (Autumn), 135.

E290. The Fir. Floating Island, (Spring), 49.

E291. Fishing East of Ashby. Moons and Lion Tailes, 1 (no. 4), 43.

E292. Frost on Window Panes. Poetry Now, 3, no. 2, p. 7.

E293. Going Out to Check the Ewes. Paris Review, no. 65 (Spring), [150].

E294. A Hollow Tree. Poetry Now, 3 (no. 2), 7.

E295. The Large Animals. Paris Review, no. 65 (Spring), [149].

E296. The Left Hand. Paris Review, no. 65 (Spring), [149].

E297. A Long Walk Before the Snows Began. Poetry Now, 3 (no. 1), 8.

E298. [The Loon]. Reproduced as a woodcut by Wang Hui-Ming. New Letters, 42 (Summer), 52.

E299. Moving Books to a New Study. Moons and Lion Tailes, 1 (no. 4), 14.

E300. Night Farmyard. Poetry Now, 3 (no. 1), 8.

E301. The Perspiculum Worm. Iowa Review, 7 (Autumn), 134.

E302. Poem in Four Parts. Floating Island, (Spring), 48.

E303. Prophets. Poetry Now, 3 (no. 1), 8.

E304. A Rock Inlet in the Pacific. Poetry Now, 3 (no. 2), 7.

E305. Snow Falling on the Water Tank. Rapport, no. 9, p. 8.

E306. Standing in a Willow Grove at Dusk. Some, no. 7/8, First Installment, p. [4].

E307.  Staying Alert. Moons and Lion Tailes, 2 (no. 1), 72.

E308.  Walking Swiftly. Paris Review, no. 65 (Spring), 148.

E309.  The Woman Priest's Hair. Boundary 2, 4 (Spring), 703.

E310.  A Wooden Hotel in Norway. New Letters, 42 (Summer), 15.

## 1977

E311.  The Blue Raft. Kayak, no. 45 (May), 7.

E312.  The Crow's Head. Ohio Review, 18 (Autumn), 21.

E313.  The Dead Seal Near McClure's Beach. Aura, no. 6 (Spring),
       41.

E314.  The Farallone Islands. Kayak, no. 45 (May), 9.

E315.  Four Poems after Bashō. Kayak, no. 45 (May), 8.

E316.  A Fragment Written Out of Admiration For James Wright's
       Poems. Ohio Review, 18 (Spring/Summer), 58.

E317.  Frost Still in the Ground. Kayak, no. 45 (May), 9.

E318.  Grass From Two Years. Aura, no. 6 (Spring), 43-[44].

E319.  The Hockey Poem. Aura, no. 6 (Spring), [42]-43.

E320.  Leonardo's Secret. Aura, no. 6 (Spring), 45.

E321.  Looking at a Dead Wren in My Hand. Aura, no. 6 (Spring),
       [44]-45.

E322.  Near Kabekona Lake. Bits, no. 6 (July), 5.

E323.  Out Picking Up Corn. Kayak, no. 45 (May), 6.

E324.  Rejoicing When Alone. Cornell Review, 1 (Spring), 73.

E325.  Tiny Spinning Wheel Concerto. New Republic, 177 (3 Septem-
       ber), 28.

E326.  A Turtle. Aura, no. 6 (Spring), [44].

E327.  Two Years After the War. Nation, 224 (21 May), 636.

E328.  Walking to the Next Farm. American Poetry Review, 6 (May/
       June), 45.

E329.  Watching a Big Shadow Move Across the Lake.  Kayak, no.
       45 (May), 7.

E330.  Watching the St. Paul Chamber Orchestra Play Bach.  American Poetry Review, 6 (May/June), 45.

E331.  A Windy Day at the Shack.  Aura, no. 6 (Spring), 45.

E332.  Written in Two Feet of Snow in a Valley at Mule Hollow, Utah.
       Grove: Contemporary Poetry and Translation, no. 3
       (Winter), 21.


                                1978

E333.  An Evening When the Full Moon Rose as the Sun Set.  Georgia Review, 32 (Fall), 512.

E334.  The Farallones Islands.  Ohio Review, 19 (Autumn), 49.

E335.  Moon On a Pasture Near Ortonville.  Georgia Review, 32
       (Summer), 332.

E336.  A Moth with Black Eyes.  Ohio Review, 19 (Autumn), 50.

E337.  A Ramage of the Man Who Is Alone.  Ohio Review, 19 (Autumn), [51]-55.

E338.  Walking the Mississippi Shore at Rock Island, Illinois.  Missouri Review, 1 (Spring), 5.

E339.  Walking Where the Plows Have Been Turning.  Georgia Review, 32 (Fall), [513].

E340.  Women We Never See Again.  Georgia Review, 32 (Summer),
       333.


                                1979

E341.  The Cry Going Out Over Pastures.  Poetry Now, no. 22,
       p. 21.

E342.  Feeling at Home in the Body (for Robert Creeley).  Georgia
       Review, 33 (Spring), 108.

E343.  Galloping Horses.  Poetry Now, no. 22, p. 21.

E344.  Listening to a Cricket in the Wainscoting.  Southern Review
       [Australia], 12 (July), 136.

E345.  Listening to a Friend's Easter Sermon (for H. Klever).
       Carleton Miscellany, 17 (Spring), 13.

E346.  Prayer Service in an English Church. Georgia Review, 34
       (Summer), 277.

E347.  Small Poem. Carleton Miscellany, 17 (Spring), 13.

E348.  What Goes Out and Returns. Agenda, 13/14 (Winter/Spring),
       32.


                                1980

E349.  The Busy Man Speaks. New York Times Magazine, 3 Febru-
       ary, p. 51.

E350.  The Call. Harvard Magazine, 83 (September/October), 14.

E351.  The Casks of Wine. Iowa Review, 11 (Spring/Summer), 209.

E352.  Covers. Ironwood, no. 16, p. 72.

E353.  Dawn in Threshing Time. Poetry Now, no. 26, p. 21.

E354.  Driving My Parents Home at Christmas. Parabola, 5 (Winter),
       80.

E355.  Driving Toward the Lac Qui Parle River. TWA Ambassador,
       (December), p. 35.

E356.  Elegy for David Wand. Poetry Now, no. 27, p. 38.

E357.  The Fallen Tree. Tendril, no. 9, p. 26.

E358.  Grief and Its Roots. Ohio Review, no. 25, p. 85.

E359.  The Grief of Man. New Republic, 183 (29 November), 32.

E360.  Listening to a Fog Horn at Port Townsend. Ohio Review,
       no. 25, p. 84.

E361.  Love Poem in Prose. Ohio Review, no. 25, p. 85.

E362.  Mourning Pablo Neruda. Harper's, 260 (May), 73.

E363.  Night of First Snow. Poetry Now, no. 26, p. 21.

E364.  October Frost. TWA Ambassador, (December), p. 35.

E365.  The Ram. Harvard Magazine, 83 (September/October), 14.

E366.  The Rough-Barked Cottonwood.  Georgia Review, 34 (Winter),
       751.

E367.  Thirst.  Harvard Magazine, 83 (September/October), 14.

E368.  Walking.  Ironwood, no. 16, p. 73.

E369.  What the Plants Do.  Harvard Magazine, 83 (September/
       October), 14.

E370.  Words Rising (To Richard Eberhart).  Parabola, 5 (Winter),
       78.


                              1981

E371.  The Altar (Twenty Poems in Homage to Max Ernst).  Kayak,
       no. 55 (January), 42.

E372.  At Midocean:  Poetry East, no. 4/5 (Spring/Summer), 21.

E373.  _____.  Images, 7 (no. 3), 3.

E374.  The Author's Goodbye to the Reader (Twenty Poems in Hom-
       age to Max Ernst).  Kayak, no. 55 (January), 51.

E375.  The Bird Headed Man (Twenty Poems in Homage to Max
       Ernst).  Kayak, no. 55 (January), 43.

E376.  A Bouquet of Ten Roses.  Poetry East, no. 4/5 (Spring/
       Summer), 22.

E377.  Crazy Carlson's Meadow.  Poetry East, no. 4/5 (Spring/
       Summer), 17-18.

E378.  A Curious Incident in the Hotel (Twenty Poems in Homage to
       Max Ernst).  Kayak, no. 55 (January), 35.

E379.  Eleven O'Clock at Night.  Poetry East, no. 4/5 (Spring/
       Summer), 23-24.

E380.  Far Out at Sea (Twenty Poems in Homage to Max Ernst).
       Kayak, no. 55 (January), 45.

E381.  Fifty Males Sitting Together.  Poetry East, no. 4/5 (Spring/
       Summer), 19-20.

E382.  Finding an Old Ant Mansion.  Harvard Magazine, 83 (May/
       June), 53.

E383.  The Flute Player (Twenty Poems in Homage for Max Ernst).
       Kayak, no. 55 (January), 50.

E384.  For My Father (Twenty Poems in Homage to Max Ernst).
       Kayak, no. 55 (January), 37.

E385.  Here Is What I Experienced.  Ploughshares, 7 (no. 1), 47.

E386.  Herons.  Poetry, 138 (August), 284.

E387.  Kneeling Down to Look Into a Culvert.  Atlantic, 248 (September), 25.

E388.  Maid Listening (Twenty Poems in Homage to Max Ernst).
       Kayak, no. 55 (January), 37.

E389.  The Man with Huge Eyes (Twenty Poems in Homage to Max
       Ernst).  Kayak, no. 55 (January), 42.

E390.  A Meditation on Philosophy.  Poetry East, no. 4/5 (Spring/
       Summer), 14-15.

E391.  The Moose.  Poetry, 138 (August), 284.

E392.  The New King.  Poetry East, no. 4/5 (Spring/Summer), 16.

E393.  An Ominous Scene (Twenty Poems in Homage to Max Ernst).
       Kayak, no. 55 (January), 43.

E394.  Poem on Sleep.  New Yorker, 57 (7 September), 36.

E395.  Prodigal Son.  New Republic, 184 (31 January), 28.

E396.  The Quai at Midnight (Twenty Poems in Homage to Max
       Ernst).  Kayak, no. 55 (January), 47.

E397.  The Railway Carriage (Twenty Poems in Homage to Max
       Ernst).  Kayak, no. 55 (January), 49.

E398.  A Ramage for Awakening Sorrow.  Poetry, 138 (August),
       283.

E399.  A Ramage for the Star Man, Mourning.  Poetry, 138 (August), 283.

E400.  A Ramage for Waking the Hermit.  Parabola, 6 (February),
       32.

E401.  The Roman Matron (Twenty Poems in Homage to Max Ernst).
       Kayak, no. 55 (January), 44.

E402.  Scene in a French Forest (Twenty Poems in Homage to Max
       Ernst).  Kayak, no. 55 (January), 45.

E403.   Scene with Respectable Men (Twenty Poems in Homage to
        Max Ernst). Kayak no. 55 (January), 39.

E404.   Skulls Among the Rocks (Twenty Poems in Homage to Max
        Ernst). Kayak, no. 55 (January), 44.

E405.   Small Scene with Winged Man (Twenty Poems in Homage to
        Max Ernst). Kayak, no. 55 (January), 36.

E406.   A Suit Hanging on a Branch (Twenty Poems in Homage to
        Max Ernst). Kayak, no. 55 (January), 41.

E407.   The Train in Mid-Ocean (Twenty Poems in Homage to Max
        Ernst). Kayak, no. 55 (January), 50.

E408.   The Whole Moisty Night. Poetry East, no. 4/5 (Spring/
        Summer), 21.

E409.   Woman Asleep Near Bridge (Twenty Poems in Homage to Max
        Ernst). Kayak, no. 55 (January), 36.

E410.   Words Rising. Poetry East, no. 4/5 (Spring/Summer), 10-11.

E411.   Written at Mule Hollow, Utah. Poetry East, no. 4/5 (Spring/
        Summer), 12-13.

## 1982

E412.   The Black Hen of Egypt. American Poetry Review, 11
        (November/December), 6.

E413.   The Boy In the Ditch. Ploughshares, 8 (no. 2/3), 209.

E414.   Fifty Males Sitting Together. New Age Journal, 7 (May),
        33.

E415.   A Glad Morning. American Poetry Review, 11 (November/
        December), 6.

E416.   The Hummingbird Valley. American Poetry Review, 11
        (November/December), 6.

E417.   Kennedy's Inauguration. Threepenny Review, no. 11 (Au-
        gust), 25.

E418.   Love Poem in Twos and Threes. New Republic, 187 (27
        December), 24.

E419.   A Love That I Have In Secret. American Poetry Review, 11
        (May/June), 18.

E420. A Man and a Woman Sit Near Each Other. Ploughshares, 8
      (no. 2/3), 208.

E421. Reading an Old Love Poem. American Poetry Review, 11
      (May/June), 18.

E422. The Stump. Ploughshares, 8 (no. 2/3), 210.

E423. There are Fiery Days.... Ploughshares, 8 (no. 2/3), 207.

E424. Tiny Concerto in the Key of "Er." River Styx, no. 13, p.
      7.


                              1983

E425. "The coarse grainy skin of the flounder...." ("A Parabola
      Bestiary"). Parabola, 8 (Spring), 44.

E426. Conversation with a Woman Not Seen for Many Years. Poetry
      East, no. 11 (Summer), 79.

E427. The Farallones Islands. Ohio Review, no. 30 (Ten Year
      Retrospective), 123.

E428. In the Month of May. Atlantic, 251 (May), 43.

E429. The Indigo Bunting. New Yorker, 59 (29 August), 34.

E430. Listening to a Fog Horn at Port Townsend. Ohio Review,
      no. 30 (Ten Year Retrospective), 122-123.

E431. A Moth with Black Eyes. Ohio Review, no. 30 (Ten Year
      Retrospective), 122.

E432. "On a mess of greenish-brown seaweed there is a rock
      crab...." ("A Parabola Bestiary"). Parabola, 8
      (Spring), 43-44.

E433. "The oyster looks impenetrable and thuggy...." ("A
      Parabola Bestiary"). Parabola, 8 (Spring), 45.


                              1984

E434. Black Tree Trunks. Kenyon Review NS, 6 (Winter), 22.

E435. Cherry Blossoms. Bluefish, 1 (Spring), 29.

E436. Dark Eyebrows Swim Like Turtles (from Poems for Max Ernst).
      Chelsea, no. 42/43 (Chelsea Retrospective 1958-1983), 181.

E437.  Ferns. <u>Kenyon Review</u> NS, 6 (Winter), 22.

E438.  The House. <u>Kenyon Review</u> NS, 6 (Winter), 21.

E439.  How Beautiful the Shiny Turtle (from Poems for Max Ernst).
       <u>Chelsea</u>, no. 42/43 (<u>Chelsea</u> Retrospective 1958-1983), 181.

E440.  In Rainy September. <u>New Republic</u>, 190 (9-16 January), 36.

E441.  Merchants Have Multiplied. <u>Chelsea</u>, no. 42/43 (<u>Chelsea</u>
       Retrospective 1958-1983), 69.

E442.  Night Winds. <u>Atlantic</u>, 253 (June), 98.

E443.  The Pillow. <u>Kenyon Review</u> NS, 6 (Winter), 21.

E444.  The Way He Turns. <u>Kenyon Review</u> NS, 6 (Winter), 21.

# F. TRANSLATIONS IN PERIODICALS

## 1958

F1. Boyson, Emil. The Child. <u>Commentary</u>, 26 (November), 382.

F2. Ekelöf, Gunnar. Apotheosis. Tr. by RB, William Duffy, & Christina Bratt Duffy. <u>The Fifties</u>, no. 1, pp. 6-7. Swedish opposite.

F3. _____. Chorus. Tr. by RB, William Duffy, & Christina Bratt Duffy. <u>The Fifties</u>, no. 1, pp. 8-9. Swedish opposite.

F4. _____. "The Fear and Flight of the Virgin." Tr. by RB, William Duffy, & Christina Bratt Duffy. <u>The Fifties</u>, no. 1, pp. 12-15.

F5. _____. "He Who Does Not Hope." Tr. by RB, William Duffy, & Christina Bratt Duffy. <u>The Fifties</u>, no. 1, pp. 10-13. Swedish opposite.

F6. _____. In the Forests of Convention. Tr. by RB, William Duffy, & Christina Bratt Duffy. <u>The Fifties</u>, no. 1, pp. 2-3. Swedish opposite.

F7. _____. Suburb. Tr. by RB, William Duffy, & Christina Bratt Duffy. <u>The Fifties</u>, no. 1, pp. 4-5. Swedish opposite.

F8. Kristensen, Tom. Anxiety. <u>The Fifties</u>, no. 1, pp. 16-17. Danish opposite.

F9. Michaux, Henri. My Life. <u>The Fifties</u>, no. 1, pp. 20-21. French opposite.

F10. _____. Repose in Grief. <u>The Fifties</u>, no. 1, pp. 18-19. French opposite.

## 1959

F11. Benn, Gottfried. Ah, That Land So Far Off. <u>The Fifties</u>, no. 2, pp. 2-3. German opposite.

F12.    _____. Night's Wave. The Fifties, no. 2, pp. 8-9. German opposite.

F13.    _____. Poems That Stand Still. The Fifties, no. 2, pp. 4-5. German opposite.

F14.  Ibsen, Henrik. The Storm Swallow. Nation, 189 (26 December), 490.

F15.  Tuma, Mirko. Letter. The Fifties, no. 3, pp. 22-23. Czechoslovakian opposite.

F16.    _____. The Pastoral Symphony. The Fifties, no. 3, pp. 24-29. Czechoslovakian opposite.

F17.    _____. Poem. The Fifties, no. 3, pp. 30-31. Czechoslovakian opposite.

### 1960

F18.  Ekelöf, Gunnar. Monologue with Its Wife. Chelsea, no. 8 (October), 33.

F19.    _____. Perpetuum Mobile. Nation, 190 (2 April), 300.

F20.  García Lorca, Federico. Home from a Walk (In New York). The Sixties, no. 4 (Fall), 26-27. Spanish opposite.

F21.    _____. Memorial. The Sixties, no. 4 (Fall), 16-17. Spanish opposite.

F22.  Machado, Antonio. "Faint Sounds of Long Robes." The Sixties, no. 4 (Fall), 4-5. Spanish opposite.

F23.    _____. "From the doorsill...." The Sixties, no. 4 (Fall), 10-11. Spanish opposite.

F24.    _____. Songs. The Sixties, no. 4 (Fall), 12-13. Spanish opposite.

F25.  Martinez, Enrique Gonzalez. Take This Swan. The Sixties, no. 4 (Fall), 2-3. Spanish opposite.

### 1961

F26.  Baudelaire, Charles. Dusk Before Dawn. The Sixties, no. 5 (Fall), 10-13. French opposite.

F27.    _____. Intimate Associations. The Sixties, no. 5 (Fall), 16-17. French opposite.

F28.    _____.  Inward Conversation.  The Sixties, no. 5 (Fall),
        14-15.  French opposite.

F29.    _____.  The Rare Perfume.  The Sixties, no. 5 (Fall),
        18-19.  French opposite.

F30.    Char, Rene.  Branching Off.  The Sixties, no. 5 (Fall), 60-
        61.  French opposite.

F31.    _____.  Four Poems on the Cave Paintings at Lascaux.
        The Sixties, no. 5 (Fall), 56-59.  French opposite.

F32.    _____.  On the High Places.  The Sixties, no. 5 (Fall),
        54-55.  French opposite.

F33.    _____.  Truth Will Set You Free.  The Sixties, no. 5
        (Fall), 62-63.  French opposite.

F34.    Elevard, Paul.  Max Ernst.  The Sixties, no. 5 (Fall), 50-
        51.  French opposite.

F35.    LaForgue, Jules.  Protest.  (Tr. as Charles Reynolds).
        The Sixties, no. 5 (Fall), 38-39.  French opposite.

F36.    _____.  Sundays.  (Tr. as Charles Reynolds).  The Six-
        ties, no. 5 (Fall), 40-43.  French opposite.

F37.    _____.  To Go By.  (Tr. as Charles Reynolds).  The
        Sixties, no. 5 (Fall), 52-53.  French opposite.

F38.    Mallarmé, Stéphane.  Sonnet (For your dear wife now dead,
        from her friend).  The Sixties, no. 5 (Fall), 22-23.
        French opposite.

F39.    Nerual, Gerard De.  Golden Lines.  The Sixties, no. 5
        (Fall), 4-5.  French opposite.

F40.    Rimbaud, Arthur.  A Comedy of Thirst.  The Sixties, no. 5
        (Fall), 28-35.  French opposite.

F41.    St. John Perse.  From Praises, Part 18.  The Sixties, no. 5
        (Fall), 46-47.  French opposite.

F42.    Supervielle, Jules.  Whisper in Agony.  (Tr. as Charles Rey-
        nolds).  The Sixties, no. 5 (Fall), 48-49.  French opposite.

F43.    Valery, Paul.  A Room.  The Sixties, no. 5 (Fall), 44-45.
        French opposite.

F44.    Vallejo, César.  Masses.  Poetry, 98 (September), 353.

F45.  Verlaine, Paul.  Autumn Song.  (Tr. as Charles Reynolds).
      The Sixties, no. 5 (Fall), 24-25.  French opposite.


                              1962

F46.  Brekke, Paal.  Mine, Though Bitter.  The Sixties, no. 6
      (Spring), 58-59.  Norwegian opposite.

F47.  _____.  Nightmare in the Noon Nap.  The Sixties, no. 6
      (Spring), 52-55.  Norwegian opposite.

F48.  _____.  Poem from the Song of Changes.  The Sixties, no.
      6 (Spring), 54-55.  Norwegian opposite.

F49.  _____.  To A Watercolorist.  The Sixties, no. 6 (Spring),
      56-57.  Norwegian opposite.

F50.  _____.  The Weight of Boughs.  The Sixties, no. 6
      (Spring), 60-61.  Norwegian opposite.

F51.  Ekelöf, Gunnar.  The Knight Has Rested.... Tr. by Chris-
      tina Bratt & RB.  Hudson Review, 15 (Winter 1962/1963),
      549-550.

F52.  _____.  So Strange to Me.  Tr. by Christina Bratt & RB.
      Hudson Review, 15 (Winter 1962/1963), 550.

F53.  _____.  There Exists Something That Fits Nowhere.  Tr.
      by Christina Bratt & RB.  Hudson Review, 15 (Winter
      1962/1963), 547-548.

F54.  _____.  Trionfo Della Morte.  Tr. by Christina Bratt &
      RB.  Hudson Review, 15 (Winter 1962/1963), 548-549.

F55.  _____.  When One Has Come.... Tr. by Christina Bratt
      & RB.  Hudson Review, 15 (Winter 1962/1963), 550.

F56.  Montale, Eugenio.  Another Labor of the Moon.  The Sixties,
      no. 6 (Spring), 74-75.  Spanish opposite.

F57.  _____.  Fragment.  The Sixties, no. 6 (Spring), 72-73.
      Spanish opposite.

F58.  _____.  On a Letter Not Written.  The Sixties, no. 6
      (Spring), 70-71.  Spanish opposite.

F59.  _____.  On the Marked-Up Wall.  The Sixties, no. 6
      (Spring), 76-77.  Spanish opposite.

F60.  Neruda, Pablo.  The Dictators.  The Sixties, no. 6 (Spring),
      10-11.  Spanish opposite.

1963

F61.    Goytisolo, Juan.  The Cross and the Face.  [fiction].  Hud-
        son Review, 16 (Spring), [61]-67.

F62.    Ibsen, Henrik.  On the Murder of Abraham Lincoln.  Nation,
        196 (16 February), 142.

F63.    Strindberg, August.  Like Doves.  [fiction].  Minnesota Re-
        view, 3 (Spring), 299-315.

F64.    _____.  Love and the Price Index.  [fiction].  Minnesota
        Review, 3 (Spring), 299-315.

F65.    _____.  The Phoenix Bird.  [fiction].  Minnesota Review,
        3 (Spring), 299-315.

1964

F66.    Al-Muntafil.  The Mole.  The Sixties, no. 7 (Winter), 33.

F67.    Aspenström, Werner.  Fall.  The Sixties, no. 7 (Winter), 40.
        German same page.

F68.    Char, Rene.  To a Tree Who Was a Brother Through Certain
        Counted Days.  The Sixties, no. 7 (Winter), 36.  French
        same page.

F69.    Hölderlin, Friedrich.  Advocatus Diaboli.  The Sixties, no. 7
        (Winter), 37.  German same page.

F70.    Neruda, Pablo.  Nothing But Death.  The Sixties, no. 7
        (Winter), 14-17.  Spanish opposite.

F71.    _____.  Sixth Poem.  The Sixties, no. 7 (Winter), 4-5.
        Spanish opposite.

F72.    _____.  The United Fruit Co.  The Sixties, no. 7 (Winter),
        6-9.  Spanish opposite.

F73.    Vallejo, César.  The Anger That Breaks a Man.  The Sixties,
        no. 7 (Winter), 64-65.  Spanish opposite.

F74.    _____.  Black Stone Lying on a White Stone.  Tr. by RB
        & John Knoepfle.  The Sixties, no. 7 (Winter), 66-67.
        Spanish opposite.

F75.    _____.  The Spider.  The Sixties, no. 7 (Winter), 58-59.
        Spanish opposite.

1966

F76.  Apollinaire, Guillaume.  The Carp.  Chicago Review, 19 (no. 1), 77.

F77.  Char, Rene.  The Oriole.  Chicago Review, 19 (no. 1), 77.

F78.  Eich, Gunter.  "From the Blue...."  The Sixties, no. 8 (Spring), 43.

F79.  Ekelöf, Gunnar.  "In dreams I have not."  The Lampeter Muse, 2 (December), 5.

F80.  _____.  The Moon.  Adam International Review, 31 (nos. 304-306), 14.

F81.  _____.  Poem.  Tr. by Christina Bratt & RB.  The Lampeter Muse, 2 (December), 5.

F82.  _____.  Portrait.  Adam International Review, 31 (nos. 304-306), 14.

F83.  _____.  Who Is Coming?  Adam International Review, 31 (nos. 304-306), 15.

F84.  Hölderin, Friedrich.  Human Applause.  The Sixties, no. 8 (Spring), 11.

F85.  _____.  To the German People.  The Sixties, no. 8 (Spring), 11.

F86.  Machado, Antonio.  Elegy for Don Francisco Giner De Los Rios.  Nation, 202 (18 April), 464.

F87.  Martinson, Harry.  On the Congo.  Adam International Review, 31 (nos. 304-306), 25.

F88.  Neruda, Pablo.  Cristobal Miranda:  Shoveller at Tocopilla.  Michigan Quarterly Review, 5 (Spring), 106.

F89.  _____.  Friends on the Road (1921).  Tr. by James Wright & RB.  Paris Review, no. 39 (Fall), 126-127.

F90.  _____.  Funeral in the East.  Holy Door, 3 (Spring), 1.

F91.  _____.  _____.  Nation, 203 (11 July), 54.

F92.  _____.  It Was the Grape's Autumn.  Tr. by RB & James Wright.  Michigan Quarterly Review, 5 (Spring), 88.

F93.  _____.  Melancholy Inside Families.  Tr. by James Wright & RB.  Paris Review, no. 39 (Fall), 125-126.

F94.  _____.  Ode to My Socks.  Nation, 203 (11 July), 53.

F95.  Nietzsche, Friedrich.  Undiscouraged.  (Tr. as Charles Rey-
      nolds).  The Sixties, no. 8 (Spring), 20-21.  German op-
      posite.

F96.  Rilke, Rainer Maria.  "Already the Ripening Barberries."
      The Sixties, no. 8 (Spring), 29.

F97.  _____.  "I Find You."  The Sixties, no. 8 (Spring), 25.

F98.  _____.  "Just as the Watchman."  The Sixties, no. 8
      (Spring), 23.

F99.  _____.  Pont Du Carrousel.  The Sixties, no. 8 (Spring),
      31.

F100. _____.  Progress.  The Sixties, no. 8 (Spring), 31.

F101. _____.  "Sometimes a Man Stands Up."  The Sixties, no.
      8 (Spring), 27.

F102. Sonnevi, Göran.  On the War in Vietnam.  Nation, 202 (30
      May), 655.

F103. Van Hoddis, Jakob.  End of the World.  The Sixties, no. 8
      (Spring), 35.

F104. Von Hofmannsthal, Hugo.  Traveller's Song.  (Tr. as
      Charles Reynolds).  The Sixties, no. 8 (Spring), 20-21.
      German opposite.


                                1967

F105. Hernandez, Miguel.  "For Pulling the Feathers From Icy
      Archangels."  The Sixties, no. 9 (Spring), 12-13.
      Spanish opposite.

F106. _____.  I Have Plenty of Heart.  The Sixties, no. 9
      (Spring), 14-17.  Spanish opposite.

F107. _____.  "You Threw Me a Lemon...."  The Sixties, no. 9
      (Spring), 10-11.  Spanish opposite.

F108. Neruda, Pablo.  Art of Poetry.  TriQuarterly, no. 8 (Winter),
      239.

## 1968

F109.  Boyson, Emil. After the Fourth Year of the War. The Sixties, no. 10 (Summer), 60-61. Norwegian opposite.

F110.  _____. Toward Sleep. The Sixties, no. 10 (Summer), 60-61. Norwegian opposite.

F111.  Bull, Olaf. Banquet. The Sixties, no. 10 (Summer), 42-43. Norwegian opposite.

F112.  _____. The Circle of Stars. The Sixties, no. 10 (Summer), 52-53. Norwegian opposite.

F113.  _____. Dream. The Sixties, no. 10 (Summer), 44-45. Norwegian opposite.

F114.  _____. Forgiveness of Sins. The Sixties, no. 10 (Summer), 40-43. Norwegian opposite.

F115.  _____. House By the Sea. The Sixties, no. 10 (Summer), 46-49. Norwegian opposite.

F116.  _____. Snowfall. The Sixties, no. 10 (Summer), 50-51. Norwegian opposite.

F117.  Gill, Claes. Maria. The Sixties, no. 10 (Summer), 62-63. Norwegian opposite.

F118.  Goll, Yvan. "Ode to Autumn." Kayak, no. 14 (April), 63-67.

F119.  Holm, Peter. The Lonely Rower. The Sixties, no. 10 (Summer), 64-65. Norwegian opposite.

F120.  Ibsen, Henrik. To My Friend, The Spokesman for the Revolution. The Sixties, no. 10 (Summer), 56-57. Norwegian opposite.

F121.  Jacobsen, Rolf. The Busses are Homesick. The Sixties, no. 10 (Summer), 70-71. Norwegian opposite.

F122.  _____. Hand and Mouth. The Sixties, no. 10 (Summer), 72-73. Norwegian opposite.

F123.  _____. Heredity and Environment. The Sixties, no. 10 (Summer), 74-75. Norwegian opposite.

F124.  _____. Rubber. The Sixties, no. 10 (Summer), 68-69. Norwegian opposite.

F125. _____. Where Do the Streets Go? The Sixties, no. 10 (Summer), 72-73. Norwegian opposite.

F126. Jiménez, Juan Ramón. Author's Club. Tennessee Poetry Journal, 1 (Winter), 17.

F127. _____. Cemetery. Tennessee Poetry Journal, 1 (Winter), 20.

F128. _____. Dawn Outside the City Walls. Agenda, 6 (Autumn/ Winter), 91.

F129. _____. Deep Night. Tennessee Poetry Journal, 1 (Winter), 21.

F130. _____. Full Consciousness. Agenda, 6 (Autumn/Winter), 93.

F131. _____. An Imitation of Billy Sunday. Tennessee Poetry Journal, 1 (Winter), 15-16.

F132. _____. In the Subway. Tennessee Poetry Journal, 1 (Winter), 19.

F133. _____. Intelligence, Give Me. Agenda, 6 (Autumn/Winter), 90.

F134. _____. Lavender Windowpanes. Tennessee Poetry Journal, 1 (Winter), 13-14.

F135. _____. The Lumber Wagons. Agenda, 6 (Autumn/Winter), 88.

F136. _____. The Name Drawn from the Names. Agenda, 6 (Autumn/Winter), 92.

F137. _____. Oceans. Agenda, 6 (Autumn/Winter), 90.

F138. _____. A Remembrance Is Moving. Agenda, 6 (Autumn/ Winter), 89.

F139. _____. Road. Agenda, 6 (Autumn/Winter), 90.

F140. _____. Walt Whitman. Tennessee Poetry Journal, 1 (Spring), 18.

F141. _____. Who Knows What Is Going On. Agenda, 6 (Autumn/Winter), 89.

F142. _____. Wrong Time. Tennessee Poetry Journal, 1 (Spring), 12.

F143. Malik, Sahl Ben. The Dawn. The Sixties, no. 10 (Summer),
      5.

F144. Martinson, Harry. Cotton. Unicorn Journal, Spring, p. 61.

F145. _____. Gypsy Lunch. Unicorn Journal, Spring, p. 62.

F146. _____. from Hell & Euclid (First Version). Unicorn
      Journal, Spring, pp. 66-67.

F147. _____. Letter From a Cattleboat. Unicorn Journal,
      Spring, p. 63.

F148. _____. Lighthouse Keeper. Unicorn Journal, Spring,
      p. 65.

F149. _____. Moon Poem. Unicorn Journal, Spring, p. 64.

F150. _____. The Ocean Wind. Unicorn Journal, Spring, p. 60.

F151. _____. On the Congo. Unicorn Journal, Spring, p. 59.

F152. Neruda, Pablo. It Was the Grape's Autumn. Tr. by RB &
      James Wright. TriQuarterly, no. 13/14 (Fall 1968/Winter
      1969), 297.

F153. _____. Ode to My Socks. Agenda, 6 (Autumn/Winter),
      97-99.

F154. _____. They Receive Instructions Against Chile. Tr. by
      RB & James Wright. TriQuarterly, no. 13/14 (Fall 1968/
      Winter 1969), [298].

F155. _____. White Toy Sheep. [Excerpt from Childhood and
      Poetry]. Harper's Bazaar, 102 (December), 114-115.

F156. Reiss-Andersen, Gunnar. Guide the Boat, Columbus. The
      Sixties, no. 10 (Summer), 58-61. Norwegian opposite.

F157. Rilke, Rainer Maria. "Oh where is the one who is transpar-
      ent...." The Sixties, no. 10 (Summer), 2.


                            1969

F158. Darío, Rubén. To Theodore Roosevelt, 1904. TriQuarterly,
      no. 15 (Spring), [238-239].

F159. Jiménez, Juan Ramón. Dawn Outside the City Walls. Nation,
      209 (7 July), 18.

F160.        .  Dawns of Moguer.  Nation, 209 (7 July), 18.

F161.        .  Full Consciousness.  Nation, 209 (7 July), 18.

F162.        .  The Lumber Wagons.  Nation, 209 (7 July), 18.

F163.        .  Oceans.  Nation, 209 (7 July), 18.

F164.        .  Road.  Nation, 209 (7 July), 18.

F165.  Tranströmer, Tomas.  Lamento.  Field, no. 1 (Fall), 62.
       Swedish opposite.

F166.        .  Night Music.  Field, no. 1 (Fall), 64.  Swedish
       opposite.

F167.        .  Open and Closed Space.  Field, no. 1 (Fall), 66.
       Swedish opposite.

### 1970

F168.  Kabir.  In the Privacy.  Kamadhenu, 1 (March), [2].

F169.        .  Inside this Jug.  Kamadhenu, 1 (March), [30].

F170.        .  Oh Friend Whom I Love.  Kamadhenu, 1 (March),
       [31].

F171.        .  "When my friend is away from me...."  Kamadhenu,
       1 (November), [25].

F172.        .  "Why should we two ever want to part?"  Kamad-
       henu, 1 (November), [26].

F173.  Tranströmer, Tomas.  Lisbon.  Doones, 1 (no. 3), 53.

F174.        .  The Open Window.  Doones, 1 (no. 3), 55.

F175.        .  Summer Grass.  Doones, 1 (no. 3), 54.

F176.  Vallejo, César.  Poem to be Read and Sung.  Tr. by RB &
       James Wright.  Crazy Horse, no. 5, p. [3].

### 1971

F177.  Jacobsen, Rolf.  The Age of the Great Symphonies.  Madrona,
       1 (June), 19.

F178.        .  Country Roads.  Madrona, 1 (June), 32.

F179.    Machado, Antonio.  For Don Francisco Giner de los Rios.
         Tennessee Poetry Journal, 4 (Spring), 67.

F180.    Neruda, Pablo.  Brussels.  Greenfield Review, 1 (Winter), 5.

F181.    _____.  Funeral in the East.  Audience, 1 (no. 4), 71.

F182.    _____.  Gentlemen Without Company.  Win, 7 (December
         15), 19.

F183.    _____.  The Head on the Pole.  Win, 7 (December 15), 18.

F184.    _____.  Hunger in the South.  Greenfield Review, 1 (Win-
         ter), 4.

F185.    _____.  Ode to Salt.  Win, 7 (December 15), 18.

F186.    _____.  The Strike.  Greenfield Review, 1 (Winter), 4.

F187.    _____.  United Fruit Company.  University Review, no. 21,
         p. [15].

F188.    _____.  _____.  Win, 7 (December 15), 18.

F189.    Rilke, Rainer Maria.  Evening in Skane.  Madrona, 1 (Novem-
         ber), 12.

F190.    Tranströmer, Tomas.  After a Death.  Granite, no. 1 (Spring),
         14.

F191.    _____.  Balakirev's Dream (1905).  Granite, no. 1 (Spring),
         12-13.

F192.    _____.  Breathing Space July.  Granite, no. 1 (Spring),
         15.

F193.    _____.  From An African Diary.  Granite, no. 1 (Spring),
         16.

F194.    Vallejo, César.  The Tennis Player.  Modern Occasions, 1
         (Winter), 210.

F195.    Voznesensky, Andrei.  Dogalypse.  Tr. by RB & Lawrence
         Ferlinghetti.  New York Times, 19 November, p. 45.

F196.    _____.  Halloween Apples.  Tr. by RB & Vera Dunham.
         New York Times, 19 November, p. 45.

1972

F197.    Ekelöf, Gunnar. Monologue with Its Wife. The Seventies,
         no. 1 (Spring), 57.

F198.    Garcïa Lorca, Federico. City That Does Not Sleep (Night-
         song of Brooklyn Bridge). The Seventies, no. 1
         (Spring), 70-73. Spanish opposite.

F199.    _____. Dance of Death. New Letters, 38 (Summer), 6.

F200.    _____. Death (for Isidoro de Blas). New Letters, 38
         (Summer), 9.

F201.    _____. Ghazal of the Terrifying Presence. New Letters,
         38 (Summer), 10.

F202.    _____. Landscape with Two Graves and an Assyrian Dog.
         The Seventies, no. 1 (Spring), 9.

F203.    _____. Little Infinite Poem. The Seventies, no. 1
         (Spring), 10-13. Spanish opposite.

F204.    _____. New York (Office and Attack). The Seventies, no.
         1 (Spring), 38-43. Spanish opposite.

F205.    _____. The Quarrel. The Seventies, no. 1 (Spring),
         50-53. Spanish opposite.

F206.    _____. Rundown Church (Ballad of the First World War).
         The Seventies, no. 1 (Spring), 34-37. Spanish opposite.

F207.    Machado, Antonio. Clouds Torn Open. Michigan Quarterly
         Review, 11 (Autumn), 279.

F208.    Neruda, Pablo. The Ruined Street. The Seventies, no. 1
         (Spring), 26-27.

F209.    _____. Sonata and Destructions. Above Ground Review,
         3 (Spring/Summer), 1.

F210.    Otero, Blas de. Loyalty. The Seventies, no. 1 (Spring),
         33.

F211.    Rilke, Rainer Maria. "I Am Too Alone in the World." Van-
         derbilt Poetry Review, 1 (Spring), 3.

F212.    _____. Sonnets to Orpheus [I, III, VI, IX]. The
         Seventies, no. 1 (Spring), 77-80.

F213.    Tranströmer, Tomas. The Name. Books Abroad, 46 (Winter),
         48.

F214. _____. The Open Window. Books Abroad, 46 (Winter),
           48.

F215. _____. Out in the Open. The Seventies, no. 1 (Spring),
           58-60.

F216. Unamuno. Throw Yourself Like Seed. Michigan Quarterly
      Review, 11 (Autumn), 280.

F217. Vallejo, César. "And so? The pale metalloid heals you?"
      The Seventies, no. 1 (Spring), 46-47. Spanish opposite.

F218. _____. "And what if after so many words...." Tr. by
      RB & Douglas Lawder. The Seventies, no. 1 (Spring),
      28-29. Spanish opposite.

F219. _____. "I have a terrible fear...." The Seventies, no. 1
      (Spring), 24-25. Spanish opposite.

F220. _____. The Mule Drivers. Modern Occasions, 1 (Winter),
           209.

F221. _____. Poem to be Read and Sung. Tr. by RB & James
      Wright. The Seventies, no. 1 (Spring), 22-23. Spanish
      opposite.


                              1973

F222. Aleixandre, Vicente. The Body and the Soul. Hawaii Re-
      view, 2 (Fall), 28-29. Spanish opposite.

F223. _____. It's Raining. Hawaii Review, 2 (Fall), 42-43.
      Spanish opposite.

F224. _____. Life. Hawaii Review, 2 (Fall), 24-25. Spanish
      opposite.

F225. _____. The Waltz. Hawaii Review, 2 (Fall), 12-15.
      Spanish opposite.

F226. Bjørnvig, Thorkild. Owl. Massachusetts Review, 14 (Au-
      tumn), 745.

F227. Ekelöf, Gunnar. Ezra Pound. Some, no. 4 (Summer), 57.

F228. _____. Paralyzed by the Light. Some, no. 4 (Summer),
           57.

F229. García Lorca, Federico. The Boy Unable to Speak. Granite,
      no. 5 (Spring), 60.

F230. _____. Ghazal of the Dark Death. Granite, no. 5
(Spring), 59.

F231. _____. The Moon Comes Out. Granite, no. 5 (Spring),
61.

F232. _____. Preciosa and the Wind (for Damaso Alonso).
Nation, 216 (28 May), 694.

F233. _____. Song of the Cuban Blacks. Granite, no. 5
(Spring), 58.

F234. _____. The Unmarried Woman at Mass. Granite, no. 5
(Spring), 62.

F235. Hauge, Olav N. Harvest Time. Massachusetts Review, 14
(Autumn), 49.

F236. _____. I Look at the Stamp. Massachusetts Review, 14
(Autumn), 749.

F237. Jacobsen, Rolf. Country Roads. Modern Poetry in Trans-
lation, 15, p. 12.

F238. _____. Glass Shop. Massachusetts Review, 14 (Autumn),
750.

F239. _____. Heredity and Environment. Modern Poetry in
Translation, 15, pp. 12-13.

F240. _____. I See Women. Stand, 14 (no. 4), 74.

F241. _____. Light Pole. Modern Poetry in Translation, 15,
p. 12.

F242. _____. The Lonesome Balcony. Modern Poetry in Trans-
lation, 15, p. 13.

F243. _____. Melancholy Towers. Modern Poetry in Translation,
15, p. 12.

F244. _____. Morning Paper. Massachusetts Review, 14 (Au-
tumn), 750.

F245. _____. Old Age. Massachusetts Review, 14 (Autumn),
751.

F246. _____. _____. Modern Poetry in Translation, 15, p.
12.

F247. _____. Towers in Bologna. Modern Poetry in Translation,
15, p. 13.

F248.   Lihn, Enrique.  Rooster.  Massachusetts Review, 14 (Au-
        tumn), 746.

F249.   Machado, Antonio.  From Proverbs and Tiny Songs.  Massa-
        chusetts Review, 14 (Autumn), 754-56.

F250.   _____.  Memory from Childhood.  Massachusetts Review,
        14 (Autumn), 753.

F251.   _____.  Songs.  Massachusetts Review, 14 (Autumn),
        753.

F252.   Martinson, Harry.  The Angleworm.  Some, no. 4 (Summer),
        58.

F253.   _____.  Creation Night.  Mundus Artium, 6 (no. 1), 27.

F254.   _____.  Landscape.  New Letters, 39 (Spring), 59.

F255.   _____.  March Evening.  Mundus Artium, 6 (no. 1), 29.

F256.   _____.  Nameless.  Nation, 217 (24 September), 282.

F257.   _____.  Old Farmhouse.  Mundus Artium, 6 (no. 1), 27.

F258.   _____.  From Poems About the Trade Winds [VII, VIII,
        IX].  New Letters, 39 (Spring), 59-60.

F259.   _____.  Power.  New Letters, 39 (Spring), [58].

F260.   Sonnevi, Göran.  Through the Open Door.  Mundus Artium,
        6 (no. 1), 85.

F261.   _____.  You are a Murderer!  Mundus Artium, 6 (no. 1),
        83.

F262.   Stanescu, Nichita.  Second Elegy.  Tr. by RB & Alexander
        Ivasinc.  Massachusetts Review, 14 (Autumn), 747.

F263.   _____.  Song (Only the Present Instant has Memories).
        Massachusetts Review, 14 (Autumn), 748.

F264.   Tranströmer, Tomas.  C Major.  Hawaii Review, 1 (Winter),
        5.

F265.   _____.  The Scattered Congregation.  Mundus Artium, 6
        (no. 1), 41.

F266.   _____.  Seeing Through the Ground.  Mundus Artium, 6
        (no. 1), 45.

F267.   _____.  Summer Grass.  Hawaii Review, 1 (Winter), 4.

F268. _____. _____. Madrona, no. 5, p. 20.

F269. _____. The Tree and the Sky. Hawaii Review, 1 (Winter), 4.

F270. Voznesensky, Andrei. Ant. Tr. by RB & Vera Dunham. New York Times, Section 4, 13 May, p. 15.

F271. _____. _____. Hawaii Review, 2 (Fall), 54.

F272. _____. Artists Dine in the Paris Restaurant Kous-Kous. Tr. by RB and Vera Dunham. New York Times, Section 4, 13 May, p. 15.

F273. _____. Ironic Treatise on Boredom. Tr. by RB & Vera Dunham. New York Times, Section 4, 13 May, p. 15.

F274. _____. Woman in August. Tr. by RB & Vera Dunham. Hawaii Review, 2 (Fall), 55.

F275. Wang Wei. The Creek By the Luan House. Hawaii Review, 1 (Spring), 31.

F276. _____. The Hill of Hua-Tzu. Hawaii Review, 1 (Spring), 30.

F277. _____. The Hill of the Hatchet-Leaved Bamboos. Hawaii Review, 1 (Spring), 32.

F278. _____. The Magnolia Grove. Hawaii Review, 1 (Spring), 31.

F279. _____. The Path with Ash Trees. Hawaii Review, 1 (Spring), 32.

F280. _____. The Walnut Tree Orchard. Hawaii Review, 1 (Spring), 30.

### 1974

F281. Baudelaire, Charles. The Rare Perfume. Counter Measures, no. 3, p. 162.

F282. García Lorca, Federico. Preciosa and the Wind (for Damaso Alonso). Counter Measures, no. 3, p. 164.

F283. Hauge, Olav N. Before I Go to Bed. Decotah Territory, no. 8/9 (Fall/Winter 1974/1975), 29.

F284. _____. Don't Come to Me With the Entire Truth. Decotah Territory, no. 8/9 (Fall/Winter 1974/1975), 28.

F285. _____. I Saw Two Moons. Decotah Territory, no. 8/9
        (Fall/Winter 1974/1975), 29.

F286. _____. You are the Wind. Decotah Territory, no. 8/9
        (Fall/Winter 1974/1975), 28.

F287. Kabir. The Jar Filling. Hawaii Review, 2 (Spring/Fall), 4.

F288. _____. The Road of Praise. Hawaii Review, 2 (Spring/
        Fall), 4.

F289. La Compiuta Donzella. In the Season. Counter Measures,
        no. 3, p. 179.

F290. LaForgue, Jules. Sundays. Counter Measures, no. 3, p.
        158.

F291. Martinson, Harry. Henhouse. Field, no. 10 (Spring), 39.

F292. _____. The Hill in the Woods. Field, no. 10 (Spring),
        37-38.

F293. _____. I See Women. Stand, 14 (no. 4), 74.

F294. Rilke, Rainer Maria. Just as the Watchman in the Winefields.
        Counter Measures, no. 3, p. 160.

F295. Tranströmer, Tomas. Along the Lines. Field, no. 10
        (Spring), 28-29.

F296. _____. Elegy. Field, no. 10 (Spring), 24.

F297. _____. Further In. Field, no. 10 (Spring), 27.

F298. _____. Sentry Duty. Field, no. 10 (Spring), 25-26.

F299. Von Hofmannsthal, Hugo. Both. Counter Measures, no. 3,
        p. 175.


                                1975

F300. Kabir. The Breath. Paris Review, no. 63 (Fall), [203].

F301. _____. The Doors are Closed. Paris Review, no. 63
        (Fall), [203].

F302. _____. "I laugh when I hear the fish in the water is
        thirsty." Street Magazine, 2 (no. 1), [23].

F303. _____. "I talk to my inner lover, and I say...."
        Street Magazine, 2 (no. 1), [26].

F304. _____. "Let's leave for the country where the guest
lives." Street Magazine, 2 (no. 1), [24].

F305. _____. Meeting the Old. Street Magazine, 1 (Spring),
[9].

F306. _____. "Oh friend, I love you, think this over." Street
Magazine, 2 (no. 1), [25].

F307. _____. "There is nothing but water in the holy pools."
Street Magazine, 2 (no. 1), [28].

F308. _____. "There's a moon in my body, but I can't see."
Street Magazine, 2 (no. 1), [27].

F309. Machado, Antonio. I Have Walked Along Many Roads. Moons
and Lion Tailes, 1 (no. 3), 58.

F310. Martinson, Harry. The Cable Ship. Atlantic, 235 (January),
[53].

F311. _____. From The Winds of Passage: "The newly discov-
ered islands grew in number." Atlantic, 235 (January),
[53].

F312. Rumi. Names. Partisan Review, 42 (no. 1), [61].


1976

F313. Kabir. The Bee. East West Journal, 6 (August), 15.

F314. _____. The Body. East West Journal, 6 (August), 15.

F315. _____. The Darkness of Night. Boundary 2, 4 (Spring),
705.

F316. _____. The Flute of Interior Time. East West Journal, 6
(August), 15.

F317. _____. Listen Friend. East West Journal, 6 (August), 15.

F318. _____. The Ruby. East West Journal, 6 (August), 15.

F319. _____. _____. Montana Gothic, 4 (Spring), [inside
front cover].

F320. Tranströmer, Tomas. Dark Shape Swimming. Moons and
Lion Tailes, 2 (no. 1), 72.

F321. _____. December Evening, '72. Moons and Lion Tailes, 2
(no. 1), 73.

F322. _____. Toward Home. <u>Moons and Lion Tailes</u>, 2 (no. 1),
      71.

## 1977

F323. Kabir. "18." <u>Moons and Lion Tailes</u>, 2 (no. 3), [inside
      front cover].

F324. _____. "11." <u>Moons and Lion Tailes</u>, 2 (no. 3), [inside
      front cover].

F325. _____. Versions of Kabir. <u>Floating Island</u>, no. 2, pp.
      40-45.

## 1978

F326. Martinson, Harry. No Name for It. <u>Moons and Lion Tailes</u>,
      2 (no. 4), 42.

F327. Rilke, Rainer Maria. From <u>Book for the Hours of Prayer</u>:
      "18." <u>Field</u>, no. 18 (Spring), 98.

F328. _____. From <u>Book for the Hours of Prayer</u>: "11."
      <u>Field</u>, no. 18 (Spring), 97.

F329. _____. From <u>Book for the Hours of Prayer</u>: "7." <u>Field</u>,
      no. 18 (Spring), 96.

F330. _____. From <u>Book for the Hours of Prayer</u>: "20."
      <u>Field</u>, no. 18 (Spring), 99.

F331. _____. From <u>Book for the Hours of Prayer</u>: "2." <u>Field</u>,
      no. 18 (Spring), 95.

## 1979

F332. Jiménez, Juan Ramón. Walt Whitman. <u>West Hills Review</u>,
      no. 1 (Fall), 12.

F333. Kabir. The Bee. <u>Southern Review</u> [Australia], 12 (July),
      135.

F334. _____. Listen Friend. <u>Southern Review</u> [Australia], 12
      (July), 135.

F335. _____. The Ruby. <u>Southern Review</u> [Australia], 12
      (July), 136.

202                                    Writings by Robert Bly

F336.  Machado, Antonio.  "The Clock Struck...."  Missouri Review,
       3 (Autumn), 12.

F337.  _____.  "It's Possible That...."  Missouri Review, 3 (Au-
       tumn), 12.

F338.  Tranströmer, Tomas.  Along the Lines.  Ironwood, no. 13,
       pp. 58-59.

F339.  _____.  Boat, Town.  Ironwood, no. 13, p. 60.

F340.  _____.  From the Winter of 1947.  Ironwood, no. 13, p.
       57.

F341.  _____.  Late May.  Ironwood, no. 13, p. 59.

F342.  _____.  A Section of Woods.  Ironwood, no. 13, p. 40.


                              1980

F343.  Jacobsen, Rolf.  Old Age.  Parabola, 5 (February), 80.

F344.  _____.  The Old Woman.  Parabola, 5 (February), 79.

F345.  Martinson, Harry.  Creation Night.  Mundus Artium, 12/13
       (1980/1981), 111.

F346.  _____.  March Evening.  Mundus Artium, 12/13 (1980/
       1981), 112.

F347.  _____.  Old Farmhouse.  Mundus Artium, 12/13 (1980/
       1981), 111.

F348.  Ponge, Francis.  The End of Fall.  Ohio Review, no. 24,
       p. 58.

F349.  Rilke, Rainer Maria.  On Music.  Parabola, 5 (May), 59.

F350.  Sonnevi, Göran.  Clarity.  Poetry East, no. 1, p. 19.

F351.  Tranströmer, Tomas.  Below Freezing.  Poetry East, no. 1,
       p. 7.

F352.  _____.  Citoyens.  Prism International, 19 (Fall/Winter
       1980/1981), 78.

F353.  _____.  The Scattered Congregation.  Mundus Artium,
       12/13 (1980/1981), 90.

F354.  _____.  Schubertiana.  Parabola, 5 (May), 16-17.

F355. _____. Street Crossing. <u>Poetry East</u>, no. 1, p. 8.

1981

F356. Rilke, Rainer Maria. Fox Fire. <u>Poetry East</u>, no. 4/5
(Spring/Summer), 27.

F357. _____. Imaginary Biography. <u>Poetry East</u>, no. 4/5
(Spring/Summer), 26.

F358. _____. Just as the Winged Energy of Delight. <u>Poetry
East</u>, no. 4/5 (Spring/Sumemr), 28.

F359. _____. Mourning. <u>Poetry East</u>, no. 4/5 (Spring/Summer),
25.

F360. Tranströmer, Tomas. After a Long Dry Spell. <u>Pequod</u>, 12,
p. 93.

F361. _____. At Funchal. <u>Pequod</u>, 12, p. 91.

F362. _____. The Black Mountain. <u>Pequod</u>, 12, p. 92.

F363. _____. From the Winter of 1947. <u>Poetry Now</u>, 5 (no. 6),
26.

F364. _____. Street Crossing. <u>Poetry East</u>, no. 4/5 (Spring/
Summer), 233.

F365. _____. _____. <u>Poetry Now</u>, 5 (no. 6), 26.

1982

F366. Hauge, Olav N. Harvest Time. <u>Ploughshares</u>, 8 (no. 2/3),
212.

F367. _____. Looking at an Old Mirror. <u>Ploughshares</u>, 8 (no.
2/3), 211.

F368. _____. There Is Nothing So Scary. <u>Ploughshares</u>, 8 (no.
2/3), 211.

F369. _____. Up On Top. <u>Stand</u>, 23 (no. 3), 15.

F370. Jacobsen, Rolf. The Silence Afterwards. <u>Stand</u>, 23 (no. 3),
10.

F371. Machado, Antonio. Country Roads. <u>River Styx</u>, no. 13,
p. 26.

F372.    _____.  The Evening is Grayish and Gloomy.  River Styx,
         no. 13, p. 24.

F373.    _____.  In the Shady Parts of the Square.  River Styx,
         no. 13, p. 22.

F374.    _____.  It's Possible that While Sleeping.  River Styx, no.
         13, p. 23.

F375.    _____.  Oh, Guadarrama Range.  River Styx, no. 13, p.
         22.

F376.    _____.  Two Poems from "The Countryside of Soria."
         River Styx, no. 13, p. 25.

F377.    _____.  The Wind One Brilliant Day.  River Styx, no. 13,
         p. 23.

F378.    Mirabai.  The Clouds.  Hampden-Sydney Poetry Review,
         (Fall), p. 11.

F379.    _____.  Why Mira Can't Go Back to Her Old House.
         Hampden-Sydney Poetry Review, (Fall), p. 11.


                                1983

F380.    García Lorca, Federico.  Dance of Death.  New Letters, 49
         (Spring/Summer), 92.

F381.    _____.  Ghazal of the Terrifying Presence.  New Letters,
         49 (Spring/Summer), 88-91.

F382.    Machado, Antonio.  Abel Martin's Last Lamentations.  White
         Pine Journal, no. 26, p. 30.

F383.    _____.  "And he was the demon of my dreams...."  White
         Pine Journal, no. 26, p. 17.

F384.    _____.  "Close to the road we sit down one day."  White
         Pine Journal, no. 26, p. 13.

F385.    _____.  "Clouds ripped open."  White Pine Journal, no.
         26, p. 16.

F386.    _____.  Field.  White Pine Journal, no. 26, p. 16.

F387.    _____.  "From the doorsill of a dream they called my
         name...."  White Pine Journal, no. 26, p. 17.

F388.    _____.  "The house that I loved so much."  White Pine
         Journal, no. 26, p. 19.

F389.      _____.  "I have walked along many roads."  White Pine
           Journal, no. 26, p. 6.

F390.      _____.  "I listen to the songs."  White Pine Journal, no.
           26, pp. 9-10.

F391.      _____.  "If I were a poet."  White Pine Journal, no. 26,
           p. 18.

F392.      _____.  "In our soul everything...."  White Pine Journal,
           no. 26, p. 22.

F393.      _____.  "Is my soul asleep?"  White Pine Journal, no. 26,
           p. 16.

F394.      _____.  "It doesn't matter now if the golden wine...."
           White Pine Journal, no. 26, p. 18.

F395.      _____.  "It's possible that while asleep the hand...."
           White Pine Journal, no. 26, p. 21.

F396.      _____.  "Last night, as I was sleeping."  White Pine Jour-
           nal, no. 26, p. 15.

F397.      _____.  "Like Anacreonte."  White Pine Journal, no. 26,
           p. 20.

F398.      _____.  Memory from Childhood.  White Pine Journal, no.
           26, p. 7.

F399.      _____.  "Oh evening full of light!"  White Pine Journal,
           no. 26, p. 20.

F400.      _____.  "One Summer Night."  White Pine Journal, no. 26,
           p. 24.

F401.      _____.  Rebirth.  White Pine Journal, no. 26, p. 22.

F402.      _____.  "The square and the brilliant orange trees."
           White Pine Journal, no. 26, p. 10.

F403.      _____.  "There In That Mountainous Land."  White Pine
           Journal, no. 26, p. 24.

F404.      _____.  Thirteen Poems Chosen From Moral Problems and
           Folksongs.  White Pine Journal, no. 26, pp. 25-28.

F405.      _____.  Today's Meditation.  White Pine Journal, no. 26,
           p. 38.

F406.      _____.  The Water Wheel.  White Pine Journal, no. 26,
           p. 14.

F407.          . "The wind, one brilliant day, called." White
          Pine Journal, no. 26, p. 19.

F408.          . "You can know yourself." White Pine Journal,
          no. 26, p. 22.

F409.   [The report of an eye-witness].  A Homage to Machado in
          1966.  [prose].  White Pine Journal, no. 26, pp. 61-63.


                              1984

F410.   Ekelöf, Gunnar.  Monologue with Its Wife.  Chelsea, no. 42/
          43, (Chelsea Retrospective 1958-1983), p. 65.

# G. POEMS IN BOOKS

[This list does not include those works edited by Bly.
See "Editions" under section "A" for titles edited and/
or compiled by Bly.]

## 1957

G1.  New Poets of England and America. Eds. Donald Hall, Robert
     Pack, and Louis Simpson. New York: Meridian Books.
     Barnfire During Church/The Man Whom the Sea Kept
Awake/A Missouri Traveller Writes Home: 1830/The Puritan on his
Honeymoon/Where We Must Look for Help

## 1962

G2.  Contemporary American Poetry. Selected and Introduced by
     Donald Hall. Baltimore: Penguin Books.
     After the Industrial Revolution, All Things Happen at
Once/Andrew Jackson's Speech/Awakening/A Busy Man Speaks/
Driving Toward the Lac Qui Parle River/Hunting Pheasants in a
Cornfield/Poem Against the British/Poem in Three Parts/The Pos-
sibility of New Poetry/Sleet Storm on the Merritt Parkway/Sunday
In Glastonbury/Where We Must Look for Help

## 1964

G3.  A Journey of Poems. Ed. Richard F. Niebling. New York:
     Dell Publishing Company.
     A Missouri Traveller Writes Home: 1830.

## 1965

G4.  A Book of Love Poems. Ed. William Cole. New York: Viking
     Press.
     Love Poem

G5. · The Faber Book of Modern Verse. 3rd ed. Ed. Michael
     Roberts with a supplement chosen by Donald Hall. Lon-
     don: Faber & Faber.

Laziness and Silence/A Man Writes to a Part of Himself/
"Taking the Hands"


## 1966

G6.   From the Hungarian Revolution:  A Collection of Poems.  Ed.
       David Ray.  Ithaca, NY:  Cornell University Press.
       The Journey of the Hungarian Dead after Death

G7.   Poems for Young Readers:  Selections from their own writing
       by poets attending the Houston Festival of Contemporary
       Poetry.  56th Annual NCTE Convention, November 24-26,
       1966.  [Champaign, IL:]  National Council of Teachers of
       English.
       Hatred of Men with Black Hair

G8.   28 Poems.  La Crosse, WI:  Sumac Press.
       After the Industrial Revolution, All Things Happen at
Once/Beginning a Book on America/Driving Toward the Lac Qui
Parle River


## 1967

G9.   Eight Lines and Under.  Ed. William Cole.  New York:  Mac-
       millan Co.
       Driving to Town Late to Mail a Letter

G10.  Heartland:  Poets of the Midwest.  Ed. Lucien Stryk.  De
       Kalb:  Northern Illinois University Press.
       After Drinking All Night with a Friend .../The Clear Air
of October/Depression/Driving Toward the Lac Qui Parle River/
Hunting Pheasants in a Cornfield/Laziness and Silence/Poem in
Three Parts/Three Kinds of Pleasures/Watering the Horse

G11.  The New Modern Poetry.  Ed. M. L. Rosenthal.  New York:
       Macmillan Co.
       Poem Against the Rich/Snowfall in the Afternoon

G12.  Poems.  [New York:]  Artists and Writers Against the War in
       Vietnam.
       Those Being Eaten [By America]

G13.  The Prose Poem:  An International Anthology.  Ed. Michael
       Benedikt.  New York:  Dell Publishing Company, Inc.
       The Dead Seal Near McClure's Beach/The Hockey Poem/
The Hunter/The Large Starfish/Looking at a Dead Wren in My Hand/
A Small Bird's Nest Made of White Reed Fiber/A Turtle/Two Prose
Poems on Locked-In Animals:  1.  Lobsters Waiting to be Eaten in a
Restaurant Window 2.  Bored Elephants in the Circus Stable

## 1968

G14.   100 Postwar Poems. Ed. M. L. Rosenthal. New York: Mac-
       millan Co.
       Romans Angry about the Inner World


## 1969

G15.   A Book of Nature Poems. Ed. William Cole. New York:
       Viking Press.
       Driving to Town Late to Mail a Letter

G16.   City In All Directions. Ed. Arnold Adoff. New York: Mac-
       millan Co.
       The Great Society/Hearing Men Shout at Night On Mac-
Dougal Street

G17.   The Contemporary American Poets: American Poetry Since
       1940. Ed. Mark Strand. New York: World Publishing
       Co.
       After the Industrial Revolution, All Things Happen at
Once/The Executive's Death/Those Being Eaten By America/Watching
Television

G18.   A First Reader of Contemporary American Poetry. Ed. Pat-
       rick Gleeson. Columbus, OH: Charles E. Merrill Publish-
       ing Co.
       Depression/The Executive's Death/Hatred of Men with
Black Hair/Looking at New-Fallen Snow from a Train/Those Being
Eaten by America/Three Kinds of Pleasures/Waking from Sleep/
Watching Television/When the Dumb Speak

G19.   The Modern Age: Literature. Comps. Leonard Lief and
       James F. Light. New York: Holt, Rinehart and Winston.
       Counting Small-Boned Bodies/Those Being Eaten by Amer-
ica/Watching Television

G20.   Naked Poetry: Recent American Poetry in Open Forms. Eds.
       Stephen Berg and Robert Mezey. Indianapolis: Bobbs-
       Merrill.
       After Drinking All Night With a Friend .../After Working/
Afternoon Sleep/Asian Peace Offers Rejected Without Publication/
Awakening/The Clear Air of October/Counting Small-Boned Bodies/
Depression/A Dream of Suffocation/Driving to Town Late to Mail a
Letter/Driving Toward the Lac Qui Parle River/The Executive's
Death/Getting Up Early/Hatred of Men with Black Hair/Hurrying
Away from the Earth/In a Train/Looking at New-Fallen Snow From
a Train/Looking at Some Flowers/Night/Old Boards/Poem in Three
Parts/Silence/Surprised by Evening/Those Being Eaten by America/
Watering the Horse/Written in Dejection Near Rome

G21.  **Pith and Vinegar**. Ed. William Cole. New York: Simon and
       Schuster.
       Ducks

G22.  **To Play Man Number One**. Comps. Sara Hannum and John
       Terry Chase. New York: Atheneum.
       Watching Television

G23.  **The Writing on the Wall**. Ed. Walter Lowenfels. New York:
       Doubleday & Co.
       Hurrying Away from the Earth


                              1970

G24.  **Beach Glass and Other Poems**. Ed. Paul Molloy. New York:
       Four Winds Press.
       Three Kinds of Pleasures

G25.  **A College Book of Verse**. Ed. C. F. Main. Belmont, CA:
       Wadsworth Publishing Co.
       Romans Angry about the Inner World/Sleet Storm on the
Merritt Parkway

G26.  **Poetry in English**. 2nd ed. Eds. Warren Taylor and Donald
       Hall. New York: Macmillan Co.
       A Man Writes to a Part of Himself/Romans Angry about the
Inner World/"Taking the Hands"

G27.  **The Voice That Is Great Within Us: American Poetry of the
       Twentieth Century**. Ed. Hayden Carruth. New York:
       Bantam Books.
       Driving to Town Late to Mail a Letter/Solitude Late at
Night in the Woods/Surprised by Evening

G28.  **The Wind Is Round**. Comps. Sara Hannum and John Terry
       Chase. New York: Atheneum.
       After Working


                              1971

G29.  **Contemporary American Poetry**. Ed. A. Poulin, Jr. Boston:
       Houghton Mifflin Co.
       Asian Peace Offers Rejected Without Publication/Come with
Me/Counting Small-Boned Bodies/In a Train/In Danger from the
Outer World/Old Boards/Poem Against the Rich/Poem in Three Parts/
Snowfall in the Afternoon/Surprised by Evening/The Teeth Mother
Naked at Last/Waking from Sleep/War and Silence/When the Dumb
Speak

G30.  **Earth, Air, Fire, and Water.**  Ed.  Frances Monson McCul-
        lough.  New York:  Coward, McCann, & Geoghegan.
        Hatred of Men with Black Hair/Hearing Men Shout at Night
on MacDougal Street/Moving in a Caravan (1 & 8)/Those Being Eaten
by America/Three Presidents/Turning Away From Lies

G31.  **Just What This Country Needs, Another Poetry Anthology.**
        Eds. James McMichael and Dennis Saleh.  Belmont, CA:
        Wadsworth Publishing Co.
        An Empty Place/Johnson's Face on Television/Pilgrim Fish
Heads/Water Poverty

G32.  **The Literature of the American West.** Ed. J. Golden Taylor.
        Boston:  Houghton Mifflin Co.
        Hatred of Men with Black Hair/A Missouri Traveller Writes
Home:  1846

G33.  **The Pleasures of Poetry.**  Ed. Donald Hall.  New York:
        Harper & Row.
        Romans Angry about the Inner World

G34.  **Poetry Brief:  An Anthology of Short, Short Poems.**  Comp.
        William Cole.  New York:  Macmillan Co.
        Love Poem

G35.  **Since Feeling Is First.**  Eds. James Mecklenburger and Gary
        Simmons.  Glenview, IL:  Scott, Foresman & Co.
        Come with Me/Driving to Town Late to Mail a Letter/Solitude
Late at Night in the Woods

G36.  **Twentieth Century Poetry.**  Ed. Carol Marshall.  Boston:
        Houghton Mifflin Co.
        Hearing Men Shout at Night on MacDougal Street


                                    1972

G37.  **Contemporary American Poetry.**  2nd ed.  Ed. Donald Hall.
        New York:  Penguin Books.
        After the Industrial Revolution, All Things Happen at Once/
Andrew Jackson's Speech/Awakening/A Busy Man Speaks/Driving
Toward the Lac Qui Parle River/Hunting Pheasants in a Cornfield/
Poem Against the British/Poem in Three Parts/The Possibility of New
Poetry/Sleet Storm on the Merritt Parkway/Sunday in Glastonbury/
Where We Must Look for Help

G38.  **An Introduction to Poetry.**  2nd ed.  Ed. Louis Simpson.
        New York:  St. Martin's Press.
        Love Poem/Poem Against the British/Summer, 1960, Minne-
sota/Waking from Sleep

212                                    Writings by Robert Bly

G39.  The Land on the Tip of a Hair:  Poems in Wood.  Wang Hui-
      Ming.  Barre, MA:  Barre.
      Wild Hay [reproduction of broadside, see A27].

G40.  The Pocket Book of Modern Verse.  Ed. Oscar Williams.  New-
      ly revised by Hyman J. Sobiloff.  New York:  Washington
      Square Press.
      Afternoon Sleep/Surprised by Sleep

G41.  Themes in American Literature.  Comp. Philip McFarland.
      Boston:  Houghton Mifflin Co.
      The Busy Man Speaks/Counting Small-Boned Bodies

G42.  What's In a Poem.  John Rylander and Edith Rylander.  En-
      cino, CA:  Dickenson Publishing Co.
      Those Being Eaten By America

1973

G43.  Contemporary Poetry in America.  Ed. Miller Williams. New
      York:  Random House.
      Come With Me/The Fire of Despair Has Been Our Saviour/
Hurrying Away from the Earth/Written in Dejection Near Rome

G44.  The Living Underground:  An Anthology of Contemporary
      American Poetry.  Ed. Hugh Fox.  Troy, NY:  Whitson
      Publishing Co., Inc.
      Lies/Mark of Jeep Tires on Graves/Mother Coming/Scene
with Respectable Men/Sea Scene/Unable to Wake Up/Woman Asleep
Near Bridge

G45.  Messages:  A Thematic Anthology of Poetry.  Ed. X. J.
      Kennedy.  Boston:  Little Brown & Co.
      Looking Into a Tide Pool

G46.  The Norton Anthology of Modern Poetry.  Eds. Richard Ell-
      mann and Robert O'Clair.  New York:  W. W. Norton &
      Co.
      Asian Peace Offers Rejected Without Publication/The Clear
Air of October/Come With Me/Evolution from the Fish/The Great So-
ciety/Johnson's Cabinet Watched by Ants/Poem Against the Rich/
Romans Angry about the Inner World/Waking from Sleep/When the
Dumb Speak

G47.  Poems One Line and Longer.  Ed. William Cole.  New York:
      Grossman Publishers.
      In a Train

## 1974

G48.  An Introduction to Poetry. 3rd ed. Ed. X. J. Kennedy.
      Boston: Little Brown & Co.
      Driving to Town Late to Mail a Letter

G49.  New Coasts and Strange Harbors: Discovering Poems. Comps.
      Helen Hill and Agnes Perkins. New York: Thomas Y.
      Crowell Company.
      Driving Toward the Lac Qui Parle River/A Late Spring Day
in My Life/Watering the Horse

G50.  Poetry: Past and Present. Eds. Frank Brady and Martin
      Price. New York: Harcourt Brace Jovanovich.
      Laziness and Silence

G51.  Poetry: Points of Departure. Ed. Henry Taylor. Cam-
      bridge, MA: Winthrop Publishers.
      Counting Small-Boned Bodies/Those Being Eaten By America

G52.  Room for Me and a Mountain Lion: Poetry of Open Space.
      Comp. Nancy Larrick. New York: M. Evans & Co.
      In a Mountain Cabin in Norway

G53.  To See the World Afresh. Comps. Lillian Moore and Judith
      Thurman. New York: Atheneum.
      Counting Small-Boned Bodies/Driving to Town Late to Mail
a Letter/Looking into a Face

## 1975

G54.  Contemporary American Poetry. 2nd ed. Ed. Al Poulin, Jr.
      Boston: Houghton Mifflin Co.
      After Long Busyness/Asian Peace Offers Rejected Without
Publication/Counting Small-Boned Bodies/Driving to Town Late to
Mail a Letter/In a Train/Looking Into a Tide Pool/Poem in Three
Parts/Shack Poem/A Small Bird's Nest Made of White Reed Fiber/
Snowfall in the Afternoon/Surprised by Evening/Waking from Sleep/
War and Silence/Watering the Horse/When the Dumb Speak

## 1976

G55.  America Is Not All Traffic Lights: Poems of the Midwest.
      Comp. Alice Fleming. Boston: Little Brown & Co.
      Three Kinds of Pleasures

G56.  Introducing Poems. Eds. Linda W. Wagner and C. David
      Mead. New York: Harper & Row.
      Solitude Late at Night in the Woods

G57.  The New Oxford Book of American Verse.  Ed. Richard Ell-
      mann.  New York:  Oxford University Press.
      Come With Me/Evolution from the Fish/Johnson's Cabinet
Watched by Ants/Looking at Some Flowers/Looking Into a Face/Poem
Against the Rich/Poem in Three Parts/Romans Angry about the In-
ner World/Sleet Storm on the Merritt Parkway/Snowfall in the After-
noon/Waking from Sleep/When the Dumb Speak

### 1977

G58.  The Sound of a Few Leaves:  An Appointment Book of Weeks
      and Anthology of Current Poetry.  Ed. Ernest and Cis
      Stefanik.  Derry, PA:  The Rook Press.
      Black Pony Eating Grass

### 1978

G59.  Fine Frenzy:  Enduring Themes in Poetry.  Robert Baylor
      and Brenda Stokes.  New York:  McGraw-Hill.
      Poem for the Drunkard President/The Puritan on His Honey-
moon

G60.  Silent Voices:  Recent American Poems on Nature.  Ed. Paul
      Feroe.  St. Paul, MN:  Ally Press.
      The Dead Seal Near McClure's Beach/Looking Into a Dry
Tumbleweed Brought in from the Snow/A Man and a Woman and a
Blackbird/Night Farmyard

### 1979

G61.  Brother Songs:  A Male Anthology of Poetry.  Ed. Jim Perl-
      man.  Minneapolis:  Holy Cow! Press.
      Finding the Father/For My Son Noah, Ten Years Old

### 1980

G62.  Tendril Magazine Presents The Poet's Choice.  Ed. George F.
      Murphy, Jr.  Green Harbor, MA:  Tendril.
      The Fallen Tree

### 1981

G63.  From A to Z:  200 Contemporary American Poets.  Ed. David
      Ray.  Athens, OH:  Swallow Press.
      Black Pony Eating Grass

Poems in Books                                                    215

G64.   Tygers of Wrath:  Poems of Hate, Anger, and Invective.
       Ed. & comp. X. J. Kennedy.  Athens:  University of
       Georgia Press.
       The Hatred of Men with Black Hair


                              1982

G65.   Gnosis Anthology of Contemporary American and Russian Lit-
       erature and Art.  Vol. 1.  Ed. E. Daniel Richie and
       Stephen Sartarelli.  New York:  Gnosis Press.
       Eleven O'Clock at Night/Four Ways of Knowledge/Kneeling
Down to Look into a Culvert/Words Rising.  [Note:  Vol. II contains
Russian translations of these poems.]

G66.   Of Solitude and Silence:  Writings on Robert Bly.  Ed.
       Richard Jones and Kate Daniels.  Boston:  Beacon Press.
       At Midocean/A Bouquet of Ten Roses/Crazy Carlson's
Meadow/Eleven O'Clock at Night/Fifty Males Sitting Together/A
Meditation on Philosophy/The New King/The Whole Moisty Night/
Words Rising/Written at Mule Hollow, Utah


                              1983

G67.   The Longman Anthology of Contemporary American Poetry.
       Ed. Stuart Friebert and David Young.  New York:  Long-
       man, Inc.
       August Rain/Driving Toward the Lac Qui Parle River/Fish-
ing on a Lake at Night/A Long Walk Before the Snows Begin/Mourn-
ing Pablo Neruda/Six Winter Privacy Poems/Snowbanks North of the
House/Three Presidents/Turning Away from Lies/Visiting Emily
Dickinson's Grave with Robert Francis


                              1985

G68.   The American Tradition in Literature.  6th ed.  Eds. George
       Perkins, Sculley Bradley, Richmond Croom Beatty, E.
       Hudson Long.  New York:  Random House.
       Driving to Town Late to Mail a Letter/Driving Toward the
Lac Qui Parle River/The Executive's Death/Looking at New-Fallen
Snow from a Train/Snowbanks North of the House/Watering the
Horse

# H. TRANSLATIONS IN BOOKS

[This list does not include those works edited by Bly. See "Translations" and "Editions" under section "A" for titles edited and/or compiled by Bly.]

## 1966

H1. From the Hungarian Revolution: A Collection of Poems. Ed. David Ray. Ithaca, NY: Cornell University Press.
Anonymous: Folk Song: I Go On/Folk Song: If I Were A River at High Water/Fragment
"C.": Poem for a Gravestone
Attila Gerecz: Fuit/My Legacy/On Bread and Water/Reflection
Gabor Kocsis: Old Peasant

H2. Three Poems by Tomas Tranströmer. Formula Series Number 3. Lawrence, KS: Terrence Williams.
After the Attack

## 1968

H3. Yvan Goll: Selected Poems. Ed. Paul Zweig. San Francisco: Kayak Books, Inc.
Ode to Autumn/The Inner Trees

## 1970

H4. The Penguin Book of Socialist Verse. Ed. Alan Bold. Harmondsworth: Penguin.
Gunnar Ekelöf: "Each Person Is a World." Tr. with Christine Paulston.

## 1972

H5. Dogalypse: San Francisco Poetry Reading. Andrei Voznesensky. San Francisco: City Lights Books.
Christmas Beaches. Tr. with Maureen Sager, Catherine Leech, Vera Reck, and Lawrence Ferlinghetti/Halloween Apples.

Tr. with Vera Dunham/Darkmotherscream.  Tr. with Vera Dunham

H6.  Miguel Hernandez and Blas De Otero:  Selected Poems.  Ed.
      Timothy Baland and Hardie St. Martin.  Boston:  Beacon
      Press.
      Miguel Hernandez:  Eternal Darkness.  Tr. with Timothy
Baland/"For Pulling the Feathers From Icy Archangels"/I Have
Plenty of Heart/"A Knife that Eats Flesh"/Letter/Lullaby of the
Moon/Prisons, Part II.  Blas de Otero:  Tr. with Timothy Baland/
"Sitting on Top of Corpses"/"Will This Beam of Light"/"You Threw
Me A Lemon"/"Your Heart?--It Is A Frozen Orange"

1976

H7.  The Contemporary World Poets.  Ed. Donald Junkins.  New
      York:  Harcourt Brace Jovanovich.
      Rene Char:  Four Poems on the Cave Paintings at Lascaux
      Gunnar Ekelöf:  Monologue With Its Wife/The Swan/When
One Has Come as Far as I in Pointlessness.  All three poems tr. with
Christina Paulston.
      Miguel Hernandez:  I Have Plenty of Heart/Lullaby of the
Moon
      Rolf Jacobsen:  The Glass Shop/May Moon/The Morning
Paper/Old Age/The Old Women/Sssh
      Juan Ramón Jiménez:  At First She Came to Me Pure/Being
Awake/Dawn Out-Side the City Walls/Full Moon/I Am Not I/Oceans
      Federico García Lorca:  Ghazal of the Dark Death/Ghazal
of the Terrifying Presence/The Guitar/Little Infinite Poem/The Quar-
rel
      Pablo Neruda:  Enigmas/Letter to Miguel Otero Silva, in
Caracas (1948)/Sexual Water
      Nichita Stanescu:  Second Elegy/Song
      Tomas Tranströmer:  After a Death/Out in the Open
      César Vallejo:  The Anger That Breaks A Man Down Into
Boys/Black Stone Lying On a White Stone/Masses

H8.  The Prose Poem:  An International Anthology.  Ed. Michael
      Benedikt.  New York:  Dell Publishing Co., Inc.
      Juan Ramón Jiménez:  Author's Club/Cemetery/Deep Night/
Lavender Windowpanes and White Curtains/Walt Whitman
      Tomas Tranströmer:  The Bookcase/Standing Up

1977

H9.  Twenty Poems of Vicente Aleixandre.  Ed. Lewis Hyde.  Madi-
      son, MN:  The Seventies Press.
      The Body and The Soul/It's Raining/Life/The Waltz

## 1978

H10.  Nostalgia For the Past.  Andrei Voznesensky.  Eds. Vera
      Dunham and Max Howard.  New York:  Doubleday & Co.
      Darkmotherscream/Shame/Ant.  Tr. with Vera Dunham/
Christmas Beaches.  Tr. with Lawrence Ferlinghetti/Halloween Apples

H11.  The Poetry Connection:  An Anthology of Contemporary Poems
      with Ideas to Stimulate Children's Writing.  Kinereth Gens-
      ler and Nina Nyhart.  New York:  Teachers and Writers
      Collaborative.
      Bashō:  "The temple bell stops--"
      Issa:  "I look into a dragonfly's eye"/"Now listen, you
watermelons--"

## 1979

H12.  An Anthology of Modern Swedish Literature.  Ed. Per Wäst-
      berg.  Merrick, NY:  Cross-Cultural Communications.
      Göran Sonnevi:  Through the Open Door

H13.  A Longing for the Light:  Selected Poems of Vicente Aleix-
      andre.  Ed. Lewis Hyde.  New York:  Harper & Row.
      The Body and The Soul/It's Raining/Life/The Waltz

H14.  Modern Swedish Poetry in Translation.  Eds. Gunnar Harding
      and Anselm Hollo.  Minneapolis:  University of Minnesota
      Press.
      Göran Sonnevi:  A Ball/The Double Movement/The Island
of Koster, 1973/On the War in Vietnam/Through the Open Door/Will
You Come in Here and Get Your Cap On/"You are a murderer"/
"You shouted to me ..."/Zero

## 1980

H15.  Editor's Choice:  Literature and Graphics from the U.S. Small
      Press, 1965-1977.  Eds. Morty Sklar and Jim Mulac.  Iowa
      City, Iowa:  Spirit That Moves Us Press.
      Vicente Aleixandre:  The Old Man and the Sun.  Tr. with
Lewis Hyde
      Rolf Jacobsen:  Old Age
      Kabir:  Friend, Hope for the Guest
      Federico García Lorca:  New York (Office and Attack)
      Rainer Maria Rilke:  The Voices
      César Vallejo:  The Black Riders

H16.  Of Solitude and Silence:  Writings on Robert Bly.  Eds.
      Richard Jones and Kate Daniels.  Boston:  Beacon Press.
      Rainer Maria Rilke:  Fox Fire/Imaginary Biography/Just as
the Winged Energy of Delight/Mourning

# I.  SOUND RECORDINGS

## 1960

I1.  Robert Bly Reading His Poems with Comment in the Recording
     Laboratory, May 2, 1960.  Washington, DC:  Library of
     Congress.  Library Work Order 3106.  Reel to reel tape.
     Contents:  Poem in Three Parts ("Oh in an early morning
     I think I shall live forever")/Thoughts on Long Journeys in Fall/
     Evening/Poem in Three Parts ("The hawk sailed over the trees")/
     Arriving Home on a Summer Evening/Dusk/Fall Rain/September Night
     with an Old Horse/Driving Through Ohio/The Pennsylvania Turn-
     pike/Thinking of Trees/The Coming of Autumn/Return to the Life
     of the Spirit/The Joy When the Leaves of the Body Fall/At the Fun-
     eral of Great Aunt Mary/After Drinking All Night With a Friend .../
     Watching the Snow and Thinking of Death/Joy/Walking About at
     Night/Restless in the Fall Afternoon/The New Snow/The Possibility
     of New Poetry/The Marriage/The Delicious Confusion/A Dream as the
     Western Movies Increase/Singing in Winter (incomplete)/Condition
     of the Working Classes, 1960/The Coming of Night/The Campaign
     of the Advertising Men/The Confusion of America/Listening to the
     Radio/Mourning for the Recent Deaths/The Tossing Seas/Poem ("The
     moon sails out over the street canyons in New York")/We Have
     Overlooked Something/The Strange Sensation of Hearing Men Who
     Shout at Night in Bleecker Street/The Chinese Coolies Who Built
     the Railroads .../The Three American Heroes/Each Day I Live/The
     World Is a Confusion of Three Worlds/Thinking of Wallace Stev-
     ens .../Remembering in Oslo.
         Cited in Literary Recordings:  A Checklist of the Archive of
     Recorded Poetry and Literature in the Library of Congress.  Comp.
     Jennifer Whittington.  Washington, DC:  Library of Congress, 1981.

## 1961

I2.  "Bly, Robert."  Audiotape #178, 179.  San Francisco:  The
         American Poetry Archive.  San Francisco State University.
         Recording of a reading at San Francisco State sponsored by
     The Poetry Center on October 25, 1961.  Contents uncataloged.

## 1966

I3.  The Poetry of Robert Bly.  New York:  Jeffrey Norton

Publishers, Inc. Cassette, 2-track, mono, 38 min. Recorded at the YM-YWHA Poetry Center on May 2, 1966. See I27.

I4. Twelve Contemporary Poets: 1966 Houston Poetry Festival Poets Reading Selections from Their Own Works. [Champaign, IL: National Council of Teachers of English]. 1 disc, 33 1/3 rpm, mono, 12 in.
Contents: Driving Through Ohio/Poem in Three Parts/ September Night with an Old Horse

## 1967

I5. "Bly, Robert." Audiotape #341. San Francisco: The American Poetry Archive. San Francisco State University.
Recording of a reading at San Francisco State sponsored by The Poetry Center on April 24, 1967. Contents uncataloged.

I6. _____. Audiotape #359. San Francisco: The American Poetry Archive. San Francisco State University.
Recording of a reading at San Francisco State sponsored by The Poetry Center on November 21, 1967. Contents uncataloged.

## 1968

I7. Robert Bly Reading. Stony Brook: Educational Communications Center, State University of New York at Stony Brook. 2 cassettes, 2-track, mono, 75 min. Recorded June 10, 1968.
Contents: Late at Night during a Visit of Friends/Looking into a Face/Taking the Hands/Chrysanthemums/Driving Through Ortonville, Minnesota/A Doing Nothing Poem/Sketch for a Renaissance Painting/Romans Angry about the Inner World/Watching Television/ Those Being Eaten by America/Counting Small-Boned Bodies/Johnson's Cabinet Watched by Ants/Foreign Policy/The Busy Man Speaks/ Hatred of Men with Black Hair/Asian Peace Offers Rejected without Publication/Driving through Minnesota during the Hanoi Bombing/ Kabir-"Student do the simple purification"/Ducks/Three Kinds of Pleasures/The Teeth Mother Naked at Last [selections]. Also recites translations of Ibn Hazm, Bashō, Issa, García Lorca, and Jiménez, and poems by Yeats, Kenneth Koch, and William Carlos Williams.
Includes introductory remarks by Louis Simpson.

I8. Today's Poets: Their Poems, Their Voices. Vol. 5. Comp. Stephen Dunning. New York: Scholastic Records. 1 disc, 33 1/3 rpm, mono, 12 in.
Contents: Awakening/Counting Small-Boned Bodies/Driving Through Minnesota During the Hanoi Bombings/Driving Through Ohio/Driving to Town Late to Mail a Letter/Driving Toward the Lac

Qui Parle River/Hatred of Men with Black Hair/Love Poem/"Taking
the Hands"/Three Kinds of Pleasures/Waking from an Afternoon
Sleep.

### 1969

I9.   Spoken Arts Treasury of 100 Modern American Poets Reading
      Their Poems. Vol. 16. Ed. Paul Kresh. New Rochelle,
      NY: Spoken Arts, Inc. 1 disc, 33 1/3 rpm, mono, 12 in.
      Contents: A Busy Man Speaks/Condition of the Working
Classes, 1960/The Man Whom the Sea Kept Awake/Snowfall in the
Afternoon.

### 1970

I10.  Poetry International '69. London: Argo Records, Spoken
      Word Division, 1970-1971. 2 discs, 33 1/3 rpm, mono, 12
      in.
      Contents: Counting Small-Boned Bodies/Tongues Whirling.

I11.  [Public Reading]. Brockport: Educational Communications
      Center, State University College at Brockport, State Uni-
      versity of New York.
      Recorded March 1970. Reel to reel tape.

### 1971

I12.  Andrei Voznesenskii Reading His Poems in Russian and Making
      Some Comment in English, with William Jay Smith reading
      English translations of the poems, in the Coolidge Auditori-
      um, October 27, 1971. Washington, DC: Library of Con-
      gress. Library Work Order 6649. Reel to reel tape.
      Contents: Christmas Beeches, tr. by Bly.
      Cited in Literary Recordings: A Checklist of the Archive
      of Recorded Poetry and Literature in the Library of Congress.
      Comp. Jennifer Whittington. Washington, DC: Library of Congress,
      1981.

I13.  [Public Reading]. Brockport: Educational Communications
      Center, State University College at Brockport, State Uni-
      versity of New York. Recorded December 1971. Reel to
      reel tape.

### 1972

I14.  Panjandrum. [San Francisco: Panjandrum Press]. 1 disc,
      33 1/3 rpm, mono, 12 in.

Contents: Another Doing Nothing Poem/Jumping Out of
Bed/November Day at McClure's/Sunday Morning In Tomales Bay.
See A28 and A32.

I15.  Tough Poems for Tough People.  Ed. Florence Howe.  New
      York:  Caedmon.
      Cassette, 2-track, mono.
      Counting Small-Boned Bodies [not read by Bly].


                                1973

I16.  Lecture on Poetry.  St. Cloud, MN:  St. Cloud State Univer-
      sity.  Reel to reel tape, 3 3/4 ips, mono, 113 min.  Re-
      corded on April 2, 1973 in Atwood Center Theatre of St.
      Cloud State University.

I17.  Robert Bly.  St. Paul:  Minnesota Public Radio.  Cassette,
      2-track, mono.  Date of broadcast, Fall 1973.
      Contents:  Bly reads his poetry and talks at Moorhead
State University.


                                1974

I18.  Black Box 3.  With Sonia Sanchez.  Washington, DC:  Poets'
      Audio Center, Watershed Foundation.  2 cassettes, 1-track,
      mono.
      Contents:  After Long Busyness/After the Industrial
Revolution, All Things Happen at Once/At Night/Climbing Up Mt.
Vision with My Little Boy/Counting Small-Boned Bodies/The Dead
Seal Near McClure's Beach/Driving Toward the Lac Qui Parle River/
Hatred of Men With Black Hair/"Inside this Clay Jug"/Letter from a
Girl/"My poetry resembles the bread of Egypt"/On a Moonlight Road
in the North Woods/A Place Prepared/Poem in Three Parts/Six Winter
Privacy Poems/Snowbanks, North of the House/Kabir-"Student, do
the simple purification"/Sufi Song-"And when I"/The Teeth-Mother
Naked at Last/Thinking of the Autumn Fields/Turtle Climbing From
a Rock/Unanswered Letters/Water Under the Earth.
      See I22.

I19.  Poetry Outland.  St. Paul:  Minnesota Public Radio.  Cas-
      sette, 2-track, mono, 37 min., 44 sec.  Date of broad-
      cast, October 9, 1974.
      Contents:  Interview and readings.

I20.  Poetry Reading.  Fort Collins:  Colorado State University.
      Reel-to-reel, 3 3/4 ips, mono.  Recorded May 6-7, 1974
      at Colorado State University, Fort Collins, CO.
      Contents:  Reading of his own works and those of Spanish
poets.

I21.  [Public Reading].  Brockport:  Educational Communications
      Center, State University College at Brockport, State Uni-
      versity of New York.  Recorded April 1974.  Reel-to-reel
      tape.

## 1975

I22.  For the Stomach:  Poems.  Washington, DC:  Poets' Audio
      Center, Watershed Foundation.  Cassette, 2-track, mono,
      64 min.  Originally released as half of Black Box 3.
      Contents:  See I18.

I23.  Mother Consciousness.  St. Paul:  Minnesota Public Radio.
      Cassette, 1-track, mono, 26 min, 13 sec.  Date of broad-
      cast, May 20, 1975.
      Contents:  Bill Siemering speaks with R.B. about the phi-
losophy of mother consciousness and the advantages it offers.
      Reprinted, in part, in A57 and P107.

I24.  Poet Robert Bly.  St. Paul:  Minnesota Public Radio.  Cas-
      sette, 2-track, mono, 41 min, 30 sec.  Date of broadcast,
      June 29, 1975.
      Contents:  Reading and lecture on the techniques and
philosophy of poetry.

## 1976

I25.  Robert Bly.  DeLand, FL:  Everett/Edwards, Inc.  Cassette,
      1/2 track, mono, 27 min.  Cassette curriculum in American
      literature, #154.
      Contents:  A Busy Man Speaks/Counting Small-Boned Bodies/
Hatred of Men with Black Hair/Poem in Three Parts/Six Winter Pri-
vacy Poems/Snowfall in the Afternoon/Taking the Hands/Where We
Must Look for Help.

## 1977

I26.  "Bly, Robert."  Audiotape #1275.  San Francisco:  The Amer-
      ican Poetry Archive.  San Francisco State University.
      A donated recording.  Contents uncataloged.

I27.  The Poetry of Robert Bly.  New York:  Jeffrey Norton Pub-
      lishers, Inc.  YM-YWHA Poetry Center Series, #23242.
      See I3.

## 1978

128. "Bly, Robert." Audiotape # 1276. San Francisco: The
     American Poetry Archive. San Francisco State University.
     A donated recording. Recorded on May 5, 1978. Contents
uncataloged.

129. A Conversation with Robert Bly. Stony Brook: Educational
     Communications Center, State University of New York at
     Stony Brook. Cassette.
     See J6.

130. Creative Writing: The Whole Kit and Caboodle. James W.
     Swanson. St. Paul, MN: EMC Corporation. 4 cassettes.
     Contents: The Dead Seal Near McClure's Beach

131. A Poet Reads His Work: Robert Bly. Stony Brook: Educa-
     tional Communications Center, State University of New York
     at Stony Brook. Cassette.
     See J8.

132. Robert Bly, May 2, 1978. St. Paul: Minnesota Public Radio.
     Cassette, 2-track, mono.
     Contents: Reads from This Body Is Made of Camphor and
Gopherwood, and talks with Bill Siemering.


## 1979

133. "Bly, Robert." Audiotape #1396. San Francisco: The Ameri-
     can Poetry Archive. San Francisco State University.
     Recording of a reading at San Francisco State sponsored
by Associated Students on October 9, 1979. Contents uncataloged.

134. The Greek Gods and Goddesses Considered as Interior Ener-
     gies. Galesburg, IL: Knox College. 2 cassettes, 2-
     track, mono, ca. 105 min.
     Lecture at Knox College, May 9, 1979.

135. New Letters on the Air: Robert Bly. Kansas City: New
     Letters, University of Missouri. Cassette, 2-track, mono,
     29 min.
     Contents: Anna Akhmatova poems: "Evening hours at
dusk"/"I did not lock the door"/"A land not mine"/Visiting Emily
Dickinson's Grave with Robert Francis/Written at Mule Hollow,
Utah/"Silent in the moonlight" (repeated)/At the Time of Peony
Blossoming/A Ramage for Waking the Hermit/Snowbanks North of
the House/For My Son Noah, Ten Years Old/"The maternal, the
fall air, all that we have learned."

136. Poetry Reading. Galesburg, IL: Knox College. 2 cassettes,
     2-track, mono, ca. 150 min.

137.  Robert Bly Reading His Poetry.  Minneapolis, MN:  North
      Hennepin Community College.  Cassette, 2-track, mono,
      30 min.

138.  The Teeth Mother Naked at Last, and Other Poems, A Read-
      ing.  St. Paul, MN:  Macalester College.  2 cassettes,
      mono.  The reading took place as part of The Vietnam Ex-
      perience and America Today, March 1-10, 1979.


                              1980

139.  Crisis in American Poetry.  Seattle:  Omega Institute West.
      2 cassettes, 2-track, mono.  Recorded May, 1980, Seattle,
      Washington.

140.  Poems and Stories.  Seattle:  Omega Institute West.  Cassette,
      2-track, mono.  Recorded May, 1980, Seattle, Washington.

141.  [Robert Bly Speaks and Reads from His Works at Michigan
      State].  Reel-to-reel tape, 7.5 ips, mono, 60 min.  Broad-
      cast on WKAR Radio, October 1980.

142.  A Poetry Reading with Dulcimer.  San Francisco:  C. G.
      Jung Institute of San Francisco.  2 cassettes, ca. 240 min.


                              1984

143.  "Bly, Robert."  Audiotape #1823.  San Francisco:  The Amer-
      ican Poetry Archive.  San Francisco State University.
      A donated recording.  Contents uncataloged.

# J.  VIDEORECORDINGS

## 1970

J1.  Robert Bly with Gregory FitzGerald and Bill Heyen.  Brock-
port:  Educational Communications Center, State University
College at Brockport, State University of New York.  Cas-
sette, 29 min, 38 sec., sound, b&w, 3/4" Umatic.  Recorded
March 17, 1970.

## 1972

J2.  The Poetry of Robert Bly.  Host, Al Poulin, Jr.; discussion,
Anthony Piccione.  Director, Francis R. Filando.  Brockport:
Educational Communications Center, State University College
at Brockport, State University of New York.  2 cassettes,
39 min, 35 sec. and 49 min, 20 sec., sound, b&w, 3/4"
Umatic.  Interview recorded February 2, 1972.

## 1973

J3.  Robert Bly.  Honolulu:  University of Hawaii.  Cassette, 30
min, sound, b&w, 3/4".

## 1974/1975

J4.  Poets Talking #5:  Robert Bly and Donald Hall.  Host, Donald
Hall.  Director, Marshall Franke.  Producer, Alma W.
Smith.  Ann Arbor:  Michigan Media, The University of
Michigan Media Resources Center.  1 cassette, 30 min.,
sound, 3/4" Umatic, 1/2" VHS-SP or Betamax I.
Contents:  Bly reads his poetry but also discusses the ef-
fects of translations on poetry and the importance of place.

## 1978

J5.  Booth and Bly:  Poets.  [Lincoln, NE:]  Netche Videotape Li-
brary.  4 cassettes, 30 min. each, sound, color, 3/4"
[also available on 1/2" reel].
Contents:  I.  A Workshop with Robert Bly; II.  A Workshop
with Martin Booth; III. Approaches to Poetry; IV.  In Performance.

J6.  A Conversation with Robert Bly. Executive producer, Louis
     Simpson. Director, Brian Byrnes. Stony Brook: Educa-
     tional Communications Center, State University of New York
     at Stony Brook. Cassette, 60 min., sound, b&w, 3/4".
     Stony Brook visiting poets series, #20. Recorded, March
     17, 1978.
     Contents: The discussion centers around Bly's ideas con-
cerning the community and the network, and his analysis of the
American psyche. Also discussed is the effect of translating foreign
poets upon his own work, the funciton of criticism, and his ideas on
the best poets of the twentieth century.
         See I29.

J7.  A Man Writes to a Part of Himself: The Poetry of Robert Bly.
     Minneapolis, MN: University Community Video. Cassette,
     57 min, 37 sec., sound, color, 3/3".

J8.  A Poet Reads His Work: Robert Bly. Executive producer,
     Louis Simpson. Director, Brian Byrnes. Stony Brook:
     Educational Communications Center, State University of New
     York at Stony Brook. 2 cassettes, 98 min., sound, b&w,
     3/4". Stony Brook visiting poet series, #19. Recorded,
     March 16, 1978.
     Contents: Mourning Pablo Neruda/Poem Against the British/
Old Boards/After Working/Sleet Storm on the Merritt Parkway/
Romans Angry about the Inner World/Watching Andrei Vosnesensky
Read in Vancouver/Shack Poem/Six Winter Privacy Poems/Neruda-
poem from "Solo la muerte": Nothing But Death/Walking Swiftly/
The Left Hand/Finding the Father/Coming In for Supper/A Man and
a Woman and a Blackbird/The Blue House/The Way the Body Loves/
Snowbanks North of the House/Silent in the Moonlight/Kabir-"Inside
this clay jug"/"The small ruby everyone wants"/"Between the con-
scious and the unconscious"/"I know the sound of the ecstatic
flute"/Whitman-I Heard You Solemn-Sweet Pipes of the Organ/[selec-
tions from Yeats].
         Introductory remarks by Louis Simpson.
         See I31.


                              1979

J9.  Poet at Large: A Conversation with Robert Bly. Director,
     Mike Colgan. Producer, Jonnet Kleinbaum. Bill Moyers'
     Journal. New York: WNET. Cassette, 59 min., sound,
     color, 3/4".


                              1981

J10. Ola and Per: The Cartoons of Peter Julius Rosendahl. Written
     and directed by Paul Burtness. Ed. by Kathy Soulliere.

Tr. by Carl Crislock. [Minneapolis, MN: Paul D. Burt-
ness]. Reel, 30 min., sound, color, 16 mm. [Also avail-
able as cassette, 29 min., sound, color, 3/4"]. Includes
an interview with R. B.

### 1984

J11. Robert Bly. San Francisco: The American Poetry Archive.
San Francisco State University. Cassette, 60 min., sound,
b&w, 3/4". [Also available on VHS]. Recorded, March 20,
1984.
Contents: Readings of his works as well as that of Macha-
do, Bashō, and Rumi. Various social and political issues are also
discussed, specifically the legacy of the Vietnam War as embodied
both in the current political atmosphere and in the psyches of the
veterans.

## K.  BOOK BLURBS

### 1973

K1.  Brainard, Franklin.  Raingatherer.  Morris, MN:  Minnesota
Writers' Publishing House.
Rear cover.

K2.  Jenkins, Louis.  The Well Digger's Wife.  Morris, MN:  Minne-
sota Writers' Publishing House.
Rear cover.

### 1974

K3.  Andrews, Jenne.  In Pursuit of the Family.  Morris, MN:
Minnesota Writers' Publishing House.
Rear cover.

### 1975

K4.  Gunderson, Keith.  3142 Lyndale Ave. So. Apt 24.  Morris,
MN:  Minnesota Writers' Publishing House.
Rear cover.

### 1976

K5.  Maloney, Dennis.  Naked Music:  Poems of Juan Ramón Jiménez.
Buffalo, NY:  White Pine Press.
Rear cover.

### 1979

K6.  Meyers, Bert.  Windowsills.  Stony Creek, CT:  Common
Table.
Rear cover.

### 1980

K7.  Waterman, Cary.  The Salamander Migration and Other Poems.

Pittsburgh: University of Pittsburgh Press.
Front flyleaf.


## 1981

K8. Ignatow, David. Whisper to the Earth. Boston: Little,
Brown and Co.
Rear of dist jacket; rear cover (paperback).

K9. Mandel, Charlotte. A Disc of Clear Water: Poems. Upper
Montclair, NJ: Saturday Press.
Rear cover.


## 1983

K10. Ignatow, Yaedi. The Flaw. New York: The Sheep Meadow
Press.
Rear cover.


## 1984

K11. Cardenal, Ernesto. With Walker in Nicaragua, and Other
Early Poems, 1949-1954. Selected and translated by
Jonathan Cohen. Middletown, CT: Wesleyan University
Press.
Dust jacket.

## L. DRAMAS

### 1968

L1. "The Satisfaction of Vietnam: A Play in 8 Scenes." <u>Chelsea</u>, no. 24/25 (October), 32-46.

## M. NOTEPAPER

M1. ["Love Poem".] Printed in light blue-gray on a yellow field on white paper. One sheet folded, 5 3/4 X 8 3/4". Woodcut by Wang Hui-Ming. In Piccione's collection.

## N. MISCELLANY

N1. <u>Ten Songs For Low Man's Voice and Piano</u>. Hillsdale, NY: Mobart Music Publications, 1978.
   "A Busy Man Speaks," pp. [13]-23. Music by R. Bruce Hobson.

PART II:

WRITINGS ABOUT ROBERT BLY

# O. BOOKS

## 1976

O1. Lensing, George S., and Ronald Moran. Four Poets and the
Emotive Imagination: Robert Bly, James Wright, Louis
Simpson, and William Stafford. Baton Rouge: Louisiana
State University Press.
    The first chapter of the book is a revised version of their
earlier article. Within the first two chapters in which the emotive
imagination is defined and its origin and development is discussed,
Bly is the central figure focused upon. His translations and criti-
cal essays are used as supportive material in the general discussion.
The actual chapter on Bly is comparatively short because of his
prominence in the preceding background chapters.
    A concise and well-balanced analysis of Bly's poetry through
Sleepers Joining Hands is given. Bly is seen as the "strongest
proselytizer" of the emotive imagination and "a vital phenomenon in
American poetry since mid-century." His contributions as critic
and theorist are emphasized over those as poet.
    See P25.

## 1977

O2. Friberg, Ingegerd. Moving Inward: A Study of Robert Bly's
Poetry. Gothenburg Studies in English 38. Göteborg,
Sweden: Acta Universitatis Gothoburgensis.
    A doctoral thesis that is the first published full-length
study of Bly's work. It uses Bly's imagery to develop what is
seen as "conspicuous and representative elements and concepts"
that recur in the poetry. The work is widely inconsistent in pre-
sentation, and there are close parallels to other doctoral disserta-
tions, e.g., Piccione and Sarge. The bibliography is poorly organ-
ized with several erroneous citations.
    See R1 and R4.

## 1982

O3. Jones, Richard, and Kate Daniels, eds. Of Solitude and Si-
lence: Writings on Robert Bly. Boston: Beacon Press.
    A reprinting, with minor deletions, of the special issue of
Poetry East devoted to Bly: no. 4/5 (Spring/Summer 1981).
    See article listings for 1981 for individual entries.

<u>1984</u>

O4.  Nelson, Howard.  <u>Robert Bly:  An Introduction to the Poetry</u>.
     New York:  Columbia University Press.
        A thorough and helpful book which presents an analysis of
     Bly's poetry in a chronological order, book by major book, through
     <u>The Man in the Black Coat Turns</u>.  Nelson relies, in part, on Bly's
     criticism to illustrate his poetry, but he is careful not to overdo
     this aspect of his analysis.  This is the single best source for an
     understanding of Bly's poetry.  It is a sympathetic but not uncriti-
     cal evaluation.

O5.  Peseroff, Joyce, ed.  <u>Robert Bly:  When Sleepers Awake</u>.
     Ann Arbor:  The University of Michigan Press.
        Reprints of B93, P2, P20-P21, P48-49, P51, P74, P78, P82,
     P94, P109, P117, P151, P158, P181, P188, P209, Q54, Q86, Q258,
     Q276, S5.  Also, P225, P230, and P234 are printed for the first
     time.

# P. ARTICLES AND PARTS OF BOOKS

## 1959

P1.  Sullivan, Dan. "Minnesotans Publish Magazine to Boost Bright
     Young Poets." St. Paul Pioneer Press, 13 December.
     Not verified, cited in Friberg (no. O2), p. 219.

## 1962

P2.  Hall, Donald. "Introduction." In his Contemporary American
     Poetry. Baltimore: Penguin Books, pp. 24-25 [17-25].
     Lines by Bly and Louis Simpson are cited as examples of "a
new kind of imagination," which reveals through images a subjective
life which is general.
     See P3. Reprinted in O5.

## 1963

P3.  Brooks, Cleanth. "Poetry Since 'The Waste Land'." Southern
     Review NS, 1 (no. 3), 498-499 [487-500].
     A reaction to Donald Hall's introduction to Contemporary
American Poetry and his example of Bly and Louis Simpson as rep-
resenting a "new imagination." There is nothing new about it. The
poetry cited by Hall is quiet poetry, leaving it to the reader's
imagination to supply any spark that will ignite it.
     See P2. Reprinted in P64.

P4.  Jones, Le Roi. "The Colonial School of Melican Poetry (or,
     'Aw, man, I read those poems before...')." Kulchur, no.
     10 (Summer), 83-84.
     A biting, scornful, humorous, and not unrealistic, assess-
ment of The Sixties and Bly based on an examination of issue no. 5.
The Colonial School of American Poetry is defined as that which pub-
lishes translations almost exclusively, suggesting that there is no
poetry new or otherwise in "our motherland." The familiarity of
Bly's choice of fourteen French poets in no. 5 rather than young,
obscure, relevant French poets is ridiculed. His choice of young
American poets in the issue is also sarcastically noted.
     Bly's statement that Charles Olson's Maximus Poems is the
worst book of the year is angrily rejected. Jones suggests that if
this is so, it is only because Bly or William Duffy did not publish a
book that year. They are dismissed as "ignorant fools."

P5.  Oberback, S. K.  "A Poet Who Listens."  St. Louis Post-
        Dispatch, 4 March, p. 4.
        Not verified, cited in Friberg (O2), p. 220.

P6.  Ossman, David.  "Robert Bly."  In The Sullen Art.  Inter-
        views by David Ossman with Modern American Poets.
        New York:  Corinth Books, pp. 39-42.
        A brief interview with Bly concerning his views on American
poetry and contemporary poets.  It presents nothing that is not
better and more fully expanded upon in Bly's essays in The Fifties
and The Sixties.


                                    1964

P7.  Hall, Donald.  "American Expressionist Poetry."  Serif, 1
        (December), 18-19.
        A discussion of the movement led by Bly, James Wright,
and Louis Simpson which uses "fantastic images, images from deep
in the imagination, either to reveal an inward world, or to under-
stand our objective existence in the light of inward knowledge."
This is an explanation of the poetry of this "movement" in general
rather than specifically Bly's poetry.


                                    1965

P8.  Garrett, George.  "Against the Grain:  Poets Writing Today."
        In American Poetry.  Ed. Irvin Ehrenpreis.  London:
        Edward Arnold, Ltd.; New York:  St. Martin's Press.
        Stratford-Upon-Avon Studies 7; p. 234.  [221-239].
        Brief, unfocused comments concerning Bly.  He has an an-
nounced plot to take over Poetry.  His success is all too obvious in
the "new" James Wright of The Branch Will Not Break.

P9.  Mills, Ralph J., Jr.  Contemporary American Poetry.  New
        York:  Random House, pp. 210-217 passim.
        In a discussion of the poetry of James Wright, Bly's close
association with Wright and the allied spirit of their poetry is ex-
amined.  Their poetry relies to a great extent on "sources below the
level of consciousness or of rational thought."  The poems have a
dreamlike, fluid construction, and reflect "a condition of intense
subjectivity, a moment of extreme perception personal to the poet
and yet capable of stirring subtle and profound responses in the
reader."

P10.  Stepanchev, Stephen.  American Poetry Since 1945:  A Critical
        Survey.  New York:  Harper & Row, pp. 175-180 passim,
        185-187, 208.
        Bly, along with James Wright, William Duffy, Robert Kelly,
and Jerome Rothenberg, institutes a movement in American poetry

toward subjectivism, influenced by the Surrealists. The concept of
the deep image in poetry is important to Bly, "who feels that an in-
ward look can vitalize any poet's work." The originality of his deep
images give his poetry an intense subjectivity and "a feeling of the
irremediable loneliness of man, who can never make contact with the
things of the world."

<u>1966</u>

P11.   Corbin, Jonathan. "Biographical Sketch." In <u>Poems for</u>
       <u>Young Readers: Selections from Their Own Writings by</u>
       <u>Poets Attending the Houston Festival of Contemporary</u>
       <u>Poetry</u>. 56th Annual NCTE Convention, November 24-26,
       1966. [Champaign, IL: National Council of Teachers of
       English, (1967?)], p. 15.
       Conventional biographical entry.

P12.   Donadio, Stephen. "Some Younger Poets in America." In
       <u>Modern Occasions</u>. Selected and edited by Philip Rahv.
       London: Weidenfeld & Nicolson, pp. 240-241 [226-246].
           A brief entry. Bly states his emotions directly with an
exuberant simplicity that makes them convincing and artistically
relevant.

P13.   Otto, Kathy, and Cynthia Lofsness. [An Interview with
       Robert Bly.] <u>Plaintiff</u> [Mankato State College], (Spring),
       15-24.
           One of Bly's more cogent and straightforward interviews;
there are few circumlocutions or bombastic political statements. He
discusses his background and start as a poet, translations, poetry
workshops, working in solitude, influences, the emptiness of poetry
and poets in the United States, and his Vietnam War protests.
       Reprinted in A57 and P53.

P14.   "Poets Hold 'Read-In' in Oregon to Protest U.S. Role in Viet-
       nam." New York <u>Times</u>, 6 March, p. 4.
           Bly is quoted regarding William Westmoreland and the con-
cept of read-ins. He and David Ray also discuss the formation of
the American Writers Against the Vietnam War.

P15.   Stryk, Lucien. "Zen Buddhism and Modern American Poetry."
       <u>Yearbook of Comparative and General Literature</u>, no. 15,
       pp. 190-191 [186-190].
           Bly's interest in Zen can easily be seen in his work. Two
examples of Bly's poems that are reminiscent of Zennists are given.

P16.   Tulip, James. "The Wesleyan Poets--II." <u>Poetry Australia</u>,
       3 (December), 40 [38-41].
           An ambivalent assessment of Bly's poetry. Based on <u>Si-</u>
<u>lence in the Snowy Fields</u>, Bly is a "connoisseur of quietness, a

miniature Wallace Stevens." There are examples of banal ecstasy
in his poems, but they are effective when the imagination finds
that facts are really metaphors.

P17.  Zweig, Paul.  "The American Outsider."  Nation, 203 (14
      November), 517-519.
      A thoughtful and intelligent examination of the Sixties
Press and The Sixties (and The Fifties).  Bly's purpose has been
a double-pronged one:  to make available, through translations, the
works of great European and South American poets of imagination
and self-exploration; and to offer a vehicle for literary criticism
concerned with the poets of imaginative insight and discovery.
"Behind the Sixties Press is a desire to test the limits of our
American poetic traditions; to weed out the dry exercises which
have often, in the past twenty years, passed for poetry, simply
because they followed a scheme of imagination familiar to all."

1967

P18.  Bowering, George.  "Answers to Correspondents."  Kayak,
      no. 11, p. 28.
      A letter pointing out that Bly missed Anselm Hollo's trans-
lations in Selected Poems of Andrei Voznesensky and that these
translations are of a far superior quality than the two books of
translations Bly previously wrote about.
      See B29.

P19.  Collins, Douglas.  "To the Editor."  Lillabulero, 1 (Fall),
      60-61.
      A letter in response to the review of The Lion's Tail and
Eyes.  The very existence of the book is more important than the
tone of the review implies.  The letter is an intelligent and impas-
sioned plea for the type of poetry represented in the book.  Bly is
seen not as a poet speaking out of laziness and silence, but as one
seeking solitude and awakening.  His voice is one of tremendous
emotional energy.
      This letter is much more insightful than the review that pro-
voked it.
      See Q68.

P20.  Dickey, James.  Spinning the Crystal Ball:  Some Guess at
      the Future of American Poetry.  Washington, DC:  Library
      of Congress, pp. 8-10.
      A vindictive and sarcastic piece that gives little quarter.
Bly believes the salvation of English poetry is to be found in non-
English poetry understood as badly as possible and translated with
as many liberties as one desires.  The salvation of American poetry
does not depend upon poor imitations of Spanish poems.  Bly's type
of poetry is "essentially a derivative, imitative, extremely lazy,
unimaginative poetry," which is easy to write.
      Reprinted in O5.

P21. Friedman, Norman. "The Wesleyan Poets—III: The Experimental Poets." Chicago Review, 19 (no. 2), 59 [52-73].

Bly is not a formal poet because his is an outside world which the speaker lives in and responds to directly as a man in the agony of searching for himself, and for whom the external world has real and objective existence. His poetry is experimental because his imagination releases startling perspectives from a bright perception of the ordinary. The faults of the poetry are that it is too taut and too economical for comfort. Bly evades ideas and feelings.

This view of Bly's poetry is necessarily narrow because of the date of publication. The series is interesting because of the continuing comparison made among the poets discussed.

P22. Harnack, Curtis. "Week of the Angry Artist...." Nation, 204 (20 February), 245-248 passim.

A report on a "Napalm Poetry Reading" at New York University and a symposium on "The War, The Artist, His Work," both of which Bly had a central part in. In the latter program, Bly denounced the climate of American literature and the idea that poetry must be kept pure of politics. This idea derives from the New Criticism which tries to divorce the world itself from the world of a poem.

P23. Hertzel, Leo J. "What About Writers in the North?" South Dakota Review, 5 (Spring), 8-10 [3-19].

Impressions of Bly as he participated in a workshop at Wisconsin State University on nature and regional writing are given. Also noted is a general description of what Bly did and the reaction to it.

P24. Hoffman, Frederick J. "Contemporary American Poetry." In Patterns of Commitment in American Literature. Ed. Marston LaFrance. Toronto: University of Toronto Press, p. 201 [193-207].

Bly's poetry is briefly characterized as one of bare imagery and statement by implication. His type of poetry, with an emphasis on simple pleasures, has a tendency to "settle into a monotony of almanac observations," and lacks drive.

P25. Moran, Ronald, and George Lensing. "The Emotive Imagination: A New Departure in American Poetry." Southern Review NS, 3 (January), 51-67.

An important early critical essay on Bly's poetry. The poetry of Bly, James Wright, Louis Simpson, and William Stafford is discussed in terms of the concept of the emotive imagination. This poetry is described as "meaningfully new." The dominant themes and characteristics of the poetry are examined. This discussion is more fully developed and specifically applied to each poet in the authors' Four Poets and the Emotive Imagination.

See O1.

242                                    Writings About Robert Bly

P26.  Rosenthal, M. L.  The New Poets:  American and British
        Poetry Since World War II.  New York:  Oxford University
        Press, pp. 320-321.
        A brief description of the poets loosely associated with
The Sixties who have promoted a new simplicity and directness in
poetry.  Bly is the most active "theorist" of the group and has
"tried valiantly to propagandize for the poetry of Lorca and Neru-
da."  His poems have the making of an essentially regional art, if
that is the direction he chooses to take.


                              1968

P27.  Curry, David.  "Correspondence."  Kayak, no. 15, pp. 51-52.
        A response to Louis Z. Hammer's review of The Light
Around the Body.  Hammer's thinking is prejudicial.  He simply
states how a book satisfies or doesn't satisfy his personal require-
ments.  Silence in the Snowy Fields and The Light Around the Body
should be taken as a sequence representing the crisis of the modern
consciousness.
        See Q50.


P28.  The Editors.  "The National Book Awards."  Nation, 206 (25
        March), 413-414.
        Bly's actions at the National Book Awards are described
and quotes from his citation for The Light Around the Body are
given.  Brief biographical information is also given.  An excerpt
from Bly's acceptance speech is included.


P29.  Haines, John.  "Letter."  Kayak, no. 13 (January), 18-19.
        A response to "The First Ten Issues of Kayak."  Bly's
criticisms were fair.  Haines refutes Bly's statement that he stands
out in the rain with pen and notebook to write.  Bly does not seem
to be aware that what he says is as true of himself as anyone.  He
should accept his own criticism.  A typical Bly poem is apt to be
cluttered and rhetorical.
        See B34.


P30.  Hays, H. R.  "Letter."  Kayak, no. 13 (January), 15.
        Bly's obvious rationalizations of his own shortcomings in
"The First Ten Issues of Kayak" must be pointed out.  He has al-
ways had the taint of dilettantism and has done practically nothing
for the contemporary American poet.
        See B34.


P31.  "Letters."  Kayak, no. 13 (January), 12-21.
        Nine letters and a poem representing a sampling of the re-
sponse to Bly's "The First Ten Issues of Kayak."
        See entries nos. P29-P30, P32-P35, P37, P39, P44, and S2
for individual citations.  See B34.

P32. Lipsitz, Lou. "Letter." Kayak, no. 13 (January), 21.
There is general agreement with the points Bly makes, but a displeasure with his excessiveness and condescension.
See B34.

P33. Marcus, Morton. "Letter." Kayak, no. 13 (January), 19-20.
Exception is taken to Bly's definition of a "Kayak poem;" it is arbitrary and fails to realize alternatives. Bly is too moralistic and Calvinistic in his viewpoint.
See B34.

P34. Meyers, Bert. "Letter." Kayak, no. 13 (January), 13-14.
Bly's critique of Kayak is really an evaluation of his own first book and the poetry he has advocated through its publication in The Fifties and The Sixties. Although he is the best critic now writing on American poetry, Bly is too narrow minded in his approach. There are more ways to achieve what he desires in American poetry than the means he champions.
See B34.

P35. Mitchell, Roger. "Letter." Kayak, no. 13 (January), 16-18.
A discussion of Richard Wilbur's lines that Bly quotes in "The First Ten Issues of Kayak." There is agreement that the lines are bad, but not for the reasons Bly states. The poets of The Sixties and Kayak share with Wilbur the same rhythmical and prosodical malaise.
See B34.

P36. "19th National Book Awards Stir Controversy in N. Y." Library Journal, 93 (April 1), 1935-1936.
A report of Bly's protestation of the Vietnam War and denunciation of the nation's institutions for their lack of protest and civil disobedience against the war.

P37. Quinn, John P. "Letter." Kayak, no. 13 (January), 21.
A brief response to Bly's "The First Ten Issues of Kayak."
See B34.

P38. Raymont, Henry. "Books Spotlight Held by Politics." New York Times, 7 March, p. 51.
Bly's speech at the National Book Awards is commented upon as is the rebuttal by William I. Nichols, chairman of the National Book Committee. Nichols states that Bly has the right to express his differences, but those differences do not automatically make his adversaries "negligent, mendacious or absurd."

P39. Rogers, Del Marie. "Letter." Kayak, no. 13 (January), 15-16.
Bly has contributed so many elements, both good and bad, to the Kayak style. His statement that a poet should spend two hours in solitude for each line of poetry written is ridiculed.
See B34.

P40.   Simpson, Louis.  "The New American Poetry."  In The Great
       Ideas Today.  Ed. Robert M. Hutchins and Mortimer J.
       Adler.  Chicago:  Encyclopaedia Britannica, pp. 86-87
       [80-89].
       A general discussion of the "Sixties poets" centered around
Bly and how they differ from the Beat and confessional poets.  These
poets are continuing the experimental "modernist" movement of Ezra
Pound and the surrealists, which had been interrupted by the con-
ventionality of the New Criticism.
       Simpson is generally considered to be among the "Sixties
poets" at this time.

P41.   Smith.  "The Strange World of Robert Bly."  The Smith, no.
       8, pp. 184-185.
       The publication of The Light Around the Body occasions
this relatively brief and acerbic review of Bly's work and poetics.
His work tends to a "pompously oracular tone and disorientedly
weird images."  His poems are sloppy and graceless as a result of
his tin ear.  The innate absurdity of Bly's thinking is comedic.  All
this is unfortunate in light of the fact that Bly has sometimes ex-
erted a beneficent influence on modern poetry by attacking academic
poetry and stressing how poetry should be concerned with the
great simplicities.

P42.   Taylor, W. E.  "The Chief."  Poetry Florida And, 1 (Sum-
       mer), 12-16.
       The object of Bly's poetry is to create a synthesis between
his two roles as protester and solitary poet:  the outer and inner
worlds.  In Silence in the Snowy Fields, one of the best books of
the decade, he is close to achieving it.  The world of suffering hu-
manity is presented as an echo of the inner world.  In The Light
Around the Body however, there is a tremendous falling off.  The
poetry is fortuitous; it is not in a stage of tension with the idea.
It propagates a "cult of Goodness" which leads to another kind of
melodramatic posturing and another kind of arrogance.

P43.   Thomas, Ben.  "Bly and Tradition:  'Lighted By Fire From
       Within'."  Tennessee Poetry Journal, 1 (Winter), 19-22.
       Bly is a metamorphic poet.  He has mastered and abandoned
the techniques of Frost and Stevens.  He extends the poetic tradi-
tion so they stand as organic rather than isolate.  He assimilates
the traditions but is not dependent upon them.  His cultural material
is both native (i.e., Minnesota, Norway, eastern United States) and
eclectic (i.e., China, Spain, Latin America, German).
       His poetic traits are discussed:  the dichotomy of light and
darkness, the land and sea, and the question of honesty.

P44.   Wilbur, Richard.  "A Postcard for Bob Bly."  Kayak, no. 13
       (January), 15.
       A sarcastic rejoinder in verse to Bly's criticism of Wilbur's
type of writing in his "The First Ten Issues of Kayak."
       See B34.

1969

P45. Bishop, Elizabeth. "Letters." Kayak, no. 19, p. 50.
In a letter to the editor, Bishop claims that Bly's three
prose poems in Kayak no. 18 ["The Hunter," "Looking at a Dead
Wren in My Hand," and "Sitting on Some Rocks in Shaw Cove,
California"] are "plainly imitations" of three prose poems of hers
in Kenyon Review, November 1967. She thinks Bly should have
mentioned the derivation of his poems.
See D2.

P46. Calhoun, Richard. "On Robert Bly's Protest Poetry." Ten-
nessee Poetry Journal, 2 (Winter), 21-22.
Objection is made not to the content of the poems, but to
the poems as poetry. The lines are too trite, flat, and unimaginative;
they are merely rhetorical. The poems lack Eliot's "aesthetic sanc-
tion": partial justification of the views of life by the art to which
they give rise. Bly fails to link the language of the outer world
with the language of the inner man.

P47. Harte, Barbara, and Carolyn Riley, eds. "Bly, Robert." In
Contemporary Authors: A Bio-Bibliographical Guide to
Current Authors and Their Work. Vol. 5-8. First Revi-
sion. Detroit: Gale Research Co., pp. 121-122.
Basic biographical and publication data. It quotes Bly and
critical passages drawn from published sources.

P48. Heyen, William. "Inward to the World: The Poetry of Robert
Bly." The Far Point, 3 (Fall/Winter), 42-50.
A personal reassessment of Bly's poetry. After an initial
dislike for Silence in the Snowy Fields--"a group of journal jottings"--
Heyen has come to believe that his original objections were only
"nigglings." Bly's poems are full of the "critical faculty." They
don't wear thin because inner lives speak in them. The supreme
and unifying subject of Bly's poetry is the Self. In Bly, personal
poetry becomes a poetry of social comment.
The essay discusses Bly as a hard Romantic and seeks to ex-
plain this sense of Self in his poetry and the journey to the inner
world that it manifests.

P49. Howard, Richard. "'Like Those Before, We Move to the Death
We Love'." In his Alone With America: Essays on the Art
of Poetry in the United States Since 1950. New York:
Atheneum, pp. [38]-48.
Bly's involvement in political events and his public per-
sonality distract from the genuine achievement and genuine aspira-
tion of his poetry. His work in his first two books is discussed in
terms of Jacob Boehme's influence on Bly's concept of the inward
and outward experiences. The other major part of this essay is the
theory that the real burden of Bly's work is "a body transfigured
by the weight of its own death."

This discussion of Bly's work in terms of life and death is effectively interwoven with Boehme's influence.
Reprinted in O5 and P167.


P50.  McMillan, Samuel H.  "On Robert Bly and His Poems:  A Se-
       lected Bibliography."  Tennessee Poetry Journal, 2 (Win-
       ter), 58-60.
       A secondary bibliography.

P51.  Matthews, William.  "Thinking About Robert Bly."  Tennessee
       Poetry Journal, 2 (Winter), 49-57.
       Random and miscellaneous thoughts on Bly, his work, and
critical reaction to it.  An incipient Bly backlash exists by those
threatened and annoyed by Bly's critical essays.  The poems of
The Light Around the Body are discussed.  A comparison between
Bly and D. H. Lawrence is made.  Bly will continue to take risks,
to overreach, and to face important questions in his poetry.

P52.  "On Bly's Poetry."  Tennessee Poetry Journal, 2 (Winter),
       16-18.
       Responses (or lack of responses) from Southern writers
and editors to a request to comment on Bly's work.  Particularly
revealing are the reproduced replies of James Dickey and Allen
Tate.

P53.  Otto, Kathy, and Cynthia Lofsness.  "An Interview with
       Robert Bly."  Tennessee Poetry Journal, 2 (Winter), 29-48.
       Reprint of P13.

P54.  Scheele, Roy.  "On Bly."  Tennessee Poetry Journal, 2
       (Winter), 19-20.
       Bly's political poems attempt to take on the grotesque
shapes of what he is talking about; the miracle is that some of them
succeed.  "Counting Small-Boned Bodies" is briefly examined.

P55.  Steele, Frank.  "Three Questions Answered."  Tennessee
       Poetry Journal, 2 (Winter), 23-28.
       Replies to three questions asked concerning Bly:  Does his
use of contemporary events hurt his Poetry?--it has deepened and
extended his poetic vision; Is Bly politically naive as suggested
in a review?--the idea is ridiculed; How good is Bly's ear?--he has
the ear of a master poet.

P56.  Yanella, Phil.  ["Two Halves of Life."]  "Interview with Robert
       Bly."  Tempest, 1 (no. 1), [1]-7.
       Topics discussed in the interview include the situation of
little magazines and the unfortunate proliferation of academic maga-
zines, how a poet learns to write and the need for an open mood that
allows the poem to come from the inside, and H. R. Hays and South
American literature.
       Reprinted in A57.

<u>1970</u>

P57.  Dodsworth, Martin.  "Introduction:  The Survival of Poetry."
      In his The Survival of Poetry:  A Contemporary Survey.
      London:  Faber & Faber, pp. 20-23 passim [11-36].
      In discussing the translatability of a poem, it is stated that
Bly and James Wright, in their Twenty Poems by Pablo Neruda, mis-
represent Neruda by the meagerness of their selection and the em-
phasis on surrealist poetry.  The translatable poem influenced the
imagist-surrealist poetry as represented by the poetry of Bly and
Wright.  While both are poets of undeniable talent and seriousness,
neither seems to be conscious of the fact that what is excellent in
one cultural situation, may not be so in another.  The influence of
Trakl in Silence in the Snowy Fields and The Light Around the Body
is overwhelming.

P58.  Janssens, G. A. M.  "The Present State of American Poetry:
      Robert Bly and James Wright."  English Studies, 51 (April),
      112-137.
      This essay is in reaction to Cleanth Brooks' statement re-
garding Donald Hall's introduction to his Contemporary American
Poetry and Moran and Lensing's subsequent article on the emotive
imagination.  The most "meaningful comparisons" can be made be-
tween Bly and Wright of the four poets focused upon by Moran and
Lensing.  An extended discussion of Silence in the Snowy Fields
and The Light Around the Body follows.  Although Bly is respect-
fully treated, he is clearly of secondary importance to Wright.  The
effect of the poems in Silence in the Snowy Fields is cumulative;
the poems are good but not really powerful.  There is a tendency
toward cuteness and preciosity.  The Light Around the Body is an
advance over the first volume because of the success of the subject
matter.  The poems are admirable and the politicalization of con-
temporary American poetry is briefly discussed.  However, the
weakness of these poems is essentially the same as the first book:
Bly fails to give objective validity to his private associations.

P59.  Kingston, Roger; Curt Greer; Peggy Rizza; and James Atlas.
      "A Conversation with Robert Bly."  Harvard Advocate,
      (February), pp. 4-8.
      An interview touching on familiar Bly topics:  South Amer-
ican poetry, the influence of Eastern philosophy, the concept of
"news of the universe," and the three-brains theory.

P60.  Ray, David.  "Bly, Robert."  In Contemporary Poets of the
      English Language.  Ed. Rosalie Murphy.  Chicago:  St.
      James Press, pp. 110-113.
      A laudatory essay which emphasizes Bly's mystical quality
in a discussion of his political theories and the differences between
Bly's first two volumes.  The Light Around the Body is more melan-
choly; the imagery is notably more complex and surreal.  Basic bio-
graphical information and a primary bibliography are also given.

There is a strong sense in the essay of its having been writ-
ten by a loving apostle for his master.

P61.  Reid, Alfred S.  "A Look at the Living Poem:   Rock, Protest
      and Wit."  The Furman Magazine, (Spring), pp. 9-11 [6-
      11, 35].
      A basic examination of three developments in contemporary
poetry.  Bly's work in The Light Around the Body is representative
of protest poetry.  Part of his National Book Award acceptance
speech is quoted.


                                  1971

P62.  Bail, Jay, and Geoffrey Cook.  "With Robert Bly:   An Inter-
      view."  San Francisco Book Review, no. 19 (April), [1]-
      32.  [Special Issue--With Robert Bly].
      An extensive interview that touches upon all of the now
standard Bly areas of concern:   inward movement in contemporary
poetry, the relationship between politics and the poet, solitude,
meditation, the four intelligences system of Jung, the three differ-
ent minds of man, mother and father consciousness, and his Na-
tional Book Award speech.  The interview is interesting for the
now dated discussion regarding the radical "Movement."  Gary
Synder, Robert Creeley, and Kenneth Rexroth are the poets dis-
cussed at length.
      Reprinted in A57.

P63.  Baker, A. T.  "Poetry Today:   Low Profile, Flatted Voice."
      Time, (12 July), 61 [61-68].
      A general discussion of contemporary poets which divides
them into five groups.  Bly and Allen Ginsberg are cited as repre-
sentative of "Polemical Roarers."  Although the compassion of such
poetry as "The Teeth-Mother Naked at Last" is praised, the general
problem with this group of poets is perceived to be the too frequent
lapsing of their sentiments into mere bombast.

P64.  Brooks, Cleanth.  "Poetry Since 'The Waste Land'."  In his
      A Shaping Joy:   Studies in the Writer's Craft.  London:
      Methuen & Co., Ltd.; New York:   Harcourt Brace Jovano-
      vich, Inc., pp. 52-65.
      Reprint of P3.

P65.  Cummings, David.  "The Collectors of Modern."  Poet and
      Critic, 6 (Fall), 39-40 [35-44].
      An omnibus review of poetry anthologies including Naked
Poetry, which includes "Looking for Dragon Smoke."  The essay is
"as delightfully readable an argument for absolute poetic freedom as
anyone could seriously disagree with."  Bly is a kind of spooked
Robert Frost.  His ideas concerning poetry are commented upon and
criticized.  Bly's inclusion within the anthologies is used throughout

the essay as a criterion for whether it includes serious contempo-
rary poetry.
     See D3.

P66.  Gitlin, Todd.  "The Return of Political Poetry."  Commonweal,
         94 (23 July), 375-380 passim.
     Bly is presented as a leading figure within an emerging
new political sensibility.  There is disagreement with Bly's theory
that a poet's inner regions are outside politics.  Bly is confusing
a poet's privacy with social isolation.  The poet only becomes fully
political when he or she accepts and expresses in "piercing language"
the political nature of his or her own life.  Bly is "one of the finest
anti-war poets of these years," and his poem "The Teeth-Mother
Naked at Last" is the first political analysis of the Vietnam War by
an American poet.  The poem is discussed and, although Bly "is in
the right neighborhood of ideas," "he is confused."

P67.  Kinnell, Galway.  "Poetry, Personality and Death."  Field,
         no. 4 (Spring), 56-75 passim.
     Bly is one of the examples of the use of the "I," or self,
in poetry.  In his earlier poetry, Bly avoided specific autobiograph-
ical details.  The "I" is an abstract, ideal one, a simplified persona
that allows him to avoid dealing with personality in his poetry.  In
his later prose poems (e.g., The Morning Glory) he gets beyond
personality by going through it.  The prose poems are moving be-
cause now Bly speaks to the reader, and for the reader, in his
own voice.  The poem is personal yet common.
     Reprinted in P168.

P68.  Mills, Josephine.  "The Home Book of Modern Verse, 1970."
         Massachusetts Review, 12 (Autumn), 701-702 [689-708].
     Not really a review of The Teeth Mother Naked at Last.
Part of the poem is quoted to demonstrate that Bly is a poet who
takes wide risks and makes big reaches to qualities of the world.

P69.  [Phillips, Barry, and Eric Mottram].  "Bly, Robert."  In The
         Penguin Companion to American Literature.  Ed. Malcolm
         Bradbury, Eric Mottram, and Jean Franco.  New York:
         McGraw-Hill, p. 36.
     A brief entry citing Bly as an important general influence
in recent poetic movements.  His poems are characterized as
"sparse, personal and observant," and as a response "in outrage to
the warfare state."

P70.  Zavatsky, Bill.  "Poets in the Avant-Garde."  University Re-
         view, no. 21, p. 9 [pp. 9, 19].
     The transition in Bly's poetry from the quiet, reflective
poems "suffused with a glow of self-realization" of Silence in the
Snowy Fields to the political poems of The Light Around the Body
was influenced by Spanish surrealism and Latin American poetry.
His new work is a poetry of moral commitment.

1972

P71.  Binni, Francesco.  "'Esterno' e 'Interno,' Nell' 'Image Poetry'
      di Robert Bly e James Wright."  Nuova Corrente, 59, pp.
      352-381.
      Not verified.  Cited in Friberg (no. O2), p. 218.

P72.  Bostick, Christina.  "The Individual and War Resistance."
      Library Journal, 97 (March 15), 1142 [1140-1145].
      Bly's The Light Around the Body is one of the twelve books
listed under "Writers Against War."

P73.  Lacey, Paul A.  "The Live World."  In his The Inner War:
      Forms and Themes in Recent American Poetry.  Philadel-
      phia:  Fortress Press, pp. 32-56.
      This is a well-balanced analysis of Bly's poetry which be-
gins by examining several of Bly's critical essays, particularly his
concept of dead world and live world, to see what he expects from
poetry.  The major focus of the essay is on the poems of Si-
lence in the Snowy Fields, The Light Around the Body, and The
Teeth Mother Naked at Last.
      There is a difference between the poetry of Bly's first two
books.  The solitude has given way to isolation, and the natural
world, through which he saw a spiritual inner world, has been re-
placed by a pale compensation for the outer world.  His pursuit of
the two worlds has taken him deeply into things, but not deeply
enough to overcome the distinction between the two worlds.  The
poetry of The Light Around the Body, exemplified by the political
poetry, is not successful by Bly's own standards of poetics.  He
is able to correct this in The Teeth Mother Naked at Last, which
has great scope and depth.  It is a sure break from the hatred,
fear, and demonology that weighted down the war poems of The
Light Around the Body.

P74.  Libby, Anthony.  "Robert Bly Alive in Darkness."  Iowa
      Review, 3 (Summer), 78-89.
      A helpful examination of the complex poetic theory and
highly articulated scheme of the psychological development of civili-
zation that lies behind Bly's poetry.  His theory of the Great Mother
is discussed at length, including how it developed out of his early
poetry, and the ongoing conflict between the Mother and Father
consciousnesses.

P75.  McPherson, Sandra.  "You Can Say That Again.  (Or Can
      You?)."  Iowa Review, 3 (Summer), 70-75.
      An examination of Bly's and James Wright's use of certain
catch words in Silence in the Snowy Fields and The Branch Will Not
Break.  The words are "dark," "sleep," "old," "alone," "heavy,"
"silence," and "small," as well as their synonyms.  The use of each
word is cloyingly examined with the point of exploring McPherson's
personal dislike for the repetition, for the choice of words repeated,

and for the "point system of word employment." The position
adopted is that the repetition is distracting from the poem itself.

P76.  Martin, Peter. "Robert Bly: Poet on the Road Home."
      Straight Creek Journal, 1 (October 24), 10-11, 16.
      An interview with Bly following some general introductory
material. The interview ranges from sexual concerns in poetry to
a discussion of the inclusion of personal life in poems, energy, and
prose poems. Bly's remarks regarding the differences between Si-
lence in the Snowy Fields and The Light Around the Body and the
spiritual roads offered by religions are of interest.

P77.  Richter, Franz Allbert, and Lew Hude. "An Interview with
      Robert Bly." Lamp in the Spine, 3 (Winter), 50-65.
      The conversation is largely centered around spiritual and/
or religious questions: the concept of God, Buddhism, reincarna-
tion, spiritualism. Toward the end of the interview, literary ques-
tions that focus on James Wright, and reasons for publishing are
discussed.

P78.  Simpson, Louis. North of Jamaica. New York: Harper &
      Row, pp. 208-216 passim.
      A discussion of Bly and the uniqueness of The Fifties
among literary magazines at the time. The Fifties was a curious
and sometimes awkward combination of eclectic theorizing and local
color. Its ideas were more stimulating and useful than those found
in such publications as The Hudson Review or The New Yorker.
Although the poets who published in The Fifties and The Sixties
were not cohesive enough to be labeled a group, they had certain
qualities in common: a desire to write about something other than
the surface of life, use of personal voice, and roots in the American
landscape. Also briefly discussed are Simpson's differences with
Bly regarding their outlooks on poetry.

1973

P79.  Cotter, James Finn. "Poetry's New Image of Man." America,
      128 (9 June), 533-534 [533-535].
      Bly's Sleepers Joining Hands is cited in a discussion of the
transition in contemporary poetry from the image of man as disillu-
sioned and lonely to man as the center of natural and spiritual
awakening, a speaker of the hopeful word. Bly's poems are inward
and visionary. Also mentioned is Bly's theory of the presence of
feminine consciousness in his generation and the return to the
primal energy and form.

P80.  Guimond, James. "After Imagism." Ohio Review, 15 (Fall),
      24-28 [[5]-28].
      This is an overview of Imagism as a general stylistic ten-
dency in twentieth-century poetry. The concluding section is

concerned with the major reaction against William Carlos Williams'
Imagism led by Bly. Bly's concept of Imagism is analyzed to under-
stand his unwillingness to acknowledge any kinship with Williams.
The conclusion of the essay is that Bly has more similarities with
Williams than readily apparent. He is turning Imagism inward and
making it express inner realities, the quality that Bly criticized
Williams' poetry for lacking.

P81.   Hall, Donald. "Knock Knock: A Column." American Poetry
       Review, 2 (July/August), 38.
       Hall, having received a form letter from Boston University
addressed to "David Hall" requesting that he consider their library
as a repository for his manuscripts and correspondence, sent a copy
to Bly. Bly responds with a satiric letter to Boston University sug-
gesting several authors they could contact in Paris, e.g., Sartre
and François Sagan. The recipient of the letter found it to be
"somewhat intemperate" and "frankly rude."

P82.   _____. "Notes on Robert Bly and Sleepers Joining Hands."
       Ohio Review, 15 (Fall), [89]-93.
       A group of thoughts and notes on Bly and writing is pre-
sented after the disclaimer by Hall that, concerning Bly, he has no
objectivity since Bly has been a friend for twenty-five years.
Sleepers Joining Hands is the best of Bly's first three books. It
recapitulates the first two books and takes a step forward.
       See Bly's essay on Hall, B55, to compare how he maintains his
objectivity after twenty-two years of friendship.
       Reprinted in P143.

P83.   Hamilton, Ian. "The Sixties Press." In his A Poetry Chroni-
       cle: Essays and Reviews. London: Faber & Faber, pp.
       122-127.
       A discussion of the poets and poetics surrounding "the
Sixties Press enterprise." The focus is on theory rather than
specific poets or poems, although Bly and James Wright are pre-
sented as the dominant figures. Bly's theory of the released sub-
conscious is doomed to either generalities or eccentricities. There
is something insidious about the "speechless approval" given the
Sixties Press activity because of guilt over the years of enslavement
under Brooks and Warren.

P84.   Libby, Anthony. "Fire and Light, Four poets to the End and
       Beyond." Iowa Review, 4 (Spring), 111-126.
       Bly, W. S. Merwin, James Dickey, and Ted Hughes' poetry
evoke a general human movement of deep crisis and cultural collapse.
Bly is the mystic of evolution. His poetry is a confluence of physi-
cal and psychological or spiritual suggesting the interpenetration of
spiritual and physical in all categories of being. It emphasizes the
chaos that results from the collision of the conflicting types of con-
sciousness surfacing in America now.

P85.  Malkoff, Karl.  <u>Crowell's Handbook of Contemporary American</u>
        <u>Poetry</u>.  New York:  Thomas Y. Crowell Co., pp. 77-81.
        The relationship between the inner and outer realities is the
central theme of Bly's poetry.  The human intellect is a barrier be-
tween the two worlds of being, and poetry is an attempt to circum-
vent that barrier and wake the inner man.  Bly's poems call for a
unity of being.  His political poetry derives from this dualism.
Public men fear a harmony with the natural world because with un-
ity of being their power would be meaningless, therefore, inner
reality is a threat to them, and the natural must be conquered.

P86.  Reinhold, Robert.  "Captain Bly and the Good Ship Lollipop."
        <u>The Smith</u>, no. 22/23 (July 4), 60-73.
        Intentionally or not, the effect of the essay is to present
Bly as pretentious and hypocritical.  He captains the middle-swell
of the American culture that lies between the beats and the aca-
demics.  He has reached this prominence not so much because of
his poetry but because he has played the politics of poetry.  Bly's
poetry does not warrant him being a "celebrated poet."  His poem
"Sleet Storm on the Merritt Parkway" is compared to Edward Zuck-
row's "Traffic."  Zuckrow has the "makings of a truly major poet."

P87.  "Robert Bly Checklist."  <u>Schist</u>, no. 1 (Fall), 48-51.
        A fifty-one-item primary bibliography prefaced by a brief
statement.

P88.  True, Michael D.  "Robert Bly, Radical Poet."  <u>Win</u>, 9 (Janu-
        ary 15), 11-13.
        Bly signifies the return of poetry to the public and brings
with it the pleasure associated with a great singer or dramatic art-
ist.  His political poetry and its derivation from "inwardness" is
briefly discussed.  The essay presents a general discussion of Bly's
appearance, the tone of his readings, and his place in contemporary
poetry.

P89.  Walsh, D[onald].  "Letters:  Donald D. Walsh Replies to
        Robert Bly."  <u>American Poetry Review</u>, 2 (July/August),
        54-55.
        A reply to Bly's "slashing and slanderous attack," regarding
Walsh's translation of Neruda and the exclusive rights provided by
the United States Copyright Law.  The "errors" Bly believes he has
discovered in Walsh's translations are corrections in faulty texts.
Walsh compares and comments upon Bly's own translations of Neruda
which reveal his "ignorance of Spanish" and that "he has a tin ear,
a sad defect in a poet."
        See D4, D5, and P90.

P90.  Walsh, Donald D.  "Letters."  <u>American Poetry Review</u>, 2
        (November/December), 39.
        Reply to Bly's letter in the September/October 1973 issue.
He disagrees that exclusive English language rights prevents the

publication of the work in any other language. Regarding Bly's
accusations of errors in reading sacred texts, Walsh states that
there are no sacred texts and that Bly is confusing the error with
Walsh's correction of the error. He finds Bly "again riding furi-
ously and nosily in the wrong direction."
See D4, D5, and P89.

1974

P91.  Emma, Joan E. "Letters." American Poetry Review, 3
      (January/February), 53-54.
      A response to Bly's article "Developing the Underneath"
and his discussion of memory and imagination, particularly what is
felt to be his failure to come to terms with Blake's use of the terms.
Bly is faulted for neglecting the fact that without memory there is
no imagination, and with generally "not thinking far enough into
the matter."
      See B75.

P92.  Libby, Anthony. "Roethke, Water Father." American Liter-
      ature, 46 (November), [267]-288 passim.
      Roethke was the dominant influence on three "new sur-
realist romantics": Bly, James Dickey, and Sylvia Plath. They
all share "striking convergences among the poetic landscapes to
which they consistently return." The poetry of these three poets
is used to examine what is central in Roethke's work through the
parallels and echoes of their poetry. The primary focus is, of
course, upon Roethke, but through the examination of his poetry,
an understanding of Bly's work, in relation to Roethke's, emerges
as well.

P93.  Lundkvist, Artur. "Ett Krig ger bismak at Kallvattnet."
      Dagens Nyheter, (May 6), p. 4.
      Not verified, cited in Friberg (no. O2), p. 218.

P94.  Mersmann, James F. "Robert Bly: Watering the Rocks."
      In his Out of the Vietnam Vortex: A Study of Poets and
      Against the War. Lawrence: University of Kansas, pp.
      113-157. Also pp. ix, x, 24, 78, 92, 95, 101, 162, 176,
      194, 205, 219, 226, 227, 230, 236, 237-238, 240, 255.
      Bly is one of four poets focused upon. This is a good
analysis of the development of Bly's poetry with particular empha-
sis on his political poetry. It is, however, an intelligent and in-
teresting essay with value beyond just an understanding of the
political works.
      See R2. Reprinted in O5.

P95.  Morris, Richard. "Romantics and Anti-Romantics or Why
      Robert Bly Doesn't Like the Poetry of Anne Waldman."
      Margins, 14 (October/November), 33-36, 88.

A response to Bly's comments on the "New York School" of poetry in The Seventies. Bly's attitude toward this group of poets is a result of his own romantic tendencies. Poetry for him must be supercharged with emotion. The Bly criticism is used as a starting point for an examination of the poetry of Charles Bukowski and Anne Waldman to see what qualities there are in it that Bly distrusts. The essay logically becomes more an examination of the characteristics of these two poets rather than an analysis of Bly's poetry or criticism, except by contrast.

See B65.

P96. Novak, R[obert]. "What I Have Written Is Not Good Enough: The Poetry of Robert Bly." Windless Orchard, no. 18 (Summer), 30-34.

In a somewhat disjointed essay four beliefs of Bly's are identified in his poetry: a qualified animism, that poets have intuited a desperation in the non-human, that good surrealistic poetry is achieved when the poet leaps from one to another of his "three evolutionary brains," and that "an executive is an executioner."

P97. Shaw, Robert B., ed. American Poetry Since 1960: Some Critical Perspectives. Chester Springs, PA: Dufour Editions, Ltd., pp. 71, 72, 77, 78, 182, 183.

Besides the Shaw and Williamson essays, other essays treat Bly briefly in relationship to the work of other poets. See P98 and P101.

P98. _____. "The Poetry of Protest." In American Poetry Since 1960: Some Critical Perspectives. Chester Springs, PA: Dufour Editions, Ltd., pp. 51-53 [[45]-54].

"The Teeth-Mother Naked at Last" is a "sort of up-dated, outward-looking 'Howl'." Some of Bly's protest poems could be viewed as satirical lyrics.

P99. Simpson, Louis. "Letters." American Poetry Review, 3 (January/February), 53.

A response to "Developing the Underneath" and Bly's belief in Jung's four-intelligences system. Simpson finds Bly's description of "thinking" types and "feeling" types to be a fairytale. He disagrees that feelings come from the unconscious. Poetry is made by thinking about feelings, and "there is something unreal about making a division between thought and feeling."

See B75.

P100. Smith, Newton. "Praise for Robert Bly." Lillabulero, no. 14 (Spring), 183-185.

A minor piece concerning a dream fantasy of Bly as a prophet, agitator, and politicizer.

P101. Williamson, Alan. "Language Against Itself: The Middle Generation of Contemporary Poets." In American Poetry

Since 1960:  Some Critical Perspectives.  Ed. Robert B.
Shaw.   Chester Springs, PA:  Dufour Editions, Ltd.,
p. 65 [55-67].
Although he is the most vocal theorist of his generation,
Bly's own poetry seems "too much the result of a design for irra-
tional poetry, too little of genuinely unconscious promptings." His
surrealistic political poetry emits "a deep voice choking on its own
anger and going shrill."

## 1975

P102.   "A Conversation with Robert Bly." [Edited from a tape of
        Bly speaking with a group of creative writing students,
        March 1975]. Street Magazine, 2 (no. 1), [15-22].
        Bly speaks on his early years in New York City, isola-
tion, poetry, poets, and Kabir.
        Reprinted in A57.

P103.   Molesworth, Charles.  "Thrashing in the Depths:  The
        Poetry of Robert Bly." Rocky Mountain Review of Lan-
        guage and Literature, 29 (Autumn), 95-117.
        This essay attempts to correct the critical situation in
which Bly's criticism all too often outweighs his poetry and to
place his criticism in relation to the poetry rather than analyzing
the poems through the polemics.  Although Molesworth does not
necessarily succeed in doing this, he does present an important
analysis of Bly's poetry, particularly his political poetry and prose
poems.  The essay is marred somewhat by its obvious commendatory
position and the too ready willingness to make excuses for Bly's
work and to place the blame on the reader rather than Bly for the
difficulty in his work.
        See P158.

P104.   Nelson, Cary.  "Whitman in Vietnam:  Poetry and History
        in Contemporary America." Massachusetts Review, 16
        (Winter), 55-71.
        Considering the subject of this essay--Vietnam War poems
and the work of those established poets whose careers were clearly
affected by the progress of the war--Bly is discussed surprisingly
little.  The essay is not important for what it presents about Bly,
but it does serve as a good background piece concerning other
poets' work on Vietnam with which Bly's work can be compared.

P105.   Nelson, Howard.  "Welcoming Shadows:  Robert Bly's Recent
        Poetry." Hollins Critic, 12 (April), 1-15.
        An examination of the development of Bly's poetry since
his first two books.  There was a radical shift between the poems
of the first two collections, but Bly did not adhere to one style or
mode.  He has developed a distinctive voice by writing different
sorts of poems simultaneously.  The poetry of Silence in the Snowy

Fields, The Light Around the Body, and Sleepers Joining Hands is
discussed, as is the concept of association and Bly's use of it.
His best recent work, however, is perceived to be in his short
poems and prose poems.  In the short poem, Bly has few contempo-
rary rivals.  Like his prose poems, the short poems have a warmer
and more varied voice.  In the prose poems he blends together his
most exact concrete descriptive writing with some of his most ar-
resting intuitions regarding the inner and outer worlds.  In these
poems he realizes his most exhilarating and graceful imaginative
leaps.

P106.  Ratner, Rochelle.  "On Writing Prose Poems."  Soho Weekly
        News, 11 December.
        A discussion with Bly that centers around the idea of the
dominance of the mind in poetry and the prose poem as a reaction
to that dominance.  The prose poem is a response to poetry that is
too abstract or too general.  It returns the poet to the physical
world where body perceptions dominate rather than mind perceptions.
This idea of breaking up the mind organization is also discussed in
terms of his translations of the Sufi poetry of Rumi and Kabir as
well as the poetry of the Spanish surrealists.
        Reprinted in A57 and P132.

P107.  Siemering, Bill.  "The Mother:  An Interview with Robert
        Bly."  Dacotah Territory, 12 (Winter/Spring 1975/1976),
        30-34.
        Excerpts from the conversation taped for the Minnesota
Public Radio Station KCCM in May, 1975.  The discussion is con-
cerned with the First Annual Conference on the Mother to be held
in July.  Bly talks about the suppression of women in society, the
impending collapse of the patriarchal society, and the need to allow
the mother consciousness to emerge.
        See I23.  Reprinted in A57.

P108.  Smith.  "The Non-Rationalist."  The Smith, no. 18 (Decem-
        ber), 152-153.
        A response to Miller Williams article on "the Anti-
rationalists."  The characteristics of the "school" are correct, but
they apply to poets today generally.  The examples given in the
article are poor and misleading.  Grander associative leaps can be
found in Ezra Pound than in the poets admired by Bly et al.  The
lack of wildness in nineteenth-century English poets was used as a
point of comparison, but there is no discussion of American writers
of the same period, specifically Thoreau.
        See P111.

P109.  Stitt, Peter.  "The Art of Poetry XIX:  James Wright."
        Paris Review, 16 (Summer 1975), 48-50 [35-61].
        In an interview, Wright briefly discusses his relationship
with Bly and the extent of Bly's influence upon his own work.
        Reprinted in O5.

P110.  Wakeman, John, ed.  "Bly, Robert."  In World Authors
       1950-1970.  New York:  H. W. Wilson Co., pp. 171-172.
       Biographical information and a brief overview of the
critical response to Bly's work is given.  The entry includes a
brief, selected bibliographical listing.

P111.  Williams, Miller.  "Intuition, Spontaneity, Organic Wholeness
       and the Redemptive Wilderness:  Some (Old) Currents in
       Contemporary Poetry."  The Smith, no. 18 (December),
       141-151 passim.
       An examination of the group or movement termed "The
Poets of Intuition" or "The Anti-rationalists."  Bly presented what
amounts to their manifesto in The Seventies issue on leaping poetry.
The characteristics of poetry they most value are delineated with
examples cited.  The essay is not specifically about Bly, but the
inference is that he is the major theorist of this movement.
       See P108.

P112.  Williamson, Alan.  "Silence, Surrealism, and Allegory."
       Kayak, no. 40 (November), 59, 61-62 [57-67].
       Several references are made to Bly in a review of the
American surrealist style.  There is a "telltale sluggishness" about
Bly's lines, "a drowning tantamount to decreation."  In his essay
on the value of community, Bly "overvalues community, and under-
values critical individualism; and so do the poems of many of his
followers."
       See B79.


                                   1976

P113.  Alexander, Franklyn.  "GLR/Bibliography:  Contemporary
       Midwest Writers Series, Nos. 1, 2--Robert Bly."  Great
       Lakes Review, 3 (Summer), 66-69.
       A forty-four-item bibliography of primary and secondary
material preceded by a brief biographical and critical introduction.

P114.  Atkinson, Michael.  "Robert Bly's Sleepers Joining Hands:
       Shadow and Self."  Iowa Review, 7 (Fall), 135-153.
       A lucid examination of Bly's book with primary focus on
the title sequence with an exploration of its relationship to Whit-
man's "The Sleepers."  The psychological mode of experience is
found to be the dominant mode of the book.  A relationship between
the poems in the book and the essay on mother culture is discussed
in order to determine the resulting focus of the work as a whole.

P115.  Benedikt, Michael.  "Introduction."  In his edition The
       Prose Poem:  An International Anthology.  New York:
       Dell Publishing Co., Inc., pp. 41-42 [[39]-50].
       A brief discussion of Bly's concept of the associative
method from "Looking for Dragon Smoke."  The imagistic factor

implied in associative leaping has contributed toward the break-
through of the prose poem in the late 1960's and 1970's.

P116.  Elliott, William D.  "Poets on the Moving Frontier:  Bly,
       Whittemore, Wright, Berryman, McGrath and Minnesota
       North Country Poetry."  Midamerica:  The Yearbook of
       the Society for the Study of Midwestern Literature, 3,
       pp. 17-38.
       A general discussion and historical overview of Midwestern
and North Country literature rather than an analysis of the indi-
vidual poets.  It provides good background material on the milieu
that Bly emerged from, but provides no analysis or discussion of
his works.

P117.  Faas, Ekbert.  "An Interview with Robert Bly."  Boundary
       2, 4 (Spring), 677-700.
       A far-ranging and insightful interview but marked by a
forced direction toward other poets the interviewer is interested in,
particularly Charles Olson, Robert Duncan, Allen Ginsberg, and
Robert Creeley.
       Reprinted in O5 and P141, and in A57 as "Infantilism and
Adult Swiftness."

P118.  _____.  "Robert Bly."  Boundary 2, 4 (Spring), 707-726.
       Bly's ability to "capture the phantasmagoria of the sub-
conscious" with convincingness and magic gives him an almost
unique position in English language literature.  The lack of a
Surrealist movement in Anglo-American poetry and Bly's attempt to
launch one through his translations and essays is discussed at
length.  His theories on poetry are related to his own works and
to his essays on James Wright and James Dickey.  There is also
speculation on the effect of Buddhist philosophy on Bly's political
and philosophical positions.
       Reprinted in P141.

P119.  Friberg, Ingegerd.  "Robert Bly:  En livsnara diktare."
       Tarningskastet, 1, pp. 35-53.
       Not verified, cited in Friberg (no. O2), p. 218.

P120.  Gitzen, Julian.  "Floating on Solitude:  The Poetry of
       Robert Bly."  Modern Poetry Studies, 7 (Winter), 231-
       241.
       An examination of the dominant images in Bly's poetry:
darkness, water, snow, and moonlight (and its relation to Boehme's
association of the spirit with light).  Natural symbols are important
as influences contributing to thoughts or emotions, or as media of
symbolic expression.  "I Came Out of the Mother Naked" is dis-
cussed as adding to Bly's spiritual quest and in terms of his so-
cial criticism.  As a social critic, he is seen to resemble Auden and
to share his moral viewpoint.

P121.  Goldman, Sherman.  "Robert Bly on Gurus, Grounding
        Yourself in the Western Tradition, and Thinking for
        Yourself."  East West Journal, 6 (August), 10-15.
          An interesting interview centered around the question of
spirituality and the influence of Eastern methods in the United
States.  The writings of Jung, Freud, and Kabir are, of course,
touched upon, as are Bly's misgivings concerning the structure of
the Naropa Institute.

P122.  Lepper, Gary M.  "Robert Bly."  In his A Bibliographical
        Introduction to Seventy-Five Modern American Authors.
        Berkeley, CA:  Serendipity Books, pp. [63]-72.
          A checklist of primary works which include seventy items.

P123.  Mills, Ralph J., Jr.  "'The Body With the Lamp Lit Inside:'
        Robert Bly's New Poems."  Northeast, series 3, no. 2
        (Winter 1976-1977), 37-47.
          An excellent review and discussion of the development
of Bly's prose poems and their relationship to his other poetry.
The Morning Glory (Harper & Row edition) is the central focus of
the discussion, and it is a "substantial accomplishment both for
Bly ... and for the prose poem in America."  In the prose poem
Bly finds a greater flexibility and lack of restrictions compared to
his other poems.

P124.  Power, Kevin.  "Conversation with Robert Bly."  Texas
        Quarterly, 19 (Autumn), 80-94.
          The central element in this interview is that of mother
consciousness and energy.  This is a good complement to Bly's
prose works on the great mother.
          Reprinted, in part, in A57 as "On Split-Brain Experiments
and the Mother," and in P231.

P125.  "Robert Bly:  Politics and the Soul."  North Country Anvil,
        no. 20 (December 1976/January 1977), 16-18.
          An interview with Bly in which he comments upon the
relationship between politics and the real world, particularly among
students.  He sees a loss of the momentum which was established
during the years of protest against the Vietnam War.  There is not
enough thinking going on among students, and they have sunk into
a tremendous despair and apathy.

P126.  Sader, Marion, ed.  "Bly, Robert."  In her Comprehensive
        Index to English-Language Little Magazines 1890-1970.
        Series One.  Millwood, NY:  Kraus-Thompson Organiza-
        tion, Ltd., Vol. 1., pp. 419-421.
          A listing of Bly's contributions to selected little maga-
zines.  Also included is a brief listing of secondary sources.

1977

P127.   Bowie, John.   "Black Flags:   America, Vietnam and Robert
        Bly."   Seneca Review, 8 (December), 13-21.
        An interesting and thought-provoking look at Bly's war
poems.   In these poems he adopts the role of a conscience doctor.
Although his heart is right, his diagnosis is asinine.   His poems
are catalogs of the national sins, ultimately laying it all on materi-
alism.   He is too willing to condemn, giving the nation no potential
for good.   His use of "we" is the rhetorical "but not me" we.   He
and the other anti-war poets were wrong because they assumed too
much.   The war was not a result of all-encompassing racism or mate-
rialism, but a general ignorance.   Bly ultimately said much but knew
little.

P128.   Friberg, Ingegerd.   "Modernsmedvetandets arketyp."
        Tarningskastet, 2, pp. 54-55.
        Not verified, citied in Friberg (no. O2), p. 218.

P129.   Investigative Poetry Group.   The Party:   A Chronological
        Perspective on a Confrontation at a Buddhist Seminary.
        Woodstock, NY:   Poetry, Crime, and Culture Press.
        An account of the altercation between W. S. Merwin and
Dana Naone and Chogyam Trungpa, Rinpoche at Vajradhatu Seminary,
and its effects on the Naropa Institute.   Bly is a secondary, but
central, figure in the story.   After receiving an account of the
incident from Merwin, Bly speaks about it publicly at a reading in
Boulder and creates a confrontation between himself and members
of the audience.   The book includes a transcript of the Bly read-
ing in Boulder and a phone interview with him regarding the in-
cident.   The book is an interesting look at Naropa, poetry politics,
Merwin, Ginsberg, Buddhism in America, and the personality of
Bly.

P130.   Malkoff, Karl.   Escape From the Self:   A Study in Contempo-
        rary American Poetry and Poetics.   New York:   Columbia
        University Press, pp. 142-143.
        Brief and general remarks on the "Deep Imagism" move-
ment.   Bly is quoted to help define the movement and its relation-
ship to Surrealism.

P131.   "Poets Initiate New Translation Award."   Coda:   Poets &
        Writers Newsletter, 5 (November/December), 10.
        In a brief article, Bly is quoted concerning the need for
a translation award given by poets themselves because of the differ-
ences in translations when poets translate.

P132.   Ratner, Rochelle.   ["On Writing Prose Poems."]   Aura, no.
        6 (Spring), 45-46.
        Reprint of P106.

P133.  Sexton, Linda Gray, and Lois Ames, eds.  Anne Sexton:  A
       Self-Portrait in Letters.  Boston:  Houghton Mifflin Co.,
       pp. 120, 300-302.
       Two letters:  the first to W. D. Snodgrass in which she
states that Bly "is the only critic with energy and a goal ... very
exciting, even when he's wrong"; the second letter, to Bly, is a
rambling commentary on The Sixties Spring 1962 issue.

P134.  Thurley, Geoffrey.  "Devices Among Words:  Kinnell, Bly,
       Simic."  In his The American Moment:  American Poetry
       in the Mid-Century.  New York:  St. Martin's Press, pp.
       217-225 [[210]-228].
       An indignant and uncompromising essay decrying what is
perceived to be the decline and repudiation of Allen Ginsberg and
the Beats with the ascendency of Bly et al.  The poetry of the
Beats is swift, intelligent, and essentially human.  Bly's poetry is
more self-assured, ruminant and safe.  In his poetry the fluency
of the poets of the 1920's is regained but it is void of human per-
sonalities.  An extended contrast between Auden and Bly, to the
detriment of the latter, follows.  There is no human voice but rather
"a factitious literary convention, an assemblage of vocables, a de-
vice among words."  Bly is irritating in his assumption of enlighten-
ment.  His vision is one-dimensional.

P135.  Williams, Harry.  "The Edge Is What I Have":  Theodore
       Roethke and After.  Lewisburg:  Bucknell University
       Press, pp. 35, 153, 155, 163-173, 201, 204.
       An examination of the influence of Roethke on the themes
and lyrical qualities of Bly's poetry.  Bly's polemics, as evidenced
in his prose, show similarities to Roethke's kind of poetry.  Bly,
like James Wright, intensifies Roethke's disenchantment with society
and its archsymbol, the institution.


                              1978


P136.  Bliss, Shepherd.  "Balancing Feminine and Masculine:  The
       Mother Conference in Maine."  East West Journal, 8 (Feb-
       ruary), 36-39 passim.
       A review of the Third Annual Conference on the Great
Mother and the New Father in which Bly participated.  Much of
what transpires at the Conference has reference to Bly's interests
in fairy tales, Jung, and the female/male dichotomy.  Poetry was
viewed as one of the integrating elements of the Conference; the
spirit of Kabir is said to be a guide for the participants and work-
shops are offered in Rilke.

P137.  Dodd, Wayne, ed.  "Robert Bly."  Ohio Review, 19 (Fall),
       [29]-66.  Special Feature--Series on Contemporary Poetics.
       See P138.

P138. _____. "Robert Bly: An Interview." Ohio Review, 19
          (Fall), 56-66.
          This is one of the single best sources for Bly's views on
the state of contemporary poetry. The interview really centers
around this one theme rather than jumping through questions not
directly relevant to one another. Topics include the lack of criti-
cism existing in poetry today, the relationship between the younger
and older poets, the concept of the MFA and writing workshops.
Reprinted, in part, in A57 as "Knots of Wild Energy."

P139. Evers, L. M. "Castaneda." New York Times Book Review,
          7 May, p. 45.
          A letter disagreeing with Bly's review of The Second
Ring of Power. See C15.

P140. Exner, Richard. "On Translating Late Rilke: Remarks on
          Some Recent Examples." Chicago Review, 29 (Winter),
          159-161 [153-161].
          In a discussion of the various translations of Rilke's later
work, Bly's translations are lauded as among the best available.
His The Voices is superbly contemporary and yet faithfully ren-
dered. Ten Sonnets to Orpheus is "perfect." A true correspon-
dence exists between Bly and Rilke.

P141. Faas, Ekbert. "Robert Bly." In his Towards A New Ameri-
          can Poetics: Essays and Interviews. Santa Barbara,
          CA: Black Sparrow Press, pp. [199]-243.
          Reprint of P117-P118.

P142. Ford, Harry. "'Travelers'." New York Times Book Review,
          30 April, p. 70.
          A response from W. S. Merwin's editor to Bly's review of
Merwin's Houses and Travelers. Bly presumes too much in his re-
marks regarding the editorial relationship that exists with Merwin.
His review ends in "windy generalities" and his judgement is trivial.
          Bly responds that he was attempting to make a general point
regarding editing in the United States and that he stands by that
assessment.
          See C16.

P143. Hall, Donald. "Notes on Robert Bly and Sleepers Joining
          Hands." In his Goatfoot Milktongue Twinbird: Inter-
          views, Essays, and Notes on Poetry, 1970-1976. Ann
          Arbor: The University of Michigan Press, pp. 137-143.
          Reprint of P82.

P144. Harner, Michael. "Castaneda." New York Times Book Re-
          view, 7 May, p. 45.
          In response to Bly's review of The Second Ring of Power,
Harner defends Castaneda from charges that he plagiarized from
his and others work on shamanism. He finds it unfortunate that

reviewers of Castaneda's books are not really experts on shaman-
ism.  He also finds Bly's position regarding primitive cultures to
smack of ethnocentrism.
   Bly replies that he amends his review in regard to the point
concerning plagiarism, but he reiterates his view that Castaneda is
pandering to a readership who follow primitive fads.
   See C15.

P145.  Komie, Lowell.  "Ecstasy and Poetry in Chicago:  A Middle-
       Aged Lawyer Goes to his First Poetry Reading."  Harper's,
       256 (March), 129-131.
   A description of a reading given by Bly in Chicago, No-
vember 1977.  Bly's use of masks and his activities and mannerisms
on stage are recounted.  It is concluded that Bly is "an ecstatic
poet."

P146.  Lockwood, William J.  "Robert Bly:  The Point Reyes Poems."
       In Where the West Begins:  Essays on Middle Border and
       Siouxland Writing, In Honor of Herbert Krause.  Ed.
       Arthur R. Huseboe and William Geyer.  Sioux Falls, SD:
       Augustana College, Center for Western Studies, pp. 128-
       134.
   The Point Reyes Poems, which appeared as a small volume
from Half Moon Bay as well as a part of The Morning Glory, are
examined as most representative of Bly's work at the time.  His
journeying through the western half of North America seems to have
offered him an opportunity to resist the "dangerous rigidity and
self-consciousness of his native northern region."  The poems pro-
duced from this journeying express a more open and unselfcon-
scious outlook.  They generate a moral clarity yet are largely free
of pretension to superior wisdom.  They offer insight rather than
judgment.

P147.  Molesworth, Charles.  "Contemporary Poetry and the Meta-
       phor for the Poem."  Georgia Review, 32 (Summer), 325-
       327 [319-331].
   One of three metaphoric images of the poem is identified
as Bly's notion of "leaping" or associatively linked clusters of non-
discursive images.  All of Bly's theories center around the key idea
that something is missing.  A conspiracy of rationality and order
keep from us a once available awareness.  Poems become a way back
to a different order of understanding.  The tension in Bly's poetics
derives from seeing the poem simultaneously as image and as leap.
Bly's movement from an image-centered poetry to a more energized
movement within the poem pointed in a direction is also discussed.

P148.  Simpson, Louis.  A Revolution in Taste:  Studies of Dylan
       Thomas, Allen Ginsberg, Sylvia Plath, and Robert Lowell.
       New York:  Macmillan Publishing Co., Inc., pp. 155-157.
   Bly's main points in his review of Lowell's For the Union
Dead are summarized and disagreed with.  Although Bly's comments

may apply to Lowell's earlier poems, they do not apply to this book.
Simpson examines several poems to support his position.
See C5.

P149.   "Tva Poeter Oversatter: Ett Samtal Mellan Robert Bly Och
Tomas Tranströmer." Bonniers Litterara Magasin, 47,
pp. 230-236.
Verified, but not translated.

P150.   Wilk, Stan. "Castaneda." New York Times Book Review,
7 May, p. 45.
A letter disagreeing with Bly's points in his review of
The Second Ring of Power. The review displays a narrowness of
vision and condescension.
See C15.

### 1979

P151.   Altieri, Charles. "Varieties of Immanentist Experience:
Robert Bly, Charles Olson, and Frank O'Hara." In his
American Poetry During the 1960's. New Jersey: As-
sociated University Presses, pp. 78-93 [78-127].
A demanding and difficult analysis of Bly's poetics and
poetry in terms of, and contrasted to, those of Robert Lowell's and
his poetry. Bly's poetic treads a delicate and often shifting bound-
ary line between traditional Romanticism and the more secular onto-
logical strategies of other postmodern poets. He, however, remains
radically postmodern by "insisting on the imaginative act as a denial
of the ego and by pointing to the immediate act of sympathetic per-
ception as the source of one's participation in this deeper life."
There is an underlying sense of acrimony throughout the essay.

P152.   Christensen, Paul. "Bly, Robert." In Great Writers of the
English Language: Poets. Ed. James Vinson. New York:
St. Martin's Press, pp. 122-124.
Basic biographical listing and brief critical entry. See
P163 and P211.

P153.   Dacey, Philip. "The Reverend Robert E. Bly, Pastor,
Church of the Blessed Unity: A Look at 'A Man Writes
to a Part of Himself'." In A Book of Rereadings in Re-
cent American Poetry: 30 Essays. Ed. Greg Kuzma.
Lincoln, NE: Best Celler Press, pp. 1-7. (This is a
triple issue of Pebble, 18/19/20.)
An original look at the basis of Bly's writing using the
poem "A Man Writes to a Part of Himself" to show what Bly is about
in his work generally. His writing is motivated by a desire to save
souls, including his own, rather than by a commitment to poetry as
an art form. Explicating the poem, and focusing on the metaphysi-
cal husband and wife pain, it is stated that Bly's theme is an

outgrowth of a nineteenth-century obsession with a desire to
achieve a union between some "High Reality" and the visible mun-
dane world.  What is important in Bly's poetry is its moral urgency.
His poems are battlegrounds for the clash of moral forces.  He is
reinterpreting the central term of his Christian heritage, love, and
urging upon us its salvific powers.

P154.  Davis, William V.  "Hair in a Baboon's Ear:  The Politics of
        Robert Bly's Early Poetry."  Carleton Miscellany, 18 (no.
        1, 1979/1980), 74-84.
        A helpful discussion of Bly's political poetry in The Light
Around the Body in relationship to the poetry of Silence in the
Snowy Fields and the philosophy of Jacob Boehme:  the notion of
two worlds, the development of public and private languages, and
the dichotomy of light and darkness.

P155.  Haskell, Dennis.  "The Modern American Poetry of Deep
        Image."  Southern Review [Australia], 12, pp. 137-166
        passim.
        A wide-ranging essay offering a solid background on the
Deep Image movement.  Bly is one of five poets concentrated on
(the others are James Wright, William Stafford, Donald Hall, and
W. S. Merwin).  The influence that Bly has exerted on the move-
ment is examined through both his poetry and his polemics.  The
failures of his poetry are usually a result of a lack of apparent
connection between the images which result in chaos and a certain
flatness.

P156.  Hoffman, Daniel.  "Poetry:  Schools of Dissidents."  In
        Harvard Guide to Contemporary American Writing.  Ed.
        Daniel Hoffman.  Cambridge, MA:  Harvard University
        Press [The Belknap Press], pp. 545-547 [496-563].  Also,
        pp. 496, 497, 512, 537, 548, 549, 551, 566.
        A brief overview of Bly's work and the influence of for-
eign poets on it.  It is suggestive of Thoreau and American trans-
cendentalism, and less successful in The Light Around the Body
than in Silence in the Snowy Fields.  He recoups with Sleepers
Joining Hands.

P157.  Magill, Frank N., ed.  Magill's Bibliography of Literary
        Criticism.  4 Vols.  Englewood Cliffs, NJ:  Salem Press,
        Vol. 1, pp. 190-192.
        A thirty-five-item bibliography of secondary material.

P158.  Molesworth, Charles.  "'Rejoice in the Gathering Dark':
        The Poetry of Robert Bly."  In his The Fierce Embrace:
        A Study of Contemporary American Poetry.  Columbia:
        University of Missouri Press, pp. 112-138.
        A melding of two previous essays:  "Thrashing in the
Depths" and "Domesticating the Sublime."
        See P103 and Q260.  Reprinted in O5.

P159.  Shepard, Richard F.  "TV:  Robert Bly, the Poet, Is Inter-
       viewed by Moyers."  New York Times, 19 February, p.
       D6.
         A preview of "Bill Moyers' Journal" program on Bly.  It
is "a fascinating and articulate visit" with Bly "who not only writes
movingly but also can speak movingly."  A viewer of the show will
learn how a poet thinks and writes, and the program is a testament
to good and intelligent conversation.

P160.  Tranströmer, Tomas.  "Letters to Bly."  Ironwood, no. 13,
       pp. 94-101.
         Letters and parts of letters from Tranströmer to Bly are
reprinted.  This is not important for what it reveals of Bly, but
is interestingly revealing of Transtömer, particularly his humor.


                              1980


P161.  Altieri, Charles.  "From Experience to Discourse:  American
       Poetry and Poetics in the Seventies."  Contemporary Lit-
       erature, 21 (Spring), 191-224 passim.
         In the hopes of clarifying "the work of many younger
poets only now developing mature voices," Altieri posits "a general
opposition between a poetics of immediate experience and a poetics
acknowledging its status as discourse...."  One group "engages in
various transformations of more surreal uses of the deep image."
Bly and Kinnell are cited as representing the style of poetry which
reveals the typical form of cultural pressure of the 1960's and
which constitutes a negative force and a stylistic norm younger
poets must resist if they are to achieve new imaginative stances.
In thus seeking to define the younger poets by examining the cor-
relation between literary changes and social changes, and using
Bly and the emotive imagination as characteristic of the sixties,
Bly's poetry is sharply criticized and dismissed to a point far ex-
ceeding Altieri's previous comments in other essays.

P162.  Atlas, James.  "New Voices in American Poetry."  New York
       Times Magazine, 3 February, pp. 18, 19, 20.
         Bly is one of a number of poets used to examine the
generation of poets "now in its early 50's."  His convictions regard-
ing the instinctual and unconscious sources of poetry have given
rise to an identifiable school of poetry, "New Surrealism."  Bly has
a weakness for the extravagant gesture, and "has become more
theatrical than ever."

P163.  Christensen, Paul.  "Bly, Robert."  In Contemporary Poets.
       3rd ed.  Ed. James Vinson.  New York:  St. Martin's
       Press, pp. 131-134.
         A variation on P152.

P164.  Dame, Enid.  "Readings:  'Like One of Your Favorite

Teachers.' Robert Bly at the New School." <u>Home
Planet News</u>, 2 (Summer), 9, 12.
A review of a Bly reading by a, at first, skeptical ob-
server. The wide extent of materials presented by Bly in his
readings is discussed. A subjective, but not unhelpful, descrip-
tion of the Bly reading experience.

P165. Froiland, Paul. "Conversation with a Poet: Of Shamans
and Solitude: Robert Bly on the Meaning of Words."
<u>TWA Ambassador</u>, December, pp. 33-36.
An informal conversation with Bly that reveals nice
touches of his "home life." Much of the article summarizes Bly's
various interests. The primary focus is upon the shaman and
the development of his role in modern civilization and consciousness.

P166. Holt, Patricia. "PW Interviews: Robert Bly." <u>Publishers
Weekly</u>, 217 (9 May), 10-11.
This is not the usual interview form of question and
answer, but an essay based on an interview. The thrust of the
piece is a discusison of <u>News of the Universe</u> and Bly's concept of
twofold consciousness and the multiconscious stream of poetry in
the United States. The character of Bly's readings is also briefly
discussed.

P167. Howard, Richard. "'Like Those Before, We Move To the
Death We Love'." In his <u>Alone with America: Essays
on the Art of Poetry in the United States Since 1950</u>.
Enlarged edition. New York: Atheneum, pp. [57]-67.
Reprint of P49.

P168. Kinnell, Galway. "Poetry, Personality and Death." In <u>A
'Field' Guide to Contemporary Poetry and Poetics</u>. Ed.
Stuart Friebert and David Young. New York and London:
Longman, pp. 204-205, 206, 212-213 [203-223].
Reprint of P67.

P169. Niikura, Toshikazu. "A Romantic Reassertion: Bly and
Haiku." In <u>The Traditional and the Anti-Traditional:
Studies in Contemporary American Literature</u>. Gen. ed.
Kenzaburo Ohashi. Tokyo: Tokyo Chapter of the Amer-
ican Literature Society of Japan, pp. 120-128.
Bly's poetry represents a greater possibility toward Ro-
mantic imagination. However, his approach to deep image poetry
owes as much to haiku as to European examples. The influence of
haiku on Bly's poetry, and the similarities between them, is dis-
cussed.

P170. Smith, C. Michal. "Robert Bly." In <u>Dictionary of Literary
Biography</u>. Ed. Donald J. Greiner. Detroit: Gale Re-
search Co.; Vol. 5, <u>American Poets Since World War II</u>,
Part 1: A-K, pp. 77-82.

A conventional biographical and critical overview of Bly's
major works.  A brief selected primary and secondary bibliography
is included.


## 1981


P171.  Alexander, Franklyn.  "Robert Bly" In A Bibliographical
        Guide to Midwestern Literature.  Gen. ed. Gerald
        Nemanic.  Iowa City:  University of Iowa Press, pp.
        148-150.
        A brief and selective overview of critical response to Bly's
work.  A listing of "Major Works" consisting of eighteen titles and
a "Checklist of Secondary Sources" listing fifteen items are included.


P172.  Andrews, Terry.  "Five Writers:  'They Bring Life to What
        We In Minnesota Have and Know and Care About'."
        Minneapolis-St. Paul, 9 (August), 73.
        Not verified, cited in Magazine Index.


P173.  Baker, Deborah.  "Making a Farm:  A Literary Biography of
        Robert Bly."  Poetry East, no. 4/5 (Spring/Summer),
        145-189.
        One of the few extended biographical essays on Bly.  It
attempts to propose the possible sources and implications of the ma-
jor themes in his literary criticism and poetry during the past thirty
years.  This is a good factual presentation that does not lose its
subject in extravagant theorizing or psychobiography.
        Reprinted in O3.


P174.  Clifton, Michael.  "Interview with Robert Bly."  Poetry East,
        no. 4/5 (Spring/Summer), 43-60.
        A typical Bly interview touching on the usual topics al-
though the thrust of the interview centers on Bly and James
Wright's concern with poetry in the late fifties and the directions
they turned under the influence of Trakl and others.
        Reprinted in O3.


P175.  Davis, William Virgil.  "At the Edges of the Light:  A Read-
        ing of Robert Bly's Sleepers Joining Hands."  Poetry
        East, no. 4/5 (Spring/Summer), 265-282.
        Sleepers Joining Hands is a synthesis of the themes and
styles of Bly's first two collections.  The development of Bly's be-
lief in the theory of the three brains and Erich Neumann's myth of
the "Great Mother culture" is discussed, and the poetry of Sleepers
is examined to determine if Bly is a poet of the "new brain."  This
collection is a poetic, religious, and psychological struggle by Bly
in an attempt to understand himself and the world around him by
exploring the substrata of the psyche.  This is an interesting and
intelligent essay.
        Reprinted in O3.

P176.  Goedicke, Patricia.  "The Leaper Leaping."  Poetry East,
       no. 4/5 (Spring/Summer), 64-84.
           An examination of Bly's belief in the nonhuman world
and the restorative powers of the natural world.  His belief in
the relationship between the human and the universe--the nonhu-
man world--is expressed through his body:  the natural movements
of his body, the passional movements of dance, and the music of
the dulcimer that are part of his readings.
           Reprinted in O3.


P177.  Haines, John.  "Robert Bly:  A Tiny Retrospect."  Poetry
       East, no. 4/5 (Spring/Summer), 190-193.
           A nicely balanced and honest reminiscence about his first
encounter with Bly through correspondence.  The position that
Haines was in at the time in regard to his poetry is discussed in
light of the influence Bly's work in The Fifties and the Sixties had
on it.  The innovative energy of The Fifties has spent itself and
disciples of it produce second and third hand pastoral sureality.
Disagreements with Bly are easy and necessary but he is respected
for his untiring efforts to push American poetry forward into the
twentieth century.
           Reprinted in O3.


P178.  Hall, Donald.  "Poetry Food."  Poetry East, no. 4/5 (Spring/
       Summer), 35-36.
           A brief personal tribute which emphasizes Bly's dissatis-
faction with his own work and his acceptance of criticism if there
is "an idea lurking in the denunciation."  Bly is willing to listen
and to develop in order to improve as a poet.
           Reprinted in O3 and P204.


P179.  Harris, Victoria Frenkel.  "Criticism and the Incorporative
       Consciousness."  Centennial Review, 25 (Fall), 417-434
       passim.
           Although this essay is not concerned with Bly's work per
se, its focus on the role of intuition in poetry and its discussion of
intuition in deep image poetry is useful for an understanding of
Bly's work.  Bly's concept of intuition is briefly discussed and his
poem, "Snowfall in the Afternoon," is explicated to show how the
intuitional imaginative content of the poem gives it symbolicity, and
a "leap" takes place.


P180.  _____.  "Landscapes of Affirmation:  Two Early Poems of
       Robert Bly."  Plainsong, 3 (Fall), 37-40.
           Silence in the Snowy Fields is an index to Bly's relation-
ship with the natural world.  By examining two poems, "Hunting
Pheasants in a Cornfield" and "Thinking of Wallace Stevens on the
First Snowy Day in December," Bly's affirmation of life is demon-
strated through the sensory impressions that reach beyond the
physical dimensions.

P181. _____. "'Walking Where the Plows Have Been Turning':
       Robert Bly and Female Consciousness." Poetry East, no.
       4/5 (Spring/Summer), 123-138.
       A cogent and thorough explication of Bly's prose poem in
terms of his handling of the concept of female consciousness. The
three paragraphs of the poem constitute a three-part metamorphosis
in which through reception, expansion, and generation Bly con-
structs a mythology of human experience.
       Reprinted in O3 and O5.


P182. Holden, Jonathan. "The Abstract Image: The Return of
       Abstract Statement in Contemporary American Poetry."
       New England Review, 3 (no. 3), 444-445 [435-449].
       "Surprised by Evening" is cited as an example of a psy-
chological pastoral which holds a simplified, schematic version of
the world. It is essentially a romantic vision. This is in contrast
to the poetic of the abstract image which tends to be compatible
with a realist view of things.


P183. Ignatow, David. "Reflections Upon the Past with Robert
       Bly." Poetry East, no. 4/5 (Spring/Summer), 197-206.
       A personal account of Bly as poet, editor, personality,
and friend. Reprinted in O3.


P184. Levine, Philip. Don't Ask. Ann Arbor: The University
       of Michigan Press, pp. 19-20, 125.
       In an interview in 1974, Levine sees Bly as a strong poet
whose contributions have been immense. Bly is described as a
"tremendous mind, tremendous spirit, a tremendous poet." Four
years later, in another interview, Bly has become "incredibly bor-
ing." He has taken his fame too seriously and become a seer, a
wise man telling people how to live.


P185. Levis, Larry. "Some Notes on Grief and the Image." Poetry
       East, no. 4/5 (Spring/Summer), 140-144.
       A discourse on the concept of "image" and a suggestion
that the condition of grief and mourning is what Bly is trying to
accomplish in some of his previous work. This is not a particularly
well-focused essay; it seems to miss its target.


P186. Libby, Anthony. "Dreaming of Animals." Plainsong, 3
       (Fall), 47-54.
       An examination of Bly's use of animals and animal meta-
phors in his poetry and poetic theories, and the relationship be-
tween the two. Bly's use of animal imagery in his poems helps to
illuminate the sense of his theories.
       This is an important essay because it is one of the few on
what is becoming recognized as an important aspect of Bly's poetry.


P187. Martin, Connie. "Some Ideas on Poetry Reading." Plain-
       song, 3 (Fall), 41-42.

The last paragraph of this brief essay on poetry read-
ings discusses Bly's readings. The job of a poet is to move the
listener into the "heart area." Bly is direct and human, and has
the ability to lead people.

P188. Mills, Ralph J., Jr. "'Of Energy Compacted and Whirling':
      Robert Bly's Recent Prose Poems." New Mexico Human-
      ities Review, 4 (Summer), 29-49.
         An in-depth examination of an important part of Bly's
canon, tracing the development of his prose poems and some of
their peculiar features and the qualities that the prose poem pro-
vides. Several of Bly's essays ("I Came Out of the Teeth-Mother
Naked," "The Three Brains," and "Wallace Stevens and Dr. Jekyl")
are used as points of comparison between the imagery of the prose
poems and his theoretical and philosophical thoughts.

P189. Nelson, Howard. "Robert Bly and the Ants." Poetry East,
      no. 4/5 (Spring/Summer), 207-215.
         Noting the importance and prominence of animals in Bly's
poetry, an examination of the use of ants in three poems is made:
"In the Courtyard of the Isleta Mission," "Ant Heaps by the Path,"
and "How the Ant Takes Part." The final analogy regarding his
use of ants is made to Lewis Thomas' The Lives of the Cell and his
concept of "the Hill" as an entity or an organism equaling it with
human evolution, the evolution of consciousness.
         Reprinted in O3.

P190. Orr, Gregory. "The Need for Poetics: Some Thoughts on
      Robert Bly." Poetry East, no. 4/5 (Spring/Summer),
      116-122.
         In each generation of poets there is a need for the poet
to serve as the reaffirmer and reinterpreter of the worth and pur-
pose of poetry. Bly's essays on poetry represent the "most in-
tense public thinking about poetry's human importance that was
taking place in English." He is the "teacher-guru of the Way of
Poetry."
         Reprinted in O3.

P191. Quam, Michael D. "Through Norwegian Eyes: Growing Up
      Among the Snowy Fields." Plainsong, 3 (Fall), 34-36.
         The author constructed a barrier to the positive aspects
of his Norwegian-American ancestry growing up in western Minne-
sota as he became influenced by the dark side of his heritage and
the "prohibition on the free expression of the realities of one's in-
ner life." He felt stifled and alone. Silence in the Snowy Fields
broke through that barrier and redeemed his childhood world. The
essay is very short in explaining just how the poetry was able to
do this however.

P192. Quinn, Fran. "An Essay in Five Disconnected Sections on
      the Great Mother Conferences." Plainsong, 3 (Fall), 43-46.

The stress is on "disconnected" in this discussion of the Great Mother Conference which grew out of Bly's interest in Erich Neumann's book, The Great Mother. The second and third sections discuss Bly's involvement in the Conference and the direction he wished it to move in.

P193.   Ray, David.   "On Robert Bly."   Poetry East, no. 4/5
        (Spring/Summer), 194.
        A brief tribute to Bly, the "archetypal crank." He has helped bring poetry back to its roots and into contact with its European heritage. It will be to poets like Bly that the world will eventually turn.
        Reprinted in O3.


P194.   Rudman, Mark.   "New Mud to Walk Upon."   Poetry East,
        no. 4/5 (Spring/Summer), 99-104.
        A disjointed essay focusing on two prose poems. After briefly starting with Bly's stated idea of a need for criticism, the essay evolves into an analysis of "The Dead Seal Near McClure's Beach" and Bly's use of similes. The awkwardness and transparency of the similes in this poem leads to a brief discussion of "Where We Must Look for Help." Bly has been able to transform his image and give it wings. Both poems present stages of life's way.
        Reprinted in O3.


P195.   Seal, David.   "Waking To 'Sleepers Joining Hands'."   Poetry
        East, no. 4/5 (Spring/Summer), 234-263.
        A helpful analysis of one of Bly's most difficult poems. The poem is clearly indebted to Jung, yet it is only apparently a Jungian drama. There is a conscious use of Jung's ideas, but also an unconscious resistance of those ideas. Each part of the poem is examined with the Jungian frame of mind, and then the anomalies in the Jungian model of interpretation are examined. These anomalies free the poem from doctrines and speak for the unconscious of Bly. This is a stimulating essay.
        Reprinted in O3.


P196.   "70 Poets on Robert Bly."   Poetry East, no. 4/5 (Spring/
        Summer), 105-115.
        Brief and essentially meaningless responses to a request for one sentence on Bly from one hundred poets. Some are amusing; too many are embarrassing.


P197.   Sjoberg, Leif.   "The Poet as Translator:   Robert Bly and
        Scandinavian Poetry."   Poetry East, no. 4/5 (Spring/
        Summer), 218-225.
        A tribute to Bly as an efficient and determined translator of Scandinavian poetry. It is senseless to nit-pick over his errors when what Bly has accomplished in general with his translations is what is important.
        Reprinted in O3.

P198.  Tranströmer, Tomas.  "Letter to Bly."  Poetry East, no.
       4/5 (Spring/Summer), 229-231.
       A letter concerning Bly's translation of "Street Crossing,"
and some reservations he has and mistakes he sees in the transla-
tion.  The give and take that is possible and necessary in success-
ful contemporary translating is nicely revealed, as is the humor,
intelligence, and warmth of Tranströmer.
       Reprinted in O3.

P199.  Turner, Frederick.  "Response to Mr. Bly."  Missouri Re-
       view, 5 (Winter 1981/1982), 196-197.
       Turner states his respect for Bly as a poet who never
gave up thinking.  He is capable of sheer logical lucidity and men-
tal discipline.  A point regarding Bly's response to the original
article is briefly argued.
       See B108.

P200.  Wright, Annie.  "Joining Hands with Robert Bly."  Poetry
       East, no. 4/5 (Spring/Summer), 37-42.
       Personal reminiscences about Bly, his family, and his re-
lationship with James Wright.  The central focus is upon a stay
with Bly on his farm in Minnesota shortly after the marriage of
Annie and James Wright.

P201.  Zavatsky, Bill.  "Talking Back:  A Response to Robert Bly."
       Poetry East, no. 4/5 (Spring/Summer), 86-98.
       Taking Bly at his word regarding his call for criticism,
Zavatsky offers his worthwhile thoughts on several standard areas
of Bly rhetoric:  object poems, prose poems, narrative poems, the
feminine, and confessional poetry.
       Reprinted in O3.


                              1982

P202.  Chaves, Jonathan.  "Chinese Influence or Cultural Colonial-
       ism:  Some Recent Poets."  Ironwood, no. 19, pp. 120-
       123 [115-123].
       Silence in the Snowy Fields is the most successful book
of American poetry to show the tradition of the Wang Wei type of
nature poetry.  In the struggle to integrate the world of the quiet
Chinese nature poem into American writing, Gary Snyder and Bly
represent two opposite poles, each equally far from the harmonious
center occupied by such a poet as Wang Wei.  In Bly's poetry
there is often a wrenching movement away from the harmonious un-
folding of nature's process.  This movement, which is so violent
that it threatens to undermine the entire world of the poem, is
caused by either a sudden assertion of personal sensation or bi-
zarre, surreal imagery.

P203.  Davis, William V.  "Camphor and Gopherwood:  Robert Bly's

Recent Poems in Prose." <u>Modern Poetry Studies</u>, 11 (no.
1/2), 88-102.
A good essay on an important Bly volume. The prose
poem is natural for Bly, both personally and poetically. Parallels
among Vico's theory of poetic development as presented in <u>New
Science</u>, Julian Jaynes' theory of mind development, and Bly's
"Looking for Dragon Smoke" are presented to establish a basis for
his affinity to the prose poem. <u>This Body is Made of Camphor and
Gopherwood</u> is a return to his beginning and the voice of <u>Silence
in the Snowy Fields</u>. The poems are as fresh and full of energy
as any in the first volume. The dominant metaphor of the book is
sleep and the waking from sleep. A number of poems are analyzed.
The danger that Bly frequently encounters in his poetry is that he
does not trust the reader to make the "leaps" the poem makes. Too
often he tries "to fill in between the cracks," violating his theory
of the mind's "associative" powers.

P204. Hall, Donald. "Robert Bly: Poetry Food." In his <u>The
Weather for Poetry: Essays, Reviews, and Notes on
Poetry, 1977-81</u>. Ann Arbor: The University of Michigan
Press, pp. 175-176.
Reprint of P178.

P205. Harris, Victoria Frenkel. "Robert Bly." In <u>Critical Survey
of Poetry: English Language Series</u>. 8 vols. Ed.
Frank N. Magill. Englewood Cliffs, NJ: Salem Press,
Vol. 1, pp. 220-228.
Brief entries under the headings of "Principal Collections,"
"Other Literary Forms," "Achievements," "Biography," and a long-
er, although concise, "Analysis" of the poetry in <u>Silence in the
Snowy Fields</u>, <u>The Light Around the Body</u>, <u>Old Man Rubbing His
Eyes</u>, and <u>The Man In the Black Coat Turns</u>. The last volume is
more sympathetic to those who are "undeveloped." Bly's voice is
nonjudgmental and more humble. A brief secondary bibliography
is included.

P206. Heller, Erich. "On Translating Rilke." <u>New Republic</u>, 186
(28 April), 3.
A reply to Bly's letter in defense of his translations of
Rilke, which were unfavorably reviewed by Heller. Bly has simply
perpetuated bad translations of Rilke which are a disservice to the
original poet as well as to the English language.
See Q146 and D8.

P207. "Interview with Robert Bly--November 1, 1982, St. Louis."
<u>River Styx</u>, no. 13, pp. 8-21.
A discussion of the changes in Bly's poetry and the grow-
ing resistance to Whitman that has been developing in him. Bly
talks about his current work with Machado's poems. Other topics
include Robert Lowell, prose poems, and the question of how poets
learn.

P208.  Lammon, Marty.  "Something Hard to Get Rid Of:  An In-
        terview with Robert Bly."  Ploughshares, 8 (no. 1),
        11-23.
        The interview centers on Donald Hall:  Bly's working re-
lationship with him, his remembrances of experiences with Hall in-
terviewing T. S. Eliot, and as literary editors of the Harvard Ad-
vocate.  The differences between their poetry is briefly discussed,
including Hall's strong English literature roots and the importance
of sound and rhythm to his poetry.  Illuminating and interesting
are Bly's comments that his own interest in South American poetry
may have thrown other poets "off their center."  He feels he will
have done a disservice if they got excited about Spanish poetry
but, as a result, neglected English literature.

P209.  Shakarchi, Joseph.  "An Interview with Robert Bly."
        Massachusetts Review, 23 (Summer), 226-243.
        The interview is strongly concerned with Bly's philosophi-
cal outlook and the influences upon it.  The influence of Eastern
thought and Eastern writers on his work and thinking is discussed,
as well as Jungian thought and the concept of twofold conscious-
ness.  Bly also talks extensively about Gary Snyder.  The con-
versation also touches upon fairy tales and Bly's use of the dul-
cimer.
        Reprinted in O5.

P210.  Thompson, Keith.  "What Men Really Want."  New Age Jour-
        nal, 7 (May), 30-51.
        A lengthy discussion concerning the contemporary male
experience.  Bly talks about the present state of the male, partic-
ularly the younger men, in relationship to the feminist/radical move-
ment of the 1960's and 1970's.  He views man as being "soft males,"
good people but unhappy; they are life-preserving rather than life-
giving.  There is a need to go beyond the unification of the femi-
nine and masculine parts of the male.  The man must make touch
with the powerful, dark energy within him, the wildman.
        See B126.


                                  1983


P211.  Christensen, Paul.  "Bly, Robert."  In American Writers
        Since 1900.  Ed. James Vinson.  Chicago:  St. James
        Press, pp. 87-89.
        Given the publication date, this is an embarrassingly out-
dated listing of primary sources and a brief, general essay on Bly.
No material after 1977 is cited.  Reprint of P163.

P212.  Davis, William V.  "'To Attend, Singing, to the Trace of
        the Fugitive Gods':  A Note on Robert Bly and the Poetry
        of Apocalypse."  Notes on Contemporary Literature, 13
        (March), 6-8.

Bly's dominant metaphors in his poetry have been ones of regeneration. Coupled with his penchant for the mystical, these have frequently moved him into the apocalyptic as defined by Paul Tillich. His metaphor of vision is itself an image of visionary experience and is the constant theme of his work.

This is a slightly disjointed essay whose thesis is not done justice by its brevity.

P213. Fredman, Stephen. Poet's Prose: The Crisis in American
Verse. Cambridge: Cambridge University Press, pp. 52-54.

A brief comparison between William Carlos Williams' "generative sentences" and Bly's prose poem, "The Dead Seal Near McClure's Beach." Bly's poem is sentimental and squarely in the tradition of Aloysius Bertrand's imaginary Flemish paintings and Baudelaire's fantasies of the city. The prose merely sets forth emotions already derived at. The poem plods in its description and meditation in comparison to Williams' improvisations. Bly's message is bold and overstated giving neither himself or the reader impetus for discovery. Williams draws a moral and then questions it.

P214. Gingerich, Martin E. "Robert Bly." In Contemporary Poetry
in America and England 1950-1975. Detroit: Gale Research Co., pp. 107-109.

A selected bibliography of books of poetry and secondary
sources.

P215. Kalaidjian, Walter. "From Silence to Subversion: Robert Bly's
Political Surrealism." Modern Poetry Studies, 11 (no. 3), 289-306.

A response to the criticism of Bly for the limitations of the immanent aesthetic evident in Silence in the Snowy Fields. In the political poetry that immediately followed Silence..., Bly developed a more rhetorically based poetic style. In Silence... he filtered his politics through a poetic language of aesthetic distance. But in The Light Around the Body and Sleepers Joining Hands, Bly abandons his earlier reliance on lyric simplicity and begins to exploit the more self-reflexive mediations of discourse. His achievement as a political poet derives from his dialogic fusion of the languages of our public and unconscious selves through the verbal techniques of surrealism.

P216. Kramer, Lawrence. "A Sensible Emptiness: Robert Bly and
the Poetics of Immanence." Contemporary Literature, 24 (Winter), 449-462.

An important article that presents a minority critical opinion that rejects Bly as a "deep image" poet and acknowledges him as a poet of bodies and spaces. Rather than being outside of a poetic tradition with his esoteric deep image poetry, Bly is part of a specifically American poetic tradition of immanence. His "genuine achievement as a poet" is not the result of his deep image

poetry, but rather his work in this tradition which has its touch-
stones in Whitman and Robert Frost.

This tradition maintains a feeling for the "numinous value of
objects divorced from all transcendental glamor." Its value de-
pends on simple, tangible, elemental things, confronted almost with-
out thought. Bly's strongest works of immanence are Silence in
the Snowy Fields and This Tree Will Be Here for a Thousand Years.
Kramer accepts Bly's statement that the two books should be seen
as one, and in emphasizing This Tree..., he gives attention to a
critically ignored Bly work.

P217.   Roberson, William H.  "Robert Bly:  A Primary Bibliogra-
        phy, Part I."  Bulletin of Bibliography, 40 (March), 5-11.
        The bibliography is divided into sections on books and
pamphlets, translations, editions, sound recordings, and videore-
cordings.
        See P232.

P218.   Thornton, Naoko Fuwa.  "Robert Bly's Poetry and the
        Haiku."  Comparative Literature Studies, 20 (Spring),
        [1]-13.
        An interesting and well-developed attempt to determine
the inception of Bly's reception of Japanese traditional haiku and
to evaluate his use of it.  Relying heavily upon his introduction
to The Sea and the Honeycomb and the poems in Sleepers Joining
Hands and The Morning Glory, the influence of Bashō is examined
on Bly's shift of focus from the form to the spirit leading to the
art of creation.

P219.   Wesling, Donald.  "Image and Measure in the Prose Poems
        of Robert Bly."  In The New American Prosody.  Ed.
        Norma Procopiow.  College Park, MD:  Sun & Moon
        Press.
        Not verified, cited in Peseroff (no. O5), p. 232.


                              1984

P220.   "Bly, Robert [Elwood]."  Current Biography, 45 (March),
        6-10.
        A good basic biographical entry with brief general dis-
cussions of each of Bly's major works.
        Reprinted in P229.

P221.   Breslin, James E. B.  From Modern to Contemporary Ameri-
        can Poetry, 1945-1965.  Chicago:  University of Chicago
        Press, pp. 1, 12, 51, 54-55, 64, 161, 176-183, 195, 242,
        254.
        Although Bly is not a central figure in this study, there
are several references to him within the context of developing lines
of thought regarding poetry.  The beginning of the chapter on

James Wright presents a good, concise statement on the "deep image" by reviewing Bly's statements on poetry in some of his essays and interviews.

P222.   Carson, L. M. Kit.   "Robert Bly Wants to Make a Man of You."   GQ [Gentleman's Quarterly], 54 (October), 301-302, 348, 349, 350.
        A personal account of the happenings at a five-day "Wildman's Workshop" conducted by Bly in Los Angeles' Temescal Canyon.
        Reprinted in P223.

P223.   _____.   "Robert Bly Wants to Make a Man of You."   Utne Reader, no. 7 (December 1984/January 1985), 46-53.
        Reprint of P222.

P224.   Davis, William V.   "'In a Low Voice to Someone He is Sure Is Listening':   Robert Bly's Recent Poems in Prose."   Midwest Quarterly, 25 (Winter), 148-156.
        A rather fawning and unfocused discussion of Bly's prose poems, which are the most personal and least mannered poems he has written.

P225.   _____.   "'Still the Place Where Creation Does Some Work On Itself':   Robert Bly's Most Recent Work."   In Robert Bly:   When Sleepers Awake.   Ed. Joyce Peseroff.   Ann Arbor:   The University of Michigan Press, pp. 237-246.
        A linkage is seen between the poems in The Man In the Black Coat Turns and those in Silence In the Snowy Fields.   The poems come from the same source and have a similar form; they share a central tone, mood, and theme.   Silence In the Snowy Fields represents the beginning of a journey, and The Man In the Black Coat Turns represents the ending, the "self-referential elegy."   The poems open doors to himself unlike he has done before.   He has returned to Boehme and his third division of reality, the dark world.

P226.   Grob, Barbara, and John High.   "An Interview with Robert Bly."   Five Fingers Review, no. 1, pp. 114-118.
        A general discussion on current political issues and their relationship to the poetry that is (or isn't) being written.   The elegance of trying to transcend evil (the legacy of Whitman, Emerson, et al.) and the lack of a steady and constant looking at grief are the reasons for a lack of political and social thought in American poetry.

P227.   Libby, Anthony.   "Robert Bly Unknowing Knowing."   In his Mythologies of Nothing:   Mystical Death in American Poetry 1940-70.   Urbana:   University of Illinois Press, pp. [153]-184; [also pp. 69, 95, 101-105 passim, 108, 117-121, 141, 149, 185-196 passim, 206, 215].

A stimulating and provocative examination of Bly's work
as it is concerned with death, or a "visionary negation," in terms
of a mysticism that seeks union between the ordinary world and
another world. Death is viewed as the physical union between the
dichotomies that Bly attempts to reconcile. Bly is placed within
the context and tradition of American mystic poetry, especially
Whitman and his views of death.

P228. Marras, Emma. "Robert Bly's Reading of South American
      Poets: A Challenge to North American Poetic Practice."
      Translation Review, 14, pp. 33-39.
      A general overview of Bly's interest in, and advocation
of, the South American poetry of Neruda and Vallejo. This is not
so much an analytic view as it is a review of Bly's writings on
Spanish surrealism and the effect South American poets had on the
Bly generation of North American poets.

P229. Moritz, Charles, ed. "Bly, Robert [Elwood]." In Current
      Biography Yearbook 1984. New York: H. W. Wilson
      Co., pp. 33-36.
      Reprint of P220.

P230. Peters, Robert. "News From Robert Bly's Universe: The
      Man In the Black Coat Turns." In Robert Bly: When
      Sleepers Awake. Ed. Joyce Peseroff. Ann Arbor: The
      University of Michigan Press, pp. 304-314.
      This book is viewed as one of the seminal works of the
1980's. Bly's theoretical distinctions are used as a means of per-
ceiving the poems. Extended readings of various poems in the col-
lection, particularly "My Father's Wedding 1924" and "The Prodigal
Son," are given.

P231. Power, Kevin. "Conversation with Robert Bly." In Ameri-
      can Poetry Observed: Poets on Their Work. Ed. Joe
      David Bellamy. Urbana: University of Illinois Press.
      Reprint of P124. [This is the Bly edited version that
appeared in A57.]

P232. Roberson, William H. "Robert Bly: A Primary Bibliogra-
      phy, Part II." Bulletin of Bibliography, 41 (June), 81-
      95.
      An initial attempt at an extended documentation of Bly's
contributions to periodical literature. The listing is divided into
sections on poems, translations, dramas, and articles and essays.
      See P217.

P233. Thompson, Keith. "Robert Bly on Fathers and Sons."
      Esquire, 101 (April), 238-239.
      A concise examination of Bly's current thoughts on
fathers and sons and modern rites of passage. There are three
stages of initiation in a man's development: the father is the first

"transformer," teaching the son to direct his energy toward work for a community; the second is the archetypal wise man, who assumes the role of shaman by introducing the boy to new values; the third stage is the intensive study of mythology, the boy learns to relate mythological figures and forces to the many levels of his psyche.

P234.   Wesling, Donald.   "Sentences as Measures in Two of Robert Bly's Prose Poems."   In Robert Bly:   When Sleepers Awake.   Ed. Joyce Peseroff.   Ann Arbor:   The University of Michigan Press, pp. 232-236.
An analysis of how sentences from "Falling Into Holes in Our Sentences" and "How the Ant Takes Part" are used to "drop the reader into deeper levels of personality."

P235.   Williamson, Alan.   Introspection and Contemporary Poetry. Cambridge, MA:   Harvard University Press, pp. 1, 4, 66, 68-69, 73, 79-80, 91-92, 98-99.
Brief discussions of Bly's utilization of language and image, and his influence on younger poets.   There are no sustained passages specifically concerned with Bly's work, but the essays are interesting and pertinent to his work and poetics.

# Q. REVIEWS OF BOOKS

## Canciones
## (Antonio Machado)

Q1.  Maloney, Dennis.  "Machado in Translation."  White Pine
     Journal, no. 26 (1983), 64-65.
     See Q278.


## The Eight Stages of Translation

Q2.  Boston Review, 9 (March 1984), 30.
     This is an enlightening glimpse behind one poem's trans-
lation; it is a privileged vantage point for the reader.


## The Fish In the Sea Is Not Thirsty
## (Kabir)

Q3.  Crazy Horse, no. 8 (September 1977), 47.
     The translations are wonderful poems in their own right.
Bly has a feeling for Kabir; the emotions are expressed directly,
powerfully, and imaginatively.

Q4.  Tapscott, Stephen.  Greenfield Review, 2 (no. 2, 1972), 60-61.
     Bly succeeds in achieving a genuine speaking voice by un-
cluttering the diction and restoring the wit of the original poems.


## Forty Poems Touching Upon Recent
## American History

Q5.  Coxe, Louis.  "Poets as Crusaders."  New Republic, 163 (14
     November 1970), 26-27.
     The anthology lacks the hate, guts, spirit, and talent
that may have made it work.  In the preface, Bly's rhetoric is em-
barrassing, and his statements concerning "inwardness" are be-
wildering.  He leaves himself too open for easy criticism and ridi-
cule.

Q6.  Kirkus Reviews, 38 (August 1, 1970), 832.
     "A Quite perfect little book" in which the nation is con-
tracted, felt, and engaged.  Bly's introduction is the core of the
work with the poems as imaginative and efficient illustration.

Q7. "Literature." The Booklist, 67 (November 15, 1970), 246.
     A descriptive review. Bly provides a "clear-cut introduc-
tion."

Q8. Moore, Stephen. "Literary Studies and Literature: The Re-
     turn of History." Michigan Quarterly Review, 12 (Summer
     1973), 287-288 [285-293].
     The selection is personal and eclectic. Even the good
poems suffer in this strident, self-righteous, and moralistic context.

Q9. Publishers' Weekly, 198 (27 July 1970), 73.
     A brief, purely descriptive notice.

Q10. Taylor, Henry. "A Gathering of Poets." Western Humanities
     Review, 25 (Autumn 1971), 367-372.
     The poems have been chosen to prove that "political real-
ities are human realities after all." Bly provides an excellent in-
troduction.

Q11. "This Week." Christian Century, 87 (7 October 1970), 1200-
     1201.
     A very brief review.

Q12. Waring, Walter W. "The Book Review." Library Journal, 95
     (September 15, 1970), 2925.
     The care shown in both selection and translation is compli-
mented. Reprinted in Q13.

Q13. _____. In The Library Journal Book Review. New York:
     R. R. Bowker Co., 1970, pp. 441-442.
     Reprint of Q12.


                    Friends, You Drank Some Darkness
                    (Ekelöf, Martinson, Tranströmer)

Q14. Choice, 13 (July/August 1976), 699.
     These excellent translations compare favorably with other
available translations. The introductions read like prose poems.
The lack of post-World War II selections (with Ekelöf and Martinson)
is a flaw.

Q15. Garrison, Joseph. "LJ: Book Review." Library Journal,
     100 (April 1, 1975), 674-675.
     A brief descriptive review. Bly is not mentioned.

Q16. Kirkus Reviews, 43 (March 1, 1975), 268.
     Now that Auden's gone, Bly is the only writer equipped for
such work as this.

Q17. Meyer, Michael. "Call of the Deep." Times Literary Supple-
     ment, 31 October 1975, p. 1287.

Bly has honorably, but unevenly, succeeded in conveying
the qualities of these poets. He does not succeed with Ekelöf at
all, but no one really can; he is vexatiously elusive. Unhappily,
Bly is an addict of the intrusive preposition in translations. He
must remain concise, but he is a good translator. One's reaction
to the book must be one of gratitude and pleasure.

Q18. Petherick, Karen. Scandinavian Studies, 48 (Winter 1976),
     114-118.
        A well-balanced and sensible review. Although Bly is gen-
erally good at getting the general sense of the poems, he under-
standably makes occasional errors of detail or linguistic nuance.
A number of instances of discrepancies between the originals and
translations concerning rhythm, rhyme, and metaphor are discussed.
Bly is at his best with Tranströmer.

Q19. Thompson, Gary. Chariton Review, 1 (Fall 1975), 75-77.
        Bly's major accomplishment may be his ability to consistently
remind other poets and critics of the confines of the English/Ameri-
can poetic tradition. This is an excellent collection of translations.
The bulk of the essay is devoted to a discussion of the three poets.

Q20. Vendler, Helen. "False Poets and Real Poets." New York
     Times Book Review, 7 September 1975, pp. 17-18 [6-7, 8,
     10, 12, 14, 16-18].
        This is "a dazzling volume." Bly's lines have a cadence
and melody of their own that are not inappropriate to their meaning.

Q21. Young, Vernon. "The Body of Man." Hudson Review, 28
     (Winter 1975-1976), 591-592 [[585]-600].
        Bly's translated selections "cannot be praised too highly."
He has done a "good thing."


                    I Do Best Alone at Night
                       (Gunnar Ekelöf)


Q22. Benedikt, Michael. "The Shapes of Nature." Poetry, 113
     (December 1968), 211-212 [188-215].
        The translations are "models of aptness and attention to de-
tail, not to mention understanding."

Q23. Meyers, Bert. "Two Poets in Translation." Kayak, no. 16
     (1968), 64-65 [62-65].
        There is no significant mention of Bly's work as translator.


                    I Never Wanted Fame
                     (Antonio Machado)


Q24. Maloney, Dennis. "Machado in Translation." White Pine

Journal, no. 26 (1983), 64-65.
See Q278.

### Jumping Out of Bed

Q25.  Chamberlin, J. E. "Poetry Chronicle." Hudson Review, 26
       (Summer 1973), 398-399.
       See Q199.

Q26.   Choice, 11 (May 1974), 434.
            The woodcuts by Wang Hui-Ming are the essence of the
       book. The poems are a matter of indifference; they are no more
       than journeyman work.

Q27.   Murray, Michele. "Talent Will Out [sic], Right? Wrong.
       Here Are Four Worthy But Neglected Books That Deserve
       Better." National Observer, 3 March 1973, p. 21.
            A brief notice. The title of the article tells more regard-
       ing the opinion of the book than the two-paragraph "review."

Q28.   Naiden, James. "Echoes Don't Lessen Poet Bly's Strength."
       Minneapolis Star, 20 November 1973, p. 2B.
       See Q215.

### The Kabir Book

Q29.   Blackman, Jennings. Midwest Quarterly Review, 19 (Winter
       1978), 219-222.
            This book is obviously a labor of love. The poems are well
       chosen. They are rendered in a spirit of energetic simplicity that
       communicates the spontaneity, the humor, and the joyous delight of
       Kabir. Bly is to be commended for the vigor of his workmanship
       and for making more accessible a fine poet.

Q30.   Blazek, Douglas. American Book Review, 1 (December 1978/
       January 1979), 9.
            This book is easily one of the highest points in recent
       poetry publishing. It is the expression of very accomplished living
       and true enlightenment. Bly has created a pure poetry not only by
       refinement of language but by affinity of heart and mind.

Q31.   Carroll, Paul. "On Bly's Kabir." American Poetry Review, 8
       (January/February 1979), 30-31.
            Bly's translations are superb. He offers Kabir as an ec-
       static, generous saint with direct and intoxicated language rather
       than the stuffy, portentous, sober, and didactic Tagore translation.
       The afterword is excellent.

## Late Arrival on Earth
### (Gunnar Ekelöf)

Q32.  Clark, Leonard.  "Motions of the Heart."  Poetry Review, 59
      (Summer 1968), 109–110 [109–111].
      Other than speculation that Ekelöf must be a difficult poet
to translate into satisfactory English, there is no mention of Bly's
translations.

Q33.  "Poetry International."  Times Literary Supplement, 7 March
      1968, p. 231.
      No mention of Bly's work.  The selection of poems is brief
but striking.

## Leaping Poetry

Q34.  The Booklist, 72 (November 15, 1975), 425.
      A short, descriptive review with no mention of Bly's work.

Q35.  Choice, 12 (January 1976), 1438.
      A descriptive review.  The volume challenges the alleged
academic grudge against surrealism.

Q36.  Kirkus Reviews, 43 (September 1, 1975), 1023–1024.
      This is "a fabulous, madly lucid, useful little book."  Such
is Bly's guileless authority that you can take him any way you want
and still come away learning something about imagination.

Q37.  Publishers' Weekly, 208 (4 August 1975), 53.
      An often dazzling, passionately personal, anthology.  Bly's
critical interpolations are arguable at times, but they are usually
acutely intuitive.

## The Light Around the Body

Q38.  Bland, Peter.  London Magazine NS, 8 (December 1968), 95–97.
      The darkness that was "overly fey and self-indulgent" in
Silence in the Snowy Fields is here real.  Bly has achieved the in-
wardness that was only suggested in the first book.  The great
strength of these poems lies in Bly's response to being an American.

Q39.  The Booklist and Subscription Book Bulletin, 64 (October 15,
      1967), 231–232.
      Brief review.  The most effective poems make their point
by understatement.  The weakest poems are shrill and more polemic
than poetry.

Q40.  Brownjohn, Alan.  "Pre-Beat."  New Statesman, 76 (2 August
      1968), 146.

The titles are more direct and forceful than the poems.
Bly's metaphors fail to effectively apply to those things he wishes
to comment upon.  "His generalized despair about the brutalities of
politics gets lost in a haze of vague, over-reaching fantasy."

Q41.  Burns, Gerald.  "U.S. Poetry 1967--The Books That Matter."
      Southwest Review, 53 (Winter 1968), 103 [101-106].
      Bly specializes in a long breathing line with surprise imag-
ist similes calculated to leave you breathless.  His combination of
conviction and perceived "puckish nuttiness" is needed so that the
poetry will not be subverted by "the message."

Q42.  Carruth, Hayden.  "Comment."  Poetry, 112 (September 1968),
      423 [418-427].
      The poems are flat and Bly's "theoretical statements are
programmistic, arrogant, and facile."

Q43.  Davidson, Peter.  "New Poetry:  The Generation of the Twen-
      ties."  Atlantic, 221 (February 1968), 141.
      Bly has persisted, on principle, in trying to exclude ego-
tism from his poetry.  While this is admirable as a moral position,
his poetry suffers because of it.  He should be, as the "true
mystics" have been, absorbed with self, for his "native personality
is a powerful one."

Q44.  Delonas, John.  "The Book Review."  Library Journal, 92
      (October 15, 1967), 3647.
      Although the rich imagery of the political statements cannot
be denied, the continual intrusion of death into poems is disconcert-
ing.
      Reprinted in Q45.

Q45.  _____.  In The Library Journal Book Review.  New York:
      R. R. Bowker Co., 1967, p. 403.
      Reprint of Q44.

Q46.  Dodsworth, Martin.  "Towards the Baseball Poem."  Listener,
      79 (27 June 1968), 842.
      "Bly's committed poems ... deal humanely, poetically, with
immediate concerns of the nation--poverty, the Vietnam War."

Q47.  Goldman, Michael.  "Joyful in the Dark."  New York Times
      Book Review, 18 February 1968, pp. 10, 12.
      The poems are superficial in the name of inwardness.  They
provide references to the inner world rather experiences of it.
"There is a curious externality, a kind of misplaced and engaging
confidence [throughout the volume] that strikes me as not only weak
poetically but dangerously alluring to young writers...."

Q48.  Halley, Anne.  "Recent American Poetry:  Outside Relevan-
      cies."  Massachusetts Review, 9 (Autumn 1968), 710-713
      [696-713].

This review centers on Bly's use of the surreal images or patterns of images. He has found a way of making the outside world feel real again, and of making lyric poetry relevant to the feel of public experience.

Q49.  Hamilton, Ian.  "Public Gestures, Private Poems."  The Observer [London], 30 June 1968, p. 24.
By now, Bly's mannerisms--a small stock of images, his measured, insidiously lilting cadences--are too familiar. They seem absurdly stock and forceless. He is at his best when he does not attempt resonant generalities.

Q50.  Hammer, Louis Z.  "Mothers in the Light."  Kayak, no. 14 (April 1968), 63-67.
There is a peculiar effect of much of Bly's poetry. One knows there is a powerful voice but one really cannot hear it. This is a disappointing collection. It lacks a consistent tone and varies in qualities.
The reviewer breaks down the contents and delineates the poems into groups of "unquestionable good," "good-but-marred," and bad or indifferent. There is a certain self-righteousness permeating this review (similar to what is sometimes found in Bly's own work), especially when the differences between "life-suffering" and "poetry-suffering" are discussed.
See P27.

Q51.  Lask, Thomas.  "Another View."  Minnesota Daily, "Ivory Tower," October 1967, p. 22.
Reprint of Q52.

Q52.  _____.  "The Public Mind and the Private Mind."  New York Times, 22 August 1967, p. 37.
Bly's style is not ideally suited to his subject matter of the Vietnam War, the callousness of American foreign policy, and the general terror of American life. He needs a powerful or moving rhetoric that could break the restraint which characterizes his work. There is a noticeable lack of energy and vitality.
Reprinted in Q51.

Q53.  Leibowitz, Herbert.  "Questions of Reality."  Hudson Review, 21 (Autumn 1968), [553]-557.
The book is "an honorable failure." The poems are generally "dispirited, inconsolable, monotonous." The failure of the work is one of "intensity and poetic structure," of not linking the "language of the inner man with the language of outer events." It is also noted that there is an absence of "any audience of his countryman" for such a work.

Q54.  Mazzocco, Robert.  "Jeremiads At Half-Mast."  New York Review of Books, 10 (June 20, 1968), 22-25.
A major review. There is a constant ebb and flow of

admiration and criticism in the essay. Bly is seemingly admired for
individualism and personal courage in comparison to his contempo-
raries, but the overall impression of the collection is a negative
one. The book should be read as a single poem or variations on a
single complaint. The poems dealing directly with the Vietnam War
are the least successful; the imaginative process gets lost in the pur-
ity of his appeal. There is a monotony in the cumulative effect and
something a little arbitrary in the book's aesthetic strategy. The
political content becomes predictable and pious. The poems are
thinner in texture and idea than those of his South American influ-
ences. The remarkable quality of the work, however, is the detail;
it is clear cut, cunningly evocative, and disturbingly imagistic, but
little is revelatory.

Q55. Mueller, Lisa. "Five Poets." Shenandoah, 19 (Spring 1968),
     69-71 [[65]-72].
     The poems are of two types. Those of the outer world,
especially political life, tend to be harsh and dissonant; their sad-
ness has a bitterly sharp edge. The poems of the inner world are
slow moving and quietly, intently joyful. Bly's approach in these
poems is essentially mystical. He is at his best when his focus is
single and concentrated and his language straightforward and in-
tense.

Q56. "Notes on Current Books." Virginia Quarterly Review, 44
     (Winter 1968) xviii.
     There are two distinct types of poems in the book. The
mystical poems, similar to those in Silence in the Snowy Fields, are
most often good. They seem to come straight and electric from the
visionary interior. The political poems are a muddle of anti-
Vietnam War sentiment and clumsy surrealism. They have the feel
of fakery and express a political adolescence.

Q57. Rexroth, Kenneth. "The Poet as Responsible." Northwest
     Review, 9 (Fall/Winter 1967-1968), 116-118.
     A review essay on The Light Around the Body and A
Poetry Reading Against the Vietnam War which is, in effect, a trib-
ute to Bly's efforts to "return American poetry to the mainstream of
international literature." An intelligent, if recognizably biased, es-
say on the state of contemporary American poetry from a Bly parti-
san.

Q58. Ruffin, Carolyn F. "From the Book Reviewer's Shelf: Three
     Poets of the Present." Christian Science Monitor, 9 Octo-
     ber 1967, p. 9.
     A brief inconsequential review.

Q59. Simpson, Louis. "New Books of Poems." Harper's Magazine,
     237 (August 1968), 74-75.
     "Bly is one of the few poets in America from whom greatness
can be expected." The poems are moving when there is a central

flow, a single feeling which holds all the poems together. At times,
however, the flow is not obvious and there is no connection of the
images. Bly should forget about images for awhile and "concentrate
on music, the way things move together."

Q60. South Dakota Review, 5 (Autumn 1967), 68.
     Bly is worth reading and applauding even when he fails to
produce a complete poem. In some ways, he is old-fashioned de-
spite his aura of newness. The essay tells very little about the
book in question.

Q61. "Special Pleading." Times Literary Supplement, 15 August
     1968, p. 867.
     A curious review because it sounds very much like Bly's
own criticism of other poets. The purity and fire of Bly's senti-
ments get too little support from the language he uses. His figures
of rage are more forced than frightening, and his declarations do
not sound fresh enough.

Q62. Symons, Julian. "New Poetry." Punch, 255 (24 July 1968),
     136.
     In this brief review Bly is cryptically referred to as "a
currently fashionable American White Hope." His best works are
semi-surrealist images that are powerfully effective in rendering his
own pain. Much of his rhetoric forces the reader to ask, "although
it sounds good, is it true?"

Q63. Tulip, James. "The Poetry of Robert Bly." Poetry Australia,
     no. 29 (August 1969), 47-52.
     A review essay that establishes a comparison to the poems
in Silence in the Snowy Fields. Three things are delineated as
marking Bly's achievement in modern poetry: a discovery of a solu-
tion for irony, rediscovery of a great tradition of sensibility in west-
ern culture, and, most importantly, a grasp and use of surrealism.

Q64. Weber, R. B. "Six Poets: Bly Most Worth Reading." Louis-
     ville, Kentucky The Courier-Journal and Times, 10 March
     1968, p. E6.
     Although Bly does not always succeed in his attempts at
creating "leaping poetry," he accurately reflects the nation's current
spiritual dream that has been troubled by a nightmare for a long
time.

Q65. Wheat, Allen. "Solitude and Awareness: The World of Robert
     Bly." Minnesota Daily, "Ivory Tower," October 1967, pp.
     19-23, 44.
     A well-reasoned examination of The Light Around the Body
and Silence in the Snowy Fields. The latter records the progress of
a spiritual journey almost without fault. The Light Around the
Body, however, has large and frequent faults. It is not as moving
and does not have the sustained feeling of poetic excitement that the
first book does.

Q66. Zinnes, Harriet. "Two Languages." Prairie Schooner, 42
        (Summer 1968), 176-178.
        A highly laudatory review. The book is "one of the most
significant American volumes to be published in years." The poetry
that Bly is writing (along with a handful of others) finally joins
Whitman to a European tradition. The political poems are not merely
doctrine, they are also deeply poetic.

Q67. Zweig, Paul. "A Sadness for America." Nation, 206 (25
        March 1968), 418-420.
        "There is a playfulness and an excitement in the poems; a
gift of praise enlivening those 'things' into which we are being tak-
en. Without the praise, the melancholy would be pale; it would be
ungenerous. The danger is real because Bly knows how precious
are those things which the 'spark' of man destroys."

## The Lion's Tail and Eyes

Q68. DNS. Lillabulero, 1 (September 1967), 61-63.
        The reviewer does not seem sure of what to make of this
"strange" book. Bly's contributions are not among his best. His
lines are complex, the images tend to be pretentious, and his rhythms
are off. There are no sustained poems.
        See P19.

Q69. Gunderson, Keith. "The Solitude Poets of Minnesota." Burn-
        ing Water, (Fall 1963), 57-61.
        A combined review with Silence in the Snowy Fields. The
majority of the essay deals with The Lion's Tail and Eyes and the
poetry of James Wright and William Duffy as well as Bly's. Bly's
poetry is consistently good; it exhibits a simplicity with a thrust to it.

Q70. Sorrentino, Gilbert. Kulchur, no. 10 (Summer 1963), 84-86.
        Continuing LeRoi Jones' attack on "Mr Bly and Co." for
their "arrogant stupidity," this essay is more a brief position paper
against Bly's "school" and a sarcastic attack on "these cornshuckers"
than a true review. The real point of contention is Bly's claim that
there is no avant-garde poetry in the United States, and the seem-
ingly condescending and pedantic attitude Bly expresses in his
writings.
        See P4.

Q71. Stitt, Peter. "Robert Bly's World of True Images." Minnesota
        Daily, "Ivory Tower," 8 April 1963, pp. 29, 47.
        Reviews of The Lion's Tail and Eyes, Twenty Poems of César
Vallejo, and Silence in the Snowy Fields prefaced by a commendation
of Bly's work as a publisher, translator, and poet in The Sixties
magazine and The Sixties Press. The Lion's Tail and Eyes presents
the opportunity to compare three poets who write similarly and yet
differently.
        See Q193.

Q72.   Smith, Ray.  Permanent Fires:  Reviews of Poetry, 1958-
       1973.  Metuchen, NJ:  Scarecrow Press, 1975, pp. 11-13.
       Brief review.


                              The Loon

Q73.   Dacey, Philip.  "This Book Is Made of Turkey Soup and Star
       Music."  Parnassus:  Poetry in Review, 7 (Fall/Winter
       1978), 34-45.
       See Q254.


                  Lorca and Jimenez:  Selected Poems

Q74.   Choice, 11 (March 1974), 98.
           The translations offer, at best, a splintered, warped, de-
       luded view of poetic reality.  The saving grace of the book is that
       Bly's "miscarriages" will send the discerning reader back to the
       "exquisite domain" of the Spanish originals.

Q75.   "Literature."  The Booklist, 70 (December 1, 1973), 364-365.
           A descriptive rather than evaluative review.  There is no
       specific mention of Bly's work as translator.  On p. 379 under "Books
       for Young Adults," the book is recommended to large high schools
       with strong Spanish departments.

Q76.   [Regler, W. G.]  Prairie Schooner, 48 (Spring 1974), 91-92.
           Bly's translations are as helpful as his introductions are not.
       The introductions are "flighty and free-blown."


                  The Man In the Black Coat Turns

Q77.   The Booklist, 78 (January 1, 1982), 582.
           Although some of these lyrics go from prose poem to verse
       and back, Bly's style is consistent; he is more interested in mood
       or attitude than form.  The poems, however, are filled with clichés,
       and they do not evoke much beyond conditioned responses.

Q78.   Christian Century, 99 (24 March 1982), 348.
           A very brief, very unimportant, positive review.

Q79.   Molesworth, Charles.  Western American Literature, 17 (No-
       vember 1982), 282-284.
           An, as usual, perceptive review of Bly's work by this
       critic.  The book reveals the diversity that Bly is now demonstrat-
       ing in his poetry.  The book's three sections consist of familiar Bly
       poems and themes, a group of prose poems (the best of which is
       "Finding An Old Ant Mansion"), and, finally, a group of demanding
       poems different from what one would expect of Bly.  These poems

extend the variety of his structures and show that he is finding different approaches to his subjects. Bly is a poet of growth.

Q80. Jarman, Mark. "The Poetry of Non Sequitor." American Book Review, 4 (May/June 1982), 13-14.
An indifferent review that damns with faint praise. Too often these poems, which are modestly at work, are interrupted by silly interjections or all together broken off. Bly is comfortable with his mannerisms. If the reader is too, then the book will be enjoyed.

Q81. Perloff, Marjorie. "Soft Touch." Parnassus: Poetry in Review, 10 (Spring/Summer 1982), 221-230 [209-230 passim].
A review essay of Philip Levine's One for the Road and Don't Ask and Bly's the Man In the Black Coat Turns and Talking All Morning. In the first part of the essay, which focuses on Levine's works, Bly is mentioned in comparison and contrast to Levine. Talking All Morning is never discussed. The thrust of the comments on Bly's book is that his current poetry no longer possesses the elements of his earlier poetry that demand attention. His turn toward the autobiographical mode he has always scorned seems to go counter to his poetics of immanent presence. The problem he faces is how to reconcile the linear story of one's life, especially one's evolving relation to one's father, with the belief that poetry depends upon the privileged moment when consciousness can enter the realm of otherness. The poem "The Prodigal Son" is examined to see how successful Bly is. The conclusion is that he is not very successful. He is now substituting sentimental commentary for image. There is no sense of real people living in the world.

Q82. Publishers Weekly, 220 (21 August 1981), 48.
These are thoughtful poems which are more accessible and personal than his previous work.

Q83. Roffman, Rosaly DeMaios. "Book Review." Library Journal, 106 (October 15, 1981), 2032.
The poems are powerful and surprising meditations. Bly's commitment is to unfolding rather than the end result.

Q84. San Francisco Review of Books, 8 (July 1983), 22.
This book is a "clear case of an established, important poet larded by his own theories and specialties of style, turning them into fetishes." He is attempting to write poems to fit his theories; the results are mannered and self-indulgent. In the entire book, there are only a few isolated lines that engage, compel, or even mildly interest.

Q85. Stuewe, Paul. Quill & Quire, 48 (January 1982), 39.
Although Bly's work can be hauntingly allusive and suggestive, his strength lies in the straightforward narrative and descriptive accomplishments. This is an impressive work in the "modern mainstream."

Q86.  Stitt, Peter.  "Dark Volumes."  New York Times Book Review,
      14 February 1982, p. 15, 37.
      Bly has produced his "richest, most complex book."  His
use of imagery derived from free association is discussed.

Q87.  Wesling, Donald.  "The Wisdom-Writer."  Nation, 233 (31
      October 1981), 447-448.
      This review relies upon Weinberger's review of This Tree
Will Last A Thousand Years as its starting point.  Although three
of the poems are among the very best Bly has written, the majority
of them are subject to Weinberger's criticism of the previous volume.
The best way to regard Bly is as a preacher or wisdom-writer.  The
wisdom is often delivered in fine parts of poems, but rarely in com-
plete poems.
      See Q274.


                       The Morning Glory

Q88.  Bedell, Thomas D.  "Book Review."  Library Journal, 100
      (November 1, 1975), 2056-2057.
      A brief, ecstatic, descriptive review.

Q89.  The Booklist, 72 (April 15, 1976), 1162.
      Collectively, these poems display "new poetic powers."
They are not to be missed.

Q90.  Choice, 13 (April 1976), 220.
      The poems are short, evocative lyric responses.  They are
experimental in design and, for the most part, command the reader's
attention.

Q91.  Davis, William V.  "Defining the Age."  Moons and Lion
      Tailes, 2 (no. 3, 1977), 85-89.
      The book represents a period of renewal and a return,
imagistically and thematically, to Bly's first collection.  The central
thesis of the work is the use of the visible to penetrate the invisible.
Through careful observation and appropriate meditation the body
experiences a new kind of birth.

Q92.  Dresbach, David.  Greenfield Review, 6 (Spring 1978), 182-
      187.
      A sometimes disjointed review that centers on Bly's ability
to reconcile the inner and outer worlds.  Although a number of the
poems are merely descriptions or recordings, Bly achieves in others
a correlation between the two worlds by focusing on the objects of
the outer world to illuminate the inner one.

Q93.  Lattimore, Richard.  "Poetry Chronicle."  Hudson Review, 29
      (Spring 1976), 128-129 [[113]-129].
      The poems have a rather emotional tone.  The reviewer

notes his own bias against the prose poem and believes there can scarcely be a worse one than "Looking at a Dry Tumbleweed Brought in from the Snow." "The Hockey Poem" and "The Hunter," however, are not to be denied.

Q94. Mersmann, James F. "Robert Bly: Rediscovering the World." Aura, no. 6 (Spring 1977), 40.

The prose poems of this volume are a culmination of twenty years of activity by Bly. They present a new poetry for him, more free, spontaneous, excited, and sensuous. These poems present Bly as both innocent and experienced. As a result the poems ecstatically rediscover "a world of profound correspondences" that realizes that all things are connected and united in a common ground and center.

Q95. Plumly, Stanley. "Books." American Poetry Review, 4 (November/December 1975), 44-45.

The book is a reminder that Bly, despite his war poetry, is a poet of solitude and snow. He is "our Thoreau ... a visionary of detail, of the small, unattended moment." The last section of the work is what the book is about. The poems are revelations, complete spiritual constructs. Plumly is critical of the shortness of many of the poems; they deny the space needed to develop and integrate the similes and metaphors of which Bly is a master.

Q96. Publishers Weekly, 208 (15 September 1975), 54.

The prose poems are marvelously personal, wholly accessible. A completely unself-conscious magnanimity of spirit underlies Bly's efforts.

Q97. Skinner, Knute. Concerning Poetry, 6 (Fall 1973), 89. See Q251.


## Neruda and Vallejo: Selected Poems

Q98. Ackerson, Duane. Concerning Poetry, 5 (Spring 1972), 79-83.

It is a valuable book for its fine translations and critical insights. The selection of poems is praised.

Q99. Choice, 9 (April 1972), 220.

In translating the Neruda poems, Bly has shown great skill with difficult material. The poems are well chosen and very representative of different periods in Neruda's poetic life. The translations and introduction to Vallejo are also good.

Q100. Coleman, Alexander. "Two Latin American Poets and an Antipoet." New York Times Book Review, 7 May 1972, pp. 4, 40.

This is less a review of the book and more an essay on the poetry and influence of García Lorca and Vallejo. No evaluation of Bly as translator or editor is given.

Q101. Eshleman, Clayton. "In Defense of Poetry." Review [Center
       for Inter-American Relations], no. 4/5 (Winter/Spring
       1971/1972), 39-47.
       This is an impassioned attack not only on the translations
in this book, but also, and perhaps more so, on Bly as poet, trans-
lator, and personality. Eshleman opposes what he sees as the mono-
lithic presentation of the Bly doctrine. This is Bly's book, and he
is presenting himself rather than the poets. There is a fundamental
disagreement with Bly's methods of translating. Eshleman enumerates
the same problems concerning this book as he did in his review of
Twenty Poems of César Vallejo. This is an important presentation
of a negative opinion regarding Bly's efforts as a translator.
       See Q286.

Q102. Fraser, G. S. "The Unfinality of Translation." Partisan Re-
       view, 41 (no. 2, 1974), 291-292 [289-295].
       A brief inconsequential review. The excellent selection of
poems is noted. Two points in a passage of Bly's translation of
"No Hay Olvida" are quarreled with.

Q103. Hays, H. R. "On Vallejo and Neruda: Another Look."
       American Poetry Review, 3 (March/April 1974), 31-32.
       There are several mentions of the poets' appeal to Bly but
no specific reference to either his editing or translations.

Q104. Murray, Philip. "Perilous Arcady." Poetry, 120 (August
       1972), 310-312 [304-312].
       An extremely positive albeit discerning review. It is a
beautiful book in both its content and form. The translations are
of "a high order." The book presents a commendable introduction
to Neruda despite "certain extravagant claims and partisan politics
surrounding Bly's presentation." His preface to Vallejo's poetry is
also sometimes "eccentric."

Q105. W[oessner], W[arren]. "Inner Passages." Abraxas, no. 6
       (1971), [34-35] [[33-36]].
       An enthusiastic review. The book should be in every
poets' collection. Nothing specifically is stated regarding the trans-
lations.

Q106. Young, Vernon. "Lines Written in Roven." Hudson Review,
       24 (Winter 1971-1972), 673-676 [669-686].
       Bly's method of exalting Neruda's importance and signifi-
cance by disparaging and minimizing other major poets is cogently
criticized. While Bly's translation projects are unarguably ambitious
and welcome, his partisanship is prejudicial to his best interests.


                          News of the Universe

Q107. Bartlett, Lee. Western American Literature, 17 (May 1982),
       66-68.

A well-balanced review that finds the book to be a celebration by Bly of his obvious joy at the possibility of a poetry of "expanded consciousness." It is also his attempt to establish an alternative to the modernist line as the major movement in twentieth-century poetry.

Q108.   Hansen, Tom.   Ohio Review, no. 28 (1982), 129-133.
The book offers a revisionist view of the history of poetry in the twentieth century. The review traces Bly's review of the course of Western thinking about nature in recent centuries. The review offers little direct evaluative material regarding the anthology.

Q109.   Janik, Del Ivan.   Aspen Anthology, (Winter 1980), 89-91.
Bly's commentaries provide an important conceptual framework for the appreciation of the poems' significance in the development of a new environmental consciousness. He leads the readers to examine their own assumptions about their relationship to the non-human universe.

Q110.   Kirby, David.   "Something Old, Something New."   Prairie Schooner, 55 (Fall 1981), 97-98.
The bulk of the review is a summarization of Bly's premise in compiling the anthology. The book is provocative and charming. Some attention is given to the flaws of Bly's translations and his sometimes pompous statements in the essays.

Q111.   Kirkus Reviews, 48 (May 1, 1980), 635.
This big, idiosyncratic colleciton will probably both delight and annoy. Bly's introductory essays and selections together comprise a cultural manifesto reminiscent of William Carlos Williams' essays--arrogance balanced by love and affection.

Q112.   Lyne, Sandford.   Poetry East, no. 3 (Fall 1980), 80-83.
A combined review of News of the Universe and Talking All Morning. Most of this almost reverential essay deals with the anthology which is termed Bly's best and most important work. The interviews make an illuminating background to the tone-shifts in the anthology.

Q113.   M. D. L.   Kliatt (Young Adult) Paperback Book Guide, 14 (Fall 1980), 19.
A concise yet perceptive review. Bly's interpretive essays are clever and interesting. The poems are well chosen. He is not above a little manipulating to suit his premises. There are also comments on Bly's own poetic contributions.

Q114.   Mitchell, Roger.   American Book Review, 4 (January/February 1982), 10.
A well-reasoned review that finds the book as much critical essay as anthology. The review focuses on Bly's theoretical positions. The book, as evidence of those theories, is both compelling and disturbing.

Q115. Publishers Weekly, 217 (14 March 1980), 62.
    An unusual and rewarding anthology that embodies a co-
herent, unified vision as it redefines our poetic tradition.

Q116. [Plath, Sara]. The Booklist, 76 (May 1, 1980), 1251.
    Bly's philosophizing is simplistic to the point of being ir-
responsible and sloppy to the point of being unintelligible. His
grasp of poetry is sure, however, and the anthology is valuable
because of the selection.

Q117. Roffman, Rosaly DeMaios. "Book Review." Library Journal,
    105 (May 15, 1980), 1170.
    The anthology is probing and powerful. Bly's essays are
brilliant. The book is essential for anyone interested in how we or-
der and are ordered by the universe.

Q118. School Library Journal, 27 (September 1980), 95.
    Bly's thesis on twofold consciousness is difficult to follow,
but its beauty and inspiration are rewarding.

Q119. Schulte, R. World Literature Today, 55 (Summer 1981), 541-
    542.
    A descriptive review of the book with the one critical note
concerning Bly's translations; they are adaptations and imitations
rather than translations in the true sense.


                         Night Vision
                     (Tomas Tranströmer)
Q120. Tapscott, Stephen. Greenfield Review, 2 (no. 2, 1972), 60-
    61.
    Tranströmer's poetry is close to Bly's associational ideal
for poetry.


                  Old Man Rubbing His Eyes

Q121. Choice, 12 (June 1975), 529.
    Although we can sympathize with what Bly is attempting,
to catch the moment of a perfected sensibility, he relies too much
on the monotonous technique of understatement. Bly is a poet go-
ing downhill.

Q122. Garrison, Joseph. "LJ: Book Review." Library Journal,
    100 (April 1, 1975), 674.
    A brief review. Bly's gifts for intuitive and subliminal
associations are eye openers.

Q123. M. K. S. "Books in Brief." Beloit Poetry Journal, 28
    (Spring 1978), 40.
    The poems involve the reader in a visionary experience;
each poem is couched in its own memorable music.

Reviews

Q124. Publishers Weekly, 207 (3 February 1975), 74.
Bly is unusual in handling material familiar in American poets with an Oriental sense of the inner meaning rising out of a simple observation.

Q125. Schjotz-Christensen, H. "Death and the Poet." Moons and Lion Tailes, no. 4 (January 1976), 70-72.
Bly has confronted death with greater urgency and imagination than anyone else in contemporary American poetry. He uses his imaginative confrontation with death to destroy the walls around his psyche and expose the inner man to the world. The resulting psychic openness in the face of death is at the center of Bly's imagination and, in his poetry, is the source of his emotions. The book's lyrical mood and rural setting continues the motives and occupations of Silence in the Snowy Fields. It provides a "strangely evocative testament to the resiliency of the lyrical imagination" in its sombre reflection on death and the impermanence of life.

A Poetry Reading Against the Vietnam War

Q126. J. L. South Dakota Review, 4 (Winter 1966), 89.
The cumulative effect of the material is propagandistic, reinforced by Bly's "introductory accusations." The selection has obviously been made in terms of content rather than literary value.

Q127. M. R. El Corno Emplumado, 23 (July 1967), 149-150 [148-151].
Bly's introduction is one of the finest pieces of writing on the Vietnam War.

Q128. Mills, Ralph J., Jr. "Five Anthologies." Poetry, 109 (February 1967), 347-348 [345-350].
A brief review that mentions that Bly's own poems are "strong."

Q129. Rexroth, Kenneth. "The Poet as Responsible." Northwest Review, 9 (Fall/Winter 1967-1968), 116-118.
See Q57.

The Sea and the Honeycomb

Q130. Clayre, Alasdair. "Recent Verse." Encounter, 29 (November 1967), 78 [74-80].
This is "one of the most valuable of recent books." It is well produced.

Q131. El Corno Emplumado, 21 (January 1967), 111.
Briefly states that this is "an extremely useful book." Bly has presented the work with infinite care.

Q132.  Gullans, Charles.  "Poetry and Subject Matter, From Hart
        Crane to Turner Cassity."  Southern Review NS, 6
        (Spring 1970), 503-505 [488-505].
            An argumentative review.  Most of the poems present
some sort of argument through imagery, but natural detail is in-
trinsically meaningless unless given some symbolic, philosophical
character by the poet, and few of these poets do.  This is what
Bly wants--poetry without ideas.  Three short poems in the Eng-
lish language are quoted to refute Bly's claim in the "Preface" that
the English language has not developed any form to respond to the
rapidity and swiftness of our emotions.  The inaccuracies of some
of the translations are noted with the explanation that Bly and his
collaborators have "long been enthusiastic about poems written in
languages they do not understand."

Q133.  Mojtabai, Ann G.  "The Book Review."  Library Journal,
        96 (November 15, 1971), 3764.
        A brief review.  Reprinted in Q134.

Q134.  _____.  Library Journal Book Review 1971.  New York:
        R. R. Bowker Co., p. 350.
        Reprint of Q133.

Q135.  Root, William Pitt.  "Anything But Over."  Poetry, 123
        (October 1973), 39-41 [34-[56]].
            A combined review of this anthology and Twenty Poems
of Tomas Transtromer.  A sense of appreciation for these works
emerges from a brief descriptive, rather than critical, discussion.

                            Selected Poems
                            (David Ignatow)

Q136.  Lask, Thomas.  New York Times Book Review, 4 May 1975,
        pp. 46, 48.
            Bly's brief introductions to the different groups of poems
are full of suggestions rather than explicit analyses.  They touch
on aspects of Ignatow's poetry not self-evident to the unprepared
reader.

Q137.  Lehman, David.  "Holocaust."  Poetry, 128 (April 1976), 37-
        45.
        No mention of Bly's contributions.

Q138.  Mazzaro, Jerome.  "The Poetry of David Ignatow."  Boundary
        2, 4 (Fall 1975), 289-295 [289-297].
            Bly's selections are examined in relationship to Ignatow's
interviews and notebooks.  The discordance between some of Bly's
views and Ignatow's is discussed and Bly's continuing bafflement
with the interpretation of some of the poems is noted.  The selections
are of an overall high quality, but the impression of the collection is

angrier, more polemical than The Notebooks, Poems 1934-1969, or
Facing the Tree.

Q139.  Moramarco, Fred.  "A Gathering of Poets."  Western Human-
         ities Review, 30 (Winter 1976), 83-84 [[80]-89].
         Bly is precisely the right person to have made a selection
of Ignatow's poems.  His introductions are prose poems themselves
and illuminate Ignatow's work unobtrusively and with great sensitiv-
ity.

Q140.  "Notes on Current Books."  Virginia Quarterly Review, 51
         (Autumn 1975), cxli.
         The poems' modest dignity is ill-served by Bly's "modish
and boring comments."  The selections of poems by Bly is small but
fine.


                 Selected Poems of Rainer Maria Rilke

Q141.  Agee, Joel.  "Pony or Pegasus."  Harper's, 263 (September
         1981), 70-72 [70-72, 74-76].
         The book is used as a case in point to protest against the
"virtual absence of critical standards now applied to the art of trans-
lation, and against ... misrepresenting great works of literature for
the sake of a good English read."  These translations are both
laughable and pathetic.  It is suspected that Bly does not really know
the languages from which he translates very well.

Q142.  The Booklist, 77 (February 1981), 743.
         A brief review.

Q143.  Choice, 18 (July/August 1981), 1550.
         Bly's meanings are accurate but they sacrifice the brood-
ing tone, color and delicacy of diction of the originals.  Granting
the difficulty of translating Rilke, Bly still, too often, misses the
mark, both semantically and poetically.

Q144.  Christian Century, 98 (20 May 1981), 598.
         A brief review of no consequence.

Q145.  Hatfield, Henry.  World Literature Today, 55 (Autumn 1981),
         669-70.
         On the whole, the translations are reasonably correct, al-
though they often miss the nuances.  Bly almost always eschews
rhyme and preserves meter only in a very approximate sense.
Granting the difficulties of translating Rilke, this is still not one of
the more successful attempts.

Q146.  Heller, Erich.  "On Translating Lyric Poetry."  New Repub-
         lic, 186 (3 March 1982), 27-31.
         Translations of lyric poems are impossible and some "are

more impossible than others." This volume is one of the latter. To
compound matters, Bly has a "very insecure sense of aesthetic dis-
crimination" in his selection of poems. An extended analysis of
Bly's translation of "Progress" (or "Moving Forward") from Das Buch
der Bilder (The Book of Pictures) is used to discuss his problems
as a translator. Bly's interpretative introductions to the individual
sections are as inadequate as his translations. He fails to fully un-
derstand "the drama played out in Rilke's development."
     This is an interesting and provocative essay, not only for the
opinions of Bly's translations, but also because of his comments on
Rilke's work and the problems inherent in translating lyric poetry.
See P206 and D8.

Q147.  Judd, Inge. "Book Review." Library Journal, 106 (Febru-
        ary 1, 1981), 358.
        Bly's comments help the reader see Rilke's work in relation
to events in his life as well as affording an awareness of Rilke's
specific inwardness.

Q148.  Kirkus Reviews, 49 (January 15, 1981), 134.
        Brief review.

Q149.  Kliatt Paperback Book Guide, 15 (Fall 1981), 28.
        A brief and unimportant review.

Q150.  Livingston, Rick. "Bly's Rilke." Harvard Advocate, 115
        (Summer 1982), 50-53.
        An analysis of Bly's translations. His point in his trans-
lations is to emphasize what the German implies. In doing so, he
loses the mysterious sense of discovery in the original. Bly
has abandoned rhyme and meter in his translations. He transforms
Rilke's sense of wonder into a kind of wisdom. He is interested
more in the results of the poetry than the process. While the
originals marvel at the ordinary, the translations aim to transform
the ordinary into the mystical. The poet and the translator are,
therefore, at cross purposes.

Q151.  McDuff, David. "Poetry in Translation." Stand, 23 (no. 1,
        1981), 62-63 [58-66].
        The translations provide literal meanings, but Rilke's voice
is not heard. Bly seems to have missed nearly all the cruelties and
subtleties of Rilke's poetic language. The commentary is useful.

Q152.  Publishers Weekly, 219 (20 February 1981), 83.
        A brief notice.

Q153.  Ratner, Rochelle. Parabola, 6 (Summer 1981), 112 [108-113].
        Bly has produced the first readable translation of Rilke's
early poetry.

Q154.  Stuewe, Paul. Quill & Quire, 47 (September 1981), 67.
        A brief notice.

## Silence in the Snowy Fields

Q155. Beloit Poetry Journal, 14 (Winter 1963/1964), 39.
        Brief review. Most of the poems are deceptively simple,
and few seem contrived. Bly uses his images with charm and in-
genuousness.

Q156. Bergonzi, Bernard. "New Nature Poets." The Guardian
        [Manchester], 3 March 1967, p. 7.
        A brief review. Despite the deliberate narrowness of his
approach, the cumulative effect of the book is that Bly is a good
poet. There is a prevailing impression that these are notes for
poems rather than poems themselves.

Q157. Blackburn, Thomas. "Three American Poets." Poetry Re-
        view, 55 (Autumn 1967), 255, 257 [255-258].
        Although Bly possesses intelligence and taste, his poetry
is profoundly dull. There seems to be no worthwhile sense of
thought or feeling behind the poems.

Q158. Boland, Eavan. "A Becoming Style." Irish Times, 17 March
        1967.
        A brief review. Bly relies heavily on description and a
type of understated impressionism with no attempt at symbolism.
This results in a lack of coherence to the book. Still, there is a
great deal of attractive and delicate expression in it.

Q159. The Booklist, 59 (December 1, 1962), 274.
        Very brief. A skillful impressive simplicity is displayed
in these poems.

Q160. "Chained to the Parish Pump." Times Literary Supplement,
        16 March 1967, p. 220.
        The poems have a heavy simplicity. They are reminiscent
of haikus but lack the potential force of a haiku that lies in its sug-
gestiveness. The poems are completely circumstantial and the vo-
cabulary is drab.
        Reprinted in Q186.

Q161. Clunk. Burning Deck, 1 (December 1962), 58.
        The majority of poems are studiously irrational, heavily
delicate, and determinedly happy. This is not where Bly's strength
lies. He is at his best with highly organized and terribly sad poems.
Despite the prevailing "crap happiness" of the book, his powerful
poems give a rather beautiful cumulative effect.

Q162. Colombo, John Robert. "Poetry Chronicle." Tamarack Re-
        view, no. 26 (Winter 1963), 93-94 [86-95].
        The total effect of these poems is strong and very much a
new facet of the American mind. Bly's effects are subtle and easily
overlooked by a hasty reader. His technique, however, leaves only

the barest of physiological responses to meet the varied stimuli of
the natural world and the world of the self.  He runs the risk of
denying the essential qualities of the poet.

Q163.   Cox, C. B.  "Ox, Mule and Buzzard."  Spectator, 217 (24
         March 1967), 342 [342-343].
         A brief review.  Noting that Bly's poetry reflects a com-
plete absorption in nature and a corresponding revulsion for soci-
ety, Cox finds it disturbing that the modern imagination should so
often express itself in terms of nonhuman life.

Q164.   Crossley-Holland, Kevin.  "On the Natural World."  Books
         & Bookmen, 12 (May 1967), 24 [24-25].
         A very brief review.  The poems are "enviably transpar-
ent," but they are lightweight as well.  The style is low voltage
and the vocabulary is colorless.

Q165.   Cuscaden, R. R.  Elizabeth [New Rochelle, NY], 5 (March
         1963), 17-18.
         The poetry is obsessed with the unbuilding of the lan-
guage, and the reduction of the poem to its highest level where the
reader can make discoveries of the imagination for himself.

Q166.   Derleth, August.  "Books of the Times."  The Capital Times
         [Madison, WI], 17 January 1963, p. 20.
         This is one of the best and most refreshing books of con-
temporary poetry.  His style is earnest simplicity which scorns the
deliberate obfuscation of much modern poetry.

Q167.   Fines, C. O.  Thin Line, 1 (Spring 1963), 26-30.
         Not verified, cited in Friberg (no. O2), p. 219.

Q168.   Fowlie, Wallace.  "Not Bards So Much as Catalyzers."  New
         York Times Book Review, 12 May 1963, p. 36.
         The poems are meditations on all that surrounds man.  "At
the end of each poem there is silence, without complaint."

Q169.   Guest, Barbara.  "Shared Landscapes."  Chelsea, no. 16
         (March 1965), 150-152.
         A combined review with James Wright's The Branch Will
Not Break emphasizing the dependence upon the Minnesota landscape
images and how this leads to a certain tedium.  Bly has a "confirmed
sort of naiveté which works very well for him."  He is "blessed with
less professionalism" than Wright, so less comes between him and the
reader.

Q170.   Gunderson, Keith.  "The Solitude Poets of Minnesota."
         Burning Water, (Fall 1963), 57-61.
         See Q69.

Q171.   Gunn, Thom.  "Poems and Books of Poems."  Yale Review,

53 (Autumn 1963), 142 [142-144].

The absence of people or human consciousness in the poems and the reliance on perception and the senses rather than concepts is commented on. Bly's "language is almost always striking; his love for a world without evil is celebrated in a voice of singular purity; he evokes things and scenes immediately and vividly."

Q172.   Hamilton, Ian.   "On the Rhythmic Run."   The Observer
        [London], 20 March 1967, p. 23.
        Bly is a sucker for dim, evocative abstractions.   When he stays close to the Minnesota landscape he can achieve a genuinely rooted kind of imagery.   The poems are, otherwise, naive and vacuously sentimental.

Q173.   Hogan, Shelia.   "Book Reviews."   Quarry, (Winter 1965),
        52-53.
        Not verified, cited in Friberg (no. O2), p. 219.

Q174.   Horton, Jane C.   "Poetry Volumes of Varying Worth."   Atlanta Journal, 6 January 1963, p. 4D.
        A very brief and insignificant review.

Q175.   Hughes, D. J.   "The Demands of Poetry."   Nation, 196 (5
        January 1963), 17 [16-18].
        The book is impressive because of its "purity of time and precision of diction."   There is a monotonous simplicity to the poems. Bly relies too much on overwhelming, at times, apocalyptic, endings which spoil the momentum the poem has built up.

Q176.   Jacobsen, Josephine.   Baltimore Sun, 13 March 1963.
        Not verified, cited in Friberg (no. O2), p. 219.

Q177.   Jerome, Judson.   "A Poetry Chronicle--Part I."   Antioch
        Review, 23 (Autumn 1963), 109-110 [109-124].
        A brief comment.   The poems are distinct in manner and sensibility, but the naiveté and simplicity of response are boring.

Q178.   Logan, John.   "Poetry Shelf."   The Critic, 21 (December
        1962/January 1963), 84-85.
        Although the subject matter of the poems could be pretty dull, Bly's handling of them makes it quite lively and beautiful.   A discussion of Bly's concern with the inner life as expressed in the poems in the book is included.

Q179.   McGrath, Thomas.   Naitonal Guardian, 28 March 1963.
        Not verified, cited in Friberg (no. O2), p. 220.

Q180.   May, Derwent.   "Lions and Fauns."   The Times [London],
        6 April 1967, p. 9.
        Bly depends too much on an excited movement in the lines; the descriptions are often vague and ordinary.   A happy preoccupation

with the senses and cheerful optimism is found in practically all the
poems. Even when the subjects are more disturbing, the happy
notes persist rather oddly.

Q181.  Mills, Ralph J., Jr.  "Four Voices in Recent American Poetry."
        Christian Scholar, 46 (Winter 1963), 340-345 [324-345].
        This is more an essay on Bly's poetics and intentions as
a poet as evidenced through his work in The Fifties and The Sixties
and using poems from the book to support the critical statements
than an evaluative review of the book.  Bly's poetry is one of con-
centrated understatement.

Q182.  Nordell, Roderick.  "From the Bookshelf:  A Poet in Minne-
        sota."  Christian Science Monitor, 23 January 1963, p. 9.
        A nicely balanced review.  Bly is better at evocative sur-
faces than ambiguous depths.  The achieved simplicity is often
freshly vivid.

Q183.  "Notes on Current Books."  Virginia Quarterly Review, 39
        (Winter 1963), xxii.
        Collected, these poems reveal weaknesses not readily ap-
parent when they appear separately.  The poems are too often
repetitions of a series of pastoral scenes with little imagination or
variation.

Q184.  Offen, Ron.  "Poetry."  Literary Times, March 1963, p. 4.
        Not verified, cited in Friberg (no. O2), p. 220.

Q185.  Ray, David.  "Notes, Reviews, Speculations."  Epoch, 13
        (Winter 1963), 186-188.
        Ostensibly a review, but, in fact, an admiring discussion
of Bly's poetics and critical judgments.

Q186.  "Robert Bly:  Silence in the Snowy Fields."  T. L. S.:  Es-
        says and Reviews from The Times Literary Supplement
        1967.  London:  Oxford University Press, 1968, Vol. 6,
        p. 151-152.
        Reprint of Q160.

Q187.  Simmons, Charles.  "Poets in Search of a Public."  Saturday
        Review, 46 (30 March 1963), 48.
        A brief review.  "There is a rare and attractive cleanli-
ness to his style."

Q188.  Simpson, Louis.  "Poetry Chronicle."  Hudson Review, 16
        (Spring 1963), 138-139 [130-140].
        "If you are bored with the status quo and hope for new
poetry, then you will find ... [this book] one of the few original
and stimulating books of poetry published in recent years."

Q189.  Smith, Ray.  "New Books Appraised."  Library Journal, 87
        (November 1, 1962), 4025.

A brief review. The book is "authentically humane and readable poetry." Reprinted in Q190.

Q190. _____. Permanent Fires: Reviews of Poetry, 1958-1973. Metuchen, NJ: Scarecrow Press, 1975, pp. 11-13. Reprint of Q189.

Q191. Stepanchev, Stephen. "Chorus of Versemakers: A Mid-1963 Medley." New York Herald Tribune Books, 11 August 1963, p. 7.
A brief review. The distinction of the poetry is in the fresh simplicity of the diction and imagery. Bly has the ability to invest a scene with intense subjectivity. The poetry does, however, neglect conflict and drama.

Q192. _____. "Eight Poets." Shenandoah, 14 (Spring 1963), 60-62 [58-69].
In stark contrast to his voice as "embattled editor" of The Sixties, Bly's poetic voice is clear, quiet, and appealing.

Q193. Stitt, Peter. "Robert Bly's World of True Images." Minnesota Daily, "Ivory Tower," 8 April 1963, pp. 29, 47.
Reviews of The Lion's Tail and Eyes, Twenty Poems of César Vallejo, and Silence in the Snowy Fields. Bly's poems show the influence of the poets he has translated. The unity of the book is achieved through the pervasive theme of death and the ever-present mood of quietness.
See Q71.

Q194. Thorpe, Michael. "Current Literature 1967." English Studies, 49 (June 1968), 277 [269-281].
A brief but cutting review. The poems are often reminiscent of translated haikus. Thorpe cryptically states that though Bly is understandably popular in the American tradition of pastoral return, he actually debilitates nature. The statement is not elaborated upon.

Q195. Williams Ward, May. The Wellington Press, 22 February 1966.
Not verified, cited in Friberg (no. O2), p. 220.

Q196. Wheat, Allen. "Solitude and Awareness: The World of Robert Bly." Minnesota Daily, "Ivory Tower," October 1967, pp. 19-23, 44.
See Q65.

Q197. White, Robert. Blue Grass, (Winter 1963), 37-38.
The book gives better voice to Bly's hopes and program for American poetry than do the "waspish ukases" he delivers in The Sixties. Bly is a "magic realist." There is a tense struggle between the hallucinatory quality of his poetic vision and the restrained and understated techniques he employs.

## Sleepers Joining Hands

Q198.   Cavitch, David.   "Poet as Victim and Victimizer."   New York
        Times Book Review, 18 February 1973, pp. 2-3.
        "Bly is not really an ecstatic or visionary or even a radi-
cal poet, and he compromises himself by posturing in these popular
roles.   He is a poet who wants intensely to put together a coherent
life out of materials that he fears are not enough:   personal identity,
moral nature, mental attentiveness.   He can make one want to hear
more about that plight."

Q199.   Chamberlin, J. E.   "Poetry Chronicle."   Hudson Review, 26
        (Summer 1973) 398-399 [(388)-404].
        Review of Jumping Out of Bed and Sleepers Joining Hands.
Bly is not a particularly candid poet and is not given to exploiting
the ironies of his own lack of candor, which is a weakness of his
work.   These works are a "curious mixture of gratuitous statement
and a contrived passiveness."
        See Q25.

Q200.   Choice, 11 (May 1974), 434.
        Bly has become pretentious and sententious.   He has sacri-
ficed poetry for message.   His essay on mother consciousness is bor-
ing, poorly written, and feeble amateurism.   Rather than visionary,
he is merely absurd.

Q201.   Cooney, Seamus.   "The Book Review."   Library Journal, 97
        (October 1, 1977), 3163.
        This book is an essential example of current poetry.   It is
a rousing collection despite periodic lapses into preachiness and
bathos.   The best poems are sociopolitical in theme, especially the
moving "The Teeth-Mother Naked at Last."
        Reprinted in Q202.

Q202.   _____.   The Library Journal Book Review.   New York:
        R. R. Bowker, 1972, p. 363.
        Reprint of Q201.

Q203.   Dawe, Charles.   Boston Phoenix, Section Three, 10 April
        1973.
        Not verified, cited in Friberg (no. O2), p. 222.

Q204.   Foster, Michael.   "On Sleepers Joining Hands."   The Shore
        Review, 11 (Fall 1973), 52-55.
        This may be Bly's finest book, representing some of the
best poetry of our best living poets.   The resemblance of much of
the poetry to Japanese forms is discussed.

Q205.   "Editor's Note on Sleepers Joining Hands."   Marquette Michi-
        gan Mining Journal, March 1973, pp. 2, 13.
        Not verified, cited in Friberg (no. O2), p. 223.

Reviews

Q206. Gilder, Gary. "Books in Brief." Kansas City Star, 22 April
1973.
Not verified, cited in Friberg (no. O2), p. 222.

Q207. Helms, Alan. "Two Poets." Partisan Review, 44 (no. 2,
1977), [284]-288.
The work is an attempt to reconcile the duality of inner
and outer worlds, to integrate them or minimally lead them towards
integration, to establish a community. The poetry fails in doing so
because Bly himself is so disintegrated. He has opted for the con-
fessional mode he as critic helped to destroy. The resulting work
is sloppy and self-conscious. The prose piece, however, achieves
what the poetry fails to do, but it is not strong enough to support
the poetry.

Q208. Hyde, Lewis. "Let Other Poets Whisper ... You Can Hear
Bly." Minneapolis Tribune, 25 February 1973, pp. 10D-
11D.
Although the poems exist of two kinds, public and private,
the public poems rise out of a closeness to other people, a closeness
discovered in private. "Sleepers Joining Hands," "The Teeth-Mother
Naked at Last" ("the best poem written during the last decade"),
and Bly's essay on mother consciousness are discussed, as is his
prose writing in general. His prose is comparable only to that of
D. H. Lawrence, García Lorca, and Thoreau.

Q209. Keating, Douglas. "Bly Collection is Noteable [sic] Achieve-
ment in Verse." Philadelphia Bulletin, 16 September 1973.
Not verified, cited in Friberg (no. O2), p. 222.

Q210. Kirkus Reviews, 40 (October 15, 1972), 1217.
The prose essay proclaims the mystery toward which Bly's
poetry has been gravitating, but he tries to renege on his own im-
plications at the end. These implications are, however, drawn out
in the staggering surrealist epic, "The Shadow Poem."

Q211. Klotz, Neil. "20th Century Survival." The Mess, 2 March
1973, p. 10.
Bly's poems are becoming more intense and ambitious.
The images in the long poems come in a strange and fast stream of
"apocalyptic one-liners."

Q212. Lindquist, Ray. New, no. 22 & 23 (Fall/Winter 1973/1974),
88-89.
This essay focuses upon "The Teeth-Mother Naked at Last"
and the central prose piece of the book. The book documents the
facts and feelings of the previous decade with impressionistic insight
and power. It is questioned, however, whether Bly's reaction to
"New Criticism, reason, the Vietnam War, every kind of social in-
justice" is not an overreaction and an excessive reaction.

Q213. Metro, Jim. Montgomery Advertiser-Alabama Journal, "Alabama Sunday Magazine," 7 October 1973, p. 10.
A brief descriptive review.

Q214. Miller, Vassar. "Poetry." Houston Post, 29 April 1973.
Not verified, cited in Friberg (no. O2), p. 223.

Q215. Naiden, James. "Echoes Don't Lessen Poet Bly's Strength." Minneapolis Star, 20 November 1973, p. 2B.
Review of Sleepers Joining Hands and Jumping Out of Bed. Bly's chief weakness is in excessive rhetoric binges; however, he renews his voice with great vigor in these works. Sleepers Joining Hands is a book of unfailing energy and audacity. Jumping Out of Bed presents imagery on a quieter, perhaps deeper, level.

Q216. "New and Recommended." New York Times Book Review, 25 February 1973, p. 53.
The book is listed.

Q217. Nicolai, Peter. "Poetry." Minnesota Daily, 5 February 1973.
Not verified, cited in Friberg (no. O2), p. 223.

Q218. "1973: A Selection of Noteworthy Titles." New York Times Book Review, 2 December 1973, p. 79.
The book is included.

Q219. Oates, Joyce Carol. "Where They All Are Sleeping." Modern Poetry Studies, 4 (Winter 1973), 341-344.
A laudatory review. Both Bly's poetry and prose are unique at the present time. His work is always directed at a moral position, yet it is curiously dramatic and mysterious. It is extremely "intellectual" but avoids argumentation or didacticism. All aspects of the book, one of the most powerful of recent memory, are highly praised.

Q220. Oppenheimer, Joel. "A Newspaper Reader's Garden of Verse." Newday [Long Island, NY], "Ideas," 5 August 1973, pp. 20, 16.
The essay on mother consciousness is an important essay for the exposure of the poetic process--seeing a poet's mind grabbing onto new material.

Q221. Piccione, A[nthony]. "Bly: Man, Voice and Poem." Ann Arbor Review, August 15-16, 1973, pp. 86-90.
This is a book of balance between the two poles exhibited in Bly's two previous volumes: the meditative and the public reality. There is the sense that Bly's calm warmth for humanity is his real psychic self speaking, not the poetic voice associated with technique.

Q222. "Pilgrim Fish Heads." National Observer, 9 June 1973, p. 23.

A brief complimentary note on Bly and Sleepers Joining
Hands prefacing the poem of the title.

Q223.   Ramsey, Paul.  "American Poetry in 1973."  Sewanee Review,
            82 (April/June 1974), 401-402.
            Bly's political poetry is "shameful even for hate propa-
ganda ... [which] is always distasteful to hear or to discuss."  The
poetry is dishonest and self-deceiving.

Q224.   "A Selected Vacation Reading List."  New York Times Book
            Review, 10 June 1973, p. 41.
            This volume is one of six titles listed under poetry.

Q225.   Shapiro, Karl.  "The New Poetry:  Still Echoing the Agony
            of the '60s."  Chicago Tribune, "Book World," Section 7,
            25 March 1973, p. [1].
            The poetry is not nearly as interesting as the prose.  A
poor synopsis of Bly's essay is given.  The essay is not worth look-
ing up.

Q226.   Skelton, Robin.  "Robert Bly's New Book."  Kayak, no. 33
            (November 1973), 66-69.
            The emotional richness of the poetry, the vision and pas-
sion of the poems, is praised but the lack of intellectual stimulation
they provide is lamented.  Much of the review is a discussion of the
emergence of Mother Consciousness over Father Consciousness.

Q227.   Sternberg, Mary.  "New Work Based on Poet's Theories."
            Escondido, CA Times-Advocate, "North Country Magazine,"
            4 February 1973, p. 13.
            An uncritical laudatory review focusing upon "The Teeth-
Mother Naked at Last," the title poem, and the prose piece.  The
reviewer is blindly accepting of all that Bly offers.

Q228.   Stitt, Peter.  "James Wright and Robert Bly."  Hawaii Re-
            view, 2 (Fall 1973), 89-94.
            An intertwined review of James Wright's Two Citizens and
Sleepers Joining Hands which touches upon Bly's influence on
Wright and the commonality of their poetry.  The remarks on Bly's
book center on the concept of the female and male consciousnesses
presented in the book's prose piece.  The book is impressive not
only as poetry, but it is also important as a statement on our na-
tional psyche.

Q229.   Walsh, Chad.  "Wry Apocalypse, Revolutionary Petunias."
            Washington Post, Book World, 1 April 1973, p. 13.
            As alive and terrifying as Bly's poetic vision is, it is in
some ways surpassed by his prose section on mother consciousness.
Bly is peculiarly the seer of the present moment and the possible
future.

Q230. Zinnes, Harriet. "Images Plunging Inward." New Leader,
        56 (July 9, 1973), 19.
        The political aspects of the poems are emphasized. Bly's
meaning is essentially political. His call for more inwardness is
equally a call for greater political awareness.


## Talking All Morning

Q231. Campbell, James. "Agony and After." Times Literary Sup-
        plement, 20 February 1981, p. 208.
        This is a readable and entertaining book despite some
dreadful editing of some of the transcripts. The book reveals Bly
as a man full of deep thought and good sense.

Q232. Choice, 18 (February 1981), 792.
        The book's value lies in the fact that almost anything of
importance that Bly has said in the past decade is repeated someway
in the essays and interviews. The pronouncements, however,. grow
stale with an excess of Bly's rage and highly subjective patter.
Users of the book understand that it is an "ironic commentary
against a once-strong poet who has become an old harpy."

Q233. Hansen, Tom. "On Writing Poetry: Four Contemporary
        Poets." College English, 44 (March 1982), 270-272 [265-
        273].
        This is not a review of the work so much as it is a dis-
cussion of Bly's attitudes toward poetry and language. Three other
works, by Donald Hall, William Stafford, and Richard Hugo, are also
discussed within the article.

Q234. Lyne, Sandford. Poetry East, no. 3 (Fall 1980), 80-83.
        See Q112.

Q235. Martone, J. World Literature Today, 55 (Autumn 1981), 680.
        This is one of the most important and provocative com-
mentaries on the relationship of poetry to life to emerge in some
time.

Q236. Perloff, Marjorie. "Soft Touch." Parnassus: Poetry in
        Review, 10 (Spring/Summer 1982), 221-230 [209-230 pas-
        sim].
        See Q81.

Q237. Punter, David. "Robert Bly: Gone Fishing For the Sign."
        Modern Poetry Studies, 10 (no. 2/3, 1981), 241-245.
        A thoughtful and intelligent review essay. After a dis-
cussion of the general ideas shaping Bly's work, the theory that
Bly's ideas are deep-rooted but few is presented. What emerges
from the pieces in the book is Bly's obsessional negativism: the
categorization and consequent rejection of anything associated with
the "academic," the "abstract statement," or the "organizing mind."

Q238. S. P. [Sara Plath]. The Booklist, 77 (November 1, 1980),
      388.
      A brief descriptive review.

Q239. Saucerman, James R. Western American Literature, 16
      (Summer 1981), 162-164.
      See Q272.

Q240. Wesling, Donald. "The Recent Work of Donald Hall and
      Robert Bly." Michigan Quarterly Review, 20 (Spring
      1981), 144-154 passim.
      A review essay of This Tree Will Be Here for a Thousand
Years and Talking All Morning, and Hall's Kicking the Leaves and
Goatfoot Milktongue Twinbird. Comments on the poets and their
works are interwoven throughout the essay focusing on their rela-
tionship, their similarities, and the influence of Bly on Hall's work.
Talking All Morning is a stronger book than Bly's volume of poetry.
It is a unified statement; a product of an organic sensibility.

Q241. Zavatsky, Bill. Meridian, 1 (Winter/Spring 1981), [1]-3.
      This is not really a review of the book but rather an in-
telligent and well-presented criticism of Bly's poetics. Zavatsky,
in the few essays he has written on Bly, shows himself to be one
of the most perceptive of those critics who have accepted Bly's call
to criticize him and other "elder" poets. Zavatsky's central concern
is with Bly's lack of involvement with human interaction and rela-
tionships in his works.

                The Teeth Mother Naked at Last

Q242. Hefferman, Michael. "Brief Reviews...." Midwest Quarterly,
      12 (Spring 1971), 355-356 [353-356].
      Bly's tactic is a perfectly consistent attempt to fit his
poem to its occasion. It is therefore a frequently unbearable poem.
It is a nightmare of a poem proposing the logic of the nightmare as
a resolution. The poem is a total experience.

Q243. Hill, Douglas. "Scattered Literature." Ambit, no. 49 (1971),
      16 [16-17].
      There is a complimentary tone for the directness and pas-
sion of the poem.

Q244. Katz, Bill. "The Book Review." Library Journal, 96 (Feb-
      ruary 15, 1971), 641.
      A brief review. This book "may be one of [Bly's] best
works to date." Reprinted in Q245.

Q245. _____. The Library Journal Book Review. New York:
      R. R. Bowker Co., 1971, pp. 350-351.
      Reprint of Q244.

Q246.  [M. D.]  "Bookmarks."  Prairie Schooner, 45 (Spring 1971),
          92-93.
          A brief review.  This is without a doubt the long-awaited
poem concerning the horror of the Vietnam War.  It is the first
anti-war poem to rise above the slogans and innuendos with political
muscle since the war poems of Karl Shapiro and Siegfried Sassoon.
          Reprinted in Q247.

Q247.  _____.  Prairie Schooner, 45 (Summer 1971), 186.
          Reprint of Q246.

Q248.  Mills, Josephine.  "The Home Book of Modern Verse, 1970."
          Massachusetts Review, 12 (Autumn 1971), 701-702 [689-
          708].
          See P68.

Q249.  Naiden, James.  "Vietnam Everyone's Fault?  Poetry Protest-
          ing War 'Crashing Bore'."  Minneapolis Star, 30 March
          1971, p. 1B.
          This is a disappointing book.  Although Bly has made a
brave and honorable stand regarding the Vietnam War, this is a
little book of bad poetry and invective with ordinary and tasteless
rhetoric.  Bly's attitude is self-righteous, and his analogies are
shrill and embittered.

Q250.  [Reinhold, Robert].  "The Bly Mother."  The Smith, no.
          22/23 (July 4, 1973), 74-79.
          Despite the statement that the essay would explore the
positive aspects of the poem, the prevailing tone of the review is
critical.  The poem is organically sick.  It is deformed by long ex-
tremities and appendages of pure didacticism which is not poetry.
The use of the "Deep Image" seems, at times, inadvertently funny.
The political elements override the poetic.  The second part of the
essay is a reply to those who believe the reviewer is out to "get"
Bly.  He delineates what he perceives to be Bly's strengths, but
proceeds to point out further weaknesses of "The Teeth Mother."

Q251.  Skinner, Knute.  Concerning Poetry, 6 (Fall 1973), 89.
          Review of The Teeth Mother Naked at Last and The
Morning Glory.  The notices of each book are extremely brief.  It
is easy to sympathize with Bly's thesis in "The Teeth Mother," but
not his rhetoric.  He is at his best in The Morning Glory.


                This Body Is Made of Camphor and Gopherwood

Q252.  Choice, 15 (April 1978), 224.
          Bly succeeds in flattening the vividness of good poetry
and diluting the strength of good prose.  This volume is added
evidence that Bly is the country's single most grossly overrated
poet.

The reviewer's statement that these are a flat, preachy group of short poems without focus shows a lack of insight into the collection.

Q253. Cotter, James Finn. "Poetry Reading." Hudson Review, 31 (Spring 1978), 214-215.
Bly does not help the reader share in his "pure isolation." The result is "not mysticism but solipsism." Too often the work is "overweight and pretentious."

Q254. Dacey, Philip. "This Book Is Made of Turkey Soup and Star Music." Parnassus: Poetry in Review, 7 (Fall/Winter 1978), 34-45.
Ostensibly, this is a review essay on This Body Is Made of Camphor and Gopherwood and The Loon, but it is used as a basis for a humorous and deflating, and sometimes insightful, essay on Bly himself, and his visions, ideas, and biases. Bly is a "crazy operatic character," given to passionate extravagance. He believes in excess and imbalance.
Of the works themselves, This Body... possesses both a prophetic quality that distinguishes it from most contemporary work and "a grandiose purpose bordering on battiness." Whereas it is intense, driving, and fervent, The Loon is relaxed, quiet, and reserved. Bly is refreshingly relaxed, not trying to write "great poetry."

Q255. Fuller, John. "Where the Cold Winds Blow." Times Literary Supplement, 14 April 1978, p. 410.
While not rating Bly "very high" in the tradition of prose poetry, the reviewer finds "an undeniable intensity and candour" in the book.

Q256. Garrison, Joseph. "Book Review." Library Journal, 102 (August 1977), 1653.
A brief review. The book celebrates the human body.

Q257. Jacob, John. The Booklist, 74 (December 15, 1977), 658.
Bly reasserts his position as one of the country's leading poets.

Q258. Kenner, Hugh. "Three Poets." New York Times Book Review, 1 January 1978, p. 10.
The poems have a hallucinatory quality. "Bly is attempting to write down what it's like to be alive, a state in which he implies, not all readers find themselves all the time."

Q259. Kirkus Reviews, 45 (October 1, 1977), 1087.
This is not much more than the "blameless blah-books of soothing aphorisms stationery stores stock." The book consists of "moony questions and muzzy pantheism."

Q260.  Molesworth, Charles.  "Domesticating the Sublime: Bly's
        Latest Poems."  Ohio Review, 19 (Fall 1978), [56]-66.
        This is a significant discussion of the poetry of this book
and its significance in terms of the overall body of Bly's work.  The
book signals a decisive change in Bly's poetry.  There is a per-
sistence and dominance of a religious impulse in the book with Bly's
vision more directly concentrated on ecstatic moments.  His poetry
is best understood as an attempt to get back to a pre-Orphic sense
of the body.  The body is the perfect universal symbol.
        Reprinted in P158.

Q261.  _____.  Georgia Review, 32 (Fall 1978), 686-688.
        Though Bly's prose has trained itself to rescue mundane
objects and action and to celebrate cosmic power, it is at the ex-
pense of being able to accept the everyday connectedness of the
world.  There is a sense of rightness in the book, a play with the
rhythms and expectations of prose that manages to garner the criti-
cal advantage of poetry.
        This is a strangely awkward review; it is as if Molesworth
cannot identify something bothersome in a work he otherwise re-
spects.
        See Q260.

Q262.  Publishers Weekly, 212 (8 August 1977), 56.
        These prose poems reflect Bly's struggle to remain simple
and concrete, and yet to draw from the observations of mind, eye,
and body a spiritual overlay that celebrates essential mystery.

Q263.  Ringold, F[rancine].  World Literature Today, 52 (Summer
        1978), 471.
        This is a beautiful book.  The poems evoke a deep image
out of a vibrating stillness.

Q264.  W. E. L. [William E. Littlefield].  Kliatt Young Adult Paper-
        back Book Guide, 12 (Winter 1978), 18.
        A brief descriptive notice.


                    This Tree Will Be Here For
                       A Thousand Years

Q265.  Carruth, Hayden.  "Poets on the Fringe."  Harper's, 260
        (January 1980), 79 [77-81].
        Bly's theory of two consciousnesses is "Swedenborgian
nonsense" which "saps our minds as it saps the beauty of the
natural world."  While admitting to a fundamental dislike of Bly's
poetry and poetics, Carruth finds himself caught by Bly's poems:
"Sometimes it is good, better than good, to guard oneself and
still be caught."

Q266.  Cotter, James Finn.  "Poetry, Ego and Self."  Hudson Re-
        view, 33 (Spring 1980), [131]-132 [[131]-145].

Too many of Bly's poems attempt to overcharge a moment that may have psychic significance but lacks poetic expression. Nothing is happening in these poems. Although Bly wants the deeper, objective self to rule the subjective, superficial ego, some of the best contemporary poetry has been written by poets who strongly embrace the earthbound ego (e.g., Robert Lowell, John Berryman, and Sylvia Plath).

Q267.  G. S.  Carleton Miscellany, 18 (Summer 1980), 228.
A brief review that tells the reader nothing substantial.

Q268.  Garrison, Joseph.  "Book Review." Library Journal, 104 (August 1979), 1569.
A disappointment is experienced at the "hermetic and elitist subjectivism in some of the poems."

Q269.  Janik, Del Ivan.  Aspen Anthology, Winter 1980, pp. 83-84.
An admiring review by an evidently strongly admiring Bly partisan: "Any new book from Robert Bly is an important event." This is just the type of blanket endorsement that Bly has railed against.

Q270.  Kirkus Reviews, 47 (July 15, 1979), 849.
This is perhaps Bly's best collection yet. His finest poems are remarkably vivid and touching. There is a sadder-but-wiser treatment of familiar Bly subjects.

Q271.  Publishers Weekly, 216 (2 July 1979), 99.
Some of the poems possess a rare simplicity and clarity of vision that restore the reader to the real world. If there is more artifice here, there is also a more piercing and compassionate vision of the human predicament.

Q272.  Saucerman, James R.  Western American Literature, 16 (Summer 1981), 162-164.
A combined review with Talking All Morning. The poems are seldom successful. Bly's perceptions are not turned into art. They lack the shaping spirit of imagination that uses images in effective natural metaphor. Talking All Morning contributes insight into the full range of Bly's creative efforts.

Q273.  Stitt, Peter.  "The World at Hand." Georgia Review, 34 (Fall 1980), 663-666 [661-670].
Bly is an important figure in contemporary American poetry but not because of his poetry. He is akin to Ezra Pound in the extent of his influence on other poets. His importance is as a teacher, preacher, and reformer. In this book, Bly's theory of two consciousnesses, as presented in the preface, fails entirely when applied to the poems. It is an uneven book, most seriously marred by its naive preface.

Q274.  Weinberger, Eliot.  "Gloves on A Mouse."  Nation, 229
        (November 17, 1979), 503-504.
        A caustic review which is also insulting to college stu-
dents who write poems.  Weinberger eases into the review by de-
claring Bly to be "a windbag, a sentimentalist, a slob in the lan-
guage," in the first sentence.  After a discussion of Romanticism
and a linkage of it to the "feminine," which Bly is seen as an
apostle of in American poetry, the specific poetry of the book is
examined in sarcastic tones.  Throughout the review it is men-
tioned that Bly is popular with college students and that he is
imitated by them because his poems are so easy to write.  A formula
is given based on the first five lines of "Women We Never See
Again."  The conclusion is that it is disturbing that so many young
writers model themselves on Bly who is an "utterly safe, cozily ir-
relevant poet."

Q275.  Wesling, Donald.  "The Recent Work of Donald Hall and
        Robert Bly."  Michigan Quarterly Review, 20 (Spring
        1981), 144-154 passim.
        See Q240.

Q276.  Williamson, Alan.  "Music to Your Ears."  New York Times
        Book Review, (9 March 1980), pp. 8, 9, 14, 15.
        Bly, as a poet, has always been restricted by a "relative-
ly weak sense of the musical and connotative value of words."  The
poems are seemingly composed of only images and ideas.  The sec-
ond of the "two presences" of consciousnesses that Bly says these
poems record, frees his poetry from an overly intellectual and doc-
trinaire religiousity.  It presents itself to him as sadness which
relieves him of the "burden of messianic overconfidence."  There
is a need for more of a historic or psychic structure to the poetry.


                            Times Alone
                        (Antonio Machado)

Q277.  Coleman, Alexander.  "A Poet of Laconic Power."  New York
        Times Book Review, 21 August 1983, pp. 12, 19.
        A combined review with Antonio Machado:  Selected Poems
translated and introduced by Alan S. Trueblood.  In comparing the
two works, Bly gets closer to "the heart of things."  His comments
are illuminating intuitions.  However, in the actual translations of
the poems, Trueblood is far superior.  Bly is looking at the secrets
of Spanish from the outside.  A number of inaccurate translations
by Bly are given and both versions of a stanza from a poem trans-
lated by Bly and Trueblood are given.

Q278.  Maloney, Dennis.  "Machado In Translation."  White Pine
        Journal, no. 26 (1983), 64-65.
        Brief reviews of I Never Wanted Fame, Canciones, and
Times Alone (Graywolf Press edition).  They are handsomely

produced chapbooks. Bly is the most successful of Machado trans-
lators discussed (Alan S. Trueblood and Willis Barnstone) at carry-
ing over the spirit of the original.

Q279. Tammaro, Tom. Library Journal, 108 (June 1, 1983), 1142.
       This work is an example of Bly, as translator, at his
best. The notes preceding each section allow the reader to enter
the spirit of Machado's world. The differences between Bly's and
Alan Trueblood's equally fine translations verify the difficulties of
capturing the subtlety and expansiveness of Machado's psychic vi-
sion.


## Truth Barriers
(Tomas Tranströmer)

Q280. Fjelde, Rolf. "Poems as Meeting Places." New York Times
       Book Review, 26 April 1981, p. 26 [pp. 24, 26].
       A combined review with Robin Fulton's Selected Poems of
Tranströmer. The introduction is sympathetically informed. Out of
his own "temperamental affinity," Bly's translations are as conson-
ant with the Swedish as one could hope.

Q281. Fulton, R[obin]. World Literature Today, 56 (Winter 1982),
       132.
       Bly's introduction is enthusiastic and well informed. The
translations have the virtue of retaining much of the life of their
originals. Unfortunately, more than half of this brief notice is a
review of other English translations of Tranströmer, including Ful-
ton's own.

Q282. Hudzik, Robert. "Book Review." Library Journal, 105 (15
       November 1980), 2417.
       A brief review with no mention of Bly except to note that
he, along with May Swenson, are the principal translators of Trans-
trömer. This collection is "intense [and] luminous."

Q283. Kliatt Paperback Book Guide, 15 (Spring 1981), 25.
       Brief review.

Q284. Publishers Weekly, 218 (26 September 1980), 120.
       The translations by Bly sound so suspiciously like Bly
that it would be better to have the originals on facing pages rather
than at the end of the book.

Q285. Ratner, Rochelle. Parabola, 6 (Summer 1981), 112 [108-113].
       One could not hope for a better match between poet and
translator than between Tranströmer and Bly.

## Twenty Poems of César Vallejo

Q286.  Eshleman, Clayton.  Kulchur, no. 14 (Summer 1964), 88-92.
This book is practically useless in revealing anything
about Vallejo's work.  Bly slightly distrusts his originals; they are
never clear enough for him.  His translations have the quality of
someone giving a student a quick running commentary.
Bly has received too much attention considering the quality
of his work.  He has continually botched his translations of those
poets who have given their best to him.  The translations lack the
dignity of hard work.  It would be better if Vallejo remained un-
known in North America than to be represented by these transla-
tions.

Q287.  Gifford, Henry.  "The Master of Pain."  Poetry, 105 (De-
        cember 1964), 196-197.
The translations read "like something real, and the idiom
has vigor without crudity."

Q288.  Stitt, Peter.  "Robert Bly's World of True Images."  Minne-
        sota Daily, "Ivory Tower," 8 April 1963, pp. 29, 47.
        See Q193.

## Twenty Poems of Georg Trakl

Q289.  Holmes, Theodore.  "Wit, Nature, and the Human Concern."
        Poetry, 100 (August 1962), 322-324 [319-324].
The translators have "been amazingly accurate and faith-
ful to the original" in light of most contemporary translating.  How-
ever, the review is critical of several line inversions without any
evident syntactical impasses of formal considerations, and the
changes in translation of several terms.

Q290.  Simon, John.  "More Brass Than Enduring."  Hudson Re-
        view, 15 (Autumn 1962), 467 [[455]-468].
Brief notice which suggests that at least one of the trans-
lators should learn German before attempting translations.

## Twenty Poems of Pablo Neruda

Q291.  "Alienation and Acclaim."  Times Literary Supplement, 14
        November 1968, p. 1285.
The quality of the translations is usually accurate, cap-
turing without strain the spontaneous proliferation of images char-
acteristic of Neruda.  The selections are too brief, however.  The
"Canto General," for one, is hopelessly mutilated by the selections.

Q292.  Palmer, Penelope.  "Through Unfathomed Waves:  Transla-
        tions from Pablo Neruda."  Agenda, 6 (Autumn/Winter
        1968), 127-128 [124-128].

The introduction is good. The selections from "Canto General" do not give a very good idea of it; other selections, however, are good.

## Twenty Poems of Tomas Tranströmer

Q293.  P. D. [Philip Dacey].  Crazy Horse, no. 9 (December 1971), 15.
        Bly continues to serve well the American poetry audience. Tranströmer's poetry is surprising and fresh.

Q294.  Root, William Pitt.  "Anything But Over."  Poetry, 123 (October 1973), 39–41 [34–[56]].
        See Q135.

# R.  DISSERTATIONS

## 1969

R1.  Piccione, Anthony.  "Robert Bly and the Deep Image."  Ohio
     University.  199 p.
     The first extensive study of Bly's poetry and a seminal
work in the examination of his use of imagery.  The concept of the
deep image is placed within a historical perspective; its development
is traced back to Eliot and Pound.  Not only is Bly's poetry exam-
ined (the date of the dissertation limits the discussion to only two
books:  Silence in the Snowy Fields and The Light Around the
Body), but his work and ideas in regard to the deep image are also
placed within the context of other poets and their work.

## 1972

R2.  Mersmann, James F.  "Out of the Vortex:  A Study of Poets
     and Poetry Against the Vietnam War."  University of Kan-
     sas.  362 p.
     A thematic and critical study of American poets' reactions
to the Vietnam War relating their protest to their poetics.  Bly is
one of four poets whose work is focused upon (the others are Allen
Ginsberg, Denise Levertov, and Robert Duncan).  Bly's poems
draw their power from the subconscious deep image; this is in re-
action to the American psyche which is overbalanced toward the
conscious, abstract, rigid, and "masculine."
     See P94.

## 1973

R3.  Justin, Jeffrey Arthur.  "Unknown Land Poetry:  Walt Whit-
     man, Robert Bly, and Gary Snyder."  University of Michi-
     gan.  189 p.
     English language poetry is divided into two modes:  cultur-
ally based and instinctually based.  Unknown-land poetry is the
term used to identify the instinctually based mode.  Following a
discussion of the characteristics of unknown-land poetry, a link is
established among Whitman, Bly, and Snyder in their mutual rever-
ence for the great mother mysteries.  Bly's prose essays are used
to explore his critical, social, and spiritual vision.  Links between
Bly and Taoism are also discussed.

## 1974

R4.  Sage, Frances Kellogg.  "Robert Bly:  His Poetry and Literary
     Criticism."  University of Texas at Austin.  228 p.
         Bly's central concern in his poetry and prose is the deep
image.  This is an extended, but introductory, examination of the
deep image as it is found in his work.

R5.  Wosk, Julie Helen.  "Prophecies for America:  Social Criticism
     in the Recent Poetry of Bly, Levertov, Corso, and Gins-
     berg."  University of Wisconsin, Madison.  199 p.
         Bly's political and social commentary as presented in The
Light Around the Body and Sleepers Joining Hands is examined.
The thesis presented in regard to Bly's work inaccurately asserts
that he largely avoids the problems of polemic and banality in poetic
social commentary by presenting his social criticism obliquely through
surrealist images.  The poetry itself demonstrates that the images
do not always save it from banality, and the extent and tenor of
much of the criticism is evidence of the problems of polemics Bly
encounters.

## 1976

R6.  Cramer, Mark Jonathan.  "Neruda and Vallejo in Contemporary
     United States Poetry."  University of Illinois at Urbana-
     Champaign.  141 p.
         The influence of Neruda and Vallejo has been primarily upon
the deep image poets:  Bly, James Wright, and W. S. Merwin.  Bly
has served as the catalyst in sparking interest in Neruda and Val-
lejo in other United States poets.  Bly's translations of Neruda are
compared to his own poetry to ascertain the impact of Neruda's in-
fluence.

## 1977

R7.  Harris, Victoria Frenkel.  "The Incorporative Consciousness:
     A Study of the Poetry of Denise Levertov and Robert Bly."
     University of Illinois at Urbana-Champaign.  415 p.
         The incorporative consciousness is defined as encompassing
both internal and external reality, integrating the self, others, and
nature into an organic whole.  The nature of incorporative con-
sciousness and its development and language is analyzed through
Bly's Silence in the Snowy Fields and Old Man Rubbing His Eyes.
These two works are seen as organically linked.  The latter volume
begins where the former ended.  They thereby reveal Bly's ex-
panding psychic awakening.
         This work is very much attuned to Bly's thinking, and it is
the basis for the later work of this increasingly important Bly
scholar.

## 1978

R8.  Elliot, David Lindsey.  "The Deep Image:  Radical Subjectiv-
     ity in the Poetry of Robert Bly, James Wright, Galway
     Kinnell, James Dickey, and W. S. Merwin."  Syracuse
     University.  280 p.
        An examination of the history and development of deep
image poetry and the work of its primary practitioners.  Bly is
seen as the figurehead of the movement and its most outspoken pro-
ponent.

R9.  Till, David Kelland.  "The Work of Robert Bly:  'The Great
     Mother and the New Father'."  University of New Mexico.
        Bly's poetry and prose is studied in regard to the move-
ment of the psyche through both the light and the dark worlds.
The dark world is the feminine consciousness, the unconscious or
inward world:  Erich Neumann's concept of the "Great Mother."
The "New Father" represents the consciousness, the light.
        This is a useful and insightful study of the importance of
consciousness, unconsciousness, and the psyche in understanding
Bly's poetry and poetics.

R10.  Wilkinson, Robert Taylor.  "The Way Into the Self:  Con-
      temporary American Poets and the Re-Discovery of a
      Tradition."  Washington State University.  211 p.
        Since World War II American poets have moved away from
modernist-academic poetry and aligned themselves with an older,
alternative culture characterized by a pre-rational, participatory,
non-Christian vision that extends beyond the solely human.  The
works of Bly, David Ignatow, and Gary Snyder are focused upon
in regard to this thesis.  Through their poetry they try to rees-
tablish the connections with a wisdom and body of experience that
they see the contemporary, materialistic, fragmented world as need-
ing to survive.

## 1979

R11.  Carrasco Galan, Alvaro.  "Influencia de la Poesia Moderna
      Espanola y Sudamericana en la Poesia Contemporanea North-
      americana:  Influencia de Lorca y Neruda en Robert Bly."
      State University of New York at Buffalo.  199 p.
        Bly emerged as the spokesman for a group of poets that
centered around The Fifties and who found inspiration and models
in the poetry of García Lorca and Neruda.  Bly's poetry is empha-
sized since it is seen, rightly or wrongly, as a model for the other
poets of the group.  The similarities in themes and images among
García Lorca, Neruda, and Bly are examined.  Text in Spanish.

## 1980

R12.   Cohen, Jonathan I.   "Neruda in English:   A Critical History
       of the Verse Translations and Their Impact on American
       Poetry."   State University of New York at Stony Brook.
       234 p.
       Part of the fourth chapter of this work examines the influ-
ences Bly's translations of Neruda have had on his own poetry.

R13.   Zweig, Ellen Marcia.   "Performance Poetry:   Critical Ap-
       proaches to Contemporary Intermedia."   University of
       Michigan.   454 p.
       Bly is one of several poets examined in this study of
poetry presentations.   Bly's use of music and masks in his readings
is discussed.

## 1981

R14.   Miller, Susan Hawkins.   "The Poetics of the Postmodern
       American Prose Poem."   University of Oregon.   135 p.
       Bly's prose poems are examples of a vestigal romanticism
which overvalues the insights and intuitions of the speaker above
all other considerations.   The discussion of Bly's prose poetry is
part of the concluding chapter of this study.

R15.   Stiffler, Harold Randall.   "The Good Darkness:   Affirmation
       in the Poems of Robert Bly, W. S. Merwin, and James
       Wright."   University of Illinois at Urbana-Champaign.
       170 p.
       Theoretically, although the subjects of Bly's poems are
ordinarily connected with fear and death, his use of them is af-
firmative.   However, in practice, he is inconsistent.   In his pastor-
al and prose poems Bly can communicate a sense of spiritual pres-
ence and continuity.   In his political poetry though, he abandons
these affirmative associations and resurrects the threatened re-
sponses this imagery usually produces.   He manipulates them to
advance his own partisan political positions.

## 1982

R16.   Kalaidjian, Walter Barron.   "Gathering in the Far Field:   The
       Aesthetics of Contemporary Midwest Regionalism in Theo-
       dore Roethke, Robert Bly, and James Wright."   University
       of Illinois at Urbana-Champaign.   218 p.
       A comprehensive comparison of the poetics and poetry of
the three poets.   Roethke's aesthetic commitment to the American
landscape served as a model for Bly's pastoral meditations on rural
Minnesota.   His use of Midwest regionalism was part of his struggle
with the influence of High Modernism and the New Critics.   Bly's

surrealistic presentation of the deep image has a forerunner in
Roethke's use of surrealism to dramatize his poetry of individuation.


1983

R17.   Gundy, Jeffrey Gene.   "I and Me Above and In All Things:
       Versions of the Self in Modern Poetry."   Indiana Univer-
       sity.   243 p.
       Bly is one of five "modern twentieth-century poets" whose
work is examined in an attempt to discern the modern poet's search
for self while avoiding "both the frustrations of narcissism and the
destructiveness of rampant egotism." The study of Bly focuses
upon the dichotomy between the inward and outward worlds and his
use of surrealistic and imagistic language that claims to bring deep
levels of self and world into the poem.

R18.   Gutchess, Elizabeth Denver.   "Four Translators 'After' Pound:
       Studies of Richard Wilbur, Robert Lowell, Robert Bly and
       Galway Kinnell."   University of Notre Dame.   153 p.
       After establishing the importance and influence of Pound's
work in translating, this study then focuses upon Bly's translations
(and others) in comparison.   Similarly to Pound, Bly has revitalized
American poetry through foreign sources.   His program, however,
is aimed exactly against Pound's "rationalist" modernism.

R19.   Monroe, Jonathan Beck.   "A Poverty of Objects:   Studies in
       the Prose Poem (France, Germany, United States)."   Uni-
       versity of Oregon.   481 p.
       Bly is one of ten writers (and one of two Americans--
Gertrude Stein is the other) used to examine the development of the
prose poem as a literary form.   The study of Bly's work centers on
his interest, following Francis Ponge, with material objects, as well
as his use of the genre to express his "utopian aspirations for the
resolution of generic/class conflicts."


1984

R20.   Smith, Douglas George.   "The Best of Both Worlds:   The
       Poetry of Robert Bly."   University of Manitoba (Canada).
       An examination of the major works in the Bly canon (Si-
lence in the Snowy Fields, The Light Around the Body, Sleepers
Joining Hands, The Morning Glory, This Body Is Made of Camphor
and Gopherwood) to establish the misclassification of his poetry as
"deep image."   The predominate image of Bly's work is not "deep
image" but a transformational image.   The sources and uses of the
transformational image are examined in each of the works cited.   In
so doing, the study offers a comprehensive discussion of the major
influences on the development of Bly's poetics.

## S. POEMS

S1. "Thinking of Robert Bly and James Wright on the First Hot Day in April After Having Stayed Up Late at Night Drinking With a Gang of Old Norwegian Trolls." In Spinning the Crystal Ball: Some Guesses at the Future of American Poetry. James Dickey. Washington, DC: Library of Congress, p. 9.

### 1968

S2. Hammer, Louis. "After Reading the Latest Criticism." Kayak, no. 13 (January), 14.
Poem in response to Bly's "The First Ten Issues of Kayak."
See B34.

### 1969

S3. Taylor, Henry. "And Robert Bly Says Something Too." The Sixties, no. 9 (Spring), 69.
Reprinted in S20.

S4. Witherup, William. "Three for Robert Bly." Prairie Schooner, 43 (Fall), 248.
[Volume incorrectly printed as vol. 44].

### 1971

S5. MacDonald, Cynthia. "Instruction from Bly." New American Review, no. 11, pp. 29-30.
Reprinted in S7 and O5.

### 1972

S6. Browne, Michael Dennis. "Robert Bly Gets Up Early." Crazy Horse, no. 12 (Autumn), 8-9.

**1973**

S7.  MacDonald, Cynthia. "Instruction from Bly." In her Am-
     putation. New York: Braziller, pp. 33-35.
     See S5 and O5.


**1977**

S8.  Hugo, Richard. "Letter to Bly from La Push." In his 31
     Letters and 13 Dreams. New York: W. W. Norton & Co.,
     p. 34.
     Reprinted in O3.


**1980**

S9.  Disch, Tom. "A Letter to Robert Bly." Times Literary Sup-
     plement, 6 June, p. 650.


**1981**

S10. Appleman, Philip. "More." In The Brand-X Anthology of
     Poetry. Ed. William Zaranka. Cambridge: Apple-wood
     Books, Inc., pp. 321-322.

S11. Cuddihy, Michael. "Harvest." Poetry East, no. 4/5 (Spring/
     Summer), 139.
     Reprinted in O3.

S12. Harr, Barbara. "Walking Through a Cornfield in the Middle
     of Winter I Stumble Over a Cow Pie and Think of the Six-
     ties Press." In The Brand-X Anthology of Poetry. Ed.
     William Zaranka. Cambridge: Apple-wood Books, Inc.,
     pp. 322-323.

S13. McCord, Howard. "Hunting Canaries with Robert Bly."
     Poetry East, no. 4/5 (Spring/Summer), 216.
     Reprinted in O3.

S14. McGrath, Thomas. "Driving Toward Boston I Run Across One
     of Robert Bly's Old Poems." Poetry East, no. 4/5 (Spring/
     Summer), 62-63.
     Reprinted in O3.

S15. _____. "Totems (I)." Poetry East, no. 4/5 (Spring/
     Summer), 61.
     Reprinted in O3.

S16. Porter, Carol. "... Finds Something in New Jersey." In

The Brand-X Anthology of Poetry. Ed. William Zaranka.
Cambridge: Apple-wood Books, Inc., p. 323.

S17. Ray, David. "In the Money." Poetry East, no. 4/5 (Spring/
Summer), 195.
Reprinted in O3.

S18. _____. "Travelling and Sitting Still." Poetry East, no.
4/5 (Spring/Summer), 196.
Reprinted in O3.

S19. Stafford, William. "Notice: A Bly Prescription." Poetry
East, no. 4/5 (Spring/Summer), 8.
Reprinted in O3.

S20. Taylor, Henry. "... Says Something, Too." In The Brand-X
Anthology of Poetry. Ed. William Zaranka. Cambridge:
Apple-wood Books, Inc., p. 322.
See S3.

# T. MISCELLANY

## 1968

T1.  Graubart, Rose. "Drawings of Nine Poets." <u>Chelsea</u>, no.
24/25 (October), [107].


## 1971

T2.  Hui-Ming, Wang. <u>The Boat Untied and Other Poems: A
Translation of Ta'ng Poems in wood with original poems in
Chinese calligraphy</u>. Barre, MA: Barre Publishers.
Dedication: "For Robert Bly who shares with me the love
of Wang Wei."


## 1973

T3.  Graubart, Rose. "Robert Bly." [drawing]. Buffalo, NY:
The "Slow Loris" Press.
Broadside. Limited edition of 200 copies, 25 of which are
numbered and signed by the author.

# APPENDIX: SPECIAL COLLECTIONS OF BLY MATERIAL

## Connecticut

Ap1. University of Con-
   necticut
   Library
   Storrs, CT   06268
   Correspondence (William
   K. Costley papers)

## Delaware

Ap2. University of Delaware
   Library
   Newark, DE   19711
   Correspondence

## Illinois

Ap3. Newberry Library
   60 W. Walton St.
   Chicago, IL   60610
   Correspondence

Ap4. Northwestern Univer-
   sity
   Library
   1935 Sheridan Rd.
   Evanston, IL   60201
   Manuscripts and cor-
      respondence

## Indiana

Ap5. Alexander M. Bracken
   Library
   Ball State University
   2000 University Ave.
   Muncie, IN   47306

   Correspondence

Ap6. Lilly Library
   Indiana University
   Bloomington, IN   47405
   Correspondence and re-
      lated documents

## Kansas

Ap7. Kenneth Spencer Re-
      search Library
   University of Kansas
   Lawrence, KS   66045
   Manuscripts and corres-
      pondence

## Massachusetts

Ap8. Mugar Memorial Library
   Boston University
   771 Commonwealth Ave.
   Boston, MA   02215
   Correspondence

## Michigan

Ap9. University Libraries
   University of Michigan
   Ann Arbor, MI   48109
   Correspondence and re-
      lated documents

## Minnesota

Ap10. University of Minnesota
   Libraries-Twin Cities

309 19th Ave.  S.
Minneapolis, MN   55455
Correspondence

## Missouri

Ap11.   Washington University
Library
Skinker and Lindell
Blvds.
St. Louis, MO   63130
Manuscripts, corres-
pondence, and re-
lated documents

## New Jersey

Ap12.   University Libraries
Rutgers University
College Ave.
New Brunswick, NJ
08903
Correspondence

## New York

Ap13.   Fales Collection (Divi-
sion of Special
Collections)
Elmer Holmes Bobst
Library
New York University
70 Washington Sq. S.
New York, NY   10012
Manuscripts and corres-
pondence

Ap14.   Ford Foundation Library
320 E. 43rd St.
New York, NY   10017
Correspondence

Ap15.   Poetry Collection
Lockwood Memorial Li-
brary
State University of New
York at Buffalo
Amherst, NY   14260

Manuscripts and Corres-
pondence

Ap16.   Special Collections
Frank Melville Jr. Mem-
orial Library
State University of New
York at Stony Brook
Stony Brook, NY   11794
Correspondence

## Ohio

Ap17.   Oberlin College
Library
Oberlin, OH   44074
Manuscripts

Ap18.   Vernon R. Alden Library
Ohio University
Park Place
Athens, OH   45701
Correspondence

## Pennsylvania

Ap19.   Fred Lewis Pattee Library
Pennsylvania State Uni-
versity
University Park, PA
16802
Correspondence and re-
lated documents

Ap20.   International Poetry Forum
Carnegie Library of Pitts-
burgh
4400 Forbes Ave.
Pittsburgh, PA   15213
Correspondence

Ap21.   Samuel Paley Library
Temple University
Berks and 13th Sts.
Philadelphia, PA   19122
Related documents

Rhode Island

Ap22. John Jay Library
        Brown University
        Providence, RI  02912
        Correspondence

Texas

Ap23. Humanities Research
            Center
        Harry Ransom Center
        University of Texas at
            Austin
        Austin, TX  78712
        Correspondence

NAME/TITLE INDEX TO PART I

"Abel Martin's Last Lamentations"
    A126, F382
"About the Conference on the
    Mother"  A57
"About to Drink Wine"  E103
Above Ground Review  F209
"Acceptance of the National Book
    Award for Poetry"  A57
"Acceptance of the National
    Book Award for Poetry,
    March 6, 1968"  B49
Acceptance Speech by Robert Bly
    On Winning the National Book
    Award for Poetry  A10
"Across the Doorsill"  A120
Adam International Review  F80,
    F82-F83, F87
Adelson, Gloria  A49
Aditya, P. K.  A91
Adoff, Arnold  G16
"Adolescence"  A74, A95
Advice to a Prophet  C2
"Advocatus Diaboli"  F69
"The Aeroplane"  E283
"Affection"  A66, E216
"After"  A102
"After a Day of Work"  A54, E252
"After a Death"  A84, A94, A102,
    F190, H7
"After a Long Dry Spell"  A118,
    F360
"After Apple-Picking"  A135
"After Drinking All Night With
    a Friend, We Go Out in a
    Boat at Dawn to See Who
    Can Write the Best Poem"
    A3, A9, E44, G10, G20, I1
"After Long Busyness"  A35,
    E189, G54, I18, I22
"After the Attack"  A84, A94,
    A102, H2
"After the Fourth Year of the
    War"  F109
"After the Industrial Revolution,
    All Things Happen at Once"
    A7, A12, E45, G2, G8, I18,
    I22
"After Working"  A3, A9, E46,

    G20, G28, J8
"Afternoon Sleep"  A3, E105, E253,
    G20, G37
"Again, Again"  H122
"Against the Evidence"  A133
"Agape"  A73, A88
"The Age of the Great Symphonies"
    A107, F177
Agenda  E90, E110, E113, E348,
    F128, F130, F133, F135-F139,
    F141, F153
"Ah, That Land So Far Off"  F11
Ai  B75
Akhmatova, Anna  A135-A136, I35
Albanese, Mary  A124
Alberti, Rafael  A74, A95
Aleixandre, Vicente  F222-F225, H9,
    H13, H15
Alexander, Floyce  A131
"All Hallows"  A135
"All I Was Doing Was Breathing"
    A114
"All My Life"  A24
"All of You Undisturbed Cities"
    A122
"All Quiet"  A133
"All the Fruit ..."  A135
"All things die and all things live
    forever"  A111
"An Allegory"  A133
"Allegro"  A84, A94, A102
Allegrone, Olivia  A44
Al-Muntafil  A130, A132, F66
"Alone"  A48
"Alone in a Blizzard"  E284
Along the Lines  A110
"Along the Lines"  A110, F295, F338
"Already ripening barberries"  A122
"The Altar"  E37
Alverdens Krybdyr  A70
"Amazed by an Accumulation of
    Snow"  A54
"The Ambassadors"  A131
"America"  A131
"America, I Do Not Call Your Name
    Without Hope"  A88
"America is Dancing"  E15
America Is Not All Traffic Lights:

E88
Crisis in American Poetry   I39
Crislock, Carl   J10
"Cristobal Miranda"   A78, A80, A88, F88
"The Cross and the Face"   F61
"Crossing Roads"   B56
"The Crow's Head"   E312
Crunk   B3, B11-B12, B15, B18, B25, B38, C1
"The Cry Going Out Over Pastures"   A49, E341
Cummings, David   D3
Cummings, E. E.   A129
"A Curious Incident in the Hotel"   E378
"The Current Administration"   A7, A12, E109
Curtis, Edward   C12

D'Accardo, Steve E.   A40
"The Daemon Lover"   A135
"Dance of Death"   A95, A131, F199, F380
Dancing Beasts   C2
Daniels, Kate   A124, B114, D7, G66, H16
Dante Alighieri,   B83
Darío, Rubén   A131, F158
"Dark Eyebrows Swim Like Turtles"   E148, E436
The Dark Houses   B11
"Dark Shape Swimming"   F320
"Darkmotherscream"   A135, H5, H10
The Darkness of Night   A104
"The darkness of night is coming along fast"   A101, A104, A106, A108, F315
David Ignatow: Selected Poems   A133
"The Dawn"   A132, F143
"Dawn in Threshing Time"   A24, A44, A54, E353
"Dawn Outside the City Walls"   A74, A95, F128, F159, H7
"Dawns of Moguer"   A74, A95, F160
"De Profundis"   A71
The Dead Seal Near McClure's Beach   A34, A135
"The Dead Seal Near McClure's Beach"   A34, A40, A43, A68a, E218-E219, E313, G13, G60, I18, I22
Dead Souls   B86

"The Dead World and the Live World"   B27
"Dear Mr. Stevens"   A6
"Death"   A95, A130, A132, E110, F200
"The Death of an Elephant"   A135
"The Death of the Wounded Child"   A126
"The Debate"   A133
"December"   E258
"A December Dream"   E274
"December Evening, '72"   F321
"Deciding to Go to Inverness for a Few Months"   E193
Decotah Territory   F282-F285
"Deep Night"   A74, A95, F129, H8
"Delfica"   A135
"The Delicious Confusion"   I1
The Delights of the Door   A115
"The Delights of the Door"   A115, A135
"Democracy"   A129
Denison, Carol   A121
Denny, Revel   C2
De Paola, Tomie   A15
"Depression"   A3, A9, G10, G18, G20
"The Depths"   A135
"The Derelict"   A133
"Descent and Defeat"   A71
De Vega, Lope   see   Vega, Lope de
"Developing the Underneath"   B75
"A Dialogue"   A133
Diary of a Poet Recently Married   A74
Dickey, James   B25, C2, C6
Dickinson, Emily   A135
The Dictators   A77
"The Dictators"   A77-A78, A80, A88, A131, F60
"Differences"   A135
Difficult Questions, Easy Answers   C13
"Difficult Questions, Easy Answers"   C13
"Difficulties of Living"   E111
Digby, John   A65
"Digging Worms"   A44, A54
"Dilemma"   A133
A Disc of Clear Water: Poems   K9
"Discoverers of Chile"   A88
Disorderly Houses   C2
"The Distant Footsteps"   A73, A88
Divine Comedy   B83
"A Divine Falling of Leaves"   A73, A88
"Doctor"   A133

348

Name/Title Index to Part I

"The Holy One disguised as an old
  person in a cheap hotel" A108
"The Holy One of the River"
  A134
"An Homage to Machado in 1966"
  A126, F409
"Home from a walk" A95, F20
"Home Grown Poets" A134, B64
"A Home in Dark Grass" A7, A12
Hope, A. D.  C2
"Hope says: Someday you will"
  A126
"Hopping" A134, B65, B102
"The Horse" A135
"The Horse Is Loose" A2
"The House of Desire" A68b
"The House" E438
"House By the Sea" F115
"The house I loved so much"
  A125-A126, F388
Houses and Travellers C16
"How Beautiful the Shiny Turtle"
  E149, E439
"How Come?" A131, A133
"How hard it is to meet the
  Guest!" A108
"How many thousands" A122
"How the Ant Takes Part" A49
"How to Begin a Poem" A2
Howard, Max H10
Howe, Florence I15
Hudson Review B21, C2-C3, E44,
  E54, E62, E65, E68, F51-F55,
  F61
"The huge sea drives" A113
Hugo, Richard C2
Hui-Ming, Wang A13, A16, A21,
  A25, A27, A35, E298, G39,
  M1
"Human Applause" F84
"Human Beings at Night" A121-
  A122
"The Hummingbird Valley" A68b, E416
Hunger A76, A98
"Hunger in the South" A88, F184
"The Hunter" A14-A15, A43, A68a,
  E155, G13
"Hunting Pheasants in a Corn-
  field" A3, A9, E52, G2, G10,
  G37
"Hurrying Away from the Earth"
  A7, A12, E138, G20, G23,
  G43
Hvass, Hans A70
Hyde, Lewis B76, H9, H13, H15
"Hymn and Return" A88

"I Am Freed" A73, A88
"I Am Going to Talk About Hope"
  A88
"I Am Not I" A74, A95, H7
I Am Too Alone In the World A116
"I am too alone in the world" A116,
  A122, F211
"I Came Out of the Mother Naked"
  A36, B89
"I can hardly believe that this tiny
  death" A116, A122
"I did not lock the door" I35
I Do Best Alone at Night A79
"I Do Best Alone at Night" A75,
  A79, A102
"I don't know what sort of a God
  we have been talking about"
  A85-A86, A91, A101, A108
"I draw near her blouse" A13
"I dreamt you guided me" A126
"I find you in all these things of
  the world" A116, A122, F97
"I have a terrible fear of being an
  animal" A88, A134, F219
"I have been thinking of the differ-
  ence between water" A101, A106,
  A108
"I have faith in all those things that
  are not yet said" A116, A122
"I have many brothers in the South"
  A116, A122
"I have never wanted fame" A111
"I Have Plenty of Heart" F106,
  H6-H7
"I have walked along many roads"
  A126, F309, F389
"I Heard You Solemn-Sweet Pipes of
  the Organ" J8
"I Know a Man" A131
"I know the sound of the ecstatic
  flute" A101, A106, A108, J8
"I laugh when I hear that the fish
  in the water is thirsty" A85-A86,
  A91, A101, A108, F302
"I listen to the songs" A126, F390
I Live My Life in Growing Orbits
  A117
"I live my life in growing orbits"
  A116-A117, A122, A135
"I Look at the Stamp" F236
"I look into a dragonfly's eye" H11
"I love Jesus who said to us" A111
"I love the dark hours of my being"
  A116, A122
"I married my Lord, and meant to
  live with him" A108
I Never Wanted Fame A111

I18, I22, J8
"Inside this jug"  F169
Instead of Squash:  A Catalog
  Apropos Swindle  A129
"The Instruments"  A120
"Intelligence, Give Me"  A74, A95,
  F133
"Interview"  A75, A79
"Interview with the Head of The
  New York Times Book Review
  (May 2, 1958, Mr. Francis
  Brown)"  B2
"Intimate Associations"  A135, F27
Introducing Poems  G56
"Introduction"  B91
An Introduction to Poetry  G38,
  G48
"Introductory Lines"  A135
"The Invisible King"  A135
"Inward Conversation"  F28
"Iowa, Kansas, Nebraska"  A131
Iowa Review  E198, E208, E213,
  E217, E235, E240, E301, E351
"Ironic Treatise on Boredom"
  F273
Ironwood  B92, B99, B109, E352,
  E368, F338-F342
"Is he from our world?"  A93,
  A122
"Is my soul asleep?"  A126, F393
Isla Negra:  A Notebook  C18
The Island  C2
"The Island of Koster, 1973"
  A63, A124, H14
Issa Kobayashi  A81, H11, I1
Issa:  Ten Poems  A81
"It doesn't matter now if the gold-
  en wine..."  A125-A126, F394
"It is good knowing that glasses..."
  A111, A132
"It is time to put up a love swing"
  A101, A106, A108
"It was a girl, really"  A122
"It was Adam who wept"  A127
"It was the grape's autumn"  A88,
  F92, F152
"It's possible that asleep the
  hand..."  A122, A125-A126,
  F337, F395
"It's Possible that While Sleeping"
  F374
"It's Raining"  F223, H9, H13
"It's spring, all right"  A132
"It's True I Went to the Market"
  A114
Ivasinc, Alexander  F262

The Jacob's Ladder  C2
Jacobsen, Rolf  A63, A107, A135,
  B48, F121-F125, F177-F178, F237-
  F247, F343-F344, F370, H7, H15
James, William  B90
"The Jar Filling"  F287
"The Jar With the Dry Rim"  A127
Jarrell, Randall  A135
Jeffers, Robinson  A129, A131,
  A135
Jenkins, Ann  A38
Jenkins, Louis  A135, B115, K2
Jensen, Gendron  A49
"The Jewel"  A2
Jiménez, Juan Ramón  A74, A95,
  A130-A132, A135, B5, B14, B51,
  F126-F142, F159-F164, F332, H7-
  H8, I7
"John Logan's Field of Force"  B59
Johnson, Lyndon B.  A129
"Johnson's Cabinet Watched by Ants"
  A7, A12, A129, E117, E139, G46,
  G57, I7
"Johnson's Face on Television"  G31
Jones, Richard  A124, B114, B124,
  D7, G66, H16
A Journey of Poems  G3
"The Journey of the Hungarian
  Dead After Death"  G6
Journey to a Known Place  C2
"A Journey with Women"  A7, A12,
  E118
"Journeys"  A135
"Joy"  I1
"The Joy When the Leaves of the
  Body Fall"  I1
"Juan Ramón Jiménez"  A95, B5
"Juan Ramón Jiménez Under the
  Water"  A74, A95
"July Morning"  A54-A55
"A July Night"  A75, A79, A102
Jumping Out of Bed  A35
"Jumping Out of Bed"  A28, A35,
  I14
Junkins, Donald  H7
"Just as the Small Waves Came
  Where No Waves Were"  A135
"Just as the Watchman [in the Wine-
  fields]"  A122, F98, F294
"Just as the Winged Energy of De-
  light"  A122, F358, H16
Just What This Country Needs,
  Another Poetry Anthology  G31

"Kabekona Lake"  A48
Kabir  A42, A85-A86, A91-A92, A99-

Main, C. F.  G25
"Malaguena"  A95
Malik, Sahl Ben  A132, F143
Malinowski, Stanley J.  A45,
    A105
Mallarmé, Stéphane  A130, A132,
    F38
Maloney, Dennis  K5
"A Man and a Woman and a Black-
    bird"  A61, A68a–A68b, G60, J8
"A Man and a Woman Sit Near
    Each Other"  E420
"The Man Awakened by a Song
    Above His Roof"  A54, A94,
    A102
The Man In the Black Coat Turns
    A59
"The Man in the Dead Machine"
    A131
"Man on North Main"  A96
"The Man Watching"  A122, A135
"The Man Who the Sea Kept Awake"
    E3, G1, I9
"The Man with Huge Eyes"  E389
A Man Writes to a Part of Himself
    A39
"A Man Writes to a Part of Him-
    self"  A3, A9, A39, G5, G26
A Man Writes to a Part of Himself:
    The Poetry of Robert Bly  J7
Mandel, Charlotte  K9
Manfred, Fred  A57
"Mankind owns four things"  A111
Maquire, Jack  A11
"March Evening"  A102, F255, F346
"The March Buds"  A68b
"March in Washington Against the
    Vietnam War; November 27th,
    1965"  E122
"Maria"  F117
"Marietta, Minnesota"  A48
"Mark of Jeep Tires on Graves"
    G44
"Marriage"  A24, I1
"The Marriage of Heaven and
    Hell"  A135
"Marsh Net"  A2
Marshall, Carol  G36
Martin, Peter  A57
Martinson, Harry  A102, A135,
    B39, B77, F87, F144–F151,
    F252–F259, F291–F293, F310–
    F311, F326, F345–F347
Martinez, Enrique Gonzalez  F25
Marx, Kevin  A70
Mary and the Seasons  A135
"The Masculine versus the

Feminine in Poetry"  A57
Massachusetts Review  E169–E170,
    F226, F229–F230, F232, F238–
    F239, F242, F249–F251, F262–
    F263
Masses  A87
"Masses"  A73, A87–A88, F44, H7
"The maternal, the fall air, all that
    we have learned"  I35
Matthews, William  A24
"Max Ernst"  F34
"May Moon"  A107, H7
"Maybe They're Shy"  A120
Mead, Alex  A116
Mead, C. David  G56
Mecklenburger, James  G35
"A Meditation on a Poem of Goethe's"
    A135
"A Meditation on a Yeats Poem"
    A135
"Meditation on Olai and Pete Bly"
    E94
"A Meditation on Philosophy"  A59,
    E390, G66
Medusa in Gramercy Park  C2
"Meeting the Old"  F305
"Meetings [of Those in Love]"
    A130, A132, A136
"Melancholia"  A7, A12, E141
"Melancholy Inside Families"  A78,
    A80, A88, F93
"Melancholy Towers"  A107, F243
"A Memorable Fancy"  A135
"Memorial"  F21
"Memories of Horses"  A107
"The Memory"  A74, A95
"Memory from Childhood"  A125–A126,
    F250, F398
Mendelson, Phyllis Carmel  B87
"Merchants Have Multiplied"  E30,
    E441
Merwin, W. S.  B15, C3, C16–C17
Messages: A Thematic Anthology of
    Poetry  G45
Meyers, Bert  K6
Mezey, Robert  A135, B50, G20
Michaux, Henri  F9–F10
Michigan Quarterly Review  C7,
    F88, F92, F207, F216
"Middle of the Way"  A135
Middleton, Christopher  C4
Midwest  E56, E92, E98
Midwest Quarterly  E195
"'Mighty Poets in Their Misery
    Dead': A Polemic on the Con-
    temporary Poetic Scene"  B108
"Mignon"  A135

Niebling, Richard F.   G3
Nietzsche, Friedrich   F95
"Night"   A3, A131, G20
Night and Sleep   A120
"Night and Sleep"   A120
"Night and Stillness"   A75, A79
"The Night-Blooming Cereus"   A135
"Night Duty"   A84, A89, A94, A102
"Night Farmyard"   A44, A54,
   E225, E300, G60
"Night Frogs"   A68b
"Night Here"   A131
"Night Journey"   A131
"The Night Journey in the Cooking
   Pot"   A68a
"Night Music"   F166
"Night of Castille"   A113
"Night of First Snow"   A54, E363
"Night Piece"   A74, A95
Night Vision   A89, A94
"Night Winds"   E442
"Nightmare in the Noon Nap"   F47
"Night's Wave"   F12
"1960"   A133
"No Complaints"   A129
"No Mountain Peak Without Rolling
   Foothills"   A67, A68b
"No Name for It"   A102, F326
"No Theory"   A133
"No Wall"   A120
"Nocturne"   A84, A94, A102
"Nonsense Poem"   E246
Norse, Harold   C2
North Stone Review   E272, E277
The Norton Anthology of Modern
   Poetry   G46
Nostalgia For the Past   H10
"Not far from the black water"
   A113
"Not Very Near the Ocean"   C7
"Note"   B41
"A Note on Antonio Machado"   B13
"A Note on César Vallejo"   A73
"A Note on James Wright"   B92
"A Note on Olaf Bull"   B42
"A Note on Trakl"   A70
"Notes for a Lecture"   A133
"Notes on Five Norwegian Poets"
   B43
"Nothing but Death"   A78, A80,
   A88, F70, J8
Novalis   A135
"November"   A21
"November Day at McClure's"
   A28, A40, A43, A135, I14
"November Fog"   A54, E158, E247
"Now listen, you watermelons--"

H11
Nowlan, Alden   B53-B54
Nude Descending the Staircase   C2
"Nurse"   A133
"Nutting"   A135
Nyhart, Nina   H11

"O Sacred Death"   A75, A79
"O you lovers that are so gentle..."
   A93, A122
"The Ocean Wind"   F150
"Oceans"   A74, A95, A135, F137,
   F163, H7
O'Clair, Robert   G46
"October Day"   A121-A122
October Day and Other Poems   A121
"October Evening in Minnesota"   A9
"October Frost"   A44, A54, E364
"Oda a unas flores amarillas"   A96
"Ode to Autumn"   F118, H3
"Ode to My Socks"   A63, A78, A80,
   A88, F94, F153
"Ode to Salt"   A78, A80, A88, A135,
   F185
Ode to Some Yellow Flowers   A96
"Ode to Some Yellow Flowers"   A96
"Ode to the Watermelon"   A88, A135
"The Odor of Blood"   A131
"Of Jeoffry, His Cat"   A135
Of Solitude and Silence: Writings on
   Robert Bly   B114, G66, H16
"Off to the Cemetery"   A133
"Often I am Permitted to Return to
   a Meadow"   A135
"Oh, evening full of light"   A126,
   F399
"Oh friend, I love you, think this
   over"   A85-A86, A91, A101, A108,
   F306
"Oh Friend Who I Love"   F170
"Oh, Guadarrama Range"   A126,
   F375
"Oh in an early morning I think I
   shall live forever"   I1
"Oh, where is the one who is trans-
   parent..."   F157
Ohio Review   E237, E242-E243, E261,
   E312, E316, E334, E336-E337,
   E358, E360-E361, E427, E430-
   E431, F348
"El ojo que ves no es"   A119
Okamura, Arthur   A40, A90
Ola and Per: The Cartoons of Peter
   Julius Rosendahl   J10
"Old Age"   A63, A107, F245-F246,
   F343, H7, H15

"The Owl"  A135
"Owning Homes"  E177
"The Oyster"  A135
"The oyster looks impenetrable
   and thuggy..."  E433

"Pablo Neruda:  Conversation
   About Hernandez"  B68
Pachano-Fombona, Jacinto  A131
Pack, Robert  G1
"Pagan Women"  A88
Pagnucci, Gianfranco  A135
"The Pail"  A49, E279
Paintbrush  E253
"Palm [of the Hand]"  A122,
   A135
Panjandrum  A28, A32, I14
"The Panther"  A122, A135
"The Paper Cutter"  A133
"The Paper Route"  A24
Parabola  E354, E370, E400,
   E432-E433, F343-F344, F349,
   F354
"A Parabola Bestiary"  E425,
   E432-E433
Paradise Lost  A135
"Paralyzed by the Night"  A102,
   F228
Paramahansa, Sri Gurudev
   Swami Muktananda  A101
Paris Review  E1-E3, E5-E6,
   E27-E28, E47, E58, E60, E72-
   E73, E93-E94, E97, E287,
   E293, E295-E296, E308, F89,
   F93, F300-F301
Partisan Review  C5, E270, E282,
   F312
"Passageways"  A126
"Passing an Orchard by Train"
   A44, A54
"Passing Remark"  A136
"The Pastoral Symphony"  F16
"Paterson:  Book II"  A131
"A Path Through Grass"  A107
"The Path with Ash Trees"  F279
"Paul Celan"  B8
Paulson, Arthur  A44
Paulston, Christina  A75, A79,
   H4, H7
"Paymaster"  A133
Paz, Octavio  C11
"The Peace of Wild Things"  A135
The Penguin Book of Socialist
   Verse  H4
"The Pennsylvania Turnpike"
   I1

"The People"  A131
"People possess four things"  A130,
   A132
Pequod  F360-F362
Perkins, Agnes  G49
Perkins, George  G68
Perlman, Jim  B110, G61
"Perpetuum Mobile"  F19
Person, James E., Jr.  B122
"The Perspiculum Worm"  E301
Peters, Robert  C17, D6
Peterson, Robert  A129
Petty, Mark  A96
Phoenix  E182, E187
"The Phoenix Bird"  F65
Piccione, Anthony  J2
Pickard, Tom  A134
"Pilgrim Fish Heads"  A36, A68a,
   E229, E248, G31
"A Pilgrim Settlement"  E159
"Pilgrimage"  A88
Pillin, William  B61
"The Pillow"  E443
Pima  A135
Pith and Vinegar  G21
"A Place in the Woods"  A118
"A Place Prepared"  I18, I22
Plainsong  B111
Plaintiff  E119, E127-E128
"Playfully"  A133
Playing the Jesus Game:  Selected
   Poems  B53
The Pleasures of Poetry  G33
Ploughshares  E385, E413, E420,
   E422-E423, F366-F368
The Pocket Book of Modern Verse
   G40
"Poem"  A2, A21, E8, E42, E60,
   F17, F81, I1
"Poem (A view of the mountain from
   the valley floor)"  A133
"A Poem About Tennessee"  A43
"Poem Adopted from the Chinese"
   E230
"Poem After Kabir"  E267
"Poem Against the British"  A3, A9,
   G2, G37-G38, J8
"Poem Against the Rich"  A3, A9,
   G11, G46, G57
"A Poem Beginning with a Line by
   Pindar"  A131
"Poem for a Gravestone"  H1
"Poem for Max Ernst"  E142
"Poem for the Drunkard President"
   E97, G59
"Poem for William Stafford at Martin"
   E204

"Rescue the Dead"  A133
Residencia en Tierra  B44, B76
Residencia One  B76, D4-D5
"Response to Frederick Turner"
    B108
"Restlessness in the Fall After-
    noon"  E32, I1
"Return for an Instant"  A74,
    A95
"Return to Solitude"  A3, A9
"Return to the Life of the Spirit"
    I1
"Returning Poem"  A67, A68a-A68b
"A Review of James Wright's Shall
    We Gather at the River"  E179
"Revolution"  E124
"Rewriting vs. Translation"  C3
Rexroth, Kenneth  A20, A63,
    A131, A135
Reynolds, Charles  E41, E67,
    F35-F37, F42, F45, F95, F104
"Rhododendron Leaf"  A24
Richie, Daniel  G65
Richter, Father  A29
Richter, Franz Albert  A30, A44,
    A56
"Riderless Horses"  A7, A12,
    E144
"Riding Around Big Stone Lake"
    E207
"The Right Meaning"  A88
"Rigorists"  A135
Riley, Carolyn  B85, B87
Rilke, Rainer Maria  A93, A109,
    A112, A116-A117, A121-A122,
    A134-A135, B72, B95, B104,
    B110, B113, C3, C8, D8, F96-
    F101, F157, F189, F211-F212,
    F294, F327-F331, F349, F356-
    F359, H15-H16
"Rilke's Book of Hours"  B95
Rimbaud, Arthur  A129
"Ritual One"  A133
"Ritual Two"  A133
The River  A131
River Styx  E424, F371-F377
Rivers, Diana  A116
"Road"  A74, A95, F139, F164
"The Road of Praise"  F288
"Roads"  A44, A54
"Road's End"  A107, A135
Robert Bly  I17, I25, J3, J11
Robert Bly, May 2, 1978  I32
Robert Bly Reading  I7
Robert Bly Reading His Poems
    with Comment in the Record-
    ing Laboratory, May 2, 1960

I1
Robert Bly Reading His Poetry  I37
Robert Bly Speaks and Reads from
    His Works at Michigan State
    I41
Robert Bly with Gregory FitzGerald
    and Bill Heyen  J1
Robert Lowell:  A Portrait of the
    Artist in His Time  C9
"Robert Lowell's For the Union
    Dead"  C5, C9
Roberts, Michael  G5
Robertson, James  A135
"A Rock Inlet on the Pacific"  A43,
    E304
Rockler, Elliot  A57
Roethke, Theodore  A131, A135
"Rolf Jacobsen"  B48
"The Rollcall of Bones"  A88
"The Roman Aqueduct"  A113
"Roman Countryside"  A122
"The Roman Matron"  E401
"Romans Angry About the Inner
    World"  A7, A12, E152, G14,
    G25-G26, G33, G46, G57, I7, J8
Romtvedt, David  A125
"A Room"  F43
"The Room"  A133
Room For Me and a Mountain Lion:
    Poetry of Open Space  G52
"Rooster"  F248
"The Roots"  A68b
Rosenthal, M. L.  G11, G14
Rothenberg, Jerome  A134
"The Rough-Barked Cottonwood" E366
"Rubber"  F124
The Ruby  A128
"The Ruby"  A128, F318, F335
"The Ruined Street"  A88, F208
Rumaker  B12
Rumi  A108, A120, A127, A135,
    F312, J11
A Run of Jacks  C2
"Rundown Church"  A95, F206
"The Runner"  A130, A132
"Running Over the River"  E125
Rylander, Edith  G42
Rylander, John  G42


"A Sacrifice In the Orchard"  A59
"The Sadness of American Unrest
    in 1961"  E126
Sager, Maureen  H5
"Sailor's Tale"  A102
St. Geraud  A130, A132; see also
    Knott, Bill

# NAME/TITLE/SUBJECT INDEX TO PART II

Q196, Q217, Q288

"Minnesotans Publish Magazine to Boost Bright Young Poets" P1

Missouri Review  P199

Mitchell, Roger  P35, Q114

"The Modern American Poetry of Deep Image"  P155

Modern Occasions  P12

Modern Poetry Studies  P120, P203, P215, Q219, Q237

"Modernsmedvetandets arketyp" P128

Mojtabai, Ann G.  Q133

Molesworth, Charles  P103, P147, P158, Q79, Q260-Q261

Monroe, Jonathan Beck  R19

Montgomery Advertiser-Alabama Journal  Q213

Moons and Lion Tailes  Q91, Q125

Moore, Stephen  Q8

Moramarco, Fred  Q139

Moran, Ronald  O1, P25, P58

"More"  S10

"More Brass Than Enduring" Q290

Moritz, Charles  P229

The Morning Glory  P67, P123, P146, P218, Q88-Q97, Q251, R20

Morris, Richard  P95

"The Mother: An Interview with Robert Bly"  P107

"Moths in the Light"  Q50

"Motions of the Heart"  Q32

Mottram, Eric  P69

"Moving Forward"  Q146

Moving Inward: A Study of Robert Bly's Poetry  O2

Moyers, Bill  P159

Mueller, Lisa  Q55

Murphy, Rosalie  P60

Murray, Michele  Q27

Murray, Philip  Q104

"Music to Your Ears"  Q276

"My Father's Wedding 1924" P230

Mythologies of Nothing: Mystical Death in American Poetry 1940-1970  P227

Naiden, James  Q28, Q215, Q249

Naked Poetry  P65

Naone, Dana  P129

"Napalm Poetry Reading"  P22

Naropa Institute  P121, P129

Nation  P17, P22, P28, Q67, Q175, Q274

"The National Book Awards"  P28

National Guardian  Q179

National Observer  Q27, Q222

"The Need for Poetics: Some Thoughts on Robert Bly"  P190

Nelson, Cary  P104

Nelson, Howard  O4, P105, P189

Nemanic, Gerald  P171

Neruda, Pablo  P57, P89-P90, P228, Q98-Q106, Q291-Q292, R6, R11-R12

"Neruda and Vallejo in Contemporary United States Poetry"  R6

Neruda and Vallejo: Selected Poems Q98-Q106

"Neruda in English: A Critical History of the Verse Translations and Their Impact on American Poetry"  R12

Neumann, Erich  P175, P192, R9

New  Q212

New Age Journal  P210

"The New American Poetry"  P40

The New American Prosody  P219

New American Review  S5

"New and Recommended"  Q216

"New Books Appraised"  Q189

New England Review  P182

New Leader  Q230

New Mexico Humanities Review P188

"New Mud to Walk Upon"  P194

"New Nature Poets"  Q156

"New Poetry"  Q62

"New Poetry: The Generation of the Twenties"  Q43

"The New Poetry: Still Echoing the Agony of the '60's"  Q225

The New Poets: American and British Poetry Since World War II P26

New Republic  P206, Q5, Q146

New Science  P203

New Statesman  Q40

"New Voices in American Poetry" P162

"New Work Based on Poet's Theories" Q227

New York Herald Tribune  Q191

New York Review of Books  Q54

New York School of Poetry  P95

New York Times  P14, P38, P159, Q52

New York Times Book Review

P139, P142, P144, P150, Q20,
Q47, Q86, Q100, Q136, Q168,
Q198, Q216, Q218, Q224, Q258,
Q276-Q277, Q280
New York Times Magazine   P162
New York University   Ap13
New Yorker   P78
Newberry Library   Ap3
"News From Robert Bly's Universe:
The Man In the Black Coat
Turns"   P230
News of the Universe   P166, Q107-
Q120
Newsday   Q220
"A Newspaper Reader's Garden of
Verse"   Q220
Nichols, William I.   P38
Nicolai, Peter   Q217
Night Vision   Q120
Niikura, Toshikazu   P169
"1973: A Selection of Noteworthy
Titles"   Q218
"19th National Book Awards Stir
Controversy in N.Y."   P36
"The Non-Rationalist"   P108
Nordell, Roderick   Q182
North Country Anvil   P125
North of Jamaica   P78
Northeast   P123
Northwest Review   Q57
Northwestern University   Ap4
"Not Bards So Much as Catalyzers"
Q168
The Notebooks   Q138
Notes on Contemporary Literature
P212
"Notes on Current Books"   Q56,
Q140, Q183
"Notes on Robert Bly and Sleep-
ers Joining Hands"   P82, P143
"Notes, Reviews, Speculations"
Q185
"Notice: A Bly Prescription"   S19
Novack, Robert   P96
Nuova Corrente   P71


Oates, Joyce Carol   Q219
Oberback, S. K.   P5
Oberlin College   Ap17
The Observer   Q49, Q172
"'Of Energy Compacted and
Whirling': Robert Bly's Re-
cent Prose Poems"   P188
Of Solitude and Silence: Writings
on Robert Bly   O3
Offen, Ron   Q184

Ohashi, Kenzaburo   P169
Ohio Review   P80, P82, P137-P138,
Q108, Q260
Ohio University   Ap18
Old Man Rubbing His Eyes   P205,
Q121-Q125, R7
Olson, Charles   P4, P117
"On Bly"   P54
"On Bly's Kabir"   Q31
"On Bly's Poetry"   P52
"On Robert Bly"   P193
"On Robert Bly and His Poems:
A Selected Bibliography"   P50
"On Robert Bly's Protest Poetry"
P46
"On Sleepers Joining Hands"   Q204
"On Split-Brain Experiments and
the Mother"   P124
"On the Natural World"   Q164
"On the Rhythmic Run"   Q172
"On Translating Late Rilke: Re-
marks on Some Recent Examples"
P140
"On Translating Lyric Poetry"   Q146
"On Translating Rilke"   P206
"On Vallejo and Neruda: Another
Look"   Q103
"On Writing Poetry: Four Contempo-
rary Poets"   Q233
"On Writing Prose Poems"   P106,
P132
One For the Road   Q81
Oppenheimer, Joel   Q220
Orr, Gregory   P190
Ossman, David   P6
Otto, Kay   P13, P53
Out of the Vietnam Vortex: A Study
of Poets and Poetry Against the
War   P94
"Out of the Vortex: A Study of
Poets and Poetry Against the
Vietnam War"   R2
"Ox, Mule and Buzzard"   Q163


"PW Interviews: Robert Bly"   P166
Palmer, Penelope   Q292
Parabola   Q153, Q285
Paris Review   P109
Parnassus: Poetry in Review   Q73,
Q81, Q236, Q254
Partisan Review   Q102, Q207
The Party: A Chronological Per-
spective on a Confrontation at a
Buddhist Seminary   P129
Patterns of Commitment in American
Literature   P24

"Pre-Beat"  P40
"The Present State of American
    Poetry:  Robert Bly and
    James Wright"  P58
Procopiow, Norma  P219
"The Prodigal Son"  P230
"Progress"  Q146
"Prophecies for America:  Social
    Criticism in the Recent Poetry
    of Bly, Levertov, Corso, and
    Ginsberg"  R5
The Prose Poem:  An Inter-
    national Anthology  P115
"Public Gestures, Private Poems"
    Q49
"The Public Mind and the Private
    Mind"  Q52
Publishers Weekly  P166, Q9, Q37,
    Q82, Q96, Q115, Q123, Q152,
    Q262, Q270, Q284
Punch  Q62
Punter, David  Q237

Quam, Michael D.  P191
Quarry  Q173
"Questions of Reality"  Q53
Quill & Quire  Q85, Q154
Quinn, Fran  P192
Quinn, John P.  P37

Ramsey, Paul  Q223
Ratner, Rochelle  P106, P132,
    Q153, Q285
Ray, David  P14, P60, P193,
    Q185, S17-S18
Raymont, Henry  P38
"Readings:  'Like One of Your
    Favorite Teachers.'  Robert
    Bly at the New School"  P164
"Recent American Poetry:  Out-
    side Relevances"  Q48
"Recent Verse"  Q130
"The Recent Work of Donald
    Hall and Robert Bly"  Q240,
    Q275
"Reflections Upon the Past with
    Robert Bly"  P183
Regler, W. G.  Q76
Reid, Alfred S.  P61
Reinhold, Robert  P86, Q250
"'Rejoice in the Gathering Dark':
    The Poetry of Robert Bly"
    P158
"Response to Mr. Bly"  P199
"The Return of Political Poetry"

P66
"The Reverend Robert E. Bly,
    Pastor, Church of the Blessed
    Unity:  A Look at 'A Man Writes
    to a Part of Himself'"  P153
Review  Q101
A Revolution in Taste:  Studies of
    Dylan Thomas, Allen Ginsberg,
    Sylvia Plath, and Robert Lowell
    P148
Rexroth, Kenneth  P62, Q57, Q129
Richter, Franz Allbert  P77
Riley, Carolyn  P47
Rilke, Rainer Maria  P136, P140,
    P206, Q141-Q154
Ringold, Francine  Q263
River Styx  P207
Rizza, Peggy  P59
Roberson, William H.  P217, P232
"Robert Bly"  P6, P117, P122, P137,
    P141, P170-P171, P205, P214, T3
"Robert Bly:  A Primary Bibliogra-
    phy, Part I"  P216
"Robert Bly:  A Primary Bibliogra-
    phy, Part II"  P232
"Robert Bly:  A Tiny Retrospective"
    P177
"Robert Bly Alive in Darkness"  P74
"Robert Bly:  An Interview"  P138
Robert Bly:  An Introduction to the
    Poetry  O4
"Robert Bly and the Ants"  P189
"Robert Bly and the Deep Image"
    R1
"Robert Bly Checklist"  P87
"Robert Bly:  En livsnara diktare"
    P119
"Robert Bly Gets Up Early"  S6
"Robert Bly:  Gone Fishing For the
    Sign"  Q237
"Robert Bly:  His Poetry and Liter-
    ary Criticism"  R4
"Robert Bly on Fathers and Sons"
    P233
"Robert Bly on Gurus, Grounding
    Yourself in the Western Tradition,
    and Thinking for Yourself"  P121
"Robert Bly:  Poet on the Road
    Home"  P76
"Robert Bly:  Poetry Food"  P204
"Robert Bly:  Politics and the Soul"
    P125
"Robert Bly, Radical Poet"  P88
"Robert Bly:  Rediscovering the
    World"  Q94
"Robert Bly:  Silence in the Snowy
    Fields"  Q186